Passion's Child

Passion's child . . .
She was one
Made but to love, to feel that she was his
Who was her chosen: what was said or done
Elsewhere was nothing.

—Lord Byron

Passion's Child

The Extraordinary Life of Jane Digby

◆————————————◆

Margaret Fox Schmidt

Harper & Row, Publishers
New York, Hagerstown,
San Francisco, London

FIRST EDITION

Designed by Janice Willcocks Stern

Library of Congress Cataloging in Publication Data

Schmidt, Margaret Fox.
  Passion's child.
  Bibliography: p.
  Includes index.
  1. Ellenborough, Jane Elizabeth Digby Law, Countess
of, 1807–1881. I. Title.
DA536.E45S35   1976   301.41'76'330924 [B] 74–15848
ISBN 0-06-013807-6

---

76 77 78 79 10 9 8 7 6 5 4 3 2 1

*This book is affectionately dedicated
to those nearest and dearest to me, in
the order of their appearance: Mother,
Dorothy Ann, Melissa, and Norman.*

Contents

Illustrations

The misfortune of my nature is to consider love as all in all; without this feeling life is a dreary void—no earthly blessing can compensate its loss, and having at first setting out in life sacrificed all without regret to one great and absorbing passion, the necessity of loving and being loved is to me as the air I breathe and the sole cause of all I have to reproach myself with.

—Jane Digby

Author's Note

I was first introduced to Jane Digby in the spring of 1970, when I came upon an intriguing footnote in Edward Crankshaw's *Fall of the House of Habsburg*. I had no inkling then that the greatest adventure of my life had just begun, but I was certain that a lady who could so enliven four lines of small print at the bottom of the page was someone I wanted to know better. As I began to unravel the tangled threads of Jane Digby's incredible odyssey, I felt there had to be more to her story than a series of highly publicized, scandalous love affairs. I tried to separate the gossip and the fiction from the facts and to present a truer, more rounded portrait of Jane than has ever been done before. Even if I have succeeded only partially in this, I have already been lavishly rewarded by Jane herself with five years of sustained excitement. She has enriched my life immeasurably with new friendships, with fascinating people and places.

There are living today in England, Germany, Austria, France and Greece many who are connected to Jane Digby by blood relationship or family names, and those I have met have been unstinting in their cooperation. Thanks to Jane's peculiar magic, I was able also to enlist a battalion of enthusiastic volunteer researchers, who provided me with an enormous amount of material I could not possibly have uncovered alone. Among these I must single out Dr. Tekla Hammer of Nuremberg, whose efforts on my behalf were tireless and whose detective work was brilliant. The many others, to whom I owe so much, can best be identified according to their geographical location.

England

Lord and Lady Digby were most generous and gracious with their help and hospitality, putting at my disposal everything pertaining to Jane in the Muniments Room at Minterne, Dorset. I am indebted to them for much of the material in this book and for permission to reproduce family portraits and Jane's watercolors. For many kindnesses and much information I am grateful to the

Dowager Lady Ellenborough, the Earl of Leicester at Holkham, Dr. W. O. Hassall of the Bodleian Library, Oxford, Ms. Sarah Graham-Brown of the Middle East Centre, St. Antony College, Oxford, Colonel and Mrs. Anthony Barne, Mr. J. L. Walford of the Public Records Office, Miss Josephine Biffen of the Foreign Office Library, Mr. Innes Rose, Mrs. Tita Theotoky Campbell and the courteous staff of the British Museum Reading Room. I am much indebted also to the late E. M. Oddie (Elinor Mary O'Donoghue) for preserving in her 1935 biography many details of Jane's life in Syria from personal papers that have since been lost. My thanks also go to Mr. Dick Ross of the BBC for his help.

Austria and Germany

To Baron Karl von Venningen and his family in Riegerding, Austria, I wish to express my thanks for their warm hospitality and for allowing reproduction of their Jane Digby miniature and their portrait of the nineteenth-century Baron. I am grateful to His Royal Highness Duke Albrecht of Bavaria for permission to work in the *Geheimes Hausarchiv* in Munich, where Jane's letters to King Ludwig I are kept; for the courtesy extended to my daughter and me I am indebted to the Archives Director, university professor Dr. Hans Rall and his assistant, Frau Johanna Häfker. Dr. Rall's careful reading of two drafts of my manuscript was an invaluable aid. From two of Jane's direct descendants, Baronin Gabriella von Venningen of Pöcking, and Frau Ilse Horner of Munich, I received help and encouragement, for which I am deeply appreciative. For their generous gifts of time and information I wish to thank the Baroness Theresia von Gebsattel of Rothenburg, Frau Marlies Drösel and Professor Joseph Fresin, both of Weinheim, Peter North of Vienna and the staff of the Schwarzenberg Archives in Murau, Austria.

Greece

No one has worked more enthusiastically to advance my research than Countess Eleni Theotoky of Corfu and Mr. Paul Marmaridis of Athens. The Countess has been a devoted friend, who did not hesitate to come flying across Europe to act as my interpreter and who arranged help and a warm welcome for me on Corfu from her equally gracious daughter and son-in-law, Dr. and Mrs. Spyros Poyagos. Mr. Marmaridis neglected his art gallery to come to my aid on several occasions, making numerous important calls to locate people I could not otherwise have found, and taking me on a breathtaking search through the *Plaka* (in the best spy thriller tradition) to find a portrait of Jane.

The Middle East

Through a chain of events incredible enough to suggest a guiding hand, I contacted Mr. John Brinton of Beirut, who trusted me with his own microfilm of

Jane's Damascus account book. I am deeply grateful to him and to Mr. John Joly of Beirut, who had the foresight to preserve this valuable record of Jane's life in Syria. To Mr. Kenton W. Keith and Mr. Ibrahim Nakhleh of the United States Information Service in Damascus I am much indebted. Mr. Keith went to a great deal of trouble to get photographs of Jane's grave for reproduction in this book, and Mr. Nakhleh made an all-out effort to find a missing portrait of Medjuel el Mesrab.

Italy

My journey to Bagni di Lucca would have been fruitless had it not been for the kindness of the village priest, Sac. Francesco Nicoli, who gathered up two strangers he found wandering through the streets. My heartfelt thanks to Father Nicoli and also to the gallant Signor Alfredo Barbagli, for their interest and memorable hospitality.

Mexico

The name of Jane Digby is now well known among the foreign colony in San Miguel de Allende, where my husband and I spend summers, thanks to those friends there who helped me with translations and performed a wide variety of missions connected with my research: the late Mrs. Helen Wale, Mrs. Betty Kempe, Sr. Jaime Ross Limantour, Sra. Nina Tabuena, Sra. Erika Sanchez de Kortlang, Mrs. Florence Johnson, the Rev. Harold Cook, Mr. Frederick Taylor and Mr. Cyrus Adams III. No one has given more encouragement to this project from its inception than Eleanor and Allan Kahn, who had been traveling companions, photographers and helpers in a hundred different ways.

Athens, Ohio

My husband's associates at Ohio University have provided invaluable assistance to me, both on campus and abroad. My warmest thanks to Doctors and Mmes. Lawrence Goldberg, Henri Seibert, Edgar Whan, Barry Thomas, Hollis Summers, Robert Ingham, and Paul Murphy; Mrs. Jacqueline Bolen, Dr. Ursula Lawson, Mr. Stanley Plumly, Dr. Carl Carrier, Mr. Phil Richardson, Dr. Alfonso Gonzalez, Mr. and Mrs. John Baldwin and Mr. and Mrs. Leslie Rollins. I am also much indebted to the staff of the Vernon Alden Library.

Here and There

I wish to thank Francie Goldberg Robbins at the Library of Congress for rising to some unusual occasions, and Professor Francis Schwarzenberg of Chicago for directing me to the Schwarzenberg Archives. I am much indebted to Sr.

Lourenço Luiz Lacombe, director of the Museu Imperial in Petropolis, Brazil, for an excerpt from the diary of Emperor Dom Pedro. I owe more than I can say to Nahum J. Waxman of Harper & Row for his friendly guidance throughout the writing of this book. For her careful reading and suggestions, which made my work much easier, I am very grateful to my typist, Mrs. Frances Dunnigan of Athens, Ohio. I am indebted also to Mr. Lawrence Durrell for his permission to quote from *Prospero's Cell.*

The four people who have been almost as deeply involved with Jane Digby as I have been during the past five years are my husband, my daughter, my mother and my sister, to whom this book is dedicated. They have each contributed more than they realize. To Norman, who sacrificed so much of his time and his own interests to further mine; to Melissa, who was "frisked in Frankfurt and martyred in Munich" on the trail of Jane; to Mother, who courageously played solitaire in a remote Austrian inn while I was having Sunday dinner with a baron; to Dorothy Ann, who plowed through my first rough manuscript and never failed to applaud my triumphs, but did not live to see this book in print; to all of you I give loving thanks and hope you think it was worth it.

MARGARET FOX SCHMIDT

Athens, Ohio
September, 1975

Passion's Child

Prologue

Passion's child . . .

She was one

Made but to love, to feel that she was his

Who was her chosen: what was said or done

Elsewhere was nothing.

—LORD BYRON

In Damascus, Anglican funerals have never been commonplace, and the one held on a sweltering August day in 1881 ended in such a dramatic manner (not at all provided for in the Book of Common Prayer) that no one who was there ever forgot it. For a woman whose life beggared fiction, there could not have been a more fitting end.

The solemn faces and somber European dress of the handful of mourners struck an incongruous note in the midst of the colors, the odors, and the raucous shouts of the native bazaars as the funeral procession threaded its way through the narrow, twisted streets. These same streets only a few years earlier had run violent red, as seven thousand Christians were massacred in a Druse uprising. The Englishwoman now being laid to rest had survived that slaughter in the "Blessed City of the Prophet" to die more conventionally, of illness, at age seventy-four. But even if her manner of dying was conventional, nothing about her life had been so.

Her Bedouin husband, Sheik Abdul Medjuel el Mesrab, had agreed reluctantly to take his place in the closed black carriage reserved for the chief mourner, and he bore the stifling atmosphere for half the way along the road to the cemetery, when suddenly, bewildered by the strange Christian rites, overcome by grief and an uncontrollable need for open space, he bolted from the trap with a strangled cry and fled in the opposite direction from the funeral cortège. The clergyman and the others in attendance exchanged shocked glances, then shrugged and renewed their pace, dismissing Medjuel's breach of funeral etiquette as the act of an unfeeling barbarian. Their judgment proved to be hasty, for just as the minister was sprinkling a handful of earth over the coffin and intoning the ritual words, "Ashes to ashes, dust to dust," the barbarian came galloping through the

1

cemetery gate on his wife's favorite black Arabian mare. No one moved or spoke while the man on horseback stared into the open grave, as though he had expected the dead woman to be awakened by the familiar sound of hoofbeats. Moments passed in this frozen tableau. Then, as abruptly as he had appeared, the Bedouin rode away.

How Jane Digby would have loved her husband's farewell! For her (in the splendid phrase of her old friend, Sir Richard Burton) "life's poetry never sank to prose." In the walled-off Protestant section of the ancient, sprawling Jewish cemetery of Damascus, her grave itself has an exotic touch entirely appropriate for its extraordinary occupant. It is marked by a simple cross bearing Jane's birth and death dates in English, but the Sheik of the Mesrabs, a devout Muslim, honored the woman he loved by carving in Arabic her Bedouin name on a stone which he placed at the base of the cross.

Visiting her burial ground a few years after Jane's death, Dr. William Wright, a missionary who had known her well, wrote, " ... and here lies the beautiful and cultured Lady Ellenborough, known at Damascus as 'the Honourable Mrs. Digby el Mesrab,' who lost her way in the seething slough of fashionable society, and after a wild, passionate and reckless career, closed her days in peace as the wife of a Bedawi sheik, and died in the Christian faith, in sure and certain hope of a Blessed Resurrection." The compassionate missionary understood and admired the scandal-haunted lady whose worst sins were an overwhelming appetite for romance and adventure, an honesty which left her defenseless, and an astonishing naiveté about men.

Few others of Dr. Wright's time and fewer since have been willing to concede Jane Digby a place in heaven. A false report of her death in 1873—and then her actual death in 1881—brought forth a deluge of highly inaccurate but pleasantly lurid obituaries to titillate the tightly-corseted society of an aging Queen Victoria (who refused to receive at court widows who remarried, but not widowers who did). Despite Jane's impeccably aristocratic lineage, a woman who had taken a fourth husband (and a Bedouin at that) while her three previous husbands were still very much alive was hardly welcome while the iron-fisted queen sat on the throne. Had Jane returned on her knees, a repentant sinner, ravaged by time and unmentionable excesses, her Victorian countrymen might have extended the hand of righteous condescension, but that was not her style, and her ageless beauty, regal manner and undiminished *joie de vivre* rendered forgiveness out of the question. In her fifty-year exile Jane made only two brief visits to the land of her birth, and felt no pangs at leaving it again on either occasion.

It was a far freer, more flamboyant England she recklessly abandoned in 1829 (leaving behind a wealthy husband, an infant son, and a sullied name) to follow the Austrian prince she loved so passionately. The London of George IV winked at adultery and played musical beds with gay abandon, but even that indulgent society turned its back on the young and incredibly lovely Lady Ellenborough when she shattered its cardinal rule of decorum. The French satirist Edmond

About brilliantly summed up Jane's social blunder: "One fine morning she climbed on the rooftops and shouted distinctly to the whole of the United Kingdom, 'I am the mistress of Prince Schwarzenberg!' All the ladies who had lovers and did not say so were greatly shocked; English prudery reddened to the roots of its hair." Felix Schwarzenberg bore one of the noblest names in Europe, and he was destined to be prime minister of his country, but such credentials meant nothing to the enraptured twenty-one-year-old Jane. (In an age of vulgar snobbery she threw away titles like confetti.) This was love as she knew it should be, and it was worth any price. The price was high indeed, but she paid it joyfully. When her prince proved unworthy of the sacrifice, she was crushed, but the defeat was only temporary, and she never allowed herself to become embittered or cynical. For her, romantic love was "all in all," and she was certain that somewhere there existed the perfect lover. It took her many years, many men and many scandals to find him, and when she did she almost failed to recognize him. Only an indomitable spirit such as Jane's could have survived so bruising a journey and emerged triumphant, without a trace of coarseness. When she left England in 1829, Jane Digby took the Romantic Age with her and kept it alive and glowing for more than half a century until she died.

In matters of the heart Jane remained an adolescent all her life, but in other areas she had a rare intellect and power of fascination. She was "a woman of extraordinary and stately beauty, with the manners of a queen"; she spoke nine languages with wit and charm and was a remarkably talented artist with watercolors and pencil. Her attraction for men never faded; it crossed all geographical boundaries and captivated three kings (including a father and son), two princes, a German baron, an Albanian brigand general and several Bedouin sheiks, to name but a few of her admirers. Writers from Honoré de Balzac to James Michener have been sufficiently intrigued by Jane Digby to incorporate bits of her story into their works. Part of her fascination stems from her refusal to fit any conventional mold. She was neither nymphomaniac nor courtesan, although she has been described as both by writers who did not know the facts. Jane never used her charms to gain wealth or power; her private income was more than sufficient to live well. She never had to strive for equality—it came naturally. She was endowed by nature and by birth to take life on her own terms. Like Haidee in Lord Byron's *Don Juan*, Jane Digby was "Passion's child," made to love and be loved, and the rest of the world be damned!

Jane and Byron never met. She was a child of nine in 1816 when the scandal of the poet's incestuous love affair with his half-sister forced him into exile, but all of England continued to read Byron's poetry with relish, and Jane's adolescent years were vividly colored by the adventures of *Childe Harold's Pilgrimage* and *Don Juan*. In these two poems Byron gave the Romantic Age its dominant character—the Byronic Hero—the proud, passionate, moody, often anguished sinner, who defied every rule that confined the human spirit. It was this hero Jane sought all her life, little realizing that she was the female counterpart. Jane

Digby was the living, breathing heroine of a genuine Byronic odyssey, determined to wrest happiness from a gloriously inviting world. She shared Byron's aristocratic disdain for any form of hypocrisy, and she followed her Byronic course with far greater success than the "little limping dandy" himself had enjoyed, for she was unhampered by his neurotic penchant for self-destruction. The trail this English beauty blazed from a marble and alabaster palace in Norfolk to the black goathair tents of the Syrian Bedouins makes the travels of Lord Byron seem by comparison as uneventful as a stroll through Hyde Park. Her life is one of the great romantic adventures of all time.

1

Cokes and Digbys

Deo non Fortuna
—DIGBY FAMILY MOTTO

Prudens qui Patiens
—COKE FAMILY MOTTO

In the eyes of Jane Digby's Victorian relations, her life was shocking beyond belief. They never considered that their scandalous kinswoman might be following in the family footsteps of a freer age. She was, after all, the descendant of two of England's most colorful, aristocratic houses: the Digbys, whose noble lineage could be traced to the eleventh-century reign of Edward the Confessor; and the Cokes, whose ancestral tree was rooted in the days of King John and the Magna Carta. For centuries Digbys and Cokes had enlivened the pages of English history.

An Everard Digby, fighting for the Red Rose of Lancaster, died on Towton Field in 1461 when the Yorkist army, headed by the new claimant Edward IV, routed the forces of the ill-fated Henry VI. Everard's seven sons fled England in the bloody aftermath, when the estates of Lancastrian lords were confiscated, but all seven Digbys returned to take their revenge at Bosworth Field on August 22, 1485.

A direct descendant of one of these seven brothers at Bosworth carved his niche in history a century later. Sir Everard Digby was described in John Aubrey's *Brief Lives* as "a most gallant Gentleman and one of the handsomest men of his time." At Cambridge, however (where he tutored Francis Bacon), Digby was said to be a noisy young man, who told rude jokes on the master of his college, "blew an horn and halloed disrespectfully." He was also careless about paying bills and was finally expelled.

Although he was knighted by James I, Sir Everard, a fiery Catholic convert, joined Guy Fawkes's group of conspirators in the bizarre "Gunpowder Plot" to blow up the king and his entire Parliament in 1605. Digby was only twenty-eight when he and seven other men, including Fawkes, were beheaded for concealing thirty-six barrels of gunpowder in a vault just below the House of Lords, intending to set it off to protest the king's anti-Catholic laws. A curious legend sprang up concerning Sir Everard's death on June 30, 1606. According to John Aubrey's version, when the executioner plucked out the heart of the prisoner and gave the traditional cry, "Here is the heart of a traitor," the indomitable Sir Everard answered, "Thou liest!"

5

More durable and even more colorful than his father was Sir Everard's son, Sir Kenelm Digby. For this Digby, who was only three years old when his father was executed, life was a series of uphill struggles from which he always emerged gloriously triumphant. His first major victory was at Oxford where, as a Catholic, Digby was ostracized, forced to enroll as a commoner, not permitted to wear the academic gown or to work for a degree. His brilliance made the outcast a favorite with his professors, and one of them, Thomas Allen (a distinguished mathematician and occultist), bequeathed to Kenelm a priceless library of rare manuscripts.

In his teens Digby fell in love with the beautiful Venetia Stanley, who was three years older and who already had a rather racy reputation. According to John Aubrey, "The young Eagles had espied her, and she was sanguine and tractable, and of much suavity (which to abuse was great pittie)." Lady Digby was not so sympathetic toward her son's beloved, and to separate Kenelm and Venetia she sent her son abroad. The plan had one consequence that Lady Digby could hardly have foreseen. While Kenelm was on his enforced grand tour, the forty-seven-year-old queen of France, Marie de' Medici, developed such a mad passion for the English youth and pursued him so relentlessly that Kenelm had to circulate a false rumor of his own death to end the chase.

Digby's letters to Venetia during this period were intercepted by his mother, and the young lady, believing her lover to be dead, became the mistress of Sir Edward Sackville, bearing him a child or two. By the time Kenelm had returned to England, the stories about Venetia could not be ignored, but he accepted the facts as he saw them and discounted the gossip. Kenelm forgave Venetia's infidelity and married her, over the violent protests of his family. As John Aubrey explained, "Digby would say that a wise man, and lusty could make an honest woman out of a brothell house." On the subject of women's chastity Sir Kenelm Digby was a very free thinker for his time. "What discreet man," he asked, "ever threw away a fair and rich garment for having a small spot in one corner of it?"

During his tour of Italian courts, Digby was asked by a childless prince to beget a son with the prince's wife, because the Italian regarded the red-haired Englishman as the measure of perfection. His physical strength was prodigious, and he once lifted with one arm "a middling-sized man," chair and all. Before he was twenty, Digby had studied art and science in Florence, where he was befriended by Galileo; accepted membership in a learned society, the Accademia dei Filomati, in Siena, where he addressed the group on secret writings among the ancients; joined a diplomatic mission to Madrid; and been knighted by King James I—the very man Kenelm's father had tried to blow up!

Despite his popularity with the English people, Digby's outspokenness continually kept him in hot water. On a not-so-diplomatic mission to the Vatican, Sir Kenelm boldly and openly upbraided the pope, who reported in return that the Englishman was "quite mad." During the upheavals of the Civil War in his homeland, Digby was imprisoned once and twice banished, returning finally with the Restoration. During his imprisonment in 1642 Sir Kenelm spent his time writing literary criticism.

The "renown Knight, great Linguist and Magazen of Arts" (Aubrey's description) died in 1665 at the age of sixty-two; such a life span was in itself remarkable in an era when forty years was the normal life expectancy. Digby requested no epitaph, but he got one nonetheless:

> Under this Stone the Matchless Digby lies,
> Digby the Great, the Valiant and the Wise:
> This Age's Wonder, for his Noble Parts;
> Skill'd in six Tongues, and learn'd in all the Arts . . .

Apparently Sir Kenelm was not the only unconventional Digby of the seventeenth century. In Graham Greene's biography of the second Earl of Rochester, there is a cryptic reference to a Digby in a paragraph describing the revels of Charles II at the Newmarket races:

> The King rode his own horses, sometimes to victory, got drunk on the road and made the fiddlers at his inn sing all the obscene songs they knew, watched Lord Digby walk five miles within the hour over the heath 'stark naked and barefoot' . . .

There is no further mention of the athletic peer, who must have been the son of the Earl of Bristol and a cousin of Sir Kenelm.

The kind of swashbuckling adventurers who decorate the branches of the Digby family tree are not to be found in the Coke genealogy, but the Cokes (pronounced Cooks) had their own style. Edward Coke, one of Jane Digby's illustrious ancestors on her mother's side, let it be known early that he was going to be out of the ordinary. On a chilly February 1 in 1551 or 1552 Mrs. Winifred Knightly Coke was sitting quietly by the parlor fire in the Norfolk village of Mileham when her thoughts were interrupted in a most bizarre fashion by the leaping forth of a man-child onto the hearthstone! There was no time for the midwife Mrs. Gamp to arrive with her traditional cry of "Bless the babe and save the mother." "Prudence through Patience" may have been the Coke family motto, but Edward Coke was not one to wait long for what he wanted.

The enormous wealth of the Cokes, which built palatial Holkham Hall on the Norfolk marshlands near the North Sea where Jane Digby spent her childhood, began to be amassed nine generations earlier by the man who made such an auspicious entrance into the world. This was Sir Edward Coke, who became attorney general to both Queen Elizabeth and James I, and Lord Chief Justice. This Coke, who claimed that he "never gave his Body to Physic, his Heart to

Cruelty, nor his Hand to Corruption," made an indelible mark on the English legal system and is still referred to as chief among the judges who made English justice famous for its excellence and impartiality. Partly through his professional earnings and partly through the large fortunes brought him by the two wives whom he chose with great prudence, Sir Edward set about to buy up a considerable portion of England. Besides large properties in Hertfordshire, Suffolk, Berkshire and what is presently Manchester, Coke acquired sixty manors in Norfolk alone.

Sir Edward fared better with queens of England than with kings, possibly because of his exceptional good looks. (The *British Compendium* said of him, "...the Jewel of his Mind was put in a fair Case, a beautiful Body with a comely Countenance...") Coke's account book records neighborly gifts of pears and fresh raspberries from Queen Elizabeth, who was godmother to one of Coke's daughters. During the reign of James I, Coke was a favorite with Queen Anne, and the inventory of his "rarities" includes "A ringe sett with a Great diamond cutt with fawcetts, given to Sir Edward Coke by Queen Anne."

Coke's relationship was not always so smooth with Queen Anne's husband, and there were more serious issues involved than Coke's real estate ventures. He lost his position as attorney general in 1617 by refusing to defer to the wishes of James I in a court decision; then, undaunted, Sir Edward got himself elected to the House of Commons, where he continued to be a thorn in the royal side. The King violently resented Coke's widely circulated "Protestation" against the royal view that the privileges of the House of Commons were derived from the king at his pleasure. This piece of audacity cost Sir Edward his freedom, and in 1621 he spent twenty-six weeks imprisoned in the Tower of London, where he occupied his time writing Latin poetry with a piece of charcoal on the stone walls.

Remarkably Sir Edward escaped the headman's axe (despite the many powerful people who would have rejoiced at his silencing), and he lived to the almost unheard of age (for his day) of eighty-two, in full command of his faculties.

The upheaval of a civil war and the vicissitudes of a rapid turnover on the English throne allowed five generations of Cokes to follow Sir Edward and nearly a hundred years to elapse after his death before the wealthy and powerful family was honored with a peerage. In 1728 King George II named Thomas Coke the Lord Lovell, and in 1744 made him Earl of Leicester. The Earl was the most cultured Coke of them all. In his youth Thomas Coke traveled for several years in Europe, beginning his own collection of rare books and manuscripts, and locating Greek and Roman treasures for the Norfolk palace he dreamed of building. When the foundations of Holkham Hall were laid in 1734, Thomas had the combined help of the greatest English architect of the age—William Kent— and the brilliant amateur, Lord Burlington, Thomas's close friend and traveling companion. All three men were admirers of the magnificent sixteenth-century Italian residences built by Andrea Palladio, and Holkham was planned to be a jewel of the Palladian style. Nothing was too good for a man whose bill for silver plate at Mr. Paul Lamerie's topped 3,000 pounds, and whose London home was Thanet House, built by Sir Christopher Wren. (According to Coke's account books, even a Wren house had its drawbacks. He records a payment of twelve shillings "To Mr. Southall for the Killing of Buggs," and Mr. Southall later became permanent "Buggman" at a salary of one guinea a year.)

The magnificent Long Library at Holkham was built to house the rare books Thomas had inherited, plus such gems of his own collection as the *Libro della Natura*, written and illustrated in Leonardo da Vinci's own hand; the Dante which had belonged to Pope Pius II, and six other manuscripts of the divine poet; the Boccaccio *Decameron* illuminated by Taddeo Crivelli for Alberto d'Este; the magnificent prayer book given by Lorenzo de' Medici to his bride Clarice Orsini; the ninth-century Cicero from Cluny; and the Gospels which Lutharius wrote for the Schütthorn monastery about 800 A.D. Some of the library's books still bear the label pasted in nearly three hundred years ago by Thomas's mother: "Cary Coke, wife of Edward Coke of Norfolk, Esq." (Cary was described by a contemporary as a "fair and accomplished woman with a true and delicate taste in art and literature.")

The great tragedy in the life of the first Coke peer was that his only son turned out to be an utterly dissolute young man who died in his thirties without children of his own. For this reason, in 1776 one of the greatest estates in England came into the possession of the Earl's great-nephew, Thomas William Coke. For more than half a century afterward, this man, known as Coke of Norfolk (and sometimes simply as "King Tom"), reigned at Holkham Hall. It was during those golden years that the Palladian palace reached the peak of its splendor and King Tom's granddaughter, Jane Digby, was born.

From an early age Thomas William Coke was groomed to be the master of Holkham Hall. Like most wealthy young Englishmen of his time he was sent to Europe for the grand tour, and while he was acquiring continental polish, his handsome face and figure caught the eyes of some very highborn ladies. He was an immediate favorite at the court of the King of Sardinia, where His Majesty's daughter, the Princess of Savoy, taught Coke to dance the cotillion and chose him to be her escort when she left Sardinia to marry the Comte d'Artois. At another royal wedding—this one in Rome—Tom made an even greater conquest. He was only eighteen in the spring of 1772 when the Princess Louise of Stolberg and Charles Edward, grandson of King James II and pretender to the throne of England, were married. During the ball following the ceremony, the pretender's "queen" became so infatuated with young Tom Coke that she commissioned his portrait to be painted by Pompeo Batoni, the most popular painter in Italy at the time.

In spite of these heady successes with the opposite sex, Tom Coke returned to England to discover that his childhood sweetheart, Jane Dutton, surpassed all the royal ladies he had met. He was determined to marry her, even over his father's opposition to the match. (The Dutton and Coke families were close friends—Jane's brother James had married Tom's sister Elizabeth. The only objection Tom's father had to Miss Dutton as a daughter-in-law was the insignificant dowry she would bring to Holkham Hall.) Tom and his father quarreled bitterly over the young man's choice, and the quarrels led to an estrangement between the two.

Tom Coke would have been perfectly content to spend all his time being a country gentleman, for he was an outdoor man who would renounce every other pleasure for a run with his hounds. He was a superb horseman and was considered one of the best shots in England. (At age seventy-nine he could still kill twenty-four birds with twenty-five shots.) By new methods of farming and breeding, Coke revolutionized agriculture and sheep raising in his part of England, and from the barren, salty marshlands on the North Sea coast he created a magnificent park.

No matter how much Squire Coke liked the rural life, he was expected to uphold the family tradition of public service, and when his father died, Tom was urged to stand for the vacant seat in the House of Commons. In 1776, the year of his first election, Coke was twenty-two, the youngest member of the House. When he retired fifty-six years later, he was the oldest. It did not take Coke of Norfolk long to make his presence known in that venerable assembly. A passionate Whig all his life, Coke often boasted that not once in all his years in the House had he voted with the government on any issue, and to emphasize his bitter opposition to the war against the American colonies, he publicly proclaimed that he drank a toast every night to General George Washington. When in 1782 the House of Commons passed by one vote the motion that the independence of America should be recognized, Coke, who had fought so hard for it, was unanimously selected by his fellow Whigs to present the result to an angry, defeated King George III. As a Knight of the Shire, Coke had not only the right to wear his spurs in the House, but the right to attend court "in his boots." On this triumphant occasion, Coke availed himself of this privilege for the first and only time, appearing in his picturesque country garb, top-boots with spurs, light leather breeches, long-tailed coat, and a broad-brimmed hat. The elegantly powdered and brocaded Tory court was horrified. Thomas Gainsborough, who came to Holkham to teach the Coke daughters painting, did a portrait of Coke in this attire, standing beneath a tree, loading a gun.

Coke of Norfolk humbled himself for no man. He knew that no one but royalty was permitted to drive as many as six horses in the London streets, so Tom harnessed a coach with five horses plus a donkey as the leader, and drove past the palace, flicking his whip at King George III as he urged the team to put on speed. In an era which doted on titles, the member from Norfolk was unique in refusing a peerage for more than thirty years so that he could keep his more influential seat in the House of Commons. "I had rather remain the first of the ducks," he said, "than be the last of the geese!"

One of Coke's considerations in turning down a peerage was that he had no son to carry the title on. The only male child he and Jane Dutton Coke produced was stillborn, and the circumstances of this tragedy were evidence that the wealthy Cokes shared at least some of the difficulties of humbler Englishmen. Lady Mary Coke wrote to a friend on December 1, 1776, "Did you hear that my cousin Mrs. Coke was brought to bed of a dead son, occasioned by a fright? A mouse got into her nightcap and demolished the heir to Holkham." There were no more boys born to Jane Coke.

Little more than a year after her tragedy, Coke's wife had a daughter, Jane Elizabeth, and the following year another, Ann Margaret. When Ann was scarcely fifteen, she married Thomas Anson (later Viscount Anson), and immediately began to produce a family of eleven children. Ann's firstborn arrived only a few months after her mother gave birth to a third daughter, Elizabeth Wilhelmina (Eliza). This unusual sequence of events caused the Anson children to share the Holkham nursery and schoolroom with their Aunt Eliza, who grew up with them.

Jane Elizabeth Coke married the man of her choice, Charles Nevinson Howard, Viscount Andover, in 1796, when she was nineteen, and no one could have wished for a more beautiful bride. A youthful portrait of her by John Hoppner shows a lovely, roguish face, softer in features than her mother's or her daughter's, with masses of auburn hair falling carelessly about her shoulders. Coke's eldest daughter was so noted for her looks that when the Prince of Wales was asked to name the most beautiful woman in England, he replied unhesitatingly, "Without a doubt, Lady Andover." The young bride was graceful and talented as well (she was said to dance the best *minuet de la cour*). She had been a prized pupil of Thomas Gainsborough, and at the age of fifteen painted a remarkable life-size study of Belisarius begging.

Life was good to Lord and Lady Andover for nearly four years until one winter day in the year 1800. The young couple was at Holkham for the hunting season when Lady Andover had one of the prophetic dreams for which she was noted in the family. At breakfast on the morning of January 8 she begged her husband not to join the hunt because she had had a vision of his being accidentally shot and killed. To humor her he stayed in that morning, but by midday the sun had dispersed the chilling fog, and the weather was so glorious that his wife relented and insisted he go out. Two hours later his horrified groom raced back to Holkham with the news that Lord Andover had been gravely wounded by an accidental discharge from the new, widely mistrusted double-barrel shotgun he was using. He died in a tenant farmer's cottage.

The nineteenth century did not begin auspiciously for the Cokes. Less than five months after her husband's tragic death, Lady Andover lost her mother, Jane Dutton Coke, who died at age forty-seven. The young widow was now needed at Holkham to act as hostess for her father and to supervise the rearing of her little sister Eliza, who was only five at the time.

The childless, widowed Lady Andover, with her renowned beauty, did not lack suitors, among them Lord Jersey, Lord Cowper and Sir George Anson, the brother of her sister Ann's husband, but six years passed before Coke's eldest daughter remarried. Her second husband was Captain Henry Digby, son of the late Dean of Durham and direct descendant of that early Everard Digby. With the snobbery that might be expected in a vulgar era, Lady Andover retained all her life the name and title of her first husband, finding it infinitely preferable to plain Mrs. Digby. By the time Henry was made an admiral and knighted, and she could have called herself Lady Digby, the habit of being Lady Andover was too deeply ingrained for her to think of changing.

Captain Digby could not offer a peerage, but he was wealthy, exceptionally handsome, and a naval hero. He had entered the Royal Navy at fifteen, and by the time he was twenty-five he was in command of a small frigate called the *Aurora*. According to his own report, Digby and the crew of the *Aurora* captured "forty-eight sail of the enemies' merchantmen, a Spanish frigate, a French corvette and several others, carrying in the whole two-hundred and fourteen guns and seven-hundred and forty-four men." This was rich booty, but nothing compared to what Digby won later, when he commanded the frigate *Alcimene*.

As he himself told the strange story, Digby was sailing between the Portuguese coast and the Azores in October, 1779, when he began to hear an insistent voice saying, "Digby, Digby, go to the northward." He tried to ignore this unusual summons until finally at two in the morning, unable to sleep, he changed course, much to the astonishment of his officers. At seven a large Spanish ship, laden with silver dollars, cochineal and spices, loomed up on the horizon and fell a prize to the *Alcimene*. Shortly afterwards two equally valuable Spanish galleons on their way to Santa Cruz were taken. Before he was thirty Captain Digby had acquired a fortune large enough, he said, "to permit me to ride in a coach and four instead of a one-horse chaise." Since part of the booty taken was distributed among the men, Digby soon became the most popular ship captain in the Royal Navy.

Although he heard no mysterious inner voices during the battle of Trafalgar, something caused Digby to make a "wrong turn" of the 64-gun *Africa*, which he then commanded, and he found himself in the middle of a large portion of the French fleet, which, undone by such daring, promptly surrendered. His conspicuous, albeit accidental, gallantry won him the praise of both houses of Parliament and a gold medal. Captain Digby may have been, as the Regency diarist and gossip Thomas Creevey described him, "a dull dog at dinner," but he was not a dull dog at sea.

The marriage of Jane Elizabeth, Lady Andover, and Captain Henry Digby was celebrated April 17, 1806, at St. James's, Westminster, and the exotic monkeys of the Digby coat of arms were joined with the proud ostriches of the Coke escutcheon. The union produced three children, the eldest of whom became one of the most colorful figures of the nineteenth century. By a strange quirk of genes, all the qualities that made so many Digbys and Cokes out-standing—their good looks, their courage, their stamina, their intellect, their love of adventure, their passionate refusal to conform, in short, their style—were passed undiluted to Jane Digby. It was an incredibly rich heritage. She made the most of it, and she added a few touches of her own.

2

◇————◇

Regency Childhood

I am very sorry for what I have done.
I will try if you will forgive me not
to do it again. . . . I will eat my
bread at dinner always.

—JANE DIGBY, AGE TWELVE

On April 3, 1807, a daughter was born to the inadvertent hero of Trafalgar, Capt. Henry Digby, and his wife Lady Andover. They were a little disappointed that Jane Elizabeth, their firstborn, was not a boy, girls being at a discount when men were dying by the thousands in the Napoleonic wars and there was a family line to be considered. When Lady Andover was told she had given birth to a girl she asked first, "What color are her eyes, for eyes do not change?" She was happy to learn that the baby's eyes were a deep blue-violet. If one had to have a daughter, having a beautiful one took out some of the sting.

The baby's father, soon to be knighted and made an admiral for his exploits, may have been a courageous commander at sea, but it was Lady Andover in charge on the home front. Her husband could afford a coach and four, but few men in England could afford a Holkham Hall, and the lady was well satisfied to keep the family residence there for the time being. She was still acting as chaperone for her little sister Eliza, but no one felt crowded in a house where a guest could get hopelessly lost coming down to breakfast.

Not only guests but the servants they brought with them (no one of fashion went visiting without a retinue of personal attendants) were continually involved in misadventures in the labyrinth of Holkham's passageways. One night, when Jane was an infant, a visiting lady's maid lost her way; after wandering about the corridors in despair, she finally arrived at a room occupied by the Duke of Sussex. The Duke's black servant, dressed in Turkish fashion complete to turban, always slept on a mat outside his master's door. When this heathen apparition sprang up from the shadows, the girl fled in terror down the hall, screaming that the devil had come through the floor to seize her.

In a time of efficiency apartments, the dimensions of Holkham Hall boggle the mind. From the gatehouses the road winds two miles through a magnificent park before the Palladian brick mansion—344 feet long and nearly 40 years in the building—appears. The great entrance hall with its semicircle of dazzling alabaster Ionic columns rises to a staggering height of 50 feet. During Jane's childhood, Holkham was so famous that it had become a popular place of pilgrimage. Arthur Bryant describes it in the *Age of Elegance*:

> ...the interminable drive, the triumphal arch, the lakes, the woods, the obelisk, the distant view of the sea, the overawed Norfolk church peering through its modest cluster of trees, the exquisite changes of autumnal leaf as the shooting parties, in green and buff and brown, moved like regiments over the landscape, the coverts with never-ending partridges rising out of wastes of sand bearded with stunted corn, and, all around, the wilderness flowering like a garden.

The splendid isolation of Holkham did not, however, shelter its occupants in the year of Jane's birth from the unsettling knowledge that Napoleon had initiated his continental blockade and, with the signing of the Tilsit treaties, now dominated the entire continent of Europe. When Jane's grandfather Coke was not in London occupying his seat in the House of Commons, he was kept well informed of outside events by the mail coaches that called twice a day at Holkham. These vehicles were a wondrous spectacle with their blood horses, their horn-blowing guards, and their coachmen with squared shoulders, multiple coats and nosegays. Everyone on the coaches was given a free glass of Holkham ale provided by servants on hand for this purpose, and the amount of ale consumed annually this way was enough to float Admiral Digby's flagship.

Jane grew up in a far more colorful England than has been seen since. There were beadles and town criers in cocked hats and flaxen wigs; postmen in red and gold uniforms; judges in scarlet and ermine driving into country towns for the Assizes, accompanied by outriders, javelin men and halberdiers, while all the church bells pealed. The arbiter of fashion was the elegant Prince of Wales (later George IV), who filled army orders with pages of instructions about epaulettes, gold lace and feathers; sent the 23rd Dragoons to Spain so overdressed they were confused with their French enemies; and rigged out his own Regiment of Hussars "like padded monkeys in crimson breeches and yellow boots." The pleasure-loving prince, according to one of his critics, would have made a splendid upholsterer.

Elaborate as were the prince's costumes, they were far surpassed by the settings he created. The oriental fantasy of the Royal Pavilion at Brighton was one of the wonders of the age with its onion domes and Eastern pagodas, looking, as Sydney Smith remarked, "as if St. Paul's had gone to the sea and had pups." The prince's crowning achievement, however, was his London residence, Carlton House, a fairly modest two-story mansion, which he transformed into a palace worthy of an oriental potentate: walls covered with painted mandarins and fluted yellow draperies, peach-blossom ceilings and canopies of tassels and bells, imperial dragons darting from every chandelier and overmantel, and a magnificent Gothic conservatory, fan-vaulted in the manner of a small cathedral.

The riches of this age of elegance were not confined to costumes, palaces and furnishings. Against the lavish backdrop created by the Prince of Wales there was a spectacular flowering of the arts, of technology, and—as might be expected—eccentricity. Wordsworth, Blake, Keats, Coleridge, Shelley, Byron, Scott, Austen, Lamb, and Hazlitt were writing, and Lawrence, Constable and Turner were painting. Marvelous new machines were revolutionizing the English economy, and nearly as fast as they were installed, a curious counterrevolutionary group who called themselves Luddites would arrive to smash the new machines to bits, claiming they were acting on orders from a mythical King Lud, who lived in Sherwood Forest.

These were revolutionary times in every sense, and few Englishmen were more aware of this fact than the members of the peerage and the landed gentry. Sensing that the days of unlimited privileges acquired by accident of birth were numbered, many English aristocrats were having a last fling, engaging in orgies of self-indulgence. This high-class hedonism was not surprising, as very recently, just across the Channel, a noble name had been good for little more than a one-way ticket to the guillotine. Despite the carnage in France, however, a title still carried enormous prestige in England and was much sought after. Admiral Digby was not one to discount the advantages of a title, and Lady Andover had already shown her regard for hers. It was natural that they should seek a peerage for one of their children.

The Admiral's first cousin—Edward, Lord Digby—was a bachelor with no male issue to carry on his title, and a son of the Admiral stood an excellent chance to become the ninth Baron Digby. This set of circumstances may have prompted Jane's parents, when Lady Andover became pregnant the second time, to take a house in Dorset, the home shire of the Digby relations. Forston Manor, an estate five miles out of Dorchester on the road to Cerne Abbas, was by no means on the palatial scale of Holkham Hall, but it was (and remains) a graceful, commodious country house dating from the time of Queen Anne. Edward St. Vincent Digby was born at Forston June 21, 1809, and his two-year-old sister, who had reigned uncontested over the household, found herself abruptly dethroned by the son and heir. This was the first time Jane was confronted with the fact that males were regarded as unquestionably superior beings.

While their children were growing up, the Digbys divided their time between Dorset and Norfolk, and in the Holkham circle there were two young men—William Coke and George Anson—who were good models for the young Edward. William, who was fourteen years older than Jane, was the nephew of Coke of Norfolk and (because it did not then seem likely that the squire of Holkham would have any sons of his own) heir presumptive to the vast Norfolk domain. Since he was being groomed for his role, William was not permitted to enter the army as he hoped, so he had to find other means of testing his courage. While he was a student at Eton, one of his legendary feats was swimming the Thames with a live hare in his mouth. He was a magnificent and daring horseman, who claimed that women in the saddle made him nervous since none of them had the proper balance—a theory his little cousin Jane would disprove in formidable fashion.

George Anson, the second son of Jane's aunt Ann Coke Anson, was not heir presumptive to anything, so he did join the army and eventually became commander-in-chief of the British Army in India, setting feminine hearts fluttering wherever he was stationed with his dark handsomeness. He and the fair-complexioned, chestnut-haired William made a striking study when they entered a room together. Despite such dashing examples, neither Jane's brother Edward nor a second brother, Kenelm, born four years after Jane, ever showed the reckless courage, independence and predisposition for adventure which was their heritage. That pretty little girl, their sister, got the lion's share; she was off and running almost before she could walk.

Jane was three, and most likely banging her silver porringer on the table for attention in the nursery, when a daring young English nobleman named George Gordon, Lord Byron, swam the Hellespont on May 3, 1810. Napoleon, meanwhile, had just married the Archduchess Marie Louise of Austria, and the French empire was at the zenith of its power.

While the emperor of France was basking in the glow of triumph, the King of England was sinking into the darkness of insanity. On November 2, 1810, George III, raving and sometimes violent, had to be confined in a straightjacket. When it became apparent that the aged monarch would never regain mental stability, his eldest son, the Prince of Wales, was given the authority to act in the king's place, and in January, 1811, the fabled Regency began. The Prince Regent was nearly fifty, but age had not tempered his notorious excesses.

To celebrate his new position (and because he loved parties) the regent gave a summer fete at Carlton House on June 19, 1811, an extravaganza the like of which England had never seen. To those who were invited the party was "an assemblage of beauty, splendor and profuse magnificence." Other Englishmen, a good many of whom were barely surviving on poor bread and half-rotten potatoes, washed down with strong tea, were less than enthusiastic about a banquet of iced champagne, hot and cold soups, fish, fowl, beef, pastries and exotic fruits served on silver trays to 2,000 guests.

At the beginning of 1813 news reached England that Napoleon had had to make a disastrous retreat from Moscow. While thousands died in Europe, the dinner bell continued to ring punctually at five every afternoon in English homes, where there were more immediate concerns than distant battle. Conversation at Holkham that spring centered around the forthcoming court presentations of Jane's eighteen-year-old aunt, Eliza Coke, and Jane's cousin Anne, sixteen. The girls' sponsor was Lady Anson, sister to Eliza and mother to Anne, and she decreed, when Jane set up a clamor to go to London, that her six-year-old niece would have to wait a while before she could take part in such gala occasions. The little Digbys and Ansons were left in the Holkham nursery and had to be satisfied with secondhand accounts of the debutantes' arrival at court in their sedan chairs, from which the tops had been removed to make room for their elaborate headdresses.

London society enjoyed a lively season in 1813, with some rich new material for gossip. The famous Madame de Staël, exiled by Napoleon, arrived in town that summer and was lionized by the aristocracy. Jane Austen's *Pride and Prejudice* had just been published, and Lady Caroline Lamb, who bore no resemblance to any of Miss Austen's reserved heroines, was sending clippings of pubic hair to Lord Byron.

That winter, Holkham Hall was blanketed with a heavy snowfall that lasted six weeks and covered all of Britain. Smoke billowed day and night from the many chimneys of Coke's palace, while shivering maids hurried through the icy corridors carrying silver warming pans to take the chill from the Cokes' feather beds, and velvet-footed butlers brought the ladies and gentlemen their steaming tankards of negus—a comforting concoction of hot water, port, lemon juice, sugar and spices. Coke's grandchildren, warmly muffled and booted, pelted each other with snowballs, and the adults skated on the small lake in front of Holkham. By the time spring finally arrived in Norfolk—when Obelisk Wood was full of sweet-smelling violets, and the park and walk around Holkham Lake were yellow with daffodils—the news came that Napoleon had surrendered. April 20, 1814, seventeen days after Jane's seventh birthday, the defeated conqueror bade a moving farewell to his Grenadiers at Fontainebleau and set out on the lonely road to Elba, while a war-weary world breathed a sigh of relief, which turned out to be a little premature.

Despite its isolation, life at Holkham Hall was never dull. Coke entertained like a monarch and the house was always crowded with guests. Jane adored the excitement of the annual sheep-shearing festival every July, called "Coke's Clippings," when visitors of every rank and station came from all over the world to see the miracles Coke had wrought with his flocks and harvests. The productivity of Norfolk had doubled in two decades, largely through the genius of its famous Squire Coke, who, dressed like his laborers, first taught himself to farm and then taught his tenants. Many of the guests scarcely saw the agricultural wonders, they were so entranced with the wonders of the house itself and the opportunity to handle the rare manuscripts collected by seven generations of Cokes in the Long Library. There were paintings by Titian, Van Dyck, Veronese, Holbein and Gainsborough, statues from ancient Greece and Rome, and magnificent medieval tapestries.

At Holkham Hall there was a great deal of high life below stairs as well as above. A staff the size of the one in Coke's palace was a community in itself, and the servants were often more strict in their protocol than their masters and mistresses. Lady Andover once heard her footman say to another in a peremptory fashion, "Exchange cards, Mitchell." It was a custom among the menservants to call each other by their masters' names, and Jane's cousin was convulsed with laughter one day as she sat in her carriage in front of Holkham and overheard the following exchange between two footmen: "Stanhope, if you see Anson, ask him if he has cleaned Digby's boots." Servants' balls were held in the Holkham audit room, and music was provided by the band from the nearby village of Wells, headed by Mr. Tysack, the Wells hairdresser, who cut quite a figure among the maids with his corkscrew ringlets. Tysack went down in ignominy the night the curls caught fire in a candle flame and turned out to be not his own.

There were never enough hours in a day for children at Holkham, where opportunities for adventure were endless. The same maze of corridors which so often undid visiting servants provided a wealth of entertainment for daring little aristocrats. Jane and her brothers and cousins shared one of the towers with their nurses, governesses and governors. Outside their rooms was a wide passage that became their playground and a dark closet that served as a "prison" for the boys when they were naughty. It was delicious fun for Jane, free on the outside, to hear cries of, "I will be good. Do let me out, Mr. Paine," accompanied by vigorous thumps, and sometimes varied by, "If you don't open the door this minute, I will kick it down!"

A more fascinating game presented itself to the children when stories of a Holkham ghost began to circulate. The eccentric Lady Mary Coke, who had steadfastly refused to allow the consummation of her marriage to the dissolute Edward Coke, son of Holkham's builder, had died in 1811, an old lady with her virginity and bitterness still intact. During the first years of her unusual marriage, she claimed that her Coke in-laws had kept her a prisoner in the turret room. Now her unhappy spirit was said to appear, weep, then vanish along the lonely corridor she had trod so mournfully in life. The ghost provided great adventures for Jane, who tiptoed down the forbidden hall, her violet eyes sparkling and her cheeks flushed with excitement, while her less daring brothers and cousins trailed behind, trembling with terror. Jane, who was totally fearless, regaled her timid followers with vivid descriptions of this specter, which to this day tradesmen claim to have encountered in the dark passageways below the great house.

In the fall of 1814, while the inhabitants of Holkham Hall were preparing for the hunting houseparties and moving, according to long-established custom, from the south dining room to the north, the delegates to the Congress of Vienna were squabbling over the partition of Europe. Lord Castlereagh, England's controversial foreign minister, was introducing his young protégé, Lord Ellenborough, to the impressive group of diplomats assembled in the Habsburg capital at about the same time that little Jane Digby was falling out of a Norfolk pear tree. Ellenborough had recently married Castlereagh's sister, Lady Octavia Stewart, and, motivated more by ambition than romance, he had selected Vienna for their honeymoon. The newlywed nobleman hoped one day to become foreign minister himself. Jane's ambition in 1814 was to learn to shoot a pheasant from the saddle at full gallop like her grandfather Coke. (She would realize that ambition, but Ellenborough would fall short of his.)

The hunting season at Holkham was on as grand a scale as everything else in Coke's palace. The *battues*, when the hunters were preceded into the field by an army of beaters, began on the first Wednesday in November and continued twice a week for the rest of the three-month season. Non-*battue* days were passed either in the turnip fields among the partridges or in the salt marshes in pursuit of snipe and wild fowl. Jane remembered the *battue* days all her life and the beautiful, stirring sight of the hunters assembled on the south lawn for the start of the day's hunt. She was often lifted onto her grandfather's horse, and paraded up and down until the company was ready to go.

On wet days, when the hunt had to be called off, large parties were conducted on a tour of the house, a favorite amusement, because visitors were anxious to see the many Holkham treasures. In the north state bedroom, which was always given to the Duke of Sussex, there was a plaque of Caesar Augustus over the mantelpiece, which bore a startling likeness to Napoleon. During one tour the guests burst out laughing to find the royal stockings warming at the fire under Caesar's haughty gaze. The duke was a frequent Holkham visitor, and had learned that not even royalty was exempt from the practical jokes and teasing which the Cokes so enjoyed. (Anyone with a thin skin had a rough time at Holkham.) Sussex was a notoriously poor marksman, and after one hunt Jane's grandfather tallied the duke's scorecard, which was presented to him with great ceremony. It read:

Killed of game	0	
Wounded in the legs	1	Foot-marker
Wounded in the face	1	Groom
Wounded on the head of a friend	1	Hat
Ditto, on the left rump	1	Horse!

At Holkham, the *battues* ran into the Christmas season, which was one long series of delights comprised of the Yule log brought in by the Holkham carpenter on Christmas Eve; mummers representing King George, the Doctor and Turkey Snipe, dressed in painted paper and floral headgear, reciting traditional lines, and banging one another with wooden swords; the famous Norfolk dumplings and smoked turkeys, along with roast beef and goose, plum pudding and mincemeat pies; rosy-cheeked carolers and red-nosed elders. The regent's sister-in-law, the Duchess of York, had introduced to England the German custom of exchanging gifts, and fashionable families were quick to adopt it. On New Year's Eve toast and ale were sent round to all the servants; there were musicians, morris dancers and the choir with garlanded wassail bowls who sang outside, regardless of the weather:

Here's to our horse and to his right ear,
God send our master a happy New Year;
A happy New Year as e'er he did see,
With my wassailing bowl I drink to thee!

It was a far milder winter that brought in the year 1815, and Holkham was visited in the spring by a curious, premature summer. A full-blown apricot blossom was gathered March 6; April 4 a honeysuckle in full bloom was plucked; and April 7 the heat was "so oppressive" that the family dined without a fire. It was a memorable year in many respects for Englishmen, and not all the memories were happy ones. A Parliament of landlords, seeking to "save the farmer," imposed the infamous Corn Law of 1815, excluding foreign corn until home-grown corn reached an average price of eighty shillings. Jane's grandfather Coke was threatened on several occasions by an angry mob for his stand with the other landlords, and in March of that year he and Lord Albermarle were saved from serious injury at a cattle fair in Norwich only by turning out an enraged bull, which dispersed the crowd while the two men made a hasty exit.

Napoleon Bonaparte was getting a far more enthusiastic reception following his landing March 1 at Golfe Juan on the French Riviera. The handful of men the charismatic ex-emperor brought with him from Elba were joined by the very soldiers who were posted to stop him. By March 20, Napoleon was once again installed in the Tuileries. With Bonaparte on the march, the threat of a French invasion loomed over England once more, and the Norfolk militia was hastily reorganized to defend the coastline near Holkham.

At eight, Jane Digby was old enough to be affected by the feverish excitement which Napoleon's return from exile created, but in June of 1815 she was creating some rather heady excitement of her own. At this stage of her life even the 43,000 acres of her grandfather's estate hardly seemed world enough for the adventurous young aristocrat. It seemed perfectly logical therefore that she should wander off one day with a band of gypsies whose free life style she found much to her liking. While most of England was holding its breath waiting for news of Wellington's battle, a small corner of Norfolk was too occupied with a search for little Miss Digby to worry about a muddy Belgian hole-in-the-road called Waterloo. The "gypsy" with the golden curls was retrieved, and not long afterward her grandfather began building a ring fence around Holkham park, which, when it was finally completed years later, measured just under nine miles in length. Jane promised in all sincerity that she would never worry her family again.

Napoleon's Hundred Days had come to an inglorious end, but England now had her hands full of domestic trouble. The only cure for social ills the regent knew was pomp and pageantry, a bread-and-circuses treatment that somehow worked for England long after it had proved obsolete in France. In 1816 a perfect occasion presented itself with the wedding of the regent's popular daughter, Princess Charlotte, to Prince Leopold of Saxe-Coburg, who had distinguished himself at the Congress of Vienna. The colorful ceremony produced the desired smoothing effect upon an unhappy populace, but it was only temporary. Jane, then a nine-year-old, was not as impressed as the rest of England by the royal wedding, but she was well aware of Princess Charlotte's death in childbirth a year later, because it was connected with one of her mother's prophetic dreams.

One morning in November 1817, Lady Andover told her sister Eliza that she was troubled by a strange dream in which she had seen a funeral procession gathered in front of Holkham Hall. The entire family appeared in black mourning crepe, but the mourning was worn for someone other than the person about to be buried. When the procession moved off, it was not in the direction of the church where the Cokes were always buried but through Obelisk Wood, where it was joined by a large throng of people.

Shortly after Lady Andover's dream, a large houseparty arrived at Holkham for the hunting season. Among the guests were Lord and Lady Albermarle, close friends and neighbors of the Cokes. When news came of Princess Charlotte's death, all of England put on mourning. Lady Albermarle, who was a lifelong companion of the Princess and who was herself expecting her eleventh child, went into shock and died at Holkham in childbirth. Her funeral procession left Holkham through Obelisk Wood and was met by a large crowd of mourners from Lord Albermarle's estate. Every detail of Jane's mother's dream came true.

That same year an attempt was made to assassinate the Prince Regent. The Whigs of Norfolk called on Coke to deliver a two-pronged speech to the regent, on the one hand congratulating him on his escape, and on the other, asking him in very plain terms to dismiss from his presence "those advisors who by their conduct had proved themselves alike enemies to the Throne and to the people." The regent was warned in advance of this sugar-coated pill. Knowing that Coke valued his position as a commoner above all else, he swore, "If Coke of Norfolk enters my presence, by God, I'll knight him!" When this threat was told to Coke, he replied, "If he dares, by God, I'll break his sword!" Jane was delighted when she heard the story of her grandfather's boast, and she initiated a new game for the schoolroom, breaking make-believe swords over the heads of her little brothers and Anson cousins. She was always the star performer, and in a delightful portrait of the three little Digbys, the painter Thomas Barber makes this obvious. Jane is in the foreground with castanets in the pose of a Spanish dancer, and Edward and Kenelm are the enchanted spectators. Barber must have been captivated by the little girl—Jane was eight or nine at the time—because he created an extraordinary portrait. At what is supposed to be the "awkward age" Jane is a poem of grace, and Barber has caught the high color which excitement always brought to her translucent skin, according to those who knew her.

Shortly after Jane's tenth birthday in 1817 she was taken in hand by a governess, Miss Margaret Steele, who was said to be a woman of puritanical correctness "with a range of vision as narrow as a needle." It was Miss Steele's first position, and she undertook in a spirit of righteousness her mission to turn little Miss Digby into a well-behaved young lady. It did not take Jane long to melt this prim young spinster's reserve. All she had to do was cry, "Dear, dear Steely!" and throw her arms around her governess in an excess of affection. Steely was delighted to discover that her little tomboy was a fascinating and unusually alert pupil. Jane had an astonishing grasp of languages and a great love of literature. She had little fondness, however, for strictly feminine tasks such as making samplers, and she begrudged every moment she spent cross-stitching such sticky verses as:

> All little girls should duteous be,
> And kind and courteous ever.
> From frivolous thoughts deliver me
> Until this life I sever.

Jane much preferred the free expression of sketching and watercoloring, and her artistic talent was so marked that Lady Andover arranged for her daughter to have special lessons in drawing and painting from Steely's sister, Miss Jane Steele. Both teachers fell under the spell of the beautiful, golden-haired mischief-maker, who could twist them around her finger. Although Jane was good at her lessons, the four walls of the schoolroom could hold her for only a limited time, and then she was off on a round of adventures. She knew the sequestered spots where hens laid their eggs, and she could climb a tall tree to examine a robin's nest. From the time she was very small she rode a horse as if she had been born in the saddle. She was the darling and the terror of the great kitchen at Holkham, for she could always find the jam pots and the cakes. She was the favorite of the stablemen, and she was the idol and the despair of her relatives, a wild and bewitching madcap who laughed at all restraint and drove her parents to distraction. Steely threatened her with every kind of punishment, but always agreed not to tell Lady Andover if Jane would promise to be good.

If being governess to a girl like Jane was not easy, at least it was never dull, and Steely had the fringe benefit of expense-paid travel. With Napoleon's armies no longer on the march, hordes of Englishmen, who had been deprived of European travel during more than a decade of fighting, "invaded" the continent once again. In 1820 Admiral Digby took his family on an extended tour that included France, Italy and Switzerland, and Steely was brought along to keep up the children's lessons. It took more than a change of scene, however, to keep Jane out of trouble, as a letter she wrote in Geneva at age twelve indicates:

Dearest Mama,
I am very sorry for what I have done. I will try if you will forgive me not to do it again. I won't contradict you no more. I've not had one lesson turned back

today. If you and Papa will forgive me send me an answer by the bearer, pray do forgive me. You may send away my rabbits, my donkey, my monkey but do forgive. I am yours ever.

J.E.D.

Send me an answer please by the bearer. I will eat my bread at dinner always.

This was Jane, the beautiful, mischievous imp, begging for forgiveness while a more daring transgression was already taking shape in her restless mind. No one who knew her ever doubted that she was always sincerely sorry for causing anyone pain; she just did what she had to and thought about it later. She always sought acceptance even when she deliberately courted rejection.

Throughout her varied relationships Jane was always extravagant, both emotionally and financially. She does not say why she wanted a forty-pound advance on her allowance one day in Florence in 1820, but as always with things she wanted badly, it was very important! She addressed this request to Admiral Digby:

Dear Papa,
I write because I have a favor to ask which I'm afraid you will think too great to grant, but as *you* at Geneva trusted me with a little—I am not ashamed, *after* you have heard from Steely my character, to ask a second time. It is to—to—to advance my pocket money to two pounds a week for twenty weeks! ! ! Counting from next Monday. I'll tell you what for if you *approve*. I'll do it but if not I'll give it up! ! ! Remember at Geneva after you advanced me twelve weeks I never teased you for money until the time was expired. I promise to do the same here. Do not tell anyone but give me the answer. I will not ask you for half a cracie until the time has expired. Think well of it and remember it is twenty weeks I ask twenty pounds extra, not a farthing more. I'll have nothing more or less ... forty pounds. Goodbye and put the answer at the bottom of this. I have long been trying to hoard the sum but I find I want it directly and then I should not have it until we were gone. If you refuse me I will not grumble and if you grant it me *je vous remercierai bien. Pensez* and goodbye *mon bon petit père*. I remain your very affectionate daughter.

Jane Elizabeth Digby

Jane's inability to wait for anything had already surfaced: forty pounds today and penniless for twenty weeks. Admiral Digby surely gave in. It was hard to resist such a winsome plea, particularly from a daughter who looked like Jane. Long before she was out of short dresses she gave promise of that exceptional beauty that combined with her defiance of convention to supply so much material for the scandal-mongers. There is a description of Jane at thirteen by a visitor to Holkham:

Her eyes were large and of an exquisite blue such as I have never seen in any other human face; her lips, parted in a merry, roguish smile, revealed teeth like flawless pearls; her face was a perfect oval, and her complexion had the delicate bloom of a peach. Her figure was instinct with vitality and an incomparable grace of movement. But her chief glory was her hair, which fell, a rippling golden cascade, down to her knees.

That same year Sir Harry Keppel wrote of the Anson and Digby cousins sharing the schoolroom at Holkham, "The Ansons, such dear, pretty children, and little Miss Digby, oh! so beautiful!"

The beautiful Miss Digby was still a tomboy, and she spent every moment she could steal from her lessons either on horseback or in the stables, where she was by this time getting some impertinent stares from the young grooms. The great coachbuilders of the early nineteenth century were turning out a wonderful assortment of carriages, and Jane could identify them all at a glance: the fashionable landau, the deep-hung barouche, the dashing curricle, tilbury and phaeton "highflyer." From the time Jane was very small, she was traveling with her family between Norfolk and Dorset, and she knew the excitement of the colorful English coaching inns with their blue-nosed ostlers who took care of the horses and the pinch-faced little boys, known always as "Boots," who cleaned the boots of the travelers. Supper was usually bread and a slice of meat cut from an enormous cold round of beef, washed down with a foaming tankard of ale.

Following the death of his octogenarian father, George III, the Prince Regent was proclaimed King George IV in January 1820, and a very sticky problem arose concerning the Princess Caroline, whom the regent had married in 1795. The marriage had been a disaster from the day the regent sent one of his mistresses, the elegant Lady Jersey, to meet his gawky German bride-to-be at Greenwich. The prince and Caroline managed to overcome their mutual dislike long enough to conceive the Princess Charlotte and then went their separate ways. George made no attempt to conceal his liaisons in the intervening years, and the princess was indiscreet from Italy to the Holy Land and back. Determined that Caroline would not be crowned queen, George bullied his cabinet into instituting a bill of Pains and Penalties against his wife on grounds of her adultery with one Bartolomeo Pergami.

It was a ridiculous situation, because while the Princess' guilt could be established with little doubt, her husband could scarcely pose as the injured innocent party. Nonetheless, coming as it did in the midst of a postwar depression, the issue threw an England already seething with discontent into a state of near-revolution.

Jane's grandfather, Coke of Norfolk, was a vehement supporter of Caroline for a variety of reasons having little to do with her innocence or guilt. Like all other Whigs, Coke saw here an opportunity to topple the Tory cabinet, and like many men of both parties, he felt the king was hardly in a position to point an accusing finger. Even an ultra-conservative like Lord Ellenborough, although he strongly condemned Caroline's conduct, could not find it in his conscience to vote for the bill. It was probably the only time in their lives that Coke and the man who was to marry his granddaughter would find themselves politically on the same side of the fence.

When the bill was finally thrown out, after an incredible amount of dirty linen had been aired, the celebrations from one end of England to another reached a fever pitch unlike anything seen since Waterloo. There were many bumpers of ale raised to Caroline at Holkham, where Jane, who was spared the ugly details, realized only that her grandfather had won an important victory over the king. (For all her temporary popularity, the acquittal was a hollow victory for Caroline. It amounted, as a Whig M.P. pointed out, to a decision that the lady was immoral and her husband a fit associate for her. The unhappy Caroline was unable to force her way into Westminster Abbey at the king's coronation in June 1821, and died a few months later still uncrowned.)

Despite his Whig rebelliousness and his staunch defense of Caroline, Coke had a rigid moral code, which would not permit him to entertain in his home the wife of his close friend and political ally, Charles James Fox, because she had lived with Fox openly before their marriage. Coke himself, however, became the butt of many bawdy jokes when his astonishing May–December marriage took place on February 26, 1822.

There are several versions of how this disparate union came about, but all agree that the idea originated with the bride, eighteen-year-old Lady Anne Keppel. Lady Anne was the goddaughter of the powerful squire of Holkham and the daughter of the Lady Albermarle whose funeral procession had been previewed in Lady Andover's dream. Since her mother's death, the young girl had been an almost permanent guest at Holkham, where she had shared the schoolroom with Jane and the other Coke grandchildren. Tom Coke had tried to arrange a match between Lady Anne and William Coke, the nephew he had chosen as his heir, but neither party showed any interest in the idea. Coke's unmarried daughter, Eliza, must have seen the handwriting on the wall, because she once asked Lady Anne bluntly whether William or Mr. Coke was the attraction that kept her at Holkham. Lady Anne had answered in equally blunt fashion that it was Mr. Coke.

It was no secret to anyone that the "White Lily" (the nickname given Lady Anne for her very fair skin) was miserably unhappy over her father's impending marriage to Coke's niece, Charlotte Hunloke, who was a respectable forty-five. Lady Anne had enjoyed her independence far too long to make way gracefully for a stepmother. After the wedding in London, she was despondently gazing out the window when she saw Coke's coach waiting at the door to take him back to Norfolk. The ideal solution to her problem must have occurred to her at that moment, for she later recalled, "I saw that coach, and I thought if Mr. Coke once gets into that, all is over—and I rushed downstairs." Crying bitterly, she threw herself into the startled man's arms, and the result was a foregone conclusion.

That Coke should marry Lord Albermarle's daughter two weeks after Lord Albermarle became the bridegroom of Coke's niece suggested an element of comedy that the public did not fail to make the most of. Even Coke's family, with the exception of the displaced Eliza, joined in the laughter.

It was Lady Anne who had the last laugh, however, and the eighteen-year-old bride who did not want to be a stepdaughter in her own house moved into the Norfolk palace to become stepmother to Lady Andover (who was then forty-five), Lady Anson (forty-three and already a grandmother), and most distressingly to the twenty-seven-year-old unmarried Eliza, who had been the mistress of Holkham Hall since her debut.

The first child, a son and heir to Holkham (displacing poor William Coke), was born to Squire Coke and Lady Anne on December 26, 1822. This time no mouse got into the lady's nightcap. Shortly after the birth of his son, the jaunty sixty-nine-year-old Whig returned to his seat in the House of Commons and was greeted with rousing cheers, even from the ministerial benches. (There were many more ovations in order, for the "Crown Prince" of Holkham was followed by three brothers and a sister—the last child born to Coke and his young wife when the master of Holkham was eighty-four!) This new family radically changed the position of Coke's children and grandchildren by his first wife. There were still visits back and forth, but the "White Lily" left no doubt in anyone's mind as to who was in charge at Holkham.

The significance of her former playmate's triumph was not lost on little Miss Digby. Just three years older than Jane and not nearly so pretty, Lady Anne reigned supreme in Norfolk with no one to tell her what to wear, what to study, when to come and when to go. If marriage could do all that for a girl, it was worth serious consideration. Although Jane's Aunt Anson had been married at fifteen, Jane had no bona fide suitors at this age. The list of her local admirers, however, could have stretched from Holkham to the sea and back. There is an unconfirmed story that about this time Jane eloped with a handsome young Holkham groom and was only rescued from Gretna Green after a wild chase over several counties. Whether or not such was the case, it is certain that Miss Digby was beginning to return some of the glances she was getting, and Lady Andover called a family conference. When "La Madre" (as she was called by her children) was under full sail, she was too formidable a foe for even the courageous Admiral Digby, and over his protests that Jane was still too young, Lady Andover launched her plans for Jane's future. It was time, she said, to get their daughter out of the stables and into the orbit of more eligible suitors.

The Digbys took a house in London and began preparations for Jane's debut into the *haut monde* of post-Regency England, where all things foreign were fashionable, and the habit of decorating the simplest English sentence with foolish little French phrases was the hallmark of the most aristocratic gatherings. The English ruling class doted on beauty, elegance, wit and a good seat on a horse. Jane Digby, at age sixteen, had more than her share of those important assets, but the wisdom, discrimination and experience to meet the "slough of fashionable society" were not yet part of her equipment.

3

◇——◇

A Debut and a Wedding

A lovely being, scarcely formed or moulded,

A rose with all its sweetest leaves yet folded . . .

—LORD BYRON

The Regency officially ended in 1820, when the Prince of Wales came to the throne as George IV, but the flamboyant character of the period continued almost undiluted for the ten years of George's reign. When Jane Digby came to town in 1823, Georgian London was at the zenith of its ordered beauty, time-mellowed and still untouched by the neo-Gothic madness. There was street after street of exquisitely proportioned three- and four-storied houses, each with the same unadorned face of freestone-bordered sash, the same white pillars on either side of the door, the same stone steps. Only in the beautifully molded doors and brightly polished door knockers with their wreaths, urns and lion masks did the English instinct for individuality break through. The Digbys took one of these houses on Harley Street, in the heart of the comparatively small area between Grosvenor Square and St. James, where fashionable Londoners lived and spent most of their time.

The London "season" officially began in the spring, but the summer months were a prime social period. (A Paris visitor was dazzled by the manner in which "this race of gods and goddesses descended from Olympus upon London in June and July . . . appeared to live on a golden cloud, spending their riches as indolently and naturally as the leaves grow green.") The debut of a young goddess required months of advance preparation, and the Digbys came to town well ahead of the season. The house on Harley Street had to be staffed and furnished. Yards of silk, Malines lace, muslin and fine linen were purchased and seamstresses engaged. There were bonnets, slippers, gloves and reticules ordered, as well as new liveries for the footmen. The new wardrobe was, in effect, a trousseau, since the presentation of a young girl at court was a formal announcement that she was ready for marriage.

King George IV, obese, gout-ridden and covered with greasepaint to hide his aging face, was too uncomfortable and too self-conscious to be seen often in public, but the society that had revolved around him during his regency was still flourishing. A few of the aristocratic women to whom the naive Jane Digby was presented were: Lady Conyngham, the king's current (and final) mistress, known disrespectfully as the "Vice-Queen"; Lady Emily Cowper, whose mother, Lady Melbourne, after spending most of her life flitting from Lord Coleraine to the Duke of Bedford to Lord Egremont, had on her deathbed commanded daughter Emily always to be true, not to Emily's husband, Lord Cowper, but to Emily's lover, Lord Palmerston; Lady Jersey, the aging autocrat whose liaison with the king when he was Prince of Wales was a matter of record; the Countess of Oxford, who had had a passionate affair with Lord Byron (though she was nearly twice his age) and whose children were known, from her family name of Harley and because their fathers were rumored to be such a mixed lot, as the "Harleian Miscellany"; and the Princess Thérèse Esterhazy, whose numerous lovers were said to enter and leave her apartments at the Austrian Embassy with the regularity of diplomatic couriers. It was a group well qualified to give a sheltered girl from the hinterlands a liberal education in a hurry.

That a society which gave tacit approval to such casual morals should impose rigid rules of decorum on other facets of life was an irony that escaped most of those involved in the charade. The protocol for a young lady's introduction into that society was immutable, and no exceptions were made even for a lovely rebel like Jane. The first order of business was the presentation at court, a heady experience for a sixteen-year-old girl just out of the schoolroom. Wearing white ostrich plumes in her hair and an elaborate gown that showed as much of her charms as was fashionable, Jane rode with her parents in a highly polished coach, accompanied by liveried footmen wearing huge bouquets in their lapels. They joined a long procession of carriages making their way down Piccadilly to St. James's Palace. In the crush of stout, painted matrons with diamonds twinkling in their wigs and blasé courtiers decorated with stars, garters, collars and cordons, young ladies often fainted from excitement while waiting to make their curtsies, but Jane was not the fainting type. For older women who had won acceptance, by fair means or foul, in the highest circles of society, a presentation at court was the apogee of success. William Makepeace Thackeray took a cynical view of the procedure:

> From that august interview they come out stamped as honest women. The Lord Chamberlain gives them a certificate of virtue. And as dubious goods or letters are passed through an oven at quarantine, sprinkled with aromatic vinegar, and then pronounced clean—many a lady whose reputation would be doubtful otherwise and liable to give infection, passes through the wholesome ordeal of the Royal presence, and issues from it free from all taint.

Jane's debut at court was followed by a series of large formal dinner parties, climaxed by a ball at the Digby home, to which as many of London's eligible men were invited as could be crammed into 78 Harley Street. The rule of thumb for an evening of dancing was established by Lady Cowper, who once told Lady Nevill, "To make a ball successful, three men should always be asked to every lady—one to dance, one to eat and one to stare—that makes everything go off well." Quadrilles were the most popular dances; there were still people who disapproved of waltzing. After each dance a partner brought his young lady back to her mother and made his bow. There was no such thing as "sitting out," and no one danced with the same person twice at any ball.

Fashionable London at the time of Jane's debut was ecstatic over Byron's *Don Juan*, and the enchanting Miss Digby acquired from one of her admirers the nickname "Aurora" after the sixteen-year-old heroine of the fifteenth canto, Aurora Raby. It was especially appropriate for the young debutante whose father's first naval victory had been won off the Portuguese coast in the frigate *Aurora*. It was far more romantic than Jane or Janet or Jenny (as her brothers called her), and name-changing was a poetic fancy much in vogue. A few years earlier Jane Austen had remarked that "No young lady of common gentility could reach the age of sixteen without altering her name as much as she could." It may not have been coincidence that the man who was "Aurora" Digby's most ardent suitor from the moment they met at her "coming out" ball fitted neatly into the *Don Juan* image with his reputation for rakishness. Thirty-four-year-old Edward Law, Lord Ellenborough, was not a popular man even among his own set. Thomas Creevey said of Edward in his diary, "Lady Anson will have it that he was a very good husband to his first wife, but all my impressions are that he is a damned fellow!" Creevey was not alone in that opinion.

Lord Ellenborough was tall and well built, with a healthy complexion, heavily arched eyebrows and a luxuriant head of brown hair. Lady Oxford once said that there was something about young Edward Law which involuntarily commanded admiration. From his portraits it is obvious that he was handsome, and, according to many of his contemporaries, he was vain. An opposing member of Parliament once ridiculed Ellenborough for his pride in his wavy brown locks:

> He would not suffer them to be cropped for twice the amount of his hereditary pension of 10,000 pounds a year. No lady rejoices more in her ringlets nor is at more pains in adjusting them.... His countenance, which has something of the Grecian about it, indicates great self-possession and coldness of manner, which are the leading attributes of his character.

Harriette Wilson, a celebrated English courtesan who embarrassed many men in high places when she published her memoirs in 1825, pointed out the same shortcomings in the man who was courting Jane Digby:

> Young Law, Lord Ellenborough's son, was a very smart, fine young gentleman, and his impatience of temper passed, I dare say, occasionally for quickness. His wig was never on straight on his head. I rather fancy he liked to show his own good head of hair under it.

Ellenborough was notorious for his acid tongue, which multiplied his enemies on both sides of the political fence. To many of his associates in the House of

Lords Edward was an arrogant parvenu, whose peerage dated back only to 1802 when his father, who had been a brilliant Lord Chief Justice of England, was created first Baron Ellenborough. Edward's family, after generations of obscurity in Westmorland, experienced a remarkable flowering of talent in the eighteenth and nineteenth centuries. Two of his uncles became bishops, and another uncle—Thomas Law—made a fortune in India and retired to America where he married the granddaughter of Martha Custis Washington.

Edward himself was an able administrator and a brilliant orator, but he believed implicitly that only the aristocracy was fit to govern. His close friend Lady Nevill wrote of Edward, "He used to say to me, 'War and women, these are in reality the only fit interests for a man!' . . . he had but small belief in the wisdom of democratic government, and dreaded the advent of new and socially inferior men in the House of Commons." In his later political career, which won him the posts of Viceroy of India and First Lord of the Admiralty, as well as an earldom, Ellenborough was accused by his associates of "overbearing demeanor," "shabby behavior," and "theatrical love of display." Even Queen Victoria, who bestowed many honors on him, said, "It is a pity that Lord Ellenborough with his knowledge, experience, activity and cleverness, should be so entirely unable to submit to general rules of conduct." For all his brilliance, Edward was lacking in humor and warmth, and he seemed to court unpopularity as if he found it gentlemanly and convenient.

It was common knowledge that Lord Ellenborough had been in the marriage market ever since his first wife, Lady Octavia Stewart, had died childless in 1819. Almost before he was out of mourning, Edward was described by Countess Granville as "evidently in search of a wife." Mrs. Harriet Arbuthnot accused him of "having flirted and made himself ridiculous with all the girls in London." Creevey claimed that Edward had been refused by a Miss Russell, along with several others. Lady Octavia's mother, Lady Londonderry, encouraged her son-in-law to take another wife, writing him in 1823, "You must marry a young and beautiful companion for an improved *noblesse*. You must again be happy in married life, for no other can make you so."

In the dazzling Jane Digby, Lord Ellenborough found the beautiful companion his mother-in-law had recommended, and it flattered his vanity to win the sensation of London society. But why with all of London at her feet did Jane choose this man to marry? His handsomeness, mature years and racy reputation would have been enough to attract an unsophisticated girl, who had been taught that the height of happiness in marriage was a house in Mayfair, a country house at Wimbledon, a fine coach, blooded horses, liveried footmen and ample "pin money." A poem in Jane's notebook provides another clue to the source of her attraction to Lord Ellenborough. It was written before her marriage, and if it is as autobiographical as the rest of her poetry, it suggests that Lord Ellenborough may have caught Jane at a vulnerable moment:

On Meeting, For the First Time

Is it then thus thou canst meet
With chilling look, averted eye,
The heart that thou first caused to beat
With love's first youthful extasy?

Ah! colder far than northern breezes
That howl across the wintry waste,
Is that repentance chill that seizes
The soul on musing o'er the past!

And tho she's to another plighted
And love t'were madness now to feel,
Yet he who first that bosom blighted
Might cast a look that wound to heal.

'Tis o'er, that form how changed alas!
That young Ianthe loved so long,
Thou art not now what once thou wast,
That gayest gallant crowds among.

And if at length when life is o'er,
Perchance my death thou'll hear,
I cannot, would not ask for more
Than Pity's silent tear!!

No one knows who the "gallant" was, but it does not sound like one of the Holkham stable boys. The most logical candidate was Jane's first cousin, George Anson. Marriage between them was taboo, but they had been strongly attracted to each other since childhood. "Ianthe," a Greek version of "Jane," is the name Lord Byron gave to Lady Oxford in the dedication of *Childe Harold's Pilgrimage*, and Jane used it often in referring to herself. It was a sobriquet that clung long after "Aurora" was forgotten.

Lord Ellenborough needed little encouragement from Jane to press his suit. With all the impatience of an adolescent but all the elegance and sophistication appropriate to his age and experience, he set out to win the lovely Miss Digby. Victory was in his pocket when he wrote a poem to her calling her "Juliet." If there was anything Jane could not resist, it was romantic poetry:

O, Juliet, if to have no fear
But that of not deserving thee,
To know no grief when thou art near,
No joy thou canst not share with me,

If still to feel a lover's fire
And love thee more the more possessed,

> *To have on earth the one desire*
> *Of making thee completely blessed,*
>
> *If this be passion, thou alone*
> *Can make my heart this passion know;*
> *Love me but still as thou hast done,*
> *And I will ever love thee so.*

Edward got his answer from Jane the following day:

> *To love thee still as I have done,*
> *Say, is that all thou ask of me?*
> *Thou hast it then, for thou alone*
> *Reign in the soul that breathes for thee.*
>
> *Edward, for thee alone I sigh*
> *And feel a love unknown before.*
> *What bliss is mine when thou art nigh!*
> *O, love me still—I ask no more*
>
> *But that thy heart may e'er remain*
> *Steadfast as mine through many a year,*
> *That I may never seek in vain*
> *To see my image graven there.*
>
> *As thou art now, O, ever be*
> *To her whose fate in thine is bound,*
> *Whose greatest joy is loving thee,*
> *Whose bliss in thee alone is found.*
>
> *And she will ever thee adore*
> *From day to day with ardor new,*
> *Both now and to life's latest hour*
> *With passion felt alas by few.*

Once Edward had won Jane's consent, her family was soon brought around. Admiral Digby got on well with his daughter's suitor. Lady Andover was aware of Ellenborough's unpopularity, but there were many things, she felt, in his favor. It was true that his peerage was quite recent, but he claimed descent from the royal families of England derived from the Plantagenets through a daughter of Edward III. Wealth and family went a long way to cancel out Edward's minus factors in Lady Andover's viewpoint. Edward's former mother-in-law, the dowager Lady Londonderry, wrote to Lady Andover congratulating her on her daughter's engagement to a man she regarded as a son, and who had made Lady Octavia very happy during their five years together. That also must have been reassuring to Jane's mother.

Lord Ellenborough appeared so anxious to carry off the prize of the London season that he asked for a special license to have the marriage performed immediately without the usual posting of the banns. Jane, the great partisan of hasty action, was in complete accord. With the right people pulling the strings, the Archbishop of Canterbury gave his consent to the proposal that "the right Hon. Lord Ellenborough and Jane Elizabeth Digby, a spinster and a minor, should proceed to speedy solemnization of a true, pure and lawful marriage by and with the consent of Henry Digby, Rear Admiral in His Majesty's Navy, the natural and lawful father of the said minor." It would never have occurred to Jane with her wildly romantic nature that Edward's haste was more a matter of expediency than ardor, that he wanted to have the honeymoon out of the way to be back in London for the political battles he knew were in the offing that autumn.

Things happened so fast that Jane's grandfather, Coke of Norfolk, had no opportunity to register his strong dislike of Edward. Having just been made a father the second time by his young wife, Coke could not get away from Holkham for the ceremony. Jane's Aunt Anson represented the Norfolk family, as Creevey reported: "Lady Anson goes to town next week to be present at the wedding of her niece, the pretty Aurora, Light of Day." The marriage was performed September 15, 1824, at Admiral Digby's house in Harley Street by the bridegroom's uncle, George Henry Law, the Bishop of Bath and Wells, who reminded the newlyweds that matrimony was ordained firstly for the procreation of children, a particularly significant part of the ceremony for Edward, who was anxious for an heir.

The Lord and his Lady made a splendid couple. The bride, tall for her age, had a perfect figure, "a most lovely and sweet-turned face, pale-gold hair, wide-apart dark blue eyes, long dark lashes and wild rose coloring." Mrs. Arbuthnot conceded somewhat grudgingly that Jane was "very fair, very young and very pretty." Edward was described in the reminiscences of Lady Dorothy Nevill: "As a young man he had been of strikingly handsome appearance; I hardly remember anyone who looked so thoroughly well-bred; the noble to his fingertips, he had the grand manner and dignified bearing which distinguished the gentlemen of the old school." In a rustle of satin, lace, brocade and fine linen, the stunning Ellenboroughs left Harley Street for their Brighton honeymoon.

The English seaside resort, described by a nineteenth-century traveler as "a clean Naples with genteel *lazzaroni*," was seven hours by coach from London. Brighton was gay and gaudy, and the prawns were excellent. Dutton's famous jellies lived up to their reputation, and the bridal suite at the Norfolk Hotel was filled with flowers. The honeymoon, however, was apparently a dismal failure. Exactly what happened on Jane and Edward's wedding trip is only conjecture, but there were unpleasant rumors that Lord Ellenborough paid more attention to the daughter of the hotel's pastry cook than to his bewildered bride. It is a safe assumption that the bridegroom, who may have shared the view of many of his contemporaries that the marriage bed was not the proper place for passion, made no attempt to be a lover to his wife. In any event, the honeymoon did not bode well for the couple's happiness together.

Admiral Digby and Lady Andover could not be blamed for their part in this misalliance. They had done their best for their daughter. They had given her in marriage to a wealthy and aristocratic man with whom she imagined herself in love. The match actually had more to recommend it than most fashionable marriages of the period. If Jane shared any of the blame, it was only because she was too inexperienced at seventeen, "a mere girl who has not seen anything of the world," as Lady Holland described her.

Edmond About, the French satirist who met Jane years later, had his own ideas of what went awry. She was, he wrote, "like all young girls of marriageable age, a book bound in muslin and full of white paper. She was waiting for a husband to form her character, her wit, and a good or bad nature. It's the story of all women; they are what one makes them.... Lord E. in matters of love was a somewhat blasé gourmet; he must have been terribly attracted by this pink and white beauty to go into such a disproportionate marriage. This man who was getting married for his own pleasure treated his wife like something he had paid a great price for."

That sort of male chauvinism was common enough in the nineteenth century, but there may have been some logic in the theory that things might have gone better for the newlyweds if Edward had been a more sensitive man. Byron in *Don Juan* may have more accurately summed up the "unnatural situation" of women in a marriage like that of the Ellenboroughs:

> *Taught to conceal, their bursting hearts despond*
> *Over their idol, til some wealthier lust*
> *Buys them in marriage—and what rests beyond?*
> *A thankless husband, next a faithless lover,*
> *Then dressing, nursing, praying, and all's over. . . .*
>
> *Some take a lover, some take drams or prayers,*
> *Some mind their household, others dissipation;*
> *Some run away, and but exchange their cares,*
> *Losing the advantage of a virtuous station.*

The Ellenboroughs returned from Brighton to Edward's country estate at Roehampton, a short distance from London. Before long the bridegroom was spending most of his time in the city. A friend of Edward's, Joseph Jekyll, visited the newlyweds less than two months after the wedding and recorded his impressions in a letter: "I dined and slept lately at Roehampton, to be presented by Lord E. to his bride. Very pretty, but quite a girl, twenty years younger than himself." Jekyll knew very well that Edward was only thirty-four, so it appears Jane's unworldliness made her appear no more than fourteen. Lord Ellenborough's frequent absences from home so soon after the honeymoon were already the subject of the young bride's complaints to Jekyll during his stay, and when asked to write a note in her album, the visitor teasingly quoted a few lines which ended, "And peers in vain by proxy love." Poor Jekyll did not intend to prove so prophetic.

In a devastating novel, *The Two Friends*, published several years later, the Countess of Blessington described the early disillusionment of the Ellenborough marriage, thinly disguising Jane and Edward as Lord and Lady Walmer:

Lady Walmer had been spoiled by a doting mother; as an only daughter and beauty, the vain parent had indulged all her caprices.... Her personal attraction gained her many suitors, from whom she selected Lord Walmer, because he was the best looking and best dressed man among them. In return, he was proud to call her his wife, she being the most admired young belle about town, whose possession all his set would consequently envy him. They fancied that they loved each other, and did not discover their mistake until nearly two months after it was irremediable. The discovery was made, like many similar ones, after a few weeks' residence, tête-à-tête, in the country, where ample time and scope is provided for acquiring a knowledge of defects, which, if detected before instead of after marriage, might prevent many an indissoluble knot from ever being tied, and save many unhappy couples from yawns, if not sighs, in after years. Lady Walmer found that her lord was very tiresome; while he felt that he was only very tired of matrimony, or of the country; which it was he had not quite determined.

Edward solved his dilemma by plunging into work, and Jane for a while was content to savor the sweets of a young matron's social life, free from the domination of family and governess. Without any mature guidance and with an unlimited budget, she revelled childishly in "dressing up," and her overly ornate gowns with too many frills and ribbons caused much laughter among the more sophisticated members of her circle. Countess Granville wrote, "Count Walewski thinks Lady Ellenborough the most divinely beautiful creature he beheld, but sickens at her dress."

It was not unusual for a man to criticize a woman's taste in clothing at a time when men gave so much time and thought to their own. The English dandy or "blood" could discuss for hours the shape of a cravat, could shrink with horror from a badly cut coat, could spend half the day choosing clothes and putting them on. It was a kind of sport, like boxing, "fives," rat-hunting and four-in-hand driving, played with mock solemnity. It was a half-defiant, half-humorous way of life for a class of men indifferent to serious matters and willing to give intense concentration to trivia. Lord Petersham, for example, was said to have a different snuffbox for every day in the year, taking care to choose one that suited the weather, and never using a light snuffbox in an east wind. It was a way of life so completely artificial that Sir Walter Scott, in London for a few weeks, expressed great longing to be back home at Abbotsford, away from fashion and pretence, away from exclusive clubs and champagne and plovers' eggs, and the innumerable gatherings where he felt "like a poodle dog compelled to stand forever on its hind legs."

Lady Ellenborough in her teens was certainly no match for the society in which she found herself, the "seething slough" of frivolity, hypocrisy and adultery, glossed over by a thin veneer of elegant mannerisms. The holy place of highest fashion for Jane's set was no longer Carlton House, which was being dismantled and incorporated at enormous expense into the rebuilding of Buckingham Palace and Windsor Castle. Carlton House had been supplanted by Almack's assembly rooms on King Street, St. James, where a far haughtier and far less cultivated circle than had graced the regent's mansion was presided over by an all-powerful group of lady patronesses. The name "Almack's" was an anagram of a Mr. Macall or McCaul, who had founded it in 1765. For nearly a hundred years London aristocracy gathered there to gossip, gamble, intrigue and hold their lavish balls.

In 1825 the six patronesses of Almack's, Lady Jersey, Lady Sefton, Lady Londonderry, Lady Cowper, Princess Esterhazy (the Austrian ambassador's wife) and Princess de Lieven (the Russian ambassador's wife) were grovelled to by the highest in the land for voucher-invitations to the Wednesday Night Balls. Great diplomacy, finesse and a host of intrigues were employed to secure an invitation to Almack's. Male guests had to have dancing skill, and knee-breeches and white cravats were *de rigueur*. The great Duke of Wellington, who had banished the threat of Napoleonic conquest from the world, was firmly refused admission one night because he was wearing trousers. Persons engaged in commerce had, of course, no hope of ever being invited, and young girls new to the fashionable world were heartbroken if they were not on the list. Henry Luttrell explained the reasons in a verse called "Advice to Julia":

> *All on that magic LIST depends;*
> *Fame, fortune, fashion, lovers, friends:*
> *'Tis that which gratifies or vexes*
> *All ranks, all ages and both sexes.*
> *If once to Almack's you belong,*
> *Like monarchs, you can do no wrong;*
> *But banished thence on Wednesday night,*
> *By Jove, you can do nothing right.*

The Princess de Lieven was not unaware of her omnipotence in the social scene; "It is not fashionable," she wrote, "where I am not." She and Princess Esterhazy were relentlessly satirized in a brilliant portrayal of their society, a novel called *Almack's*, published anonymously in 1827. The book was dedicated:

To that most distinguished and despotic conclave composed of their High Mightinesses, the Ladies Patronesses of the Balls at Almack's, the Rulers of Fashion, the Arbiters of Taste, the Leaders of Ton, and the Makers of Manners, whose sovereign sway over the "world of London" has long been established on the firmest basis, whose Decrees are Laws, and from whose judgement there is no appeal....

The characters in this *roman à clef* were in many cases only thinly disguised, and the Almack's set assumed that the author, who dared to laugh at them, was a man. Her contemporaries never knew that the witty, audacious author was Miss Marianne Spencer Stanhope, sister-in-law to Jane's aunt Eliza Coke Spencer Stanhope. Eliza helped correct the manuscript and kept the secret well although many of her own family were treated humorously. She recognized in the silly and immature Lady Glenmore a composite study of her young stepmother, Lady Anne Coke, and her niece, Lady Ellenborough.

Despite the fifty-year age difference between Lady Anne and Jane's grandfather, the Coke marriage gave every appearance of being a happy one. That could not be said for the Ellenboroughs', as that handsome couple were seldom seen together. Jane could not understand what had happened to the ardent suitor who had written such romantic poetry during their courtship. Things were not working out as Ellenborough had glowingly predicted in 1824:

> *To feel existence is itself a bliss*
> *And think, while joyous in the present day,*
> *That life will get happier than this!*
> *And each new sun shine with a brighter ray.*
>
> *To love as if we only lived to love*
> *And think that life and love will ever last,*
> *That every vision will prophetic prove*
> *And each new joy be greater than the past!*

Jane decided that Edward's coldness toward her meant that he still loved his first wife, and in the second year of their marriage she wrote a touching poem after he had criticized her melancholy moods:

TO EDWARD, ON HIS COMPLAINING OF MY WANT OF GAIETY

> *Forgive me, dearest beloved, if jealous fears*
> *Distract my most devoted heart,*
> *To feel that she, thy love of former years*
> *Still enjoys thy fondest dream's part.*

While every thought and wish of mine
Is breathed for thee and thee alone.
My life, by being, only thine,
Will allow no kindred transport own.

But mournfully with tearful eye.
With sinking voice and bearing sad,
However faithful, how much I try,
I cannot overcome the dead.

And she who still is mainly dear,
Say, did her passion equal mine?
Her joy the same when thou art near?
If not, what memories do so bind?

O, bend those angel eyes on me
And smile my jealous fears away.
Say, "Ne'r loved I aught as I do thee,"
Then and then alone thou wilt see me gay.

Most men would have been deeply moved by such a declaration, but Lord Ellenborough had no time now for romantic foolishness. The courtship was over, and he saw no need to cater to a childish demand for assurance and affection. Having bestowed his name and fortune on Jane, he was satisfied that he had fulfilled his part of the marriage. The satisfaction, however, was not mutual, and at nineteen the lovely Lady Ellenborough was hardly ready to put romance behind her. Once she had given up on Edward, she did not have to look very hard for someone who could accept the affection her husband seemed to value so little.

4

A Dazzled Librarian

Thus, though righteous Heaven above
Forbids this rebel heart to love,
To love is still its fate!
—JANE DIGBY, AGE NINETEEN

If she felt so inclined, a wealthy London lady in 1826 had plenty of time for extramarital mischief. Her large household staff was administered by a house-keeper and head butler, so her mornings could be devoted to deciding what to wear for the daily drive, the round of visits and the shopping that filled her afternoons. While Edward spent long hours in pursuit of the cabinet post, Jane had not only her mornings and her afternoons to herself but her evenings as well. It did not occur to Lord Ellenborough to insist upon a chaperone for his young wife, as Viscount Anson had done for Jane's aunt Ann. (Lady Anson's virtue was never questioned, but she had picked up an addiction for gambling from the older women with whom she was forced to spend her time at evening parties.)

The routine of the fashionable English matron did not take long to pall on Jane. In a year and a half of marriage she had acquired a wardrobe full of expensive morning dresses with the popular gigot sleeves that fit tightly from wrist to elbow and then ballooned out over the upper arm with yards of fullness. She had bared her admirable breast in a number of elaborate, Empire-waisted ballgowns. She had custom-made silk slippers in every color with matching ribbons to wind around her shapely ankles. She had seen prints of her portraits offered for sale in the windows of Colnaghi's, alongside one of King George IV in a frock coat with a fur collar simpering on a sofa from under his brown wig. But there was nothing very adventurous in any of this, and she was bored and lonely.

Many of the aristocratic ladies of the Almack's Wednesday Night Balls thought it *démodé* to be faithful to one's husband, and it is hardly surprising that Jane was tempted to follow their example. The intrigue, the fevered glances, the secret meetings of a clandestine love affair promised all the excitement that had been missing from her life. When or with whom Jane first cuckolded Edward is not known (it seems likely the man was her cousin, Col. George Anson), but the love affair began (or was resumed) sometime before September 23, 1826, when she wrote this poem:

O! it is heaven thus to love thee!
O! it is rapture to be near thee
And live to call thee mine!
If, dearest, if the joy thou feelest
But half approaches that thou givest
Then what extasy is thine!

Thus, though righteous Heaven above
Forbids this rebel heart to love,
To love is still its fate!

In mercy be my sins forgiven,
And at the last may pitying Heaven
A pardoned spirit wait!

A longer poem—this one undated—strengthens the possibility of a long-running affair with her first cousin. One verse in particular suggests a forbidden love:

What tho' the cold world proclaim it as wrong,
The feelings of youth are as lasting as strong,
And the image which love has traced on the heart
May fade for a while but cannot depart.

In January of 1827 Lady Anne Coke presented Jane's aging grandfather with a third son, and members of Coke's family by his first wife came in succession to Holkham to offer their congratulations. Jane's illicit romance was apparently either over or in decline at the time. Lady Andover was already in Norfolk, and Jane decided to join her and pay her respects to her new infant uncle. If the long winter evenings at Holkham were not glittering, they were far more cheerful than those at the Ellenboroughs' with Edward constantly away. There were usually more than enough guests at Coke's palace for the games that were much in fashion—whist and écarté, or for charades and the inevitable amateur musicales and sketching sessions. Holkham hospitality had not flagged under the reign of the determined and fertile young Lady Anne Coke. One custom she had instituted—that of family prayers after dinner—caused some amusing complications. Her brother, Sir Harry Keppel, recalled that the menservants used to go around the room afterwards, helping those whose "copious libations at dinner prevented them from rising when they had once knelt down."

When Jane came to Holkham in early spring 1827, Frederick Madden, a handsome young scholar and official of the British Museum, was temporarily in residence there, engaged in the tedious task of cataloguing the famous Long Library. For several weeks Madden had been spending long hours poring over the Greek poets in the daytime, dining and playing cards with the Coke family in the evening, and bemoaning the distance that separated him from his fiancée Mary. All that appears to have changed on March 13 when he wrote in his diary: "Lady Ellenborough, daughter of Lady Andover, arrived to dinner, and will stay a fortnight. She is not yet twenty, and one of the most lovely women I ever saw, quite fair, blue eyes that would move a saint, and lips that would tempt one to forswear Heaven to touch them." It was a remarkable change of tone from the terse entry of March 10, when he had recorded other arrivals: ". . . found in the house Lady Andover, Lady Anson and Miss Anson."

The subsequent events unfold inexorably from day to day, recorded in Madden's spidery handwriting:

Friday, March 16. Lady Ellenborough is such a charm that I find the library become a bore, and am delighted to be with her, and hear her play and sing, which she is kind enough to do.

Saturday, March 17. . . . with Lady E. in the Saloon; she sings to me the most bewitching airs, the words of which are enough to inflame one, did not the sight of so lovely a creature sufficiently do so. Her drawing books were lent me in the evening to look over.

Sunday, March 18. Lady Ellenborough has promised to take a tête-à-tête walk with me around the lake, but just as we were setting out, Capt. Greville came in and joined us. This was a bore!

Monday, March 19. In library until 4, then with Lady E. til past 5 hearing her play the guitar and sing. In the evening drew a picture for Lady Anne Coke from Lady E.'s book and am to draw something for her.

Tuesday, March 20. . . . Lady E. played to me til past 5. I am quite happy except that at times memory, like a scorpion's sting, tells me it is hollow and fleeting.

Wednesday, March 21. Lady E. generally rides in the morning with Miss Anson. She asked me to ride to Houghton with her, which I wd. like to do. Played écarté with Lady E., Lady Andover and Capt. Greville. Won the pot.

Thursday, March 22. In library til 4. Then out with Lady Ellenborough. Mr. and Mrs. Stanhope arrived.

Friday, March 23. In library til 3. Then with Lady Ellenborough and Miss Anson in the grounds.

Saturday, March 24. In library til 4. Then out. In the evening drew pictures for Lady Anne Coke and Miss Anson. Also played whist and won. Lady E. lingered behind the rest of the party, and at midnight I escorted her to her room——Fool that I was!——I will not add what passed. Gracious God! Was there ever such good fortune!

Madden could not have known that Jane, whom he could never bring himself to call by her first name, was so restless and so starved for affection she was ready to fall like a ripe peach into the arms of any man with courage to shake the branch. No matter what branch-shaking events occurred on Saturday night at Holkham, the Sunday schedule was rigid:

Sunday, March 25. Chapel in the morning. In the afternoon walked out with Lady E. She pretended to be very angry at what passed last night, but I am satisfied she——

Whatever Madden was satisfied about, a coolness seems to have developed between the lovers, for he failed to mention Jane on the following day, and on Tuesday only briefly, "Lady and Miss Anson left Holkham. Lady E., I am sorry to find, follows them on Thursday." There was a reconciliation on Jane's last full day in Norfolk, as Madden recorded:

Wednesday, March 28. In library til 2 o'clock. Then went with Lady E. tête-à-tête round the lake and remained in one of the hermitages with her til 5 o'clock. We have completely made it up. She is a most lovely fascinating woman. Whist in evening. Won. Afterwards drew a picture in Lady E.'s album.

The day of Jane's departure was a gray one for Frederick, who had little hope of their meeting again. He wrote on Thursday, March 29, "To my infinite regret Lady E. left Holkham this morning. Since I parted with dear M. never felt more melancholy or vexed." The librarian was far removed from Jane's exclusive circle at Almack's, and they never saw one another after that brief interlude in an enchanted Norfolk springtime. She is only mentioned once more in the journal, in April of the same year: "Lady Ellenborough, I find, is not at Brighton."

Madden married his Mary on February 26, 1830, and ten months later lost both her and their newborn son in the rigors of childbirth. A few weeks after their deaths the inconsolable Frederick covered a page of his journal with black ink, leaving only a small white space in which he scrawled an anguished note, "I feel I have been—Oh God, am I to confess it!—Guilty——!"

No one knows if Madden ever saw a copy of a poem in Jane's notebook dated "Holkham, March 1827":

> *Ah me, is passion's dream then o'er?*
> *Is tenderness with love then fled?*
> *Too soon cast off, beloved, no more,*
> *Forgot, as numbered with the dead.*

Yes, enough, if all I've ever done for thee
Will ne'er awake a pitying sigh,
If, should my name remembered be,
Even friendship's tear thou wilt deny.

It was then a crime to love too well!
Ah, when did man show gratitude
To her whose heart has dared rebel
Against the laws of man and God?

But still I'll weep and pray for thee,
And waft thy name on high,
Just say thou'll sometime think of me
And heave a gentle sigh.

The affair between Coke's beautiful granddaughter and his young librarian was a well-kept secret until forty years after Jane's death. In 1920 the voluminous journals of Sir Frederick Madden, which he bequeathed to Oxford's Bodleian Library, were unsealed, according to his instructions. Only then did this romance come to light.

Less than a week after Jane left Holkham that spring, she celebrated her twentieth birthday. There was enough excitement now in London to distract her thoughts from the Long Library. The fascinating story of her Jacobean kinsman's adventurous life and his deathless love for Venetia had just been published by Sir Harry Nicholas under the title of *The Private Memoirs of Sir Kenelm Digby*. (Although Nicholas left out intimate love passages and what was considered subversive philosophy in this first edition, these deletions received the maximum amount of attention when they were privately issued by Nicholas the following year under the provocative title of *The Castrations of the Private Memoirs of Sir Kenelm Digby*.) Jane was enjoying immensely the stir created by her unconventional ancestor in the spring of 1827 when she received the sad news of the death of Henry Anson, her cousin and dear friend almost from the day of her birth.

Henry and John Fox-Strangways had left some months earlier for a tour of the Holy Land and the Syrian desert. They had planned to disguise themselves as Arabs in order to enter the sacred city of Mecca, and had they succeeded, they would have anticipated by twenty-five years Sir Richard Burton's fabulous adventure. Unfortunately the young men made the unbelievably foolish mistake of entering a mosque without removing their shoes, and they were seized and flung into prison by a group of worshipers who were infuriated by this unspeakable sacrilege. It was some time before Henry and John were able to get word to the French consul, and the official machinery was slow in effecting their release. While in prison Henry contracted the plague, and freedom came too late for him.

He staggered out of his rank dungeon a dying man, and though his companion nursed him with utter disregard for his own well-being, Henry lived only a short while and was buried at Aleppo.

Before the true circumstances of Henry's death were brought to his family by Fox-Strangways, the wildest rumors had raced about London. One version, right out of the *Arabian Nights*, had the young Englishmen discovered by a Turkish official in his seraglio, whereupon they were given the choice of poison or mutilation. Henry, so the story went, had chosen the former without hesitation, and John was on his way home, having lost his eyes, ears, nose and tongue.

The tragedy of Henry's death brought Jane back in close touch with the Anson family and particularly with Henry's older brother, George. The two may have been secret lovers before, but now the attentiveness of Colonel Anson, the best-looking and most sought after bachelor of the Almack's set, to his beautiful cousin lit fires of jealousy in many an overexposed bosom, and for the first time there was ugly gossip circulated about an affection that was more than cousinly. George and Jane were together everywhere that summer: garden parties, the races, balls and receptions. It was the "Year of the Giraffe," when Londoners could talk of nothing but the animal that arrived in August, accompanied by two Nubian attendants, as a gift to the king from the Pasha of Egypt. There were giraffe medals struck, giraffes painted on fine china; no household was without some memento of the exotic creature that captured everyone's imagination. Colonel Anson escorted Lady Ellenborough on frequent excursions into the country for purposes of zoological instruction, and when Jane gave birth to her first child on February 15, 1828, the wags at Almack's were eager to give George the credit.

Lord Ellenborough, however, appears to have been completely satisfied that the child was his own, for the day after his wife gave birth he wrote in his diary:

Janet has brought me a boy. I put this down as a political occurrence because I shall make him if he lives and I live a Political Character. I shall ask the Duke of Wellington and Dudley to be his Godfathers. Princess Esterhazy is to be his Godmother. A good diplomatic introduction to the world.

Edward's singlemindedness concerning politics and his lack of tenderness, as revealed in these lines, support the gossip claiming that he married Jane more for an heir than for love. Jane disclosed later that from the day of her son's birth the Ellenboroughs gave up all pretense of conjugal life and moved into separate suites. (The arrangement was at her request, and her husband appears to have consented without a murmur of protest or even puzzlement.) Arthur Dudley Law was christened on February 28, 1828, and Lady Anne Coke sent a letter of congratulation to her step-granddaughter that had more than a hint of smugness.

"Now you, dear Janet, have had your first experience of motherhood," she wrote, "while I am somewhat ahead of you with my three small sons." (The smugness was undoubtedly lost on Jane, who had no intention of entering a baby derby.) The Ellenboroughs appeared together at Arthur's christening and again a month later at a dinner given by the Duke of Wellington, but the Lord and his Lady were freer than ever to go their separate ways.

Edward was well pleased with himself. Within one month two of his greatest ambitions were realized—he had got an heir and he had received a cabinet post as Lord Privy Seal in Wellington's newly formed ministry. The Duke's choice of the unpopular Ellenborough, however, caused screams of outrage from such fellow peers as their lordships Wharncliff, Grey and Holland. Lady Holland, that great Whig "minister-without-portfolio," was said to be so angry when she received news of Ellenborough's appointment that she set upon the hapless messenger who brought it with a flurry of unladylike blows. However few friends he had, Edward's hard work and undeniable capability were beginning to be rewarded.

Jane was showing progress too. The birth of her child had added the new dimension of maturity to her beauty, and even her taste in clothes was improving. Her relationship—whatever it may have been—with her cousin George was not resumed after her confinement with her infant son. Perhaps the ugly gossip convinced Colonel Anson it was best to end their association. There may have been family pressure. At any rate, as soon as she could get her stays fastened again, Jane was back at Almack's famed Wednesday Night Balls.

One Wednesday in April 1828, Lord Ellenborough escorted his wife to the entrance of Almack's, saw her safely inside, and then left, as was his custom, to spend his evening elsewhere. The ballroom was ablaze with the new gas lamps, and Lady Ellenborough, just turned twenty-one, was the most dazzling creature among the fashionable and brilliantly lighted assembly. The orchestra was playing *Ah quel plaisir d'être en voyage*, a favorite air from Boieldieu's *Jean de Paris*, and Jane needed an amusing new dancing partner to take George Anson's place. She did not have long to wait. After all her years on the patronesses' dais at Almack's, the Princess Esterhazy was a fair judge of what ingredients were necessary to promote a little dalliance, but she could scarcely have dreamed what she was setting in motion that night when she presented her husband's new attaché, Prince Felix Schwarzenberg, to the Lady Ellenborough. Certainly the princess was not acting in the best interests of her infant godson, Arthur Dudley Law, but how was she to know?

All the elements were there—the breathtakingly beautiful young wife, frustrated and restless, and the handsome foreign prince. Felix Schwarzenberg looked like the Byronic hero of Jane's most unbridled romantic fantasies—dashing, intense, with a spectacular black mustache and hypnotic dark eyes. In a rich, deep voice, charmingly accented, Felix could say it was a warm evening or ask for a waltz and make the words sound like a declaration of love. Unlike

Frederick Madden, the Prince was a connoisseur of women, and he could measure one's availability with a glance. Before the last strains of *Dormez, dormez, chers Amours* closed the ball that April night, Jane had committed herself irrevocably to a passionate love affair which was to have far-reaching repercussions. This foreign prince would call the tune she danced to for years to come.

5

A Prince from Bohemia

I loved, I love you, for this love have lost

State, station, heaven, mankind's, my own esteem,

And yet cannot regret what it has cost,

So dear is still the memory of that dream.

—*LORD BYRON*

Prince Felix Ludwig Johann von Nepomuk Friederich zu Schwarzenberg was born October 2, 1800, at Castle Krumlov on the Moldau River in Southern Bohemia. He was the second son of Prince Joseph and Princess Pauline (née Duchess of Arenberg), and his chief Christian name, Felix, was chosen to signify the luck which befell the family with the birth of a second guarantee to the family line. (Johann Nepomuk, Bohemia's patron saint, was regarded as the family's special protector.) The history of Felix's family was closely bound up with the histories of the Holy Roman Empire, the Austrian monarchy and the German nation; the family estates, among the largest properties on the continent, were often referred to as the "Schwarzenberg Kingdom." If Lord Ellenborough was "an aristocrat to his fingertips," Felix Schwarzenberg was one to his toes.

The family name was well known in England years before Felix Schwarzenberg arrived there. His uncle, Field Marshal Karl zu Schwarzenberg, had been Austrian ambassador to the court of Napoleon until hostilities broke out between his country and France. Then the soldier-diplomat was named commander-in-chief of the Austrian forces, and he gave the French emperor a sound drubbing at the battle of Leipzig in 1813. Field Marshal Schwarzenberg marched back into Paris with the victorious allies in 1814 and again after Waterloo. Like his uncle, Felix was successfully combining a diplomatic career with a military one. When he came to London in 1828, the prince was a captain in the Second Uhlans (mounted lancers), called the "Schwarzenberg Uhlans" after the Field Marshal.

The impressive credentials of the new attaché at the Austrian Embassy were of no importance whatsoever to Jane, who had fallen wildly, ecstatically in love for the first time. She had lost some of the innocence that belonged to the seventeen-year-old bride, but she was still remarkably naive in many respects. She had never really understood the rules of the game of love as played at Almack's, with its feints and subterfuges, and the overwhelming passion the prince awakened in her had nothing to do with rules or games. Felix Schwarzenberg at age twenty-seven was the most obvious choice imaginable for Jane to lose her head over. All his life he had been irresistible to women; he arrived in London leaving a trail of romantic conquests from St. Petersburg to Lisbon to Rio de Janeiro, and when he dropped dead in Vienna in 1852 at the age of fifty-one, he was dressing for a ball where he had arranged a rendezvous with a young officer's wife.

On the streets of London the mere sight of this dark-eyed foreign aristocrat in his dress uniform, with tasseled boots and the hussar jacket worn with studied casualness over one shoulder, evoked sighs from women of all ages, and there was more than pure physical attraction to Felix's charm. He literally breathed adventure with his background of faraway places and his restless temperament. His philosophy he summed up in one sentence: "To live is to travel; to travel, to live." That was heady wine for a would-be gypsy whose world was then bounded by Norfolk, Brighton and Dorset. How infinitely more appealing than the outlook of her child's godfather, Lord Dudley, who once sniffed, "Abroad is a poor place compared with England." Felix, like Jane, had a beautiful singing voice. He and his sister, Princess Mathilde, often sang high mass together in the village churches of their native Bohemia. He had grown up speaking German, French and Czech, and his lifelong avocation (besides women) was Latin. His military and diplomatic posts had brought him in contact with Russian, Portuguese and English, all of which he mastered with ease. There was an intriguing duality to his nature, an air of mystery that was magnetic. He was half ascetic, half womanizer, at once swaggering and melancholy, languid and fierce—a reckless playboy who somehow managed never to compromise his deadly serious ambition. It all added up to delirious excitement—and disaster—for Jane.

Almost from the moment Felix took her in his arms at that April ball, the two were lovers, and Almack's was not long in taking notice. Jane's passion for the handsome foreigner was so obvious, in fact, that only one month after their introduction Felix earned a nickname among the Almack's regulars, who were careful not to let him know about it. A horse named "Cadland" had just won the Derby, beating the favorite, "The Colonel." Because Jane had shown a marked preference for Colonel George Anson before the prince took over, it was inevitable that Felix would be called "Cadland," for having beat out the Colonel.

Before long all of London society was in on the "secret" romance of Jane and Felix. Count Rodolphe Apponyi, who joined the Austrian Embassy staff shortly after Schwarzenberg, set down in a journal his impressions of Jane after his first Almack's ball:

> Among all these people one lady especially attracted my attention. It was Lady Ellenborough, one of the most beautiful women I have ever seen, blond hair, magnificent complexion, big blue eyes, young, with the figure of a nymph; in fact, she is everything desirable. It is she whom Schwarzenberg adores, and I did not fail to have myself presented. I was not impressed by her intellect, it's true, but one cannot have everything. The expression of her face is as soft as the

sound of her voice, and her whole personality has something of modesty and innocence which enchanted me.

The coldness and formality of a first acquaintance did not last very long between us, and she spoke to me with childish candour about her husband, whom she accuses of being jealous and unkind. She obviously enjoys saying this, but my impression is that Lord Ellenborough is too busy with his political career to give his young wife good counsel.

Jane's description of Edward as "jealous and unkind" seems more childish than candid. She could hardly admit to herself or to others that rather than being jealous of her, her husband scarcely gave her any thought at all. Had Edward really been jealous, his young wife would not have been attending Almack's balls without him. No one would have been more surprised than Lord Ellenborough, who gave Jane so much wealth and freedom, to hear himself so described. Count Apponyi was far more accurate in his assessment of things when he said Ellenborough was "too busy." If Jane's husband had not been too busy to notice such things, he might have observed the change in her, the feverish excitement, the high color of that delicate complexion which always gave her emotions away. Count Apponyi had heard of the affair between Jane and Felix even before he arrived in England, and Lord Ellenborough was in constant contact with the Esterhazys and the Lievens, who had watched the affair progress. Edward was well insulated indeed in his self-centered world. He had other things on his mind.

The winds of change were sweeping English politics, and the new cabinet formed by the Duke of Wellington had its hands full, trying to appease the reformers on the one hand without offending the old-line Tory conservatives on the other. Edward was completely caught up in his only passion—politics—and his devotion to his new responsibilities was impressing even some of his former critics. Wellington's confidante, Mrs. Harriet Arbuthnot, reflected the change of attitude when she recorded in her journal that the Duke "thinks Ld. Ellenboro' very clever, and much improved by having his own office."

The post of Lord Privy Seal was mostly ceremonial with no really important duties attached, and Edward disliked it from the first, but he kept himself well occupied with work he loved—drafting dispatches for Lord Dudley at the Foreign Office. This pleasant arrangement did not last long, however. In May of 1828 (just as the affair of Lady Ellenborough and Prince Schwarzenberg was off to a roaring start) a dispute over borough reform caused part of Wellington's cabinet, including Lord Dudley, to resign. Dudley was replaced as Foreign Minister, not by the hopeful Lord Ellenborough but by Lord Aberdeen. Edward was crushed, and he sent word to the Duke that he too was ready to resign. Wellington tried to placate his Lord Privy Seal, saying that Edward had ten times more ability than Aberdeen, but Edward wanted more than flattery. "All have something to do but me," he lamented with unconscious irony that summer in his political diary.

Finally, in September the Iron Duke was able to give Edward more than sweet words. After considerable difficulty, Wellington persuaded the Royal Duke of Clarence, heir presumptive to the throne, to resign as Lord of the Admiralty. Lord Melville was then transferred to the Admiralty post, freeing his former cabinet job as President of the Board of Control for India, which was offered to Edward. "Upon the whole," Edward wrote in his diary, "I am satisfied with this arrangement. Undoubtedly the Foreign Office is the object of my ambition, and had the late Administration been beaten down in the field I must have had that office. It is now placed in very weak hands; but I may overestimate my own powers, and I excite less envy and jealousy by taking at first the *incognito* office of President of the Board of Control."

Now busier than ever, Edward was seldom to be seen at Roehampton. Certainly he devoted little time to his wife, but he was hardly the only man in the aristocracy to be guilty of this particular oversight. A contemporary, Capt. Rees Howell Gronow, noted that "... female society amongst the upper classes was most notoriously neglected, except by romantic foreigners, who were the heroes of many a fashionable adventure that fed the clubs with ever-acceptable scandal." Gronow would have been more precise had he pointed out that most Englishmen neglected only their *own* wives. Such "pillows of society" as Lady Melbourne, Lady Caroline Lamb, the Duchess of Devonshire, the Countess of Oxford and Lady Bessborough were notoriously unneglected by other women's husbands. As a rule, however, these cautiously loose peeresses managed to contain their affairs and the gossip about them within their small circle. Lady Melbourne, who was careful never to flaunt her affairs in public, made the sage observation that "Anyone who braves the opinion of the world sooner or later feels the consequences of it."

For the moment Jane and Felix were willing to let the consequences be damned. Although they made the small concession of arriving at social gatherings in separate carriages, there was little other effort to conceal their romance. While Lord Ellenborough complained of having "nothing to do," Lady Ellenborough and Prince Schwarzenberg found a great deal to do. They were quite obviously together at the Jockey Club dinner at St. James's in June, which marked the king's first public appearance in many months. The summer for the two lovers was one long idyll of breakfast parties in pastoral mansions among the Middlesex meadows and the Surrey woods; water parties in carpeted boats with bands playing under delicately colored awnings; elegant suppers catered by Gunter's, the famous confectioner; masked balls and musicales. The golden-haired lady and her darkly handsome prince made an eye-catching pair on horseback during the Sunday parades in Rotton Row and Kensington Gardens, and Jane's pictures were more popular than ever in the print shops and *Heath's*

Book of Beauty, where the common Englishman could choose his favorite pin-up.

During that summer of 1829 Jane sat for a new portrait, one which more than any other captures the essence of "Passion's child." The artist was James Holmes, who excelled in miniatures and was a great favorite of George IV. He had also painted Lord Byron in 1816, just before the poet left England in disgrace. The portrait is only about a foot square, but unlike most miniatures is full-length. Wearing a romantic (and revealing) peasant costume, Jane is reclining seductively with what appears to be a love letter in her hand. In the background are Grecian columns and a hazy moon. It is clear from these appropriate touches that Holmes understood his subject well.

Jane and Felix were too young to be a part of the intimate "cottage clique" surrounding the king and Lady Conyngham at the Royal Lodge in the summer months, and thus were spared the devastating schedule bemoaned by many of the participants. Lady Shelley described the endless days:

> They meet at three o'clock, at which hour five or six phaetons come to the door to receive a lady and gentleman who drive about the country until five. At that hour the whole party dine in a hut on the shore of Virginia Water.... The party sit at table until between nine and ten o'clock, then they return to the cottage, dress *presto,* and go into the saloon where they play écarté and other games until midnight. It is every day the same: Oh! monotony!

The lovers did, however, immerse themselves in the London social life, the feverish round of parties so detested by Sir Walter Scott. Every evening during the season, between six and eight and again from ten to midnight, the streets of the West End were filled with a stream of carriages, whose wheels made a deafening roar on the cobblestones. Every night there were a dozen or more receptions in Mayfair, and they furnished far more entertainment for those who were not invited than for those who were. Crowds of onlookers stood in front of the brilliantly lighted houses, gaping at each arrival, at the elegantly uniformed and powdered footmen who lined the steps, and at the tall windows framing a sea of nodding feathers under sparkling chandeliers. As there was generally no music, no place to sit, no cards and nothing that could pass for conversation, the guests were condemned to run an obstacle course, elbowing their way from room to room through a crush of magnificent clothes and jewelry, until finally they were back at the entrance hall waiting for their carriages to pick them up. It was not at all unusual for the guests at these assemblies to spend more time among the footmen than they spent with their hosts. What constituted boredom for others, however, provided opportunities for Jane and Felix to be together without arousing Edward's suspicion. When they attended the receptions where 1500 people were jammed into what would have been a comfortable space for 200, they were amused and delighted to be pressed against each other by the crowds.

Afternoons provided their private hours. Felix shared lodgings with Count Dietrichstein, a brother to the count who was guarding Napoleon's son at Schönbrunn Palace in Vienna. The noblemen's bachelor quarters were at 73 Harley Street, just a few doors from 78 Harley Street, where Jane and Edward had been married and where her parents were still in residence. Almost daily during that summer of 1828 a young groom named William Carpenter accompanied Lady Ellenborough from Roehampton to London in her elegant green phaeton high-flyer, drawn by two sleek, black, long-tailed ponies. Carpenter's fashionable olive-drab livery matched the upholstery of the carriage; his uniform was trimmed in sky blue, and he wore a tall black hat banded with silver lace. The lady wore filmy summer dresses in white or pastel colors, and her flower-trimmed bonnets were tied on with delicate veiling that concealed her face. The destination was always Harley Street, but Jane rarely got past number 73. One day she would arrive by Chandos Street, another day by Wimpole Street, and sometimes the groom and phaeton would be left in Cavendish Square while Jane walked to meet her lover. The numbers have long since been changed, but at the time of Felix's residence, number 73 was the house second from the corner of Harley and Queen Anne Streets, overlooking the house and gallery of the noted artist J. M. W. Turner. No matter from what angle she approached, Felix would be waiting for her, looking out the window of the first-floor drawing room. He always opened the door himself.

It never occurred to the young lovers that the residents of this quiet neighborhood had begun to watch them, and it probably would not have mattered if they had known. But there were those who soon realized that something unusual was taking place at number 73, and there were even those who took special interest in the bedroom window facing Harley Street. One was a domestic servant named John Ward, who later claimed that he had actually seen Prince Schwarzenberg lacing Lady Ellenborough's stays.

If Jane and Felix had spent most of their time indoors, the gossip about them might have been contained "below stairs" for a while, but they insisted upon being in each other's company constantly. In August all of London society turned out for the Egham Races, where the king was to put in one of his rare appearances. The crowd's attention, it was reported, was divided almost equally between two spectacles: George IV so swollen by gout that he was unable to get his ballooning right arm into his sleeve and so painfully stiff that he had to be lifted in and out of his carriage; and the beautiful Lady Ellenborough promenading unashamedly with her foreign "whiskerando." The lovers also appeared together to inspect William Wilkins's recently completed domed and turreted building on the north side of Trafalgar Square, which had been commissioned by the king to house the new National Gallery.

By the time summer had passed, vague rumors of Jane's indiscretion had reached her family, and even her former governess Margaret Steele felt obliged to step in. During one of her frequent visits to Roehampton, she summoned all her courage to confront Lord Ellenborough to tell him she feared his lady's reputation might be suffering from the company she was keeping. Edward laughed at this effrontery and told the shocked and dismayed Steely he thought she was being "over scrupulous." He apparently shrugged off other warnings as well, for Jane's aunt Eliza Spencer-Stanhope wrote to a friend at the time, "As to my right worshipful nephew-in-law, he has unfortunately all the arrogance of an upstart and will listen to no remonstrance."

Some said that Lord Ellenborough chose to ignore his wife's adultery in order to enjoy his own, but Edward would scarcely have subscribed to such equality of the sexes, and, in any case, his obsession with politics did not leave him much free time for romantic adventures. That is not to say, however, that he was living a totally celibate existence. Veiled hints in the Princess de Lieven's letters suggest that Edward was indulging in a little casual dalliance with the Countess St. Antonio, an innuendo that does not appear to be otherwise substantiated. The countess was a well-known figure at Almack's, where her husband, who ignored her completely except to draw on her large bank account, was one of the dandies-in-residence.

Several times during the summer of 1828 Jane and Felix attended dinner parties at the St. Antonio home on Wimbledon Common. On those days Jane would drive from Roehampton to London in midmorning, get out near Harley Street and send the groom home with instructions to pick her up at the Countess St. Antonio's house late in the evening. In that way she was able to spend many uninterrupted hours with her lover. When the dinner party was over, Jane would leave in her own carriage, then change to Felix's to ride the mile or more to the Green Man, where the road divided, going one way back to London and the other to Roehampton. At that point she would return to her own carriage and go home. The Windmill Inn on Wimbledon Common served as a "post office" for the exchange of messages between Jane and Felix, when they were unable for one reason or another to meet. The romantic lady would sometimes enclose a few wildflowers in the notes she left for Felix's servant to pick up.

By November of 1828 there was scarcely anyone in London society who was not aghast at Jane and Felix's rashness. Joseph Jekyll, author of that prophetic line about peers loving by proxy inscribed in a young bride's book four years earlier, wrote to his sister, "Torrents of scandal afloat! ... They call Schwarzenberg 'Cadland' because he beat the Colonel out of Lady Ellenborough's good graces. It is added that she talks publicly of her love and moreover is turned Catholic and never misses her Sunday mass...." (Jane, in fact, never converted to Catholicism, but there is little doubt she would have done so if it could have made her Felix's wife.) The rumor concerning her religious activities prompted the Bishop of Bath and Wells, who had performed the marriage ceremony for Jane and Edward, to talk to his nephew. He was the first of Lord Ellenborough's own family to advise him of the gossip, but once more Edward turned a deaf ear.

The stubborn refusal of Jane's husband to become alarmed by these warnings did not mean that he was stupid or callous. Neither recklessness nor romantic passion was part of Edward's makeup, and he must have found it hard to associate either of these qualities with that innocent young creature he had married. An arrogant man, moreover, is undoubtedly the last to accept the fact of his wife's infidelity. The servants in the Ellenborough household knew a great deal more about her ladyship's habits than did her husband. Some of the Roehampton maids on their Sunday outings had seen their mistress riding with a handsome, mustachioed stranger in Hyde Park, and the Ellenborough footmen had noticed that when milady went to the opera or theater or a ball without milord, she invariably came out on the arm of a man the other footmen identified as Prince Schwarzenberg.

During the winter of 1828, many London aristocrats who would normally be at their country seats for the hunting parties and the holidays remained in town for a special event. That December, with all the pomp and pageantry he so loved, George IV accepted a set of gilded keys in a crimson velvet bag from his architect, Sir Jeffry Wyatville, and made his formal entry into Windsor Castle, which had been completely remodeled to his order. Lord and Lady Ellenborough were not among the invited, because the king had never forgiven Edward for what he considered two acts of disloyalty. One dated back to Edward's defense of the tragicomic uncrowned Queen Caroline in 1820. His more recent misstep was his opposition to the third reading of the King's Property Bill in a speech that caused great offense to Lady Conyngham by questioning the sovereign's right to leave property to someone other than his successor.

There is no evidence that Jane was disturbed over being excluded from the Windsor Castle "housewarming." A poem in her notebook "to F. S.," dated December 22, 1828, reveals that she was very much preoccupied with her love life at the time:

> *Oh say not that my love will pass*
> *And all this fondness be forgot.*
> *Oh say not that this cannot last,*
> *That love but binds what love has wrought.*
>
> *Cold words that cruelly on my heart*
> *From thy lips fall with deadly still.*
> *It cannot be, we cannot part.*
> *I'm thine all time through good or ill.*
>
> *My love is not the love of one*
> *Who feels a passion for a day.*
> *Each look, each thought is all thine own,*
> *Unchanged, unchangeable will stay.*

Oh say no more or doubt again
That aught from thee this soul can sever.
Fixed as my fate it will remain
And wander, dearest, never!

The poem suggests that Felix was becoming apprehensive over the intensity of Jane's feelings and the dangerous direction their affair was taking. If he tried to tell his mistress that theirs was only a passing fancy, he failed spectacularly to convince her, and subsequent events show that he did not convince himself either. Whatever resolutions the Austrian attaché may have made for the new year appear to have dissolved in another passionate embrace, for in the early months of 1829, the lovers continued to meet almost daily.

During this period, Jane's absentee husband was deeply embroiled in the preliminary skirmishes over the Catholic Relief Bill, which Wellington planned to introduce when Parliament reconvened. Edward had always advocated Catholic emancipation as a simple act of justice, and it now appeared to him that passage of the bill was necessary to restore national unity.

The cabinet was in almost continuous session trying to salvage the Catholic Relief Bill when Parliament opened February 5, and Lord Ellenborough scarcely noticed when his wife announced her intention of joining their infant son in Brighton, where Arthur's nursemaids had taken him for a change of air. The rendezvous Jane and Felix planned at the seacoast resort was only one of many, but it was the first time they had dared to spend the night together. It was a costly adventure—seldom have a few hours in the lives of two lovers been so subject to public scrutiny as were theirs on the evening of February 6, 1829, in Brighton's Norfolk Hotel. If the two of them had set out with the avowed purpose of providing documented divorce evidence, they could not have been more successful at it. Jane was well known at the Norfolk, and when she arrived that afternoon, she was given the same drawing room apartments in the east wing that the Ellenborough family always occupied. It was, in fact, the suite in which she had spent her honeymoon. The memory of that occasion, though it was not one she treasured, gave Jane a twinge of conscience, and she dashed off an affectionate note to her husband at his London residence on Connaught Place, calling him by an intimate nickname which appears nowhere else in her correspondence:

Brighton, Friday night.

Dearest Oussey,

I am just arrived, and will only write you one line, as I am tired to death with my journey; the roads were so very heavy. I found Arthur looking REALLY PRETTY; you may believe it if *I* say so, and appears to me much improved in strength, but he greeted me with such a howl!! We shall improve upon ac-

quaintance. If you go to Mrs. Hope's tonight, have the thought to make my
excuses to save me the trouble of writing them.——The post is ringing——

Good night, dearest.

Janet

This message, which Edward kept, was later used to point up Jane's duplicity,
but she could hardly have been expected to write her husband that she was
meeting her lover in Brighton. The letter is also interesting as a commentary on
maternal patterns in English society of the period. Little Arthur Dudley Law, a
delicate child anyway (he lived only a year longer), was so constantly surrounded by nurses and other attendants that he barely knew his mother. It was
not entirely facetiously that Jane suggested her relations with her son would
improve "upon acquaintance."

Three hours after Jane was greeted with a howl, Felix Schwarzenberg arrived
at the hotel in a bright yellow hired carriage, and made an immediate and
apparently unforgettable impression. He was observed to be heavily accented
and mustachioed, exuding foreign intrigue and carrying a magnificent carpet bag
embroidered with the Schwarzenberg crown and—lest there be any mistake—the
initials F. S. There were few other guests to obscure the lovers' movements,
February not being the most popular month at an English seaside resort, and the
staff of the Norfolk was more than willing to give the few their fullest attention.

Felix, it must be said, did try to be somewhat circumspect. He asked the man
who saw him to his rooms what other families were in the hotel, and when Lady
Ellenborough's name was mentioned, he asked if it were the Dowager Lady Ellenborough. When the waiter said it was the younger lady, Felix told him they were
acquainted and asked that his card be taken up to her. She replied with an
invitation to tea, which was properly served to them in her sitting room. The
prince retired quite properly to his own quarters at half past ten. Up to that point
no suspicions had been aroused, and at midnight Felix thought it safe to return
to Jane. He did not reckon, however, with the mental processes of the English
domestic.

One Robert Hepple, a hotel waiter, was dozing in the pantry at the foot of the
west wing staircase as he waited for a group of guests to return from a late party.
Hearing Felix start down the steps he stepped out to see who it was. Felix beat a
hasty retreat, waited ten minutes, then tried again. This time there was no one in
sight, for a very good reason. Hepple had hidden himself behind the pantry door
and put out the light because, as he explained later, "I was conscious that this
gentleman wanted to do something that he did not want anybody to see, and I
wished to let him have his wish in that respect, and I kept out of sight."

It seems, however, that one noble gesture a night was all that Hepple could
muster, and he soon cancelled that one out. It was clearly Hepple's duty to
protect the hotel's guests by making sure this mysterious stranger was not up to
robbery or assault, so of course he followed Felix down the main hall and up the
east wing stairs to Jane's room. It is also understandable that he would want to

listen for a moment at the door after Felix had gone in to make sure that Lady Ellenborough's midnight visitor was not an unwelcome one. This point was undoubtedly cleared up for Hepple when he distinctly heard the prince get into bed. It was disappointing that the conversation was in a foreign tongue which Hepple could not understand, but the tone was obviously friendly.

The waiter then returned to his post by the pantry and spent about an hour pondering the ways of the upper classes until temptation overcame him and he went back to listen again.

It would be more than a year before the intimate details of Lady Ellenborough's Brighton rendezvous with Prince Schwarzenberg became public property, but long before that happened the Austrian ambassador to London tried to stem the tide of events. Prince Esterhazy had become increasingly nervous about his attaché's romance. Lord Ellenborough, it seemed to Esterhazy, had thus far preferred to look the other way, but who knew when he might decide to act the part of the outraged husband? A public scandal involving an embassy official and the wife of a cabinet minister could do incalculable harm. Esterhazy asked Count Dietrichstein for a report, and what Schwarzenberg's fellow lodger at 73 Harley Street had to say about the lovers' brazen behavior caused the ambassador to deliver a stern warning to his attaché. Felix was apparently shaken by this rebuke, and to appease Esterhazy he moved his quarters to 11 Holles Street and pretended to carry on a flirtation with another lady. The flirtation was a serious error on his part, for Jane immediately retaliated by claiming to all who would listen that she had been heartlessly abandoned by her lover. None of this sat very well with the Almack's regulars, as Count Apponyi wrote in his journal in March of 1829: "The accusation of Lady Ellenborough against Schwarzenberg shocks all of London society. In the meantime he is ardently courting the Countess of Hatzfeld. They say that Prince Esterhazy is furious with our attaché...."

Evidently Felix quickly gave up his efforts to break off with Jane, because they were soon seeing each other again on the old basis. However, as Apponyi pointed out, the Austrian ambassador was not the only person in London who had ceased to be amused by the Ellenborough-Schwarzenberg affair. Those social currents that later became known as "Victorian morality" were already being felt, and none of the aristocrats wanted to see an open scandal in their ranks that might provide ammunition for the middle-class forces of reform. The indefatigable gossip Thomas Creevey wrote in his diary a scathing commentary on Jane and her companions when he described a party on March 10, 1829, at Lady Sefton's:

Our small and early last night was quite as agreeable as ever, but I must be permitted to observe that considering the rigid virtue of Lady Sefton and the profound darkness in which her daughters of from thirty to forty are brought up as to even the existence of vice, the party was as little calculated to protract the delusion of these innocents as any collection to be made in London could well be. There were Mrs. F——— L——— [Mrs. Fox Lane] and Lord Chesterfield, who came together and sat together all night, Lady E——— [Ellenborough] and the Pole or Prussian or Austrian or whatever he is they call Cadland, because he beat the Colonel [Anson]. Anything as impudent as she or as barefaced as the whole affair I never beheld. Princess Esterhazy, ——— and Lady ———; Lady C——— [Cowper] and Palmerston; in short by far the most notorious and profligate women in London.

From that collection of "notorious and profligate women," one, Emily Cowper, by far the least haughty and best-liked of the Almack's patronesses, came out smelling like a rose. She took her mother's deathbed advice and remained true to her lover, Lord Palmerston, had several illegitimate children by him and finally married him after her husband died. She settled down with grace and dignity as Lady Palmerston to become one of London's most popular hostesses, despite Queen Victoria's stiff-necked disapproval of her past. There was another sidelight to this cozy gathering: more than twenty years after Lady Sefton's party Lord Palmerston became Foreign Secretary to the reluctant Victoria, and Prince Schwarzenberg was named Prime Minister to the young Austrian emperor Franz Josef. Their opposing policies made the two former comrades-in-illicit-arms such bitter enemies that when Palmerston was dismissed from office in 1851, Felix gave a ball in Vienna to celebrate.

During that spring of 1829, however, Palmerston and Schwarzenberg were simply two rising diplomats, each in love with other men's wives, and Lord Ellenborough was being as accommodating about his wife as Lord Cowper was about his.

By April, Prince Esterhazy felt he had reached the limit of his authority in dealing with the Schwarzenberg-Ellenborough romance, and in the face of mounting pressure he turned to the formidable Prince Metternich in Vienna for help. The affair was no surprise to Metternich, who was kept *au courant* of all the London gossip by his former mistress and devoted correspondent, the Princess de Lieven. All the high-level anxiety Felix was causing might well have cost him his diplomatic career, and had he been anyone else it undoubtedly would have. But Metternich, it happened, was very fond of the impetuous young prince. It was he who had persuaded Felix to enter the Foreign Office in 1824; he had made Felix his protégé and still saw great potential in him. Metternich agreed with Esterhazy that Schwarzenberg should get out of London, and Felix was notified that he was being recalled to Vienna. It was not the first time Felix had to leave a post in a hurry because of his own reckless behavior, nor would it be the last. In his early twenties, as a spirited young man stationed in St. Petersburg, he had befriended a group of equally spirited young Russian officers who were involved in the Decembrist plot to overthrow Czar Nicholas I. The plot failed, and Felix barely got out of Russia in time to avoid an embarrassing confrontation between his country and the Czar's.

When Felix told Jane early in May of 1829 that he had to leave England, his mistress had some bad news of her own to announce. She had come to the unhappy realization that she was three months pregnant, and it hardly seemed likely that Edward, who had not enjoyed his conjugal rights for a year, would accept the child as his. The ideal solution, as Jane saw it, was for her to leave with Felix and sort out the knotty legal arrangements later, but this idea did not appeal to her lover at all. It was up to the twenty-two-year-old Lady Ellenborough to pull the chestnuts out of the fire—she had little choice but to ask her husband for a separation, hoping to conceal her condition from him and eventually to join Felix in Europe. The showdown at Roehampton came on the evening of May 22, while the gallant Prince Schwarzenberg was heading for the nearest Channel port.

Exactly what Jane told Edward during that painful conversation is not known, but however Edward may have been affected by it, his work was not neglected. He dined as planned that evening with Lord Hills, and his political diary for that day deals in detail with his annoyance at Lord Melville's conduct in the Admiralty and with his concern over the London Bridge Approaches Bill. There are no references to his personal affairs.

Edward and Jane agreed she should stay at Roehampton until some course of action could be decided upon. The next morning, after writing a note to Lady Andover advising her of the separation and asking her to come at once to her daughter at Roehampton, Lord Ellenborough left for a cabinet meeting at Sir Robert Peel's and turned his attention to the appointment of his successor as Lord Privy Seal. Lord Rosslyn and Lord Chandos were both being considered, and Edward was particularly anxious that Chandos should not have it. First things first with Edward.

For Jane's family there were no such distractions from this devastating news. Poor Lady Andover, on the verge of collapse over her daughter's disgrace, somehow managed to dispatch her sister, Lady Anson, to reason with Lord Ellenborough, while she herself sped to Roehampton. Lady Anson was less surprised but scarcely less upset than Jane's mother over these developments; she had strong reasons of her own for wishing to keep the family from being dragged through the mud of a divorce. An inkling of Jane's early attachment to her son George had reached her, and she had little desire for these rumors to be publicly aired.

It was Lady Anson's suggestion that Jane write to Edward asking for time. The letter was later introduced as evidence in Edward's divorce suit.

> Roehampton, May 23, 1829
> Saturday night
>
> Forgive me if I do wrong in writing you. A note just received from Lady Anson seems to imply that you have expected it. I began a letter to you this morning, thanking you from the bottom of my soul for your unbounded kindness

in act and manner. I again renew all the assurances I gave you last night that in act I am innocent.

I hardly know what or how to write. I dare not use the language of affection; you would think it hypocrisy. But, though my family naturally wish all should be again as once was between us, those feelings of honor which I still retain towards you make me still acquiesce in your decision. I continue to think it just and right. I have not been able to speak to them on the subject I confessed to you last night. I have spoken little today, but I never for an instant swerved from my original opinion. I write this to you if it is possible for you to keep what I have said from them. Do, as they would only set it down as another proof of unkindness on my part.

Could you write me a line through Henry, were it only to tell me your opinion, be assured I should think it right. But, oh Edward, dear, dear Edward, ought not time, solitude and change of scene be tried by me to conquer or obliterate sentiments inimical to our mutual peace? Pray write to me all you think upon the subject—all you wish me to do. I will now answer you candidly, and without a shade of deception. God bless you dearest Edward.

Janet

P.S. If my aunt has misunderstood your expression, and you did not wish to hear from me personally, forgive me; although I long to tell you how gratefully I feel towards you, yet I confess I should have never ventured to write—
Ever yours.

It is a puzzling letter. It appears that Jane told her husband she was in love with another man, but had not been guilty of adultery. Later events revealed that Jane asked Edward's permission to go abroad ("a change of scene") and he flatly refused to give it. Edward was a man of sophistication—he must have been a little skeptical about his wife's claim of innocence, and he could surely have deduced her intention to join Prince Schwarzenberg in Europe. Nonetheless, Lord Ellenborough treated Jane with unusual kindness, which suggests that he felt some responsibility.

It is unlikely, however, that Edward's vanity would permit him to seek a reconciliation—Jane clearly did not want one—and his "decision" seems to have been for a legal separation. Lord Ellenborough's brother, Henry Law, was living at Roehampton at the time, and he served as a go-between for the estranged couple. Although many more messages passed between them, there is no evidence that, after the evening of May 22, 1829, Jane and Edward ever saw each other again.

In an utterly futile attempt to save the Ellenborough marriage, Jane's family converged on Roehampton and the battle of wills began. Lady Anson joined Lady Andover late in the afternoon of May 23, and on Sunday, May 24, reinforcements arrived in the person of Miss Margaret Steele. Fond as Jane was of Steely, it did not set well with her to be treated as if she were a naughty child. Lady Andover and Lady Anson meant well, but as families are apt to do in such unsettling circumstances, they handled things badly. They should have known Jane well enough to realize she thrived on opposition. The more they pointed out Lord Ellenborough's virtues, the more obvious his shortcomings appeared to Jane; the more they dwelt on the horrors of her life as a ruined woman, the more challenged she felt to prove them wrong. Roehampton was awash with tears, but Jane stood firm in her decision to leave her husband. On May 30, drained from six days of emotional upheaval, Lady Andover and Lady Anson packed Jane and Steely off to a seaside cottage in the isolated village of Ilfracombe in Devon. What they hoped to accomplish by this move is not clear, but they selected the west side of England for Jane's retreat, as far as possible from any access to Europe.

While this domestic drama was taking place at Roehampton, the London high season was in full swing. The king came out of seclusion to give his annual children's ball, which was attended by the ten-year-old *de jure* Queen of Portugal, Donna Maria de Gloria, who fell down and cut her royal nose on one of her own diamonds. In June there was a concert at St. James's Palace, where Maria Malibran sang, and a few days later the annual Jockey Club dinner was held. At all these gala events there were whispers about Lady Ellenborough and her Austrian prince, who were conspicuous by their absence.

One of the missing pair was walking the beaches of Devon, agonizing over her uncertain future. Jane knew before she left London that her lover had left her to face alone the consequences of their affair, but she was too blinded by love to see the implications of his flight. It had not occurred to her that the dashing prince was as bound by ambition as her husband and that he was surely no Sir Kenelm Digby who did "most joyfully undergo any censure, any disgrace" for the woman he loved. Jane wrote letters to Schwarzenberg daily, but she had yet to receive an answer, and she was becoming more restless as each day passed with no word.

On June 20 a cousin of Lord Ellenborough met with Edward's London solicitor, James William Freshfield, setting in motion an investigation into the conduct of her ladyship and the foreign diplomat. Edward had decided that Jane's information was a little sketchy, and he was looking for some that was perhaps less biased. Mr. Freshfield at first advised strongly against such an investigation on the grounds that there was too little hard evidence in Lord Ellenborough's possession, but Edward insisted.

Neither Freshfield nor Edward knew at that time that Lady Ellenborough was carrying the most damning evidence of adultery with her, but Jane's pregnancy was becoming painfully obvious to her former governess. The first day of July Jane and Steely left Ilfracombe for Minterne House in Dorset, the home of Admiral Digby's sister, where they were to meet Jane's parents for another family conference. Before the Admiral and Lady Andover arrived, Steely broached the subject of Jane's condition, and by then Jane was desperate to confide in someone. According to the later recollections of the governess, Jane was terribly distraught. "My situation will soon become visible!" she told Steely.

"God knows what will become of me! The child is not Lord Ellenborough's but Prince Schwarzenberg's!"

This was a confession for which the prim spinster was totally unprepared, and there was more to come. Steely listened in stunned silence to the details of the Norfolk Hotel rendezvous; she was dumbfounded to learn that Jane and Edward had not slept together since before young Arthur was born; she wept when Jane told her she could not bear the thought of life without Felix. Steely promised Jane that she would not reveal any of their conversation to the Digbys or Lord Ellenborough until given permission.

While Jane was finding life unbearable without Felix, the prince was finding life not at all unpleasant without Jane. He was back among family and friends; he was spending a long holiday pampered and fussed over by his adoring, dominating sister, Princess Mathilde, and, now that he had left England behind him, no one, including Prince Metternich, saw fit to judge his behavior there harshly. Even Jane did not rebuke him for his flight, although she could not have failed to reveal her suffering in her letters. The rigidly Catholic Schwarzenbergs —and especially Mathilde—urged Felix to terminate his costly affair with Lady Ellenborough for good, but this he refused to do. Apparently he still cared for Jane, and a gentleman was supposed to accept responsibility for his children, legitimate or not. Sometime in July he wrote Jane at Minterne, advising her to leave England as soon as possible and suggesting several places in Europe where she might go for her confinement. (Someone in the Digby family made a synopsis of this letter, which is still at Minterne, but the original is lost.) The prince warned Jane not to come near him, because he claimed all his movements were being watched by agents of Lord Ellenborough. It is unlikely, however, that Jane's husband went to this trouble and expense; more likely Schwarzenberg simply did not want his pregnant mistress arriving at the family residence. Felix deplored the position Jane found herself in, but, he explained, it was impossible for him to marry her *for the sake of his own future.* Nevertheless, he saw no reason why they could not devote their lives to each other.

It was not a very promising offer, if it was an offer, but it was all Jane had. By late summer of 1829 her family, and probably Lord Ellenborough as well, knew that she was pregnant with Schwarzenberg's child. Edward reluctantly concluded that divorce was the only means by which he might salvage his honor, even though it might cost him his political future. The financial arrangements he made for his wife were unusually generous; he told Freshfield that he did not wish Lady Ellenborough to be "without those comforts and conveniences to which her rank in life entitled her." When Jane was notified of this settlement, she wrote to her husband with gratitude:

My dearest Edward,

I hope you will believe me when I say that I felt myself utterly unequal to writing to you today. I cannot thank you enough for your kindness but entreat you will not think of making me such an allowance. Indeed it is more than I can possibly want. I will send back the green box tomorrow.

Ever, ever yours,
Janet

There is no clue to what the green box contained, but the note does indicate that Jane had very little idea of what it cost to live in style. Edward, who had a sound knowledge of these expenses, ignored his wife's protestations and gallantly stuck to his original agreement.

There was nothing now to hold Jane in England, and even her family had to agree that she would be better off out of the country when the divorce proceedings began. Basel, Switzerland, was one of the places Felix had suggested Jane stay, and this was the city she chose for her exile. Lady Andover was nearly prostrate at the idea of her daughter's difficult journey, and she insisted that Steely accompany Jane as far as Brussels. It is not certain whether Kenelm and Edward Digby, who were eighteen and twenty at the time, were allowed to say goodbye to their sister—one or both of them may have gone with the family to Ramsgate to see Jane and Steely safely on the packet to Ostend. Little Arthur Dudley Law was probably unaware that his mother had left him. No one, including Jane herself, had any notion of how long it might be before she would set foot in England again, and those who loved her in spite of her disgrace were deeply disturbed by the parting. On the last day of August, when London newspapers were cruelly caricaturing George IV and Lady Conyngham weeping over the death of the king's beloved giraffe, many genuine tears were being shed at the Ramsgate docks. Once the packet was underway, however, Jane did not look back. Crossing the Channel, the exhilaration she felt at the prospect of seeing her lover again was so strong that it blotted out all thought of the husband, son, reputation and homeland she was giving up forever.

6

A Parliamentary Divorce

*. . . what reason did Lady Ellenborough assign
to anybody for separating from her husband's
bed; and how came Lord Ellenborough to
agree to such a proposition from so young and
lovely a woman?*

—EDITORIAL IN THE TIMES

*Would anybody believe that a lady dressed to
go out to dinner could be guilty of anything
improper?*

—PARLIAMENTARY DEBATE
ON ELLENBOROUGH DIVORCE BILL

In nineteenth-century England the severing of the marriage bond was considered so grave a step that a private act of Parliament was required for an effective divorce, no matter for what reason it was sought. It was a cumbersome and costly process. A "wronged" husband had first to obtain in the ecclesiastical courts a decree *a mensa et thoro*, which was a judicial separation. Then he had to win a preliminary action at common law for the recovery of damages from the erring wife's partner in adultery. If he failed here, the case was usually closed. If this action was successful, he could then apply to the House of Lords for an absolute divorce with permission to remarry. After examining the evidence, the House of Lords would prepare a bill and forward it to the House of Commons, where the entire sum of evidence would be considered before another committee. Finally the bill required the royal assent.

In the Ellenborough case, all these legal machinations provided a bonanza for the English press and exposed Jane to ribald jokes and derision that would follow her for her lifetime.

Honoré de Balzac, who met Jane several years after her divorce, roundly denounced the English system for victimizing women. In *Le Lys dans la vallée*, a novel in which one of the main characters is partially drawn from Lady Ellenborough, Balzac wrote:

66

Never did a nation more elaborately scheme for the hypocrisy of a married woman by placing her always between social life and death. For her there is no compromise between shame and honor; the fall is utter, or there is no fall; it is all or nothing—the To Be or Not To Be of *Hamlet*.

It was a high price to pay for a love affair. Lord Byron said in *Don Juan*, "And oh! that quickening of the heart, that beat!/ How much it costs us!" In nineteenth-century England it was the woman who paid.

Before the divorce action brought all the lurid details of Jane's infidelity into public domain, the news of the Ellenborough separation had leaked out in London society, and Jane was being subjected to some private pillorying. Some of the very people who had previously expressed little fondness for Lord Ellenborough now saw him as the injured, innocent party. Mrs. Harriet Arbuthnot, who kept a gossipy journal when she was not exchanging notes with her constant companion, the Duke of Wellington, made two uncomplimentary and inaccurate entries concerning Jane during the summer of 1829:

> There has been an explosion in the house of Lord Ellenborough. He has found out all or at least a part of the improprieties of her conduct. Her lover, Prince Schwarzenberg, is gone back to Austria and at just the same time Lord Ellenborough took her to her father and refused to live with her any longer. She has been boasting of her own infamy and ridiculing Lord Ellenborough's blindness, but she now protests that however foolish and indiscreet she may have been, she is not criminal. I understand she has gone down to Roehampton, where he has allowed her to be for the present. What will be the end of it I don't know.

> Lord Ellenborough is now engaged in investigating his wife's conduct and certainly, if the stories she used to tell of herself are true, he will not have great difficulty in proving her guilt. It is quite melancholy that so beautiful a creature only two and twenty, should be so depraved. She used to boast that she used to go to Schwarzenberg's lodgings and find him in bed and go up to his rooms. She met him at all kinds of houses and places in the neighborhood of London, and not satisfied with doing so, told her stories to anybody who would listen to her. Esterhazy told me he had himself seen her coming out of Schwarzenberg's lodgings.

Since Mrs. Arbuthnot seems coolly to have accepted the illicit liaisons of other women in her set, it appears that to her way of thinking Lady Ellenborough's cardinal sin lay not in what she had done but in having had the bad taste to talk about it. There is little doubt that Jane had, in effect, "climbed on the rooftops and shouted to the whole of the United Kingdom" that she and Felix were lovers. But it is highly unlikely, however reckless and thoughtless she may have been, that Jane was guilty of deliberately ridiculing her husband.

Two major topics of conversation among aristocratic Londoners in the autumn of 1829 were the Ellenborough separation and the King of England's failing health. It was reported that George IV was too ill to sign state papers. He could still, however, summon enough strength to confer with his tailors about providing the Guards and the infantry with new uniforms and to consult a taxidermist about the possibility of stuffing the late lamented giraffe. Princess de Lieven appeared to be more concerned about the diplomatic implications of the Ellenborough divorce. Unaware that Jane was at that moment in Basel awaiting the birth of Schwarzenberg's child, the princess was not nearly so well informed as usual about who was doing what to whom. In a letter to Lord Grey dated September 29 she repeated a totally groundless rumor as fact: "Have you heard, my dear Lord, that Lord Ellenborough has instituted divorce proceedings against Mr. Anson? He has just discovered that the latter has been his wife's lover! So Austria is safe!"

The Princess de Lieven's lighthearted attitude toward marital fidelity was revealed clearly in her comments on the suicide in February, 1830, of Lord Graves, who cut his throat when he learned that the Duke of Cumberland had been his wife's lover:

> The dreadful catastrophe of Lord Graves' death is the subject of general comment and horror.... It is really difficult to decide what is true and what is fault [sic] in the beginning of the story. But even if it all be true, you must admit that the Duke has had very bad luck in coming across a husband who goes and cuts his throat for matters of this kind.... The ladies who declaim so loudly against the Duke of C. have not that I have heard of banished George Anson or any of that *confrèrie* from their society. And yet, what difference is there (or if any it is in favor of the Duke!) except that Lord Ellenborough didn't shoot himself.

Jane's husband obviously did not feel that marital infidelity was sufficient cause for suicide, but another tragedy which befell him early in 1830 appears to have shaken him deeply and almost caused his driving ambition to expire within him. Two-year-old Arthur Dudley Law, the little boy for whom Lord Ellenborough had such high hopes, died of a convulsion February 1. In a touching poem found many years later among his papers, Edward mourned his only child with an uncharacteristic show of emotion:

> *Poor child! Thy mother never smiled on thee*
> *Nor stayed to soothe thee in thy suffering day!*
> *But thou wert all on earth to me,*
> *The solace of my solitary way.*

The news of Arthur's death and the almost simultaneous announcement that the first action in the Ellenborough divorce trial was set down for Consistory Court brought speculation at Almack's that Lord Ellenborough was courting

Lord Clare's sister with an eye to another heir, but nothing came of it. Many conflicting rumors were repeated in London drawing rooms as to what would be brought out in the Ellenborough divorce.

To the annoyance of those who had their appetites whetted for shocking revelations, Sir Henry Jenner, representing Lady Ellenborough, did not oppose the suit, and as a result, scarcely any evidence was heard in the opening session. After the facts of the marriage had been established and certain depositions read, Dr. Lushington, the judge, pronounced a decree of separation. Only six lines appeared in the next morning's papers. The Sunday publications were more generous, however. They padded out the story considerably with much biographical and imaginative detail, and more grist for the mill was shortly forthcoming.

The smooth sailing received by Lord Ellenborough's petition in Consistory Court ended abruptly in the House of Lords. On February 22 the Earl of Shaftesbury presented a bill entitled "An Act to Dissolve the marriage of the Right Honourable Edward Baron Ellenborough with the Right Honourable Jane Elizabeth Baroness Ellenborough, his now Wife, and to enable him to marry again; and for other purposes therein mentioned." The same day, the bill was read for the first time and witnesses were summoned to appear at the second reading on March 9. At the second reading all the evidence was to be presented to satisfy the House that there had been no collusion on the part of the petitioner.

The proceedings that day were opened with a long speech by Mr. Adam, counsel for Lord Ellenborough, full of references to the "noble lord and his faithless lady." Mr. Adam recalled that the couple's problems began shortly after the birth of their child, when Lady Ellenborough, "a lively woman possessing many captivating qualities, felt the enchantment of fashionable society." This weakness, he continued, led her to make the acquaintance of Prince Schwarzenberg, then living with Count Dietrichstein in Harley Street, and she often visited the two bachelors, one of whom was never at home when she called.

"I have seldom, my lords," said Mr. Adam, "been engaged in a case in which the impropriety has been so clearly established, and in which so distinctly has been brought home the criminality of the parties. The unhappy lady herself acknowledges her fault. I engage to show all these circumstances, if your lordships think it necessary. I hope, however, you will not require such proof. I am not anxious to feed that appetite which now rages in this country for slander and censure of persons moving in the highest ranks of society."

Mr. Adam's hope was quite in vain. Their lordships wanted proof and plenty of it, and so began the parade of peeping toms, the waiters, grooms, housemaids and coachmen. Robert Hepple of the Norfolk Hotel gave his version of the February night in Brighton, and his evidence should have sufficed to prove Lord Ellenborough's charge, but the House of Lords wanted more. Instead of referring to the hotel register to establish Prince Schwarzenberg's identity, a half-dozen witnesses were called to verify that Felix had hired a certain carriage from a certain livery stable on a certain date for a trip to Brighton. There is no question that Lord Ellenborough's political enemies were making the most of this perfect opportunity to nail the unpopular peer to the cross, and they cared little that they were nailing Jane more brutally in the process.

The testimony moved from Brighton to Harley Street, and John Ward, the valet in the house directly across from number 73, was called. After an ambling prologue, Ward electrified his listeners with his description of the prince lacing the lady's stays. Surely, Mr. Adam felt, this was proof enough, but their lordships said no. The next parade of witnesses, mostly Jane's former servants, were asked to testify concerning the incidents at Wimbledon where Jane and Felix were obviously together.

When the petitioner's case was finally closed, Mr. Dampier, counsel for Jane, declined to call rebutting evidence. The Earl of Rosslyn moved that the bill be read a second time. It was and was passed without a dissenting voice. At the required third reading, however, the Earl of Radnor voiced strong opposition, flatly declaring that Lord Ellenborough's failure to look after his wife was so serious as not to entitle him to relief.

So anxious was Lord Radnor to pin the blame on Lord Ellenborough that he quoted a passage from St. Matthew: "He that putteth away his wife for any cause other than adultery causeth her to commit adultery." He was willing to concede that the lady had indeed misbehaved, but it had not been proved to his satisfaction that Lord Ellenborough had protected her as an older man should look after his young wife. How was it, demanded the Earl of Malmesbury, coming to Radnor's support, that Lady Ellenborough had been free to leave her house every day for Harley Street, "to prostitute herself in the most indecent manner" while her husband asked no questions as to how she spent her days? For a moment it looked as if the Ellenborough Divorce Bill would be thrown out of the House of Lords, but Radnor and Malmesbury were in the minority, and it was finally resolved that the bill should be forwarded to the House of Commons for concurrence.

The final debate in the House of Lords was printed verbatim in the *Times* on April 1, 1830, covering the entire front page and most of the second page of that staid newspaper. Tucked away in the editorial section of the same edition was a small announcement that Fanny Kemble was appearing that evening as Portia in *The Merchant of Venice* at Covent Garden. In the spring of 1830, however, the twenty-year-old Fanny was taking second billing to Lady Ellenborough.

On March 31 the Ellenborough divorce was taken up by a committee of Commons with Sir George Clerk as chairman, and once again, the Ellenborough divorce evidence was considered point by point. No one wished to miss a word of testimony from the parade of witnesses who had so enlivened the month of March for the House of Lords. For the benefit of those interested Londoners who were not members of Parliament, the verbatim transcript of this hearing was printed, according to House of Commons procedure. The tryst at the Norfolk Hotel in Brighton provided 41 pages of a total 120 in *Ellenborough Divorce: Report of the Minutes of Evidence.* Copies of this report sold for three shillings, and the printer, John Miller of 23 St. James Street, had a best seller on his hands.

Although most of the testimony before the House committee was merely a repetition of what the Lords had heard, there were some interesting new twists. Robert Hepple, the hotel waiter from Brighton, created a sensation with his story of listening outside Lady Ellenborough's door after he had seen Prince Schwarzenberg enter. "I could hear them kissing and a noise that convinced me that the act of cohabitation was taking place between them." Then William Walton, brother of the Norfolk Hotel's owner, was baldfaced enough to admit to the committee that he had called on Lady Ellenborough the morning after the foreign gentleman had spent the night in her room and told her he knew from Hepple what had transpired. The object was clearly blackmail, as the questioning revealed:

Q. Did you receive any reward in February for not divulging what had passed?
A. A present was made to me.
Q. By whom was the present made to you?
A. By Lady Ellenborough.
Q. Did she desire you not to divulge what had passed?
A. She wished me not to do so, not even to her maid.

Walton had kept Jane's "present" of twenty pounds, but not her secret. To add insult to injury, he had not even shared his windfall with Hepple, his informant. Subsequent testimony showed that the owner of the Norfolk Hotel fired both his brother and Hepple for their cooperation with the divorce investigation.

Ann Lewis, chambermaid to Prince Schwarzenberg while he lived in London, was questioned closely about Jane's visits to 73 Harley Street, and she told the committee that Lady Ellenborough spent two or three hours several times a week with Felix in his bedroom.

Q. After they were gone, used you to go to the bedroom?
A. Yes.
Q. In what condition did you find the bed?
A. I found there had been two persons in bed.
Q. Do you mean between the sheets?
A. Yes.
Q. Did it always appear so, or sometimes only?
A. Yes, mostly.

The chambermaid testified that after the prince moved to 11 Holles Street in March of 1829, his lady visitor apparently did not wish to be seen entering the house. She often slipped in through the back door, although it meant walking through the mews, which was heaped with dunghills and piles of rubbish. Following Ann Lewis's appearance, the ubiquitous valet, John Ward, cheerfully repeated his story of Jane's stays being laced by Felix, which always got a warm reception.

Not all the witnesses were so eager to give damaging testimony against Jane. William Carpenter, the young groom who had so often driven her to Harley Street, was described by Lord Ellenborough's solicitor as "An extremely unwilling witness; a more unwilling witness I never had to deal with in the course of my professional life. . . . We found so much difficulty in obtaining information from that boy that it was only by first getting access to one person who knew his father, then access to the father, and influencing the father to induce him to speak to the son, and to tell the boy to tell the truth, that we could obtain the slightest information from the boy. At first he knew nothing. Subsequently he knew as little as possible." On the witness stand young Carpenter displayed a touching loyalty to the beautiful lady who was his former employer and only two years older than himself. His answers were, where possible, yes and no. Without perjuring himself, he declined to say anything harmful to Jane and stubbornly refused to admit that he knew of any place on Harley Street she had visited other than her father's house.

The devotion her young groom felt for Jane was further shown when he admitted that he had often lied to the other servants in the Ellenborough household to protect his lady's reputation. The coachman at Roehampton had, according to William, been very persistent (far more so than the lady's husband) in wanting to learn how Jane spent her time:

Q. Did he [the coachman] ever ask you why the horses were kept out so long?
A. Yes, he asked me that.
Q. Did he ask you frequently?
A. Sometimes he has; but I never used to satisfy him of that when he asked me.
Q. You never gave him an answer?
A. Sometimes I have; sometimes I told him we had a very long ride. . . .
Q. Do you mean to say you told him you had been for a long ride when the carriage was put up in the stable near Wimpole Street?
A. Yes.
Q. Do you mean to say you told that deliberate story?
A. I have told him that.

Another unwilling witness before the House of Commons was Miss Margaret Steele, Jane's former governess, who was only persuaded to testify by the assurances of the Digby family that it was the right thing to do. Her revelation of Jane's confession that she was carrying Prince Schwarzenberg's child led the committee members to question Steely closely about the marital relations of Lord and Lady Ellenborough:

Q. Had you any further conversation on this distressing subject?

A. Yes; I remember my saying to Lady Ellenborough, "You talk a great deal in your sleep, and groan very much;" she replied, "I do. Lord Ellenborough has always told me I spoke in my sleep, and has told me of things that I said." I said, "What sort of things?" She said, "Of no sort of consequence, but he has said, 'Janet, you often talk in your sleep.'" I supposed from that that they slept together.

Q. Did she ever state to you that she and Lord Ellenborough had for a considerable time previously slept in separate beds?

A. She did.

Q. For how long a period?

A. She said from the time—when she was in that situation.

Q. For how long a period did she say she had not slept with Lord Ellenborough?

A. She never said more than that it [the child] was not Lord Ellenborough's, because from that time—she did not say what time—she had not slept with him.

Q. What did she state about not sleeping with Lord Ellenborough?

A. She said that the child could not be Lord Ellenborough's, because from the time she was with child—in short, she had not slept with Lord Ellenborough.

Q. Do you mean that she said that she had not slept with Lord Ellenborough from the time of her first child being born?

A. I think I have made it very clear.

Surprisingly, this exchange was not the most sensational part of the governess' appearance as a witness. What the newspapers and the committee members seized upon was Steely's testimony that she had warned Lord Ellenborough of the unsuitability of Jane's companions, and he had *laughed* at her! Under the questioning of Mr. Adam, Steely admitted she had heard disturbing reports about Jane's behavior that prompted her to go to Lord Ellenborough. When Mr. Adam asked what kind of reports, she answered, "That she was giddy and very regardless of consequences, which she always was." It was established that the bad company the governess had warned Jane's husband about were both men and women known to be "gay and profligate." They were high ranking in fashionable society, and the governess said of them, "I did think them bad associates for everyone, but for Lady Ellenborough singularly so." In spite of sharp questioning, Steely steadfastly refused to name names, saying, "I might implicate many persons."

Jane's governess was longer before the committee of the House than any other witness, and the proper spinster was clearly mortified at having to discuss such unmentionable matters with a group of strange men. Her testimony was followed by that of four inconsequential witnesses, and the hearing was completed before noon on Thursday, April 1. That same day the Ellenborough Divorce Bill was introduced to the entire House of Commons by Sir Charles Wetherell, the unpopular Protestant fanatic whom Wellington had sacked as attorney general a year earlier. Wetherell had been known to work himself into such passions of oratory that he would unbutton his braces and allow his waistcoat to ride up and his breeches to fall down, his only "lucid interval," according to the Speaker, being between those two garments. On this particular occasion he was limited to explaining procedure:

> On the subject of divorce, I beg leave to add, that every man has a right, when an act of adultery is proved against his wife, to obtain a sentence of divorce in the Ecclesiastical courts; not so, however, with respect to a Parliamentary divorce. That rests not on the mere proof of an act of adultery: other and scarcely less important matters are required to be satisfactorily proved by the individual who applies for it, and one most indispensable ingredient is the total absence of neglect, misconduct, connivance or collusion on the part of the husband who complained of his wife's adultery.

With his "indispensable ingredient" Sir Charles was throwing down the gauntlet to his pro-Catholic antagonist, Lord Ellenborough. There had already been much talk of collusion, most of it stemming from the letter Jane had written Edward from Roehampton at her aunt's request. It was noted that Edward's brother, Henry, mentioned in Jane's letter as her mediator and one of the witnesses at the Ellenborough marriage, was the only person Lord Ellenborough could call to the bar of the House to testify that the marriage had been a happy one prior to the coming of Prince Schwarzenberg. Henry was an odd choice, since he had been abroad during most of the past four years and had seen little or nothing of his brother or his brother's wife.

Jane's unexpected champion in Commons was Mr. Joseph Hume, the Member for Montrose, who had never met Lady Ellenborough but who objected on principle to anyone's having a divorce, and in particular to Lord Ellenborough's having one. Despite his reputation for "speaking oftener and longer and greater nonsense than anybody else," he appeared to be seriously pleading the cause of social justice for women. "In this country," Mr. Hume argued, "a woman is punished severely for faults which in the husband are overlooked. For a single slip she is banished from society. And yet if justice is to be done to Lady Ellenborough, can anyone overlook the gross neglect on Lord Ellenborough's part that has led to the unhappy events of the past couple of years? Ought not the charge to be read as one of criminality against Lord Ellenborough, who has permitted and even encouraged his wife's association with the persons responsible for her downfall, rather than one of marital infidelity against an unfortunate lady whose youth and immaturity ought to have been safeguarded by her natural protector? ... What is a young lady to do who is neglected by her husband?" he demanded. "Is she to stop at home all day long?"

Unfortunately Mr. Hume damaged his cause considerably during a discussion of Jane's drive back from Wimbledon in Schwarzenberg's carriage, when he asked, "Would anybody believe that a lady dressed to go out to dinner could be guilty of anything improper?" The question met with much laughter from the members, who were astonished at Mr. Hume's simplicity.

Simple or not, Mr. Hume was not alone in his objections to the passage of the bill. The Marquess of Blandford, although he allowed that adultery had been committed, said he could not in conscience vote for the bill because he believed that there was collusion between the two parties. He also went on record as believing that Lady Ellenborough had been "neglected, abandoned and sacrificed," and that he could see no good proof that Lord Ellenborough had enjoyed marital felicity or the "comforts of matrimony." Blandford expressed the belief that the petitioner had not enjoyed these things through his own fault.

Another of Jane's champions, Alderman Matthew Wood, had nine years earlier been a passionate defender of Queen Caroline when that unfortunate lady had been charged by George IV with adultery. Wood, an extremely radical member of Parliament for the City of London and son of a Devonshire serge maker, had left Exeter to make his fortune in the city as a chemist and hop merchant. It was Wood who had accompanied Caroline from France to England to make her unsuccessful bid for a crown. He and Lord Ellenborough had been in accord on that one occasion, but were far from accord on this one. When Wood voted against the Ellenborough Divorce Bill, he declared that he did not feel his lordship was entitled to the relief he sought, and he described as "nonsense" the charge that Ellenborough's unpopularity was influencing opposition to the bill. "I have never heard," he added pointedly, "anything about his lordship's unpopularity with this House, with the country or with the ladies!"

This innuendo brought Sir Henry Hardinge, a staunch supporter of Edward's, to his feet in protest. "Lord Ellenborough," he said, "has been unjustly and unfairly attacked, and the morality and decency of some of the objections advanced are so coarse I wonder where the Honourable Member could have picked them up. Good God! To use any unnecessary delay in passing this Bill, after it has been sifted in so unusual, and I might say in so unprecedented, a way, would be hurting the feelings and trifling with the honor of both the noble families who are interested in its progress." Sir Henry was not only a close personal friend of Edward's, but his wife was sister to Edward's deceased first wife, Lady Octavia Stewart. It was understandable that he would try to represent Edward as a model husband, but members of the House committee resented his attempt to prove it by presenting as evidence the letter written by Jane's mother, Lady Andover, absolving Edward of all guilt in the marriage breakup. The committee refused to allow the letter read.

Before the House of Commons finished this stormy session, some members demanded to know what financial provision had been made for the unfortunate Lady Ellenborough before she was severed from her husband's purse strings. They were assured by Edward's counsel that a settlement had been made which was agreeable to her family. Finally, on April 6 the Commons returned the bill to the House of Lords with a mesasge that "We have agreed to the same without amendment." The following afternoon the committee was officially summoned to be notified that the royal assent had been given, and the clerk of the House made the traditional announcement in solemn tones: "*Soit fait comme il est désiré.*" The only recorded comment Lord Ellenborough made on the merciless diatribes against him during the divorce hearings was his complaint that "There seems to be a fashion in the House of Commons to consider me a fool."

Two days after the bill was passed, Edward signed an agreement to pay Jane an annuity of 330 pounds a year in two payments, one on April 8 and one on October 8, for her lifetime. This appears to have been only a token sum, as Edward had already promised to continue Jane's generous allowance (a figure never named), and the amount she received from him enabled her to live abroad in comparative luxury. There is no evidence that Ellenborough ever tried to collect damages from Prince Schwarzenberg, although *The Complete Peerage* claimed he received 25,000 pounds from his wife's lover. With Felix out of the country this seems very unlikely.

Lord Ellenborough now had his divorce and was free to marry again, a privilege of which he never chose to avail himself. Parliament was especially lenient to Jane. Because the members felt that the circumstances of the case justified such a concession, they set aside for her benefit the usual penalty clause which forbade the guilty party in a divorce to marry the person with whom adultery had been proved. Long before this news reached Jane, however, it had become apparent to everyone, except the lady herself, that the man for whom she gave up everything would never marry her.

The case was finished so far as the law was concerned, but the press was far from through with it. The newsboys were shouting Jane's indiscretions on every street corner in London and doing a brisk business. Almost the only newspaper to have a good word for the wronged husband was the *Morning Post*, which said, "Lord Ellenborough appears to have conducted himself in a manly and honourable fashion." He did not fare so well elsewhere. A radical sheet commented sarcastically, "The royal assent has been given by commission, and the *privileged* Cabinet Lord is at liberty to enter for the *third* time into the 'holy estate of matrimony.' He may now make a legalized offer of his valuable attachment to some other youthful beauty in fashionable society."

In an editorial that covered most of a page, the *Times* conceded that "the last crime against the marriage vow was (perhaps frequently) committed by that lost creature, scarcely more than just arrived at womanhood," but wondered if the lady's husband had not been guilty of the same crime. "Whether such a charge against Lord Ellenborough could be effectually sustained, we cannot answer; but it seems to us, from reports which are current, that an inquiry might be advantageously directed to what is called by one of our correspondents 'the Brighton affair'—an affair, for the reality of which we do not certainly vouch, but which, if real, was beyond all question monstrous...." (Someone at the *Times* had heard of Edward's alleged dalliance with the pastry cook's daughter while he was honeymooning with Jane.) Not only did the editorial question Ellenborough's morals but his judgment as well. For ignoring the warning of Miss Steele, the *Times* accused Jane's husband of "reckless, inconceivable negligence. . . ." "Public opinion," the editorial continued,

> is, we believe, made up as to the name of one, we might say more than one, of the female profligates against whom Lord Ellenborough was warned by his lady's governess . . . because their vices have been notorious, and their habits of life are understood in general society to have long been depraved and infamous.

(Private correspondence and journals of the period suggest that Princess Esterhazy and Countess St. Antonio most closely fit the description of the "female profligates" in the *Times*.) "We forgot to mention," the editorial concluded, "that there is one part of the case already before the public which requires some further elucidation,—viz., what reason did Lady Ellenborough assign to *anybody* for separating from her husband's bed; and how came Lord Ellenborough to agree to such a proposition from so young and lovely a woman?"

On the same page with the Ellenborough divorce editorial that day were two announcements: Mr. Sotheby and Son were advertising the auction of the complete library of the late Major-Gen. Sir John Dalrymple at Wellington Street in the Strand, and an unusual program was listed for that evening at the Theatre Royal, Adelphia. During the latter, Mr. C. H. Adams was to deliver a lecture on astronomy; Mr. H. Childe promised to administer "Laughing Gas" to anyone in the audience who "may wish to inhale it," and a Mr. Tate was scheduled to play "several admired airs on his newly invented harmonica, which has been honoured with the decided approbation of the first musical professors." To top off the evening at the Adelphi, Mr. Childe (he of the laughing gas) would give a "grand display of FAIRY DREAMS." The April 6 edition of the *Times* had something for everyone—the Ellenborough divorce, however, continued to provide the favorite entertainment for all Londoners who could read.

The *Age*, a rather disreputable organ, had these comments: "The debate on Lord Ellenborough's business was almost obscene; and the delicate question, what was the exact extent of a husband's conjugal duties, was discussed by Sir H. Hardinge in a very scientific manner. Matters became a little personal in the end. Sir G. Clerk told Hume that he was an ass, incapable of understanding anything; on which Joe told Sir George that he was very impertinent. . . . On the whole, it was well worthy of the Cabinet which carried it through. It was a little strong, after all, for Lushington, as the judge who had pronounced the divorce, to get up as a legislator, or rather a counsel, to plead on behalf of one side of the question. But all squeamishness is now out of fashion."

The *Standard* carried the following item: "We cannot understand how his lordship could have tired of his wife, especially as evidence before the House of Commons shows that his Lordship gave her none of his society during the day and reposed himself on a distant couch by night."

There is little doubt that the saturation coverage of the Ellenborough affair in the press gave an uneasy twinge to a young librarian at the British Museum. Frederick Madden married his doomed Mary just four days after the Ellenborough Divorce Bill was introduced in the House of Lords.

Cashing in on the newspaper publicity, London printmakers turned their talents to the Ellenborough story, and one of their most popular items was a picture of Jane taken from the Colleen miniature, with her bare bosom outlined in a lacey frill and the rest of her figure obscured in a blue mist. Under the title, "A View of Ellenborough," it was subtitled, "Has been lately represented in Parliament," followed by a rhyme:

> *Never fancy time's before you,*
> *Youth, believe me, will away*
> *And then, alas, who will adore you*
> *Or to wrinkles tribute pay?*

The astonished governess Steely found herself the darling of the press and the anathema of the aristocracy. The former demanded that she name Jane's unsuitable companions; the latter were outraged that one of her class could have the unspeakable audacity to pronounce moral judgment on her betters. The repercussions of Steely's testimony were the subject of comment by the Princess de Lieven in writing to Lord Grey. The Princess wrote:

> Here nothing is talked of for the moment but the divorce of Lord Ellenborough. They are worrying this poor man in a cruel way. I foresee that the affair will be very annoying to various members of London society. Already allusions more than indirect are considerably compromising my colleague's wife [Countess St. Antonio]. It is a most disagreeable affair, the more so as there is truth at the bottom of it. The world says that Lord Ellenborough is going to leave the Cabinet, to be replaced by the Duke of Buckingham. However, at present this is only gossip.

What the "world said" notwithstanding, Ellenborough managed to survive the scandal, and his political career later flourished. The publicity given to the divorce hearings, however, tended to crystallize animosity to him in the public mind, animosity which was never completely erased. History has attested to the brilliance of Lord Ellenborough as an administrator, but during his lifetime few persons outside of official circles could ever evaluate his worth with any degree of fairness. When he was Viceroy of India in 1844, Lord Palmerston wrote of him, "Lord Ellenborough is behaving with incredible stupidity and causing his government a great deal of embarrassment. Even the *Times* writes against him, and everyone thinks he is mad. He imitates Napoleon's style...." Edward never lost his arrogance.

Many believed that the humiliation Ellenborough suffered in the divorce hearings was the main reason he never married again, anxious though he was for an

Sir Kenelm Digby (1603–1665), Jane's most spectacular ancestor—a swashbuckling and colorful adventurer and intellectual.

Chief Justice Sir Edward Coke (1551?–1634), Attorney General to Queen Elizabeth I and founder of the Coke family fortune.

Admiral Sir Henry Digby (1763?–1842), Jane's father, decorated for bravery at the Battle of Trafalgar.

Jane Elizabeth Coke (Lady Andover 1777–1863), Jane's mother. She was a noted Regency beauty.

Thomas William Coke (1754–1842), Jane's maternal grandfather, known as "Coke of Norfolk" and later Earl of Leicester.

View of Holkham Hall, Norfolk, seat of the Coke family and Jane's birthplace.

The imposing entrance hall at Holkham, with its alabaster columns and spectacular ceiling.

Jane, about eight years old, with her brothers, Edward, six, and Kenelm, four.

Jane at thirteen, painted in Switzerland when
she was wintering abroad with her family.

Edward Law, Lord Ellenborough, Jane's first husband. The inset of Jane is from the miniature by Henry Collen, prints of which were sold during the Ellenborough divorce.

Cruikshank cartoon (*ca.* 1820) of a Wednesday night ball at Almack's, where London society gathered during the Regency and the reign of George IV.

Prince Felix Schwarzenberg, attaché at the Austrian Embassy, named by Lord Ellenborough as Jane's partner in adultery.

Innocent employment for Foreign Princes

— Harley - St. } vide evidence on the Swartzenburgh affair

Newspaper cartoon (1830) of Prince Schwarzenberg lacing Jane's stays, based on evidence given at the divorce hearings.

Sketch of Jane at twenty, made by W. Slater and sold at Colnaghi's print shop. Inset: Mathilde Selden, at twenty, the illegitimate child of Jane and Prince Schwarzenberg.

heir. His personal papers reveal, however, that he had three illegitimate children —two sons and a daughter—by an unnamed woman with whom he carried on a long liaison after his divorce. In a letter to his mother in October 1841, Edward expressed a great affection for his "two beautiful boys." It was rumored that his daughter was the Madame Hamilton who became the mistress—the *Petite Mouche Blanche*—of Victor Emmanuel II, king of Sardinia and the first king of Italy.

As Edward grew older, he professed an undying devotion to his first wife, Lady Octavia Stewart. In the village of Oxenton near his Gloucestershire estate, he restored an ancient Saxon chapel and erected in it an elaborate memorial to Lady Octavia, attributing whatever good he had thought or done to her influence. In his last years he became the kindly country squire, the Dante scholar, the gallant nobleman so fondly and flatteringly portrayed in the memoirs of Lady Dorothy Nevill. As he neared eighty, he was said to be "younger in spirit and more likeable than he had been at twenty." He died on December 22, 1871.

7

Paris Interlude

Put not your trust in princes.
—PSALM 146

For soon or late Love is his own avenger.
—LORD BYRON

On a warm day in late August, 1829, the packet boat to Ostend left Ramsgate with a full complement of passengers ready to invade the continent in pursuit of health or pleasure or a combination of the two. Some were bound for the spas of Ems and Wiesbaden to take the waters and recover from the lavish dinners of the summer high season while enjoying a little roulette and *trente-et-quarante*. There were university students with their tutors; rosy-cheeked children with their nursemaids; ladies in pretty pink bonnets; gentlemen in caps and linen jackets, with mustachios they'd just begun to sprout for the "continental look." The decks were heaped with hatboxes and silver-fitted dressing cases.

The passenger list included a "Madame Einberg" and her companion, Miss Margaret Steele, neither of whom chose to mingle with the other travelers. Jane was carefully veiled to avoid recognition. As Steely watched the children playing on the deck, she must have recalled with some nostalgia a trip to Europe nine years earlier with the Digby family. Who would have dreamed in those carefree days of 1820 that the governess would be accompanying a disgraced and pregnant Jane on such a different journey?

The weather at Ostend was perfect for bathing, but the ladies were in no mood to enjoy the beach. Jane and Steely spent only one night at the fashionable seaside resort before taking a coach for the final part of their journey together. By the time they reached Brussels, seventy miles and eight miserable hours from the coast, both women were badly in need of rest. Jane was in her seventh month of pregnancy, a dangerous time for travel. She had never been delicate, however, and her recuperative powers were phenomenal. Travel, even under the most trying circumstances, never failed to stimulate her, and the prospect of a reunion with Felix made her almost giddy with excitement. Jane may have tried for Steely's benefit to behave like a repentant sinner, but the governess knew from long experience that there was little repentance behind those sparkling violet eyes and flushed cheeks.

Brussels in the late summer of 1829 was filled with English tourists, many of whom came to see the battlefield of Waterloo ten miles away, and Jane, not knowing what old acquaintance she might run into, rarely left her lodgings. Wearing a veiled bonnet, she would sometimes stroll in the nearby Grand' Place, admiring the flamboyant seventeenth-century guild houses and the Gothic Hôtel de Ville with its towering belfry. Jane's only business in Brussels was the hiring of a *femme de chambre* to take with her to Basel. She had not brought her English maid, preferring to engage a foreigner who knew nothing of her past situation. Steely spent her free time shopping. The child Jane was carrying might not have a proper name, but the governess was determined it would start out in life with a proper wardrobe. While she would have conceded that Brussels was an excellent place to buy linen and lace, Steely was never entirely comfortable on foreign soil. England, in her view, was the only fit place for Englishmen. The prim spinster had her low opinion of foreign morals confirmed when she wandered one day into the Rue de l'Étuve and came face to face with the *Manneken-Pis*, Duquesnoy's famous statue of a naked little boy performing a basic function. By the second week in September when she put "Madame Einberg" and the new maid into a hired coach for Basel, Steely was more than ready to go home. It was nonetheless a sad parting, for neither the governess nor Jane knew when they might meet again, and Jane's future was, to say the least, uncertain.

Basel, founded by Roman armies in the third century, was in 1829 a beautiful spa, rich in history. Bordered by the fabled Black Forest, the town spread itself out on both banks of the sparkling green Rhine where the river made a crescent bend. Dominating the landscape from a terrace high above the river was the picturesque red sandstone Münster, the ancient cathedral with its two slender towers, Gothic facade and Romanesque north portal. Basel had been a center of medieval culture, and its German-speaking population was still devoted to learning, art and music. Under different circumstances Jane might have enjoyed her stay in Basel. Her Swiss neighbors were lively, friendly people, too well-mannered to ask a beautiful expectant English mother where the child's father was, but that was a question Jane herself would have undoubtedly liked answered.

Felix Schwarzenberg did not get to Basel until November 10, 1829, nearly two months after Jane arrived there. The woman who greeted him did not much resemble the nymph-like belle of Almack's he had last seen in May. The birth of their child was by then overdue, and Jane was surely feeling awkward and unattractive. Felix was unchanged in appearance. He was still slender, tall and dashing—the complete Austrian aristocrat. But there were subtle differences. His precipitous flight from London had sobered him, and he had already begun to shed his frivolous Prince Charming role for the mantle of statesmanship. He was a little closer to the formidable Prime Minister Schwarzenberg of 1848, the image of detachment, contained arrogance and icy self-discipline. (That was the Schwarzenberg who, when asked to show clemency toward some captured Hungarian rebels, is said to have answered, "Yes, yes—a very good idea. But first we will have a little hanging.")

The lovers' reunion in Basel was not exactly what Jane had hoped for. Felix could not but admire her courage in giving up everything for him, but he could not help wishing she had not. The burden was too much for him. Lord Byron had written in *Don Juan*, "Alas! the love of women! it is known / To be a lovely and a fearful thing...." No one knew that better than Prince Schwarzenberg. He loved his English beauty better and longer than he was to love any other woman, but he was simply incapable of Jane's degree of intensity. With Felix self-love came first, and he had no wish to jeopardize his career any further. Jane saw immediately that her lover regretted her sacrifice, and the realization must have crushed her, but there was no turning back.

On November 12, 1829, just two days after Felix arrived in Basel, a daughter was born to Jane. The little girl, named Mathilde after Felix's favorite sister, had her mother's lovely mouth and violet eyes and her father's black hair. She was registered as "the Einberg child," and Felix gave her the nickname of "Didi." A few months later she was baptized in Paris under the name of Mathilde Selden. Felix scarcely had time to become acquainted with his daughter before he was due to report to his new diplomatic post in Paris. He promised to return at Christmas, and he kept his word, but that visit was also a brief one. Of the five months Jane spent in Basel, Felix was with her a total of less than two weeks.

There is no personal record of Jane's stay in Switzerland before and after Didi's birth, but it was undoubtedly a lonely time without family or friends. The winter weather was too cold for her to enjoy the outdoor cafés overlooking the river, and it was not the season for strolls along the Rheinweg, the fashionable right bank esplanade. A woman of the aristocracy with neither home nor husband had few entertainments besides sightseeing, writing letters, shopping and handwork. Jane, who never traveled without a sketchbook, must have turned to her pencils and watercolors to pass the long hours of waiting. But sketching, sightseeing and patronizing the shops of Basel's ribbon-weavers, however, were not very satisfying diversions for a passionate lady whose lover was in Paris, and in February of 1830, Jane and Didi left Basel to join Felix. It was not a very opportune time for their arrival, but arrivals of mistresses with illegitimate children are seldom opportune.

Paris in the winter of 1830 was seething with political intrigue—revolution was in the air, and the Austrian Embassy staff was working feverishly to maintain the status quo in France. By appointing Felix to this sensitive diplomatic mission, the powerful Prince Metternich had indicated that his confidence in his young protégé was not shaken by the Ellenborough affair, and Felix was determined to justify that faith. When the attention of all Europe (and most especially of Metternich's Holy Alliance) was nervously focused on Paris, Schwarzenberg had little time for the afternoons of romantic dalliance he had enjoyed in London. Diplomats in the French capital were very uneasy, wondering who would fill the vacuum if the shaky throne of King Charles X collapsed, as it showed every sign of doing. No one outside France was ready for another

Napoleon just fifteen years after Waterloo, but there were plenty of Frenchmen who looked back longingly from that comfortable distance to the misty grandeur of the Napoleonic era. Some of them were actively conspiring to replace their Bourbon king with Napoleon's son, the Duke of Reichstadt, who was being held by the Austrians at Schönbrunn Palace near Vienna. Street vendors were openly offering prints of Napoleon and the Duke along with other souvenirs of empire. One of their most popular items was a print of a young man who strongly resembled Napoleon, declaiming in large block letters, "France is my mother; Austria is but my nurse."

The irregular status of Lady Ellenborough made it impossible for her to be received at the French court, and she was excluded from many of the functions which duty compelled Felix Schwarzenberg to attend. No one, not even Jane herself, questioned the protocol that prevented her from being presented to Charles X. True, the French were generally a little more relaxed than the English in such matters, but even they demanded that certain amenities be observed. By living openly with Felix, Jane consigned herself to the demimonde, and not only the court but many noble houses in Paris were closed to her. She was not even among the guests at a dinner party given in the spring of 1830 by Lady Blessington in honor of Captain William Anson. William was one of Jane's numerous Anson first cousins, and he had often shared the schoolroom at Holkham Hall with her, but there is no indication that he called on her while he was in Paris. "A very remarkable young man," Lady Blessington wrote of William, "indeed a worthy descendant of his great ancestor who might well be proud of such a scion to this ancient stock." Of Jane, who came from the same ancient stock, there was no mention, and Lady Blessington later used Jane's story very cruelly in one of her novels.

However limited her social engagements may have been, Jane was settled quite stylishly in the Faubourg St. Germain, where numbers of eighteenth-century mansions, closed during the revolution and Napoleonic era, had been reopened in the years of the Bourbon restoration. This was the heart of fashionable Paris at a time when the Arc de Triomphe was still unfinished, the Madeleine only half-built and surrounded by wasteland and the Champs-Élysées a sinister cutthroat district. Jane lived briefly on the Rue de Grenelle, a short distance from the beautiful Fountain of the Four Seasons, sculpted by Bouchardon a century earlier. She may well have nodded good day to a neighbor, the twenty-year-old Alfred de Musset, who was then living in a house adjoining the fountain, where he wrote most of his poetry. After two or three months on the Rue de Grenelle, Jane and Didi moved to a larger house at 99 Place du Palais des Députés (later renamed Place du Palais Bourbon) on the square opposite the Palais Bourbon. The palace, built in 1722 by the Duchess of Bourbon, daughter of Louis XIV and Madame de Montespan, had since 1827 housed the Legislative Assembly of France. The location of Jane's house could hardly have been chosen to preserve anonymity, but the time for concealment had obviously passed.

In the beginning Felix Schwarzenberg seemed pleased enough with the arrangement. There was no shortage of places in Paris where a man might take his stunningly beautiful English mistress, and it certainly did not lessen the prince's appeal to the ladies when the romantic story of his conquest was whispered among them. The government of France may have been about to topple in the spring of 1830, but in Paris people managed to enjoy themselves as usual. Boulevard des Italiens was the center of nightlife for wealthy Parisians, and the less affluent patronized the many small theaters on the Boulevard du Temple. Parisians of all classes loved masked balls, and the hardier revelers could often be seen dancing along the boulevards in the small hours of the morning after the balls had ended. Just as aristocratic Londoners imitated everything French, the upperclass Parisians wanted everything *à l'anglaise*. The French Jockey Club had just been founded by Lord Henry Seymour, whose father, Lord Hertford, gave the most spectacular entertainments at his palatial house on the site of the present Opéra. The French romantics had just discovered Shakespeare, and the young composer Hector Berlioz fell madly in love with an English actress, Harriet Smithson, who was playing the role of Juliet at the Odeon.

Within walking distance of Jane's house on the Place du Palais were the student haunts of the Left Bank, where a remarkable collection of young writers, musicians and painters gathered. The names of Berlioz, Liszt, de Musset, George Sand, Frédéric Chopin, Prosper Mérimée, Alfred de Vigny, Charles Augustin Saint-Beuve, Victor Hugo and Eugène Delacroix were not widely known when Jane came to Paris in 1830, but they soon would be.

There was one giant talent of that generation, however, who had already tasted fame, and who preferred high society to the cafés of Montparnasse. Some of the same glittering salons from which Lady Ellenborough was ostracized during the winter and spring of 1830 were scenes of triumph for an inelegant, pot-bellied, bright-eyed, gap-toothed French writer. Honoré de Balzac, whose success was established with the publication in December 1829 of his *La Physiologie du mariage*, was being lionized by Paris's *haut monde* and loving every minute of it. No amount of sartorial extravagance—the jeweled walking stick, the dozen pairs of straw-colored kid gloves, the solid gold buttons, the white dressing gowns with gold-tasseled cords, the violet carriage rug with his monogram and someone else's coronet emblazoned on it—could make Balzac handsome, but when he entered a drawing room and turned his gold-flecked eyes upon the assembled guests, it was as if a tempest had swept in. He may have been, as a contemporary described him, "a shapeless mass resembling a dancing bear," but he had magic.

Like many Parisians, Jane was fascinated by Balzac's brilliant, uninhibited book about marriage, in which he dealt compassionately with unfaithful wives. Few people understood the complex nature of sexual attraction better than this

French author. In a later novel, *Le Lys dans la vallée*, Balzac used Jane as a model for one of his characters, and he made some astute suggestions on how to keep a passionate affair from burning itself out, none of which Jane had followed:

> Lovers who are obliged to live in the world of fashion are always wrong to break down the barriers insisted on by the common law of drawing rooms, wrong not to obey implicitly all the conventions demanded by good manners; more for their own sake than for that of others. Distances to be traversed, superficial respect to be maintained, comedies to be played out, mystery to be kept up—all the strategy of a happy love-affair fills up life, revives desire and preserves the heart from the lassitude of habit. But a first passion, like a young man, is by nature profligate and cuts down its timber recklessly instead of economizing its resources.

The "lassitude of habit" Balzac warned against began to afflict the Ellenborough-Schwarzenberg romance almost from the moment Jane arrived in Paris. The mystery and excitement of a clandestine affair disappeared as soon as the lovers had unlimited access to each other, and for Felix the challenge was gone as well. He had written Jane in plain terms that marriage was out of the question for them, but she was foolishly optimistic enough to believe that when they were together she could rekindle his ardor and persuade him to make her his wife. Rekindling the ardor was all too easy. Within a few weeks she was pregnant again, but there was no wedding in sight. The physical attraction was still there, but the love Felix had for Jane was first diluted with sympathy and then dissolved in resentment.

In April stories of the Ellenborough divorce hearings reached Paris, and *Galignani's Messenger*, the newspaper (printed in Paris) which throughout the nineteenth century kept English travelers in Europe abreast of current events at home, gave the racy testimony generous coverage. One of Felix's former colleagues on the Austrian Embassy staff in London thoughtfully sent him an English cartoon entitled "Innocent Employment for Foreign Princes," which caricatured Schwarzenberg lacing Lady Ellenborough's stays. This was hardly the kind of publicity a rising young diplomat needed, and Felix was furious. Why should he be publicly mocked and made the villain in a love affair with a woman whose husband had shown so little interest in her? Who among his peers had not been guilty of the same thing?

Almost as soon as the English and French newspapers had wrung the last morsel from the Ellenborough divorce scandal, a novel was published in England, reviving the gossip. Its publicity-shy author, Lady Charlotte Bury, besides keeping a diary as lady-in-waiting to the queen, which was later published, wrote sentimental novels, always anonymously, into which she wove a tapestry of the social life of her era. In *The Exclusives*, which appeared in 1830, the Ellenboroughs were easily recognizable in the characters of Lord and Lady Glenmore, names borrowed from the popular earlier novel *Almack's*. The heroine, like Jane, had her good name destroyed by an affair, but Lady Bury showed compassion when she wrote,

> There are few women on whom this stain is cast who could, like Lady Glenmore, plead perfect innocence of intention, but she had been almost from the outset of her marriage thrown alone in the midst of the most dangerous society in London. She had certainly not to complain that Lord Glenmore had willfully deserted or neglected her. His absence was a necessary consequence of the duties he had taken upon himself in a public career.

It took very little time for *The Exclusives* to cross the Channel and to be discussed in Paris diplomatic circles.

All this notoriety did nothing to enhance Jane's qualifications as a bride for the prince. The proud Catholic Schwarzenbergs were not at all in favor of the match. Princess Mathilde, who had lavished all her affection on Felix since their mother's death, did not consider any woman good enough for him, least of all that shameless English baggage. Felix's younger brother Friederich had just entered the priesthood, and this Schwarzenberg, who was to become Cardinal Archbishop of Salzburg and then of Prague, would hardly have been overjoyed to have a scandalous divorcée for a sister-in-law, no matter how impeccable her lineage.

While his family was advising him against marriage, Felix had pressure in the opposite direction from an unexpected source. The Marquis of Londonderry, acting on behalf of Lord Ellenborough, came to see Schwarzenberg in late April of 1830 and urged him to marry the woman he had disgraced, now that her divorce was final. From his conversation with Felix, Lord Londonderry got the distinct impression that the Austrian prince had no intention of marrying his mistress, and he went immediately to Jane with this disturbing news. Londonderry, Edward's first wife's brother, was genuinely fond of Jane (they corresponded for many years), and he begged her for her own sake to make a life for herself away from Felix. He had no idea that she was pregnant at the time with a second Schwarzenberg child, but it is unlikely that she would have taken his advice even had she not been pregnant. There is no question that she was still deeply in love with Felix, and that she would have been willing to continue indefinitely as his mistress, had not the arrangement begun to pall on him.

Felix continued to maintain his private quarters in Paris, more for his own freedom of movement than for the sake of discretion, and as summer approached, he began to spend less and less time at the house on Place du Palais. He had an excellent excuse: rumors of open rebellion were mounting daily, and the Austrian Embassy in Paris was a scene of frantic activity. Metternich's agents tried to keep track of the constantly shifting political currents and manipulate them when they could.

Through the spring, political conditions progressively worsened, until by summer Charles, becoming increasingly repressive, had reached a point of no return. During the "Three Glorious Days" of July 27, 28, and 29, a popular revolution forced his abdication, and on July 30, shortly after the last shots were fired, the throne was offered by the National Assembly to the Duke of Orléans, Louis Philippe.

From her house at 99 Place du Palais, Jane Digby watched history being made that summer. She could smell gunsmoke, hear shots being fired, even see the street barricades, but the Revolution of 1830 meant only that she was often deprived of Felix's company. Jane never took an active interest in politics, which represented a kind of competition to her, and she was feeling neglected, pregnant and very peevish. Freedom to Jane was an individual rather than a collective matter, and she certainly did not identify her personal freedom with the battle of the barricades.

Felix Schwarzenberg was no more inspired by the bourgeois revolutionaries than was Jane—to the prince they were rabble, worthy only of his contempt—but he was intensely interested in the power they represented and how it might be directed. His careful observations during the uprising were to pay off handsomely. In 1831 he wrote a long treatise on the July Revolution for his government, a work acclaimed as brilliant, and he acquired from his experiences in Paris a philosophy of dealing with mobs that he effectively used to seize power in the Austrian crisis of 1848, when the young Franz Josef came to the throne. Felix was a very busy man during the tumultuous summer of 1830, and he had little patience with Jane's complaints of neglect. This was the beginning of the end for their costly love affair.

By fall the situation had worsened as Louis Philippe's position in France weakened, in turn, and as the possibilities of a new European war increased precipitously. Prince Schwarzenberg was totally immersed in the rapidly changing events and in the delicate negotiations being carried on to try and keep the peace. When, by mid-November, the intense pressure on the diplomats in Paris was finally relieved, Felix had grown quite out of the habit of spending his evenings at 99 Place du Palais des Députés.

It was a cold and rainy autumn in Paris, a dismal and unhappy time for Jane. Two pieces of news from England did nothing to cheer her: on November 30 Colonel George Anson, her constant escort before she met the prince, married the Honourable Isabella Weld-Forrester, a reigning beauty of London society with a spotless reputation; the same month George's younger brother, William (who had so impressed Lady Blessington the previous spring), was killed in a shipboard accident while on naval duty. The worst was yet to come. By December of 1830, when Jane was too far advanced in her pregnancy to leave the house, Prince Schwarzenberg gave up all pretense of fidelity to his mistress and began publicly romancing other women. If Jane was not immediately aware of her lover's betrayal, everyone in diplomatic circles was. The Countess Granville, wife of England's ambassador to France, wrote to her brother, the Duke of Devonshire, "Poor Lady Ellenborough is just going to be confined; Schwarzenberg going about flirting with Mme. d'Oudenarde." Once Felix decided to put himself on the available list, he did not let any grass grow under his feet.

The passionate affair between Lady Ellenborough and her prince was obviously in a rapid decline, but for a ridiculously long time Jane refused to accept this fact, and she forced herself through a series of painful last gasps. When a son was born to her in late December of 1830, she named him Felix and cherished the illusion that this male child would be an inducement for her lover to marry her. It was a vain hope—the little boy lived only a few weeks. Felix was attentive for a while, out of sympathy, but the attentiveness did not last. During the first months of 1831 Jane and Felix were still "together" in a sense, but the prince was keeping to his own quarters. Jane was eager for some amusement after her long confinement, but she seldom had an escort. While she sat at home unhappy and bewildered, Felix was enjoying to the hilt the role of eligible bachelor. Count Rodolphe Apponyi, who had recently come from London to be Austria's ambassador to France, wrote in his diary early in 1831, "Felix Schwarzenberg is paying court to Mme. de H——. They are inseparable in the salons. Mme. de O——, to whom our attaché paid his first homage, is very jealous and cannot believe he would drop her for a red-haired German."

It was a gala season in Paris, with everyone caught up in a new and exotic fashion. In the midst of the political upheavals of the previous summer, hardly any Frenchmen had absorbed the fact that French troops had taken the city of Algiers in July after a three-year blockade of the port, but now Parisians went Algerian with gusto. Delacroix began painting sultry Algerian beauties, George Sand temporarily abandoned her well-cut men's trousers for the flowing harem style, and Franz Liszt wore blue Turkish bloomers when he entertained. On the evening of March 9 a Genoese violinist, Niccolò Paganini, gave his first concert in Paris and electrified his audience with his double-stops, flying staccatos and left-handed pizzicati. Paganini could be seen almost any afternoon that spring sitting in a music shop in the Passage de l'Opéra, a rather diabolic figure wearing a voluminous fur-lined overcoat, no matter how balmy the weather.

All this color and gaiety in Paris during the first months of 1831 went on without Jane, and an explosion was building in the house on Place du Palais. Matters came to a head sometime in May, but exactly what happened is not clear. There was apparently a violent quarrel, and Felix fled Paris for his native Bohemia, leaving his mistress without a word of farewell. The Austrian Embassy version of the quarrel—a vicious story—was recorded five years later in the journal of Count Apponyi, when it was called to his mind by an accidental meeting with Jane. Apponyi claimed that a cousin of Schwarzenberg's had accused Jane of infidelity to Felix. "The cousin," Apponyi wrote, "discovered one day that Milady was entertaining an officer of the guard. He spoke to her about this and warned her if she did not put a stop to this relationship immediately he would be obliged to inform S. Lady E. promised, but did not keep her word. S. was immediately informed, which caused him to break off with her and leave Paris within forty-eight hours. Lady E. cried either little or much but kept her officer of the guard, who was succeeded by another and then another. . . ."

Apponyi's story is highly suspect. This accusation against Jane was later denied by Felix himself, and there are several other inaccuracies in Apponyi's journal involving Jane. The Hungarian diplomat, who was so enchanted with Jane's beauty at an Almack's ball in 1828, claimed in his journal in the year 1836 that he had had no knowledge of her having followed Felix to Paris six years earlier. "I learned," he wrote, "that she had been living here in a very retired manner and visiting absolutely nobody except S. and one of his cousins." A strange statement from a man who wrote in his Paris journal of 1830, "Today I am going to the 'at home' of Lady Granville, wife of England's ambassador, and from there to Lady Ellenborough's."

There is no record of Jane's version of the quarrel of May of 1831, but she maintained her innocence in later correspondence and indicated that the Schwarzenberg family had instigated both the trouble between her and Felix and the slanderous stories that followed. Felix's documented flirtations during the winter of 1831 make it appear likely that he was waiting for an excuse to break off with Jane, and he merely seized upon the quarrel as a way out.

It is an interesting footnote to the story that in a biography written by the statesman's great-great nephew, Adolph Schwarzenberg, Felix is seen as victim rather than villain:

> In 1831 he returned to his native country. He needed a rest; he was in poor health and low spirits. The Ellenborough affair and the perpetual whirl of activity and excitement had left their mark. The sojourn with his family and the quiet life in the Bohemian forests restored his physical and psychic well-being. The consequences of the unfortunate crisis with regard to his psyche were, however, remarkable. Concomitant with a certain frivolous and flirtatious tendency, he had an inclination to piety. It may seem surprising that the man who was so fond of the fair sex should instruct his valet always to pack in his luggage at least one Latin classic and the *Imitatio Christi* by Thomas à Kempis.

Castle Krumlov, rising from a rocky cliff overlooking the Moldau River and surrounded by hundreds of acres of forests, was a perfect place for Felix's retreat. The castle where the prince was born was of staggering proportions— previous generations had continued to add to it until the architecture ranged from Gothic to baroque. There was more than enough room for solitude and contemplation, and the welcome was warm.

Jane had no such retreat. For a few days after Felix left her she remained secluded in the house on the Place du Palais, stunned and disbelieving. When she learned that Prince Schwarzenberg was no longer attached to the Austrian Embassy, she had no reason to remain in Paris, but she had no idea where to go. In desperation she wrote her mother that Felix had left her, and Lady Andover suggested a meeting at Dover to decide what to do. Before Jane left Paris, she paid a final visit to the grave of her infant son Felix, in whom she had placed such high hopes, and she wrote a poem (a touching mixture of grief, sentiment, remorse and pride that was uniquely Jane's), which is the only remaining record of the child's brief existence:

Paris 1831

TO FELIX

And thou art gone, my precious boy,
To join the one that went before,
An angel in those realms of joy,
Thy pilgrimage on earth is o'er.

Plead for thy mother, cherub child,
Plead that her errors be forgiven.
Now at the feet of Jesus mild
I implore the clemency of Heaven.

And thou, too, pity and forgive
Thy tainted birth, dishonored name.
Alas, t'is best thou dost not live
To share my destiny of shame.

For this lost soul remains,
That heart whose idol is thy sire,
Had rather than renounce its claims
Dared its Creator's threatened ire.

Yet were its dreams for thee most blest,
When purified at wedlock's shrine,
Sanctioned by heaven's holiness,
Her aim were joined to thine.

But thou art gone, the vision's passed,
Alas, its grave alone I view;
T'was fleeting bright, too bright to last
And quenched is now its meteor hue.

Thy will be done, but sorrow's tears
Flow o'er the lowly, verdant sod
For one who's saved from earthly cares
And, pure, returns to God.

There is no record of Jane's reunion with her mother in the summer of 1831 other than a notation in the Digby family's synopsis of her letters stating that Jane brought her daughter to Dover to meet Lady Andover and Miss Steele. It was apparently the only time any of Jane's family saw Didi. Out of that meeting came a decision by Jane to go to Munich, but the reasons for that move are not explained. It was most likely arrived at by process of elimination. The divorce scandal had made living in England unthinkable for her, and there is a strong possibility that she had made a promise to Lord Ellenborough to live abroad to save him further embarrassment. Paris had too many painful associations, and Jane needed a fresh start. Lord Erskine, the British ambassador to the Bavarian court, was an old friend of the Coke family, and that connection may have been the deciding factor. There are confusing stories that Jane arrived in Munich accompanied by an "innkeeper's son" who, according to one biographer, later became king of Sweden, but this oblique reference to Bernadotte seems to be completely without foundation in fact.

It is difficult to understand, in the light of Schwarzenberg's behavior, how Jane could have believed in the summer of 1831 that there was hope of a reconciliation, but the prince himself contributed to this illusion. Inexplicably Felix kept Jane dangling two more years with vague promises sprinkled throughout affectionate letters, but he nimbly managed to avoid a meeting in all that time, a meeting for which Jane would have traveled any distance. It would be some time before she could look with any degree of objectivity on her disastrous pursuit of her lover, but she summed it up thirty years later when she wrote to a friend, "Waiting was never my forte. Where it might have served and saved me most I could not bend my wayward spirit to wait. And Felix avenged most awfully Heaven's outraged laws."

8

Letters to a King

I will never judge you harshly, even if all the world does!
I cannot condemn you, because I understand it all.
You deserve more respect than many who seem guiltless.
The world judges one way, God another.

—KING LUDWIG TO JANE DIGBY

There was no livelier city in Europe in the 1830s than Munich. Sculptors, painters, architects, artisans, scholars and musicians from all over the continent crowded the streets and cafes. In every direction massive scaffoldings arose, masking new buildings being erected or old ones being rejuvenated. Leo von Klenze, one of Europe's greatest architects, had undertaken the herculean task of unifying the maze of structures that made up the Bavarian royal palace (the Residenz) so that a single, imposing, classic facade might overlook the Hofgarten and Max Joseph Platz. With dizzying speed Klenze's army of workmen was pulling down one building after another and in their places beginning new ones. Other architects—Gärtner, Ziebland, Ohlmüller and Volz—were engaged in a host of other royal projects—museums, churches, triumphal arches and obelisks —which were changing the face of Munich. Peter von Cornelius, the outstanding Nazarite painter who had been brought from Rome to direct the Royal Academy of Painting, was training such promising young German romanticists as Moritz von Schwind and Wilhelm von Kaulbach. The brothers Franz and Ludwig von Schwanthaler were deep in plans for a monumental patriotic sculpture to be called the *Bavaria*. The university, which had been moved from Landshut to Munich in 1826, was drawing scholars from all the German states and bursting at the seams. The building boom had revitalized Munich's traditional crafts, and the wood carvers, the glass stainers, the silversmiths and the bronze foundrymen were working furiously to keep up with their orders.

Munich boasted more theaters than any other city in Germany, and the entertainment fare was greatly varied. Plays by Bavarian and Viennese authors alternated with the light operas of Mozart and Domenico Cimarosa. Choruses were formed to sing the music of Handel and Haydn, and aristocrats played the sonatas of Beethoven and Mendelssohn on their pianofortes. Even the church bells, which rang at frequent intervals to call Bavarians to prayer and meals, were melodiously in tune.

This was a golden age for Munich, and one man was largely responsible—

King Ludwig I of Bavaria, scion of forty generations and nearly a thousand years of Wittelsbach rulers, warriors, poets and art patrons. Ludwig had a burning ambition to do for Munich what Lorenzo de' Medici had done for Florence, and he very nearly succeeded. When Jane Digby came to Munich in 1831, Ludwig was forty-five years old and had been on the Bavarian throne less than six years, but he had already initiated a remarkable renaissance of culture and learning and was well on his way to creating a Bavarian *Griechenland* in the old city that sat like a half-moon on the west bank of the Isar River.

Ludwig, who held the throne from 1825 to 1848, is often deprived of his rightful place in history by those who either confuse him with his tragic grandson, Ludwig II (the "mad king" of 1864 to 1886, who built fairy-tale castles in the Alps), or dismiss him as a foolish woman-chaser, forced to abdicate because of his infatuation with the dancer and courtesan, Lola Montez. In actuality Ludwig was a talented and intelligent man; he was also impetuous, enthusiastic, patriotic, devoted to beauty, stubborn, and deeply religious. Although he escaped the intermittent madness that plagued the Wittelsbachs, Ludwig had his share of eccentricity, mixed with a touch of genius. He was a study in contradictions. He was strongly, sometimes violently anti-Semitic, yet he offered financial and personal help to a number of young Jewish writers, composers and painters. He was as fluent in French, Italian and English as he was in his native tongue, but in 1840 he suddenly forbade the use of anything but German at court and banished any subject who spoke any other language in his presence. He used his own money to build canals, encourage new industry and improve methods of agriculture, but he would never allocate state funds for these purposes. He spent fortunes on buildings for his beloved university but refused to authorize the purchase of new textbooks for the students. "I read secondhand books when I was a student," he said, "and I am the King." He owned priceless paintings and a collection of Cinderella-like gilded carriages for state occasions but wore suits of clothes until they were threadbare, and he was fanatically economical in the royal household, where the cooks complained that the kitchen budget would not permit the luxury of onions.

From his youth Ludwig had been hard of hearing, and his deafness gave him a tendency to shout in normal conversation. The deafness and a slight speech impediment caused him to speak in measured phrases, his carefully chosen words separated by frequent pauses. Smallpox in his childhood had left his face pockmarked, and he had a rather long nose, but his thick, wavy blond hair and an interesting cleft chin gave him a handsome, youthful appearance even in middle age. Luise von Kobell, daughter of Franz von Kobell, a Munich University professor and popular poet, described Ludwig in *Unter den vier ersten Königen Bayerns* as she remembered him:

> ...the intelligent expression of his face with its finely chiseled features was attractive, and his grey-blue eyes were honest and very penetrating. He was of

medium height and good proportion. . . . His lively gait, his sudden stops never seemed mechanical, but always connected with a thought that just occurred to him. Very different things may have caused that: a building, a painting, a face, a veil. He could not abide a veil hiding a lady's face, and the women of Munich knew it so well that they pulled up their hat veils as soon as they saw the King coming. If they didn't, they were reproached by him for "lack of etiquette." Even though this was done in a joking manner, the ladies tried to avoid being scolded, because Ludwig shouted so that other people heard his remarks and were tempted to add their own comments. Although the King often walked alone, he was always followed at a respectful distance by a curious crowd of people. When he would stop to talk to someone, the crowd would also stop and gather round to listen. Whenever I had a chance, I joined one of these groups, because it was entertaining and educational to hear the King, especially when he stood with his favorite architects, Klenze and Gärtner, before one of their joint creations and passed judgement on the whole effect or some detail of the building.

It was during one of these daily "inspection tours" in the late summer of 1831 that Ludwig first saw Jane Digby. She had been in Munich only a few days, and on this particular morning she was having coffee at Tambosi's. According to *Ein Jahrhundert München*,

> Only one place can claim to be fashionable like the French or Viennese coffee houses: *Tambosi's*, under the arcades at the entrance to the *Hofgarten*. This is a cafe handsomely decorated by local artists, a gathering place for the young. There you can get to know the best actors, musicians, painters, writers, students, distinguished officers, interesting foreigners, the best card and billiard players. There is gambling and conversation available at *Tambosi's*. Manners are casual but respectable. You can be sure to see every adventurer. In front of the buffet under the chestnut trees (where no smoking is permitted) there are green tables set aside for the beauties of society. Beginning in May those are always well filled on Sundays, holidays and Wednesday evenings when the military band plays.

It is not difficult to imagine the impact a stunning stranger with large blue-violet eyes and flawless complexion made on Ludwig, who was, in any case, a slave to beauty. The details of this first meeting are not known, but it is certain that the king of Bavaria lost no time in introducing himself and receiving permission to call.

With characteristic frankness Jane explained the unusual circumstances that had brought her to Munich, and Ludwig was sympathetic and kind. "My acquaintance with you seems a dream," she wrote him two months after they had met. "I can scarcely conceive how you have contrived so completely to win my heart and make me thus at ease by setting aside the differences of rank and all the barriers that the conventions of the world have raised between us." Despite his fondness for Jane, Ludwig was enough bound by conventions that he could not arrange a formal court presentation for a divorced woman, but his friendship at least assured her of a better place in Munich's society than she had enjoyed in Paris.

To the king, an obsessive Grecophile, Jane was always Ianthe, from the Greek version of her name, and he permitted her to call him Lewis or Basily (from the Greek word *Basileus*, or king). He sent a collection of his own poems to Jane with an introduction written especially for her:

> *What a loving heart once felt glowingly*
> *These poems show you, show you my innermost feelings.*
> *You who became a victim of love, you will understand me*
> *As I understand you, dear, whom the world has exiled.*
> *I will never judge you harshly, even if all the world does!*
> *I cannot condemn you, because I understand it all.*
> *You deserve more respect than many who seem guiltless.*
> *The world judges one way, God another.*

Jane always treasured Ludwig's poems and the affectionately inscribed prayer book he gave her.

From the very beginning of their friendship almost everyone in Munich was certain that the Bavarian king was Lady Ellenborough's lover, and none of Jane's chroniclers has ever questioned this. Nevertheless, the more than seventy notes and letters from Jane to Ludwig preserved in the secret archives of the Wittelsbach family, never before available, raise the intriguing possibility that Ludwig was to Jane exactly what she called him—"my best and dearest friend" —and nothing more.

Ludwig's obsession with beautiful women could scarcely be denied; over a period of twenty-three years he had thirty-six of them, including Jane, painted by the court portrait artist, Joseph Stieler, to create his personal gallery of beauties. (This gallery, the Schönheiten, is today one of the major attractions of the Nymphenburg, the summer palace of the Wittelsbachs on the outskirts of Munich.) But the conclusion that the king enjoyed the favors of all these women is patently absurd. Some are members of his own family; some are ladies of his court with impeccable reputations; some are wives and daughters of foreign diplomats. Despite Ludwig's many alleged romances, he appears to have been more passionate generally about things than women, and his romantic poetry is far more spiritual than erotic.

In his early twenties he fell in love with Princess Theresa of Saxe-Hildburghausen, who was described by Napoleon Bonaparte as the most beautiful and accomplished young princess in Europe. Ludwig and Theresa were married in 1810. The princess met all of her husband's requirements: she was handsome; she spoke several languages; she played the piano with professional skill and was a talented painter; and she bore Ludwig seven healthy children. There was, however, one flaw. Theresa was liberal in her views, and when Ludwig's policies became increasingly repressive (he even allowed a system of surveillance to be introduced into Bavaria following the Paris Revolution of 1830), she used her influence for the first and only time in an attempt to modify his harshness. Ludwig was deeply resentful of her interference, which might explain why almost overnight his attitude towards Theresa changed. He announced to his intimates that she had acquired the drabness of a middle-class German housewife, and he made it plain in public as well as private that she bored him. According to court gossip, Queen Theresa moved to separate quarters in another wing of the *Residenz*, and rumors began to circulate that Ludwig was entertaining in his suite a succession of pretty young women—usually actresses of little note. If the Queen was concerned over these rumors, she never let it show. She refused to permit any mention of them or any criticism of Ludwig to be uttered in her presence. For this reason it is not likely that Theresa was informed that her husband was spending a great deal of time at the house of Lady Ellenborough, an intelligent and aristocratic beauty who did not fit the pattern of his actresses.

Whatever their true relationship, Jane and Ludwig obviously enjoyed each other's company. In December of 1831 she sat for her portrait by Stieler at the request of the King, who was present for most of the sittings. From late August of 1831 through March of 1832 Jane saw Ludwig almost every day, except for a short period when she was out of Munich. During these months the brief messages she wrote to the king are couched in affectionate terms and deal with her daily schedule of riding and paying calls so Ludwig would know when to find her at home. In many respects the Bavarian monarch and the English lady were kindred spirits. They were both incurable romantics who loved the courtly gestures. To both of them being "in love" was a necessity all their lives. (At age sixty Ludwig wrote a poem titled *Not in Love*, about a strange malady that was depressing his spirits. Shortly afterwards he met Lola Montez.)

The king sent Jane violets; she made him an embroidered cap. They delighted in exchanging highly personal poetry and flowery letters. Both enjoyed the theater, music and painting, and Ludwig was likely responsible for the interest Jane later showed in architecture and archaeology. From the beginning the king was intrigued by this highborn English beauty who had thrown away her reputation and become an exile for a passionate love. Such a magnificently reckless, romantic gesture was bound to appeal to the poetic monarch, but he was also practical enough to realize that his young friend was in need of some mature guidance to avoid being compromised further by her impetuous nature. Jane, whose family and close friends were far away, was grateful that Ludwig was willing to act as her confidant and advisor. The earliest dated letter in the Wittelsbach archives is one of many in which Jane asks the king to counsel her about her personal affairs:

Your kindness having inspired me with an unbounded confidence, I feel an imperious obligation to open to you my whole heart. Since your last visit circumstances have occurred which make it necessary I should have better advice than what my own head might alone suggest.

If anyone needed good advice at that time it was Jane, for in the autumn of 1831 it appeared as if the men in her life were about to stumble over each other. Felix Schwarzenberg had written that he was coming to Munich to see her. The king of Bavaria was calling almost daily, and, if that weren't enough, a German nobleman, Baron Karl Theodore von Venningen Üllner, was courting her passionately.

Karl Venningen had met Jane in September when they were both riding in the Hofgarten. For him it had been love at first sight. For Jane, who was still in love with her Austrian prince, it was not, although she could hardly have found a more eligible bachelor than the baron. Karl was a tall, handsome man with dark red hair, a luxurious mustache, and the gentle expression of a poet. He was from a noble family whose title went back to the eleventh century, and he owned valuable estates in Baden, Hesse-Darmstadt and what is now Upper Austria. A superb horseman, dashing in his military uniform, Karl could have had his pick of all the society beauties who sat at Tambosi's green tables, but he had the misfortune to pick the one who could not return his love. He took Jane to the opera, the masked balls, the outdoor cafes—all the public places where the king could not accompany her—and he offered her marriage, which Ludwig was hardly in a position to do. Karl was even undaunted when Jane told him she was in love with Felix Schwarzenberg. The baron was perhaps shrewd enough to guess what Jane was still unwilling to concede: that a man who had abandoned her in such a fashion was not likely to come back. At any rate, his subsequent behavior showed that Karl Venningen was the kind of man who fell in love once in a lifetime, and he was willing to wait for Jane to change her mind.

From Jane's letters to Ludwig it is obvious that the king knew all about Karl Venningen's courtship and Felix Schwarzenberg's proposed visit. Ludwig, like Karl, appears to have had little faith in Schwarzenberg's good intentions, and he urged Jane not to resume her affair with Felix unless marriage were guaranteed. The king suggested that she meet the Austrian diplomat at Schloss Berg, a Wittelsbach castle on Lake Starnberg, where the two could be assured of privacy and avoid creating further gossip. So, late in October of 1831 Jane went to Berg to wait for the prince, and the lovelorn Karl Venningen followed a day or two later. Whether he had Jane's permission to visit her there is uncertain, but he returned to Munich very shortly and delivered in person one of the several letters Jane wrote to the king from Schloss Berg. "If my stay here is prolonged," she told Ludwig,

the time will doubtlessly hang rather heavy on my hands, but I have much to think upon. My whole future fate depends on the present moment, and the solitary rambles in your beautiful woods will assist in strengthening my mind for that interview which is to decide or terminate all.... Rest assured nothing shall be decided by me without your knowing everything; I cannot yield confidence by halves, and that which I repose in you is entire, unbounded. In no circumstance will I ever deceive you, and even were I sure to incur your censure, still would I confess to my own dear kind friend every action and every thought.

When Jane first arrived at Berg, she wrote a poem about her anticipated meeting with Felix. As literature her poetry leaves much to be desired (the same could be said of Ludwig's), but it provides a valuable insight to her feelings:

EXPECTATION

How wilt thou meet me? Will thy look
  As of old, be bent on me
In loving tenderness, or must I brook
  A change I never thought to see?

Canst thou with cold averted eye
  Receive the loving, once beloved?
Canst not hear the stifled sigh
  From the heart thy love had soothed?

Blind canst thou be to that fond grief
  Which suffering and sorrows bears
In secret anguish, that the breath
  Of shrilling slander tears?

She loves but thee, regardless what they say;
  Trust but those tears that mark her paling cheek,
Ruined and lost, fast sinking to decay.
  Restore thy love, or soon her heart will break!

Early in November Felix wrote that he was not coming to Berg after all, and Jane poured out her grief in another poem:

DISAPPOINTMENT

He comes not, t'was but fancy's dream
Which mocked my hopes with visions bright
And threw athwart life's darkened stream
A ray of former light.
That ray is quenched, that light is gone,
Forever lost to me.
"He comes not"—in those words alone
Read my sad destiny.

Why Prince Schwarzenberg continually gave Jane false hopes only to dash them so cruelly is a mystery, but his hot and cold letters kept her in a perpetual state of emotional upheaval during this period. She returned from Berg completely crushed, and not even the knowledge that a king and a baron were waiting in Munich to console her could compensate for a prince's defection.

The mystery of Jane's relationship with Ludwig deepens with Karl Venningen in the picture. At first the baron was willing to ignore the court gossip and accept Jane's assurance that her relationship with the king was platonic, but eventually he began to have doubts. Three of Jane's letters to Ludwig during the first months of Karl's courtship add more puzzles to this complex triangle.

A note written November 11, 1831, just after Jane had returned from Berg, is maddeningly ambiguous:

Forgive me, dearest Lewis, if our last night's conversation pained you, but your openness, affection and sincerity encourage mine. It is not to be denied that rapture, untasted for six months, has reawakened passions I flattered myself were nearly if not quite extinguished. Still, dearest, I repeat my intentions remain unchanged, and such as you exhort me to entertain as the only ones worthy of our attachment and *myself*. My word of honor I ever regard as a sacred vow, and I dare not, dare not, give it lightly. What would he whose noble sentiments so enchant me, of whose esteem I am now so proud, what would he think if after all my promises to the contrary I fell a victim?—Do not be thus unhappy. I vow not to deceive you, I never will. Therefore while with me you may be assured you know all, that in my heart there *lurks no hidden thought concealed from him* whose warm and frank attachment would ill deserve such a return.

The "six months" refers to Jane's separation from Schwarzenberg, and certainly it was Ludwig whose noble sentiments and esteem she valued, but her "promises" and "falling a victim" clearly point to someone other than the king providing the "rapture." Since Jane did not see Felix at Berg, the only logical candidate was Karl Venningen. The baron was in the right place at the right time, and what could be more natural than for Jane to succumb to Karl's ardent advances when she was so depressed about Felix? A few lines scrawled hastily on the same green paper as this letter, but not dated, tend to support the Venningen theory:

Dearest Lewis, I am ready to give my word not to yield any more, for I feel you are in the right—and to cut with *you*, I cannot, will not—Do not be angry with him for I'm *sure* his intentions are good.

The most provocative letter of all was dated March 25, 6 o'clock:

The Baron was here yesterday evening, dearest Lewis, and I communicated to him word for word what I had settled. It was in vain. Neither entreaties nor threats could prevail upon him. He answered that upon such a subject it was *morally impossible* for him to give his *word of honour*, that all he could promise were his resolutions never to ask more, but a vow he could not and would not give. At the same time he told me he could not help suspecting that you had more than friendship for me, as this last sentiment could not be mixed with jealousy. He added too that he plainly perceived that I was ever more ready to follow your advice in the slightest circumstance than to listen to his most earnest prayers. At the same time he felt that the greatest joys would have no value if yielded with regret. He promised all that depended on his will. After staying two hours he left, half crazy at the discovery he believes to have made on the true nature of the sentiments we have, or *have had*, one for the other. All this you may be sure I denied. Here I send you the result of my conversation with him. Knowing the Baron as I do, I confess I never thought yesterday morning that he would refuse to give me his word. It is not my fault. I dictated word for word my conditions, but I cannot ask more. I trust you are better today and that you will see me at least to tell me your opinion.

It is little wonder that Karl Venningen was "half crazy." The woman he adored, after having accepted him as a lover on at least one occasion, asked him to promise not to make any more advances, and it was obvious to him that the king of Bavaria had instigated this unusual request. How could Karl *not* be suspicious of Ludwig's motives? Nonetheless, it is not certain that the king was, in fact, acting out of jealousy. It was, after all, Ludwig who had offered a romantic setting for Jane's anticipated rendezvous with Prince Schwarzenberg; it was Ludwig who had permitted her to send letters to Felix through Bavarian diplomatic couriers; it was Ludwig to whom Jane had spoken constantly of her undying love for the Austrian prince. If he was a true friend, the king had no choice but to advise Jane against becoming the baron's mistress. Such an affair would only add the *coup de grâce* to her reputation and was a foolish risk when she was not even in love with Karl.

There is a gap in the archives correspondence from the intriguing letter of March 25, 1832, to one dated July 13, 1832. (Ludwig was traveling during this period, and Jane's letters to him in transit were not preserved.) At the end of March the king left Munich for Italy, where he spent several months. At the end of April Jane became pregnant for the fourth time, the third time without a husband, and the child was unquestionably Karl Venningen's. By midsummer Jane was surely aware that she was pregnant, and not by Felix Schwarzenberg, whom she had not seen in more than a year, and yet her July letter to Ludwig expressed the hope that she and her prince would still eventually be reunited. Her optimism was running away with her again. She wrote the king that she had received encouraging reports from someone (name illegible) who had just returned from the Austrian capital:

... he told me Felix's father often came to him at Vienna and spoke of nothing but me, asked a thousand questions of my manner of life here, whether *you* really took as great an interest in my fate as people said and many other things.... Princess Esterhazy wrote to Mme. de Cetto from Marienbad that the *father* [Schwarzenberg] she thought would consent to the marriage. You ask me if I love him still. Alas, yes, and I feel convinced I shall never be able to marry another. There exists something in a *first* passion, especially in one such as mine has been, which has dared all and sacrificed all for its object, that no time, no subsequent ill treatment can efface.

There is no mention in this or her following letters that she is expecting a child, but Jane does announce her plans to go to Italy, a trip certainly intended to conceal her pregnancy from everyone in Munich. On July 24 she was writing from Salzburg, and sending the letter by Karl Venningen, who had apparently by this time decided Ludwig was not a threat to his courtship of Jane. Karl came from Riegerding, one of his family's estates, to press his suit again, and Jane told the king:

He is more than ever wishing to marry me and I have at last been obliged to assure him I never can nor will, giving F. [Felix] as my reason for refusing. I fear my dear friend will blame me as foolish if I confess F. has once more created a sparkle of hope in my heart that one day he will return to love me; I have received a letter in which he speaks of a future which I trust in Heaven is yet in store... and that sooner or later I shall reap the reward of patience in a union with him I have so long worshipped.

Jane was still dancing to whatever tune Felix Schwarzenberg chose to call. His renewed interest in her (even from a distance) was enough to make her happy, despite her unwelcome pregnancy, and she could write Ludwig lighthearted accounts of her sightseeing tours of Salzburg and an expedition to Berchtesgaden, "... scenes you have so often described. I need not say I thought much, very much of you to whom my attachment and gratitude is unbounded." From Salzburg Jane traveled to Innsbruck and then by the "new road" over Mount Ortler ("in all my life I never saw anything so magnificent!") to Milan. In her letter to Ludwig of August 11 she mentions for the first time a dog the king gave her: "I am in a constant fright of having him stolen." Milan was distasteful to her: "The heat here is almost too great to bear, and the noise and gaiety of this town remind me too much of Paris.... Yesterday I drove down to the Corso, but the people stare at a stranger as though she were a wild beast!"

It is apparent that Ludwig expected his Ianthe back in Munich by September, and she was obliged to give an explanation. She wrote from Naples September 12: "I assure you it was not my intention to go farther than Genoa. There, however, as I still continued not very well, the physician ordered me to try a sea voyage, and as I dislike any undertaking without an object, I embarked in a vessel for Sicily." This was not the only explanation Jane felt was necessary:

And now I must tell you what greeted my arrival. B.V.V. [Baron von Venningen] has followed me day and night, travelling under a different name. He says he is believed to be at Paris but that's when he learnt I had left or was about to leave Genoa for Sicily. He could no longer endure the separation, combined with the idea that I was now alone in Italy. By abandoning his affairs he has added this proof of his devotion to all the rest. I confess that his unceasing love, in spite of all my refusals, touches my heart, without inspiring that *passion* it is in my nature to feel. I tell him that before I can give the least hope or answer to his constant prayer for marriage everything must be finally settled between me and Felix, that also I must see the latter once more. You are the only person to whom I shall mention these circumstances as I should fear the judgements of the world.

Jane was right in believing Ludwig would be disturbed to learn that Karl Venningen had joined her. "You seem to think my journey was prearranged," she wrote him from Palermo on October 21. "I give you my word it was not. When I saw the Baron at Salzburg, he begged to come, it is true, but I positively refused on account of the world and principally of F., and thinking then my absence would not be so long, as it was only at Genoa it was settled I should take a sea voyage. He returned to Munich and hearing of my further intentions, he could not bear I should be quite alone in a strange country." Loyal and gallant Karl Venningen! None of the other men in Jane's life was so considerate. To Jane's credit she tried to be fair to Karl. Even though she became, in effect, his mistress, she made it plain that her heart still belonged to Felix. Pregnant and needing a husband badly, she continued to hold out against marriage to the baron. But as the time of her confinement drew near, she was weakening. To Ludwig she wrote:

To say that I am *angry* at so many proofs of devotion on the Baron's part would be untrue, and to you and you *only* I confess that without being the least in love, his attachment now well tried, disposes me to listen more favorably to his prayers for ultimate marriage than I have ever done before. But the time for decision is not yet come. Should I marry, I would fain make him a good wife, and that I feel I am not yet prepared to do. F., in spite of all, is still too dear.

At the time this letter was written from Palermo, Jane was six months pregnant, but she was riding on muleback to see the Sicilian countryside. Her time, she said, was passed in these excursions, sketching and taking singing lessons. At the opera one night she saw the "best society" of Palermo and decided the women were "ugly, so black and dirty." The men, though, were a different matter, and one reminded her so much of Felix that she was startled when she saw him. Despite her advanced pregnancy, Jane continued to attract a string of admirers. She told Ludwig she had received an offer (what kind she failed to specify) from "a young French peer of *L'Ancien Régime*, rich and one of the first names of France." One Sicilian gentleman was so carried away by Jane's beauty that he disguised himself several times in order to be admitted to her house, first as a friar, then as a woodcutter, then a musician and finally as a vendor of goat's milk, leading the goat to her door one morning! Jane was trying to convince her royal friend, who did not know it was too late for caution, that she was behaving herself. "I have forgotten none of my promises, although temptation here is not wanting. It is to you and your magnanimity I may say that I owe my salvation on that head, for to have lost your friendship altogether would have driven me headlong into the gulph."

There were several reasons why Jane might have been reluctant to write Ludwig about the child she was expecting. She doubted the privacy of their correspondence ("If I did not know from experience that all my letters are opened, there would be a thousand things I would give worlds to tell you...") and she was afraid that she would lose Ludwig's friendship if he learned she had given in to Karl after all his advice to the contrary. Jane missed greatly her conversations with the king, even though she failed spectacularly to follow his counsel. "What would I give," she wrote him on November 10, "if I could now hear you repeat as you have so often done that love, such as I pictured and have felt it, is not necessary in marriage. Would that I could indeed believe it, for the Baron's whole conduct towards me is faultless."

If Felix Schwarzenberg had not continued to keep Jane dangling, she might have decided to marry Karl Venningen before their child was born, but for some obscure reason, Felix refused to let go:

> The Baron still at Palermo and intends remaining probably as long as I do. I must confess I have the greatest reason to praise his conduct towards me in every respect; he dreams but of marriage, and I should be ungrateful if I were totally insensible to such tried and constant devotion, but alas! in love I am not and while F. continues to write as he does, assuring me that his is not extinguished, I fear much I never can be.

The vacillations of Felix Schwarzenberg seem more and more mysterious in the light of his long (and what was to be permanent) separation from Jane. She was certainly not fantasizing his continued interest in her, for more than 200 letters from him, later destroyed, were among her papers when she died. There is no way of knowing if the prince genuinely wished at times for a reconciliation, or if he maintained this lengthy correspondence to keep in touch with his daughter. Whichever was the case, it was devastatingly cruel not only to Jane but to Karl Venningen. The baron had been head of his family since his father's death sometime before he met Jane, and he had the responsibility of managing the several Venningen estates. He turned his back on all his duties to follow the woman he loved to Sicily, in utter defiance of his mother, a very strait-laced provincial German Catholic. The dowager baroness did not know Jane but had apparently heard enough gossip to abhor the idea of having her for a daughter-in-law. In many respects Karl was as much a romantic as Jane. His brand of romanticism, however, was not exciting enough to overcome her passion for Prince Schwarzenberg. The baron had no illusions about this, but he faithfully looked after Jane while she waited for their child to be born.

In December Jane heard from Felix that he planned to join his sister in Italy, and she told Ludwig that she intended to meet him there. "I confess I dread the interview and probable *final* adieu, but cost what it may, and I know it *will*, you may depend upon my promise given not to remain near him as his mistress." A close connection of the Schwarzenbergs, Prince Alfred Schönburg, wrote Jane that the obstacles in the way of her marriage to the Austrian prince were more of Felix's own making than anyone else in the family. "If that is so," she wrote the king, "my pride must conquer my too long victorious passion."

On the first day of 1833, less than a month before her child was born, Jane announced to Ludwig her tentative decision to marry Karl Venningen, but she was still hedging a bit:

> ... no longer hoping for much happiness myself, or what I once thought such, with the New Year I have taken at last the resolution to exist for that of another. The conduct of Bn. Charles [Karl] is such as to excite my warmest gratitude and merits my attachment. Therefore I have at length said that upon seeing the Prince, I am able to say that first passionate love no longer exists, I will be his. A more positive promise I dare not at present give.... From Felix's letters, which are written in the same tone of attachment and as though he still considered me his property, I cannot be entirely free from all engagements towards him, particularly as much must be settled first with regard to his child [Didi]. While on the other hand, as he never speaks of marriage, my scruples at taking this step are much lessened. As I promised at Munich, you are the first person I have acquainted with this determination.

Only a week before her child was born, Jane was writing Ludwig a chatty note about the weather and her companions in Palermo, with still no mention of her condition: "... excuse the stupidity of my letters, remembering I live at the world's end out of reach of all interesting news..." Violent storms had left Sicily so deep in mud, she said, that it was impossible to stir out of the house, "but the whole country is a brilliant green and the valley between this, Parco and Monreale is golden with orange and lemon trees—how magnificent!" Besides Karl Venningen and Monsieur de Laurin, the Austrian consul in Palermo, Jane wrote, her "society" included two Sicilian composers and a German painter who was traveling under the patronage of Prince Frederick of Saxony. Her only female companion was her personal maid, named Emma, who appears for the first time in the correspondence: "Emma is too flattered by *votre* gracieuse..."

Jane told Ludwig she had heard that the Countess Teresa Guiccioli, "Lord

Byron's love," was expected in Palermo. "I shall be curious to see her, as they say she is anything but 'chaste and pure' as he terms her." For someone who had been the victim of gossip herself, Jane showed surprisingly little charity toward Teresa, who in 1819 had left a titled husband to become Byron's mistress. (Evidently the Countess did not come, as she was not mentioned again.) In Jane's letter to the king, she gave the details of a lovers' triangle in Palermo that had ended in tragedy:

> An instance of passion has happened here a day or two since, which is quite in unison with my emotions of love: a young and handsome girl had been for two years in love and promised to a painter, who upon a slight pretext left her and went to Trapani, and returned married to another! His first love would not believe it, went to his house and was denied admittance. Half distracted, she returned home, disguised herself as a peasant, and in the evening, posted herself under his balcony and began to sing. He recognized her voice, approached the open window, upon which she drew two pistols from under her veil, with one shot him dead and with the other attempted to kill herself but missed. In a few hours she went raving mad, and the wife, married only a few days, is equally so. What a fine subject for a poem or a tragedy! I almost envy her!

Although Jane told Ludwig that her return to Munich was delayed by the weather, the real reason for the delay was "Filippo Antonio Herberto Venningen," who was born on January 27, 1833. His birth was recorded in Palermo on January 31, and his parents were listed as "Venningen Carlo e Digby Giovanna Elisabetta." Unlike Felix Schwarzenberg, Karl Venningen had no scruples about giving his name to a child born out of wedlock. Little "Herberto" (Heribert, as he was called in German) is not mentioned in Jane's letters to Ludwig until fully three years later, when she writes that she and the baron are going to pick him up in Marseilles. This suggests that the future Baron Venningen passed his infancy far removed from his real parents and did not make his appearance on the family scene until times were more propitious and perhaps until he had learned to hold a fork properly. (From 1833 to 1836 there is no record whatsoever of the child's existence.)

Scattered throughout Jane's letters to the king are continuing references to a mystery woman, for whose name a tiny rectangle is substituted. However, one mention of the lady places her at Colombella, identifying her beyond doubt as Marianna Florenzi, an Italian Marchesa who was said by Munich gossip to be Lady Ellenborough's rival for Ludwig's affections. Marianna, a dark Tuscan beauty, was linked with the king long before Jane came to Munich, and was the inspiration for many of Ludwig's poems. Jane was well aware of the king's attachment for the Marchesa, and knew that he was on his way to see her when he left Munich for Italy in the spring of 1832. In her letters Jane appeared to accept this romance with good grace, but when Marianna first heard of Ludwig's friendship with Lady Ellenborough, the Italian's reaction had been swift and fiery. She refused to follow the king to Ischia, writing, "My health forbids it. Besides I do not wish to bore you. I fear that I am not in the exclusive possession of your love anymore." Ludwig even felt the ire of the Marchesa's maid, Gita, who wrote, "How could this Lady Ellenborough, whose scandalous life is known to all the world, have deceived you, Your Majesty?" The King of Bavaria was apparently so chastened by these attacks that he wrote his wife Theresa, "I repeat, of all I know, I find only you worthy to be my wife."

Jane knew that she rankled Marianna badly and was afraid the marchesa would try to prevent Ludwig from meeting his Ianthe in Italy, where their proposed travel plans were to bring them close together: "...one thing alone, I beg, dearest Lewis—give [   ] no promises respecting me. The first place I yield however reluctantly, the *second*—may it not be mine?" How Ludwig answered this letter is not known, but he must have complained that he was lonely and depressed, for Jane was all sympathy. "I grieve more than I can say," she wrote, "that at this moment perhaps when you might have wished the society of a sincerely attached friend, I, who am bound to you by every tie of affection and gratitude, was not near to help divert your thoughts." Whether Jane was referring to platonic companionship or something more is open to interpretation. The most difficult fact to reconcile with the gossip that Ludwig and Lady Ellenborough were lovers is Jane's constant avowal in her letters of her love for Felix Schwarzenberg. It does not seem likely that a man with Ludwig's ego would take as a mistress a woman who continually threw in his face her "great passion" for another man.

By late February of 1833 Jane had completely recovered from the birth of Heribert, for she wrote Ludwig of attending a performance of Vincenzo Bellini's new opera *Norma*. All Palermo society turned out to honor Bellini, who was a native-born Sicilian, and Jane described the music as "magnificent." She apparently was still limiting her social engagements, however. "The Portannas have often asked me to call," she wrote, "but the young men here are so behind hand and impertinent that I thought it best to decline altogether." She told Ludwig that she had recently seen a young and pretty Sicilian woman take the nun's veil, "a most melancholy sight, particularly since she had no vocation and persisted only from a false point of honor!" She spoke of plans to leave Palermo the beginning of April with "a large company to see all Sicily and perhaps Malta. M. de Laurin, the Austrian Consul, has promised to be of the party, for which I am very glad, as he has been very amiable all winter." These plans were abruptly cancelled early in March when Jane received another emotional jolt from Prince Schwarzenberg.

In an agonized letter to Ludwig, she revealed that she had once more been expecting a meeting with Felix, who was then in Nice, and once more he had disappointed her, claiming he was too pressed for time, "...but he begs me at the same time to *join his sister* who is very ill, who *wishes to make my ac-*

quaintance and who will be in Italy the months of April and May. Is not this wish on his part extraordinary? Could he have done more at the time when we were on the best footing together, whereas now I am no longer his mistress, nor even engaged to him, he *volunteers* to introduce me to his unmarried sister!!" The only thing encouraging to Jane about this strange request of the prince was that, in the eyes of "the world,"

> the visit must have the good effect of justifying me as to the supposed cause of our rupture at Paris, as no one with common sense would believe after that that he would seek my connection with his sister... I feel a pre-sentiment she will propose my remaining with her until she returns to her family; this offer would have been accepted with joy and gratitude 18 months ago—now what can, what ought I to say? I know not—I feel quite bewildered. The poor Baron behaves quite well on this occasion and says not a word to hinder me from going, although I can see what it costs him.

Karl Venningen, when he said goodbye to the woman he loved so unselfishly, at least had the small comfort that her rendezvous was with the Princess Schwarzenberg and not with the prince. Before she left for Rome, Jane wrote Ludwig, "How very painful this visit will be to me, you, who understand so well all that concerns the affections of the heart, may well guess." In subsequent letters to the king, she said nothing of how she got along with Felix's sister Mathilde, but the visit was ominously shorter than Jane's "pre-sentiment" had led her to expect. Had she received any warmth or encouragement from the princess, she would surely have been eager to pass on such good news to her royal confidant. All she told Ludwig of the meeting was that at the urging of the princess, she had left Didi "temporarily" with her aunt and namesake.

Didi's visit turned out to be as long as her mother's was short; after June of 1833 she never left the custody of the Schwarzenbergs again. This apparently was what Mathilde had in mind all along. The princess had no intention of promoting the marriage of Felix and Jane, and she believed that by keeping their child she would relieve her brother of all obligation. When the princess returned to Austria with her niece, the child's name, plus her strong resemblance to the Schwarzenbergs, gave rise to the rumor in Vienna that little Mathilde was actually her namesake's illegitimate daughter. Such gossip did not bother the princess. With this brilliant stroke she bound to her for life the brother she adored. Neither she nor Felix ever married, and the two Mathildes made their home with Felix most of his life. As the little girl grew up, she was told that her parents had been friends of the princess and had died in a typhoid epidemic. Didi always called the princess "mother" and Felix "uncle." Just before she was married, the true identity of her parents was revealed to her, but her loyalty was to the Schwarzenbergs, and she never attempted to contact her mother.

Besides allowing Didi to travel back to Austria with Mathilde, Jane had separated herself from her only other living child, Heribert, leaving him in Palermo with a Sicilian family. Thus, in the summer of 1833, Jane, who had given birth to four children in five years, was once again unencumbered by any, and if it pained her, she did not mention it to Ludwig. She had hoped to see the king while they were both in Italy, but he was obviously a bit apprehensive about a meeting. "Be assured, my dear Friend," Jane wrote, "that in spite of my longing to see you again, nothing shall induce me to risk causing you a moment's uneasiness." It is not clear if Ludwig worried about gossip ("the world," as Jane called it), or about the Marchesa's feelings, but he managed to avoid his devoted Ianthe at a time when she was very short of friends.

Nothing is known of Jane from the time she left Rome early in June of 1833 until two months later, when she turned up in Paris with only her maid Emma as a traveling companion. Karl Venningen had returned to the duties he had neglected for a year; Ludwig was avoiding her; her infant son was behind in Palermo; her daughter was with the Princess Schwarzenberg; and Felix was as inaccessible as ever. This had to be an unhappy, unsettled time for Jane. There was no one to turn to but her family. Jane wrote Ludwig that she had met her mother in Paris, but she revealed no details of their reunion, which was a brief one. Subsequent events, however, suggest that Lady Andover was urging Jane to accept Baron Venningen's marriage proposals. For Jane the return to the French capital brought a flood of painful memories, which she later described to Ludwig: "How glad I am to have left Paris I cannot say. I too there felt most strongly the truth of all you once said to me on the power of *localities* and the empire they exercise over the heart and memory."

By the first of September the wanderer was back in Germany, but not in Munich. "My reason for choosing Heilbronn as a residence," she told the king, "was simply that it is near Grombach, where the Baron is at present and that it is on the high road towards Felix if I am ever to see him again." Jane's erstwhile lover, though he continually claimed to be prevented by press of duty from meeting her, was enjoying himself at Teplitz-Schönau, a Bohemian spa in the valley of Bilina noted for its thermal waters.

At Heilbronn, Jane had a caller, Prince Alfred Schönburg, who had just passed some time with Felix and who tried to convince Jane that her love was wasted on the Austrian diplomat: "...his visit has been of painful service to me," she wrote Ludwig, "as in spite of myself he shows me Felix as being utterly unworthy of regard; he had a good opportunity of judging him at Teplitz..."

Hearing these charges from Schönburg in person prompted Jane to announce to the king her intention of giving up Felix forever, although "it is no easy task to tear a long worshipped idol from its place out of a conviction of unworthiness." In the very next sentence, however, she said she would give Schwarzenberg "one more chance" to prove his love for her. She told Ludwig she was writing Felix of her intention to marry the baron: "If his answer is not wholly satisfactory, I will break with him at once." (It did not strike Jane as ludicrous

to threaten a "break" with a man she had not seen in more than two years.)
"This done," she continued, "may Heaven efface his image from my remembrance and help me to keep my resolution of making Karl a good and faithful
wife and showing my gratitude at last for all he has done."

Karl Venningen's mother had little faith that heaven would succeed with
Karl's beloved, and she remained intractable in her opposition to the marriage.
Without the consent of the dowager baroness, Jane told Ludwig, the ceremony
would have to be delayed several months unless the legal complications involved
could be set aside by the Grand Duke of Hesse-Darmstadt, under whose jurisdic-
tion Karl was then living. For this reason Jane asked the king of Bavaria, whose
country bordered the grand duke's domain, to intercede. The delay would not
have been important to the bride-to-be, who dreaded taking this step ("to me
marriage is an awful engagement!"), but Jane explained that her father had
come all the way from England for the wedding to "sign his reconciliation by his
appearance," and he could not easily remain so long. (Admiral Digby apparently
had not been so forgiving as Lady Andover, and this occasion was probably the
first time he had seen his daughter since she had left England in 1829.) Jane's
father had brought with him papers from England stating that the Ellenborough
marriage was "null," papers that cleared the way for a Catholic ceremony. The
Digbys, who had obviously gone to a great deal of trouble and expense to insure
that their daughter could be returned to respectability through a proper marriage, were unaware that even at this late stage Jane would have thrown away
everything again if Felix Schwarzenberg had given her the slightest encouragement.

That encouragement never came. Instead the prince gave a curious sort of
blessing to Jane's marriage to Karl. The baron, according to a note in the Digby
papers, had challenged Felix to a duel unless Schwarzenberg would formally
declare Jane innocent of misconduct in Paris with a "M. Taboutier," the officer
of the guard mentioned in Count Apponyi's journal. Karl appears to have been
deeply incensed over this slight to Jane's "honor," about which she had complained on many occasions, and he wished to have the record set straight. In a
letter to the baron, Schwarzenberg denied having ever made the accusation and
claimed that he only refused to marry Jane because of "incompatibility of their
tempers." The prince generously wished the couple well, which no doubt infuriated Jane. She wrote Ludwig: "Felix Schwarzenberg seems to have succeeded in
his mission; his ambition is now gratified, and he is free from me! He has written
a letter to the Baron at which I am surprised, but it only shows what conscience
and injustice can force from a man at last."

The King of Bavaria appeared as anxious as Felix and the Digbys to get Jane
married. He not only persuaded the Grand Duke of Hesse-Darmstadt to clear the
way for the Venningen wedding, but he bestowed upon Karl the "chamberlain's
key," which made the baron an official member of the Munich court. Jane's
presentation at court was thereby assured, after four years of being excluded

from royal functions, both in Paris and Munich. She was delighted and promised the king that the Venningens' first duty and pleasure following their marriage would be to come to Munich and thank Ludwig personally.

For two years, almost from the day he met her, Karl Venningen had courted Jane with patience and determination, but when he finally won her, it was by Felix Schwarzenberg's default. With her father as a witness, Jane became the Baroness von Venningen in a civil ceremony in Darmstadt on November 16, 1833. A few days later in Sinsheim the Bishop of Rothenburg performed the Catholic marriage rites for the Venningens, and Admiral Digby returned to England vastly relieved. On the eve of her wedding, Jane wrote Ludwig that she would turn all her energy to making a success of her new life. She closed her letter with one of those ambiguous passages which so intrigue and confound a biographer:

> I must end, altho' so many, many subjects upon which I can speak with you *alone* are still in my heart. My best and *Dearest* Friend, what I am *now*, what my resolutions *now* are is *your work*. Without you I should have been inevitably lost or plunged into an abyss of misery from which nothing could have raised me but a Providence like yourself. Never shall I forget you, and let me, Dearest Lewis, once more say, perhaps for the last time before I am chained to another, that your noble, generous conduct towards me on one occasion made a deeper, more indelible impression on my heart than a thousand triumphs of vanity or self love, and made you dearer than a thousand lovers. Would I could prove my devotion in deeds not words.

What happened on that mysterious "one occasion" only Jane and Ludwig knew, but once more the possibility is suggested that the two had not been lovers up to that time. Jane's marriage to Karl, however, did nothing to change the popular opinion that she was the king's mistress. In fact, Ludwig's intercession with the Grand Duke of Hesse-Darmstadt led some members of the Munich court to suspect that the marriage had been arranged for the convenience of the lady's royal lover. When the Baron and Baroness von Venningen arrived in the Bavarian capital in December of 1833, the gossip about Jane and Ludwig, which had smoldered during her two-year absence, soon flared up into a bonfire.

9

Balzac and the Baroness

*This beautiful English lady, so slender, so
fragile; this peaches and cream woman, so soft,
so mild-mannered, with her refined brow
crowned by shining chestnut hair; this creature
who glows with a strange phosphorescence, has
a constitution of iron.*

—HONORÉ DE BALZAC

Ludwig's affection for Jane had in no way been diminished by their long separation, and his eagerness to see her was apparent when she wrote to him, "You
desired me to name the exact day and time if possible." Jane dispatched a note
from Augsburg in response to this request: "I hope to arrive at Munich tomorrow about five or a little after.... Farewell, my best and kindest friend, you
cannot conceive the delight with which I look forward to the bliss of seeing you
once more!" The only obvious change Jane's marriage to the baron made in her
correspondence with Ludwig was in the way she sealed her letters. Previously
they were stamped with a seal bearing the name Ianthe beneath a seven-pointed
coronet. Now her seal combined the Digby and Venningen crests under a coronet with nine points. When the Venningens arrived at their Munich lodgings, a
bouquet of violets and a note from the king were waiting. Ludwig asked if he
might call that evening, and Jane replied, "Dearest, Dearest, how happy I shall
be to see you!" The unusual warmth of this message might be interpreted as
marking a change in the relationship between the king of Bavaria and his Ianthe,
even though their first meeting in nearly two years was undoubtedly chaperoned
by Karl Venningen. Whatever Ludwig's feelings for Jane had been in the past,
there had been obstacles in the way of a love affair. From Jane's letters it is
evident that in the early days she and the king had spent a great deal of their
time together comparing notes on their romantic problems with other people—
hers with Schwarzenberg and his with the Marchesa Florenzi. Now, in the winter
of 1834, things were different. Felix was at last out of the picture, and Ludwig's
romance with Marianna had cooled. Further, Jane had acquired a husband, and
a husband was a great asset to a lady who had developed a tendency to become
pregnant at the drop of a petticoat.

Whether or not Jane and Ludwig were ready to fall into each other's arms, the mere presence of the English beauty in Munich was enough to generate the unkindest talk. The gossipy Joseph Jekyll, always eager to relate the latest Jane stories to his sister, Lady Sloane Stanley, may have been the source of the rumors in London that Jane was Ludwig's mistress with these two items in his letters:

A friend of mine tells me today he saw the ci-devant Lady E. last summer at Munich; she has married a Bavarian Baron, whose name I can neither spell nor pronounce. She is received at court and everywhere. The ladies of the Bavarian Almack's know all her pranks and say the poor child was sacrificed in marriage in London to an old, rich, ugly Lord. Her liaison with the King is never denied. The King is a man of talents. My friend saw in one of his palaces a fine painted ceiling of the "Triumph of Neptune," and among the sea-nymphs discovered the portrait of Lady Ellenborough, which the King had given orders to introduce, and which the guide reported readily.

Volume the second of the ci-devant Lady E:
"My dear Queen," said His Majesty of Bavaria, "I wish you would permit her to be presented."
"My dear King," said the Queen, "it is impossible. Consider her position with respect to yourself. Why don't you get her married, and then she would be presented, of course."
"That may be difficult," quoth the King.
"Not the least," rejoined Her Majesty. "Order one of your marshals or barons, and the man will be flattered by the mark of your favor."
The thing was done. A baron was instantly found; old loves preserved; and three people made happy.

Jekyll's witty little anecdote was repeated with gusto wherever London society gathered, and no one dreamed of questioning its authenticity. The story that she was a king's mistress made the former Lady Ellenborough almost respectable in England again.

The version Jekyll wrote his sister was, in fact, very close to the one being circulated in Munich following Jane's formal presentation to Queen Theresa in February 1834. As soon as she received the royal invitation, Jane sent an urgent note to the king, asking him to meet her beforehand and give her pointers: "Her majesty has given me an audience at half past four.... I am now at *Tambosi's*, to which there is a quiet entrance by the arcades." Evidently Ludwig heard from Jane in person the details of her court presentation, for there is no further mention of it in her letters.

Following the audience with Queen Theresa, Jane was received enthusiastically by Munich society, even by those who had scrupulously avoided her in the past. The fact that she was English undoubtedly enhanced her popularity, for in the 1830s, Bavarian aristocrats, like their French counterparts, greatly admired all things English. Members of Munich's "Old England Club" included scholars, government officials, established artists and such noble gentlemen as the dukes of Leuchtenberg, Count Wilhelm of Württemberg, and the Bavarian dukes Maximilian and Theodor. At their festive dinners the chairman ("The Lord Mayor") wore a powdered wig, and the other members came dressed as English peers. There was an "English Cafe" which stood on the Duld Platz (now Maximiliansplatz), where thirty-six young artists, who called themselves the *Neu-England Club*, gathered to practice chorals. The *Neu-Englanders* "sang for their supper" at many balls and banquets which Jane attended at the Odeon. A green oasis in the heart of Munich was the Englischer Garten, and even the eighteenth-century baroque gardens of the Nymphenburg palace had been transformed into an English-style park by the brilliant landscape artist, Baron von Sckell.

Despite the "instant" popularity of the English Baroness von Venningen, Jane's closest Munich friends continued to be the ones who had accepted her before she became "respectable." During her long absence from the capital, she had kept up a steady correspondence with a Countess de Cetto and the papal nuncio to Ludwig's court. The nuncio, to whom Jane referred only by title, was mentioned in her letters as a faithful friend who had offered his help in making a Catholic marriage possible for the Venningens. Lord Erskine, Britain's ambassador to Munich, and his large family had accepted the beautiful English exile without reservation from the time of her first arrival in the Bavarian capital. In the winter of 1834, however, it was still Ludwig who was Jane's main confidant, and she consulted him on a variety of matters, including the estrangement she had caused between Karl and his mother. "I wish to ask your advice upon a reconciliation Mme. de V. has begged through Mme. de Cetto," she wrote. Scattered throughout her notes during January and February were references to the violets Ludwig frequently sent her, and sometimes her notes accompanied little gifts for the king. ("I send this drawing, and I am only sorry it is not better worthy of your acceptance.") Neither Jane nor Ludwig was unaware of the scandal their close association had revived, but Jane's notes suggest that the king was a little more sensitive about their relationship than his incautious friend. "Take care not to increase your cold," she admonished him, "for if you are confined to the house, could I again come to see you as in former days? I fear you would answer, 'No, Ianthe.'"

How Karl Venningen felt about the gossip that again linked his wife and the king Jane's letters do not reveal, but for one reason or another he took her away from Munich sometime in March of 1834. From Grombach on April 22 Jane wrote Ludwig that the dowager baroness ("my sweet-tempered mother-in-law") had asked them to Mannheim a few days earlier for the long-awaited reconciliation. "Nothing could be stiffer than the interview on both sides, and during the short time I was there she and the other Mme. de V. tried every possible means to estrange Charles and me." Afraid that Ludwig's letters might go to one of her in-laws, Jane asked him to address them to "Bnne. de Venningen Üllner, née

Miss Digby." She suspected her maid of disloyalty, and she told the king: "I have just dismissed Emma for many good reasons."

By far the most fascinating news in the first letter from Grombach was the casual announcement that Jane was pregnant again: ". . . as to me, I expect to be confined in August or September." A month later she wrote to Ludwig:

> My pregnancy till now goes on prosperously and I have great hopes will end the same. Unless any alteration occurs, I intend to be confined at Weinheim; tell me, my dear friend, if I may name it after you. It would be a great honour as well as pleasure to the Baron as to me if you would be godfather, but if disagreeable to you for any other reason that may not occur to me at present, of course you will tell me with the frankness that has always reigned between us.

There was still no indication that Ludwig knew about the child born out of wedlock in Palermo, but Jane had no hesitation in announcing this one, and the king sent her his best wishes: "In your last letter you were good enough to congratulate me on my pregnancy which is now rapidly advancing. . . ." Ludwig appears to have been less enthusiastic, however, about having the child named for him, and Jane tried to allay his apprehension in a letter from Weinheim on August 18:

> As I shall be confined so far from Munich, no gossip can arise on the subject, and if you *prefer* its not being called Ludwig at all, it is easy to give it one of your other baptismal names if a boy. At the christening if you permit it (as someone must hold the child) we have thought of our neighbor, Count Alfred Oberndorf—he is one of the Chamberlains, is a devoted Bavarian and one of the few good Royalists in this part of the country, but of course I would not propose it to him until I had your authority for it. I shall hardly be confined before the beginning of September, so there is plenty of time to let me know what you think about it.

What the king thought about it is not known, but the child turned out to be a girl, who was named Bertha. The fact that the unfortunate Bertha had to be confined in an asylum before the age of twenty convinced many people, who attributed her mental illness to the Wittelsbach strain of insanity, that Ludwig, not Karl Venningen, was her father. Jane's letters to the king give no clue.

Shortly before Bertha was born, Jane showed that she did care for her husband, even though she felt none of the passion that Felix Schwarzenberg had aroused. "The last fortnight I have passed almost in despair," she wrote Ludwig, "at the great danger the Baron has been in with an inflammation and rheumatic fever." Karl recovered, but their marriage remained in delicate health; it was not helped any by the other Venningens, who never really liked or accepted Jane. How different she was from Karl's sister was made comically clear when she told the king, "It is believed here that my sister-in-law Mimi has never consented to live with her *spiritual* Ct. Waldkirch, and what is fact, to prevent the possibility of a too tender tête-à-tête she sleeps in her maid's room!' "

Weinheim, where Jane and Karl came to live in 1834, was a picturesque watering spot eleven miles north of Heidelberg. The small town was first mentioned in chronicles of the eighth century as a fief of the Abbey of Lorsch, and when Jane saw it, it was still encircled by its ancient walls. The ruins of the medieval castle of Windeck, overlooking the valley, provided as romantic a setting as anyone could wish. What Jane lacked in Weinheim, however, was excitement and a man with whom she was passionately in love. Whether or not Munich offered such a man, it at least offered excitement, and Jane found Weinheim a poor substitute for the Bavarian capital. She constantly repeated to Ludwig her desire to be in Munich, "for this country abounds with disagreeables."

In the spring of 1835 the oppressive boredom and isolation of the Schloss Venningen were relieved briefly by an unusual visitor. Jane wrote Ludwig, "During the absence of the Baron I made an interesting acquaintance in the person of M. de Balzac, the French author, who was on his road to Vienna with Prince Alfred..." Honoré de Balzac, up to his eyebrows in debt, as usual, in spite of his considerable fame, was indulging in the budget traveler's art of houseguestmanship when he came to Weinheim. He had borrowed the money from Baron James de Rothschild to meet his beloved Eve Hanska in Vienna and was cutting economic corners wherever he could. His host and traveling companion was Jane's old friend, Austria's Imperial Envoy-Extraordinary to the court of Württemburg, Prince Alfred Schönburg.

Before the prince took Balzac to meet the celebrated Baroness von Venningen, he gave the writer a thorough briefing on Jane's colorful past. Despite his friendship with Jane, Alfred could scarcely have been expected to omit some of the more lurid details, and his information, undoubtedly derived from sources other than the lady herself, was probably in part fictitious.

What Balzac heard intrigued him and his visit to Weinheim was especially fruitful for two reasons: First, he found in Jane the model he needed to round out Lady Arabella Dudley, a character in his novel-in-progress, *Le Lys dans la vallée.* Second, while sitting on a bench in the Venningen castle park he composed the first draft of the new "Pensées," which he added to *Louis Lambert* in the edition of December 1835. (On one sheet of his notes for "Pensées," according to Balzac scholar H. J. Hunt, the novelist scrawled "Wiei–," struck it out and wrote "Wyne–," struck that out also; then finally wrote "Weinheim, près Heidelberg," and underneath that, "Baronne de Venningen, née Miss Digby.")

For the "Baronne," the meeting proved to be a mixed blessing. Her identification with Lady Dudley was not flattering, and it inspired the myth of a passionate love affair between Jane and Balzac, supposed to have taken place while she was in Paris in 1830 to 1831. The story appears groundless, but continues, nonetheless, to be repeated and embellished. By the time she actually did meet Balzac,

Jane had probably realized that she was ill-suited for the life of a German *haus-frau*, and might have welcomed a new romance, but the fat and frankly ugly Frenchman does not seem a likely lover for her. Their meeting in Weinheim was their only known encounter, and, according to Balzac's account, Prince Alfred was the one carrying on a flirtation with his hostess at the time.

Balzac and Jane parted on good terms. Before he left he apparently promised to write something for Jane as a keepsake, for Prince Alfred mentioned it in a note to the author when they were both in Vienna: "Allow me to pass on a message to you. A promise of an 'autograph' is being reminded to me. The complaint comes to me at this moment from the picturesque borders of the Neckar." (Weinheim is on the edge of the Neckar River valley.) On Balzac's return trip from Vienna he kept his promise to Jane and left the "autograph" for her in Munich, sending a note to her in Weinheim to let her know that the package was waiting for her in *poste restante*. Jane thanked him in her flawless French in a letter from Munich dated July 18, 1835. She addressed him as "Monsieur le Comte," which suggests that Prince Alfred, knowing Balzac's hunger for nobility, had facetiously introduced him to Jane with that title. Jane's letter is hardly that of a lady to her lover:

> I am blushing at my long delay while I take my pen in hand to thank you as best I can for the pleasant note which I received a few weeks ago. I should have, and I wished to do so much sooner, but as I had planned to journey to Munich from one day to the other, I wanted to await my arrival here, in order to be able at the same time to acknowledge the receipt of the package which you had the kindness to leave for me at the post office here. I thank you from the depths of my heart, and I will keep these pages at the same time as a precious souvenir and as a token of your kindness. I await with great impatience the publication of the work in question, curious to learn the ending of this adventure so well begun.
>
> The hope of seeing you again in Germany next year gives me the greatest pleasure, on condition that from now til then you do not forget a promise which means a lot to me.
>
> Prince Alfred has given me news of you, and tells me that you were satisfied with your stay in Vienna. I hope that my adoptive country will provide sufficient attractions to encourage you to come back. Awaiting the pleasure of seeing you again, Monsieur le Comte, I entreat you to believe all the sentiments of friendship with which you inspire me.
>
> J. E. de Venningen

What other promise Jane extracted from Balzac is not known, but any small favors Balzac did for Jane were more than repaid by the inspiration she added to the fictional Lady Arabella Dudley, called by H. J. Hunt "one of the most fascinating women of the *Comédie Humaine*." Women of high station gratified Balzac's vanity, and he was always in search of those whom he could use in his writing. In Weinheim he had, with a combination of his uncanny perception and fertile imagination, found what he needed for *Le Lys*.

His physical description of Lady Dudley, whose blue eyes "flashed like diamonds," is a perfect portrait of Jane:

> This beautiful English lady, so slender, so fragile; this peaches and cream woman, so soft, so mild-mannered, with her refined brow crowned by shining chestnut hair; this creature who glows with a strange phosphorescence, has a constitution of iron.

Balzac did not fail to notice the superb riding of the baroness when Jane accompanied him and Prince Alfred part of the way from Weinheim to Heidelberg, and this provided him with another key to his intriguing Lady Arabella Dudley:

> No horse, however fiery, can defy her sinewy wrist, her hand that seems so weak, and that nothing can tire. She has the foot of the roe, a small, wiry, muscular foot of indescribable beauty of form. Her strength has no rival; no man can keep up with her on horseback; she could win a steeplechase riding a centaur; she shoots a stag without checking her horse. Her body does not know sweat; it radiates a glow in the air . . .

Lady Dudley's rival in the book, the saintly Countess Henriette de Mortsauf, turns the Englishwoman's magnificent horsemanship into a weakness: "But she rides too well; she must love to exert her strength; I fancy she is energetic and violent; then, too, she seems to me too defiant of conventions; a woman who recognizes no law is apt to listen only to her own caprice. Those who are so anxious to shine, to be always moving, have not the gift of constancy." The hero, angry with his English mistress, agrees: "I have since noted that women who ride well are never tender; like the Amazons they have lost a breast, and their hearts are petrified in one spot, I know not which."

Le Lys is written in the form of a letter from a young man, Felix de Vandenesse, to his current lady love, Natalie de Manerville, in which he confesses and describes in detail his two previous romances, one with Arabella Dudley ("the mistress of my body") and the other with the spotless Henriette de Mortsauf ("the wife of my soul"). Arabella was not at all intended to be a sympathetic character, yet, almost in spite of himself, Balzac made her vivid and vigorous, while her antithesis, Madame de Mortsauf, appears as lily-livered as she is lily-white.

Balzac apparently felt that his treatment of Arabella may have been somewhat unfair, and he acknowledges in the book "the magnanimity of the woman who wrecks herself, renounces all future hope and makes love her sole virtue." His Arabella sounds very much like Jane Digby when she expresses a desire "to love, unabashed, in opposition to the law . . . to bring earth and heaven into subjection to a man and thus rob the Almighty of His right to make a god." "These," Arabella says, "are the heights to which vulgar women cannot rise; they know only two roads—the highway of virtue or the miry path of the courtesan."

Balzac's fictional Englishwoman gave herself totally to love: "...when she loved it was with intoxication; no woman of any nationality could be compared with her; she was as good as a whole seraglio..." For Arabella's behavior Balzac offers a fascinating rationale:

> What she longed for, like many Englishwomen, was something conspicuous and extraordinary. She craved for spice, for pepper on which to feed her heart, as English epicures insist on pungent condiments to revive their palate. The lethargy produced in these women's lives by unfailing perfection in everything about them, and methodical regularity of habits, reacts in a worship of the romantic and difficult.

The most remarkable part of Balzac's book insofar as it relates to Jane is its strangely prophetic association of Arabella with the desert. The French writer died many years before Jane reached Syria, but he wrote of his Lady Dudley, "Her passion is quite African; her desires are like a tornado in the desert—the desert, whose burning vastness is mirrored in her eyes—the desert, all azure and love, with its unchanging sky and its fresh, starry nights." Balzac even made Arabella the owner of an Arab stallion, which he explained was a gift to her from Lady Hester Stanhope, a nonfictional English eccentric who made Syria her home long before it was Jane's.

Like Jane, Arabella was seldom burdened with a nagging conscience. The spiritual heroine of *Le Lys*, Madame de Mortsauf, when she sees the Englishwoman unashamed, waiting for Felix in the moonlight, cries, "Oh, what a delight to wait like this for one's lover when one can do it so guiltlessly!" This was one of Jane's unusual qualities. While leading a life that was scandalous and shocking to her contemporaries, she maintained a curious air of innocence that impressed all who knew her, from Count Apponyi at Almack's to missionaries in Damascus fifty years later. It was a quality much envied not only in fiction but in life.

Lady Dudley's affair with Felix (whose career—he was a diplomat—was as suggestive as his name) caused a sensation very similar to the one Jane and Schwarzenberg had spawned: "This scandal was heard of in England, where the aristocracy was in as much consternation as heaven at the fall of its highest angel." Like Jane, Arabella could not keep her love affair a secret: "Madame de Mortsauf would have hidden her happiness from every eye; Lady Arabella wanted to show hers to all Paris, and yet with horrible dissimulation she maintained the proprieties even while riding with me in the Bois de Boulogne."

When *Le Lys dans la vallée* was published in 1836, and for some years afterward, speculation about Balzac's models was a popular topic of conversation in the salons of Paris. It has long been felt that Felix de Vandenesse bore a closer resemblance to Balzac himself than to any of his other fictional heroes. So it was no wonder that the passionate affair between Felix and Arabella was believed by many to be more fact than fiction, and the unsuspecting Jane Digby was credited with one lover she could scarcely have deserved.

Nonetheless, rumors of an affair did reach Eve Hanska, Balzac's "intended," who was courted by the French author mostly long-distance—from Paris to the Ukraine—for eighteen years before they finally married. Almost certainly the stories came to Madame Hanska through one of her correspondents, the Princess Aloisia Schönburg, Felix Schwarzenberg's sister, who was then living in Paris and had rented part of the house in which Balzac himself was living at 13 Rue des Batailles, Chaillot. Eve got, of course, the "Schwarzenberg edition" of the Lady Ellenborough story, and it is hardly likely that the cautious woman who kept Balzac dangling so many years while she held on to her aging husband, her wealth and her reputation, would have any warm feelings for the incautious Jane.

Four years after *Le Lys* appeared, the long-distance lover was still trying to clear himself, and he wrote to Eve on May 15, 1840: "Never have I seen so well that I had in *Le Lys* very well explained women of that country in a few words. What I guessed of Lady Ellenborough during the two hours when we strolled in her park with the silly Schönburg flirting with her, and during dinner afterwards, was the exact truth."

The last mention of Jane in their correspondence appeared in a letter Balzac wrote on April 23, 1843: "... as for Lady Ell.! ... another of those accusations which make me laugh. Ah! When you are right, I bow my head and I feel a tightening of the heart which makes me pale, and I admit having been severely and harshly punished. But this miserable prince, as genuine as a counterfeit coin, invited me to go to Weinheim and left me in the garden for five hours, which he spent with his mistress.... And what I saw on the return from Heidelberg would have discouraged love if love there had been! I have never spoken to you of this. My God, why do you listen to such stupidity! I laugh; I have neither resentment nor anger. I only deplore the time which it took me to read the two pages of your letter."

Having forgotten what he wrote three years earlier, Balzac stretches the two hours to five, has himself abandoned in the park and makes lovers of Jane and Prince Alfred, all for the sake of unruffling Eve's feathers.

There was no statement in the novels of Balzac's era to the effect that any similarity to persons living or dead was coincidental. In English fiction particularly such similarity was, in fact, often quite intentional, and the excitement of recognizing the characters' real life models was an important part of the reader's enjoyment. In 1835, shortly after Jane's meeting with Balzac, and just before *Le Lys* was published in France, a book called *The Two Friends* appeared in England, and in it Jane Digby was caricatured far more cruelly than she was by Balzac. The author was an Irish novelist, Marguerite Gardiner, Countess of Blessington, who had long been the center of a fashionable literary circle at Gore House, Kensington, in the London suburbs. The countess had come up the hard way from an unhappy, impoverished childhood and a first marriage at age fifteen to a Captain Farmer, whose drunkenness brought him to debtor's prison, where he died in 1817. The young widow Farmer was beautiful, charming and witty, and within a year she became the wife of Charles John Gardiner, Earl of Blessington. With her husband, whose extravagant tastes she soon learned to share, she spent several years in Europe, where she became a close friend of Lord Byron at Genoa. Depending far more on titillation than talent, the countess had a different approach to writing from Balzac's. Of her books Lady Blessington said, "They are written on the everyday business of life without once entering the region of the imagination. I wrote because I wanted money, and was obliged to select the subjects that would command it."

Lady Walmer, a main character in *The Two Friends*, was immediately identified by London society with the absent Jane, thereby exhuming and recirculating the lurid stories of her elopement and divorce which only now, five years later, had been forgotten. One reviewer of Lady Blessington's book called attention to the fact that the novelist had used the Ellenborough case quite recognizably but with questionable taste. After quoting from the book, the reviewer in *Fraser's Magazine* of April 1835 commented:

> We have many allusions such as the above to the story of Lady Ellenborough whom the authoress has caused to sit for her sketch of Lady Walmer and whom as such she takes care to discredit and punish after a fashion which is more creditable to her morality than to her good taste and charity. Lady Walmer, after being repudiated by her husband, goes abroad and marries a loving prince who soon neglects and ill treats her; and finally murders her brother at the lodgings of an opera-dancer, upon which her ladyship goes mad and so dies miserably in a foreign land among strangers.... It is a sad doom to shadow forth for a fellow creature not more guilty than many of her old companions, but only more unfortunate in the emblazonment of her guilt. The misdeeds of her past life and probable miseries of her future were no fitting theme for a female novelist. When she had once crossed over the seas, their floods should have suffered to roll between her and her native England and, as her returning footsteps heavy with shame and sorrow pressed on our shores, it would have well become Lady Blessington, as a Christian and a countrywoman, to have dismissed her in the words of the judge who punishes the offense but hates not the offender: "Erring sister, part in peace!"

Lady Blessington seems to have paid for any lack of charity to her "erring sister." When she wrote the tragic end to Lady Walmer, she might have been prophesying her own, for at age sixty she followed her lover, Count d'Orsay, her own stepdaughter's husband, to Paris, where he had fled to escape heavy debts in England. She died shortly afterward in the poverty and obscurity above which she had fought so hard to rise.

Balzac in *Le Lys* came far closer to capturing some of Jane Digby's essence than did Lady Blessington in *The Two Friends*. But even Balzac, with his gargantuan imagination, might have been dumbfounded at the scale of Jane's odyssey had he lived to know the whole story. The teapot tempests stirred up by Jane's pale reflections in literature were another source of chagrin for her family in England, but had little effect on Jane herself. For while English and French readers were amusing themselves at her expense, the lady in question was about to write the opening chapter in a new series of adventures that would make her past and the fiction it had inspired seem, by comparison, positively unimaginative.

10

A Count from Corfu

'Tis melancholy, and a fearful sign

Of human frailty, folly, also crime,

That love and marriage rarely can combine . . .

—LORD BYRON

Before the Venningen marriage was a year old, there were signs of domestic friction. Karl could not understand the restlessness that plagued his wife, and once during a quarrel he reproached her for behaving more like a frivolous young girl than a twenty-eight-year-old matron. Jane herself seemed unable to put her finger on the cause of her dissatisfaction, but she evidently believed that a move to the Bavarian capital was the solution. "Munich is the place of all others I love best," she wrote to Ludwig in July of 1834, "but I can say with truth that you, my best and really true friend, are the charm that attaches me to it in so strong and peculiar a manner." In another letter, written late in that same year, she told the king: "O, my best beloved friend, if there is a feeling between exalted devotion and something more tender, then it is exactly what you have instilled in me. My whole ambition is to settle in Munich one day."

It seems unlikely that Karl Venningen shared his wife's enthusiasm for Ludwig's capital, but the serious illness of his brother Phillip (who appears in Jane's letters as "Phila") necessitated the Venningens' return to Munich in the summer of 1835. Jane announced this news to Ludwig in a letter written June 26 of that year:

> I too am looking forward with the greatest pleasure to seeing you soon again, although one of the motives which brings us to Munich is most melancholy. Dr. B—— gives us no hopes whatever of Phila's recovery.... When I arrive, I shall again turn to you, my Best and Dearest Friend, for your counsel and advice on several points, which in the case of the sorrowful event which I fear, I fear awaits us, will be most necessary to me and which will entirely decide our plans for the future.

The meaning of Jane's last sentence is not clear, but it appears that the impending death of Phillip Venningen had a bearing on whether or not she and Karl would be able to remain in the Bavarian capital.

Although Jane had never before spent a summer in Munich, she must have been aware that Ludwig and his court usually spent July and August at a castle in the Bavarian Alps. Either she had her dates confused, or the departure from

Weinheim was delayed, for by the time the Venningens got to Munich, the king had already left. Jane was undoubtedly disappointed not to be greeted with a bouquet of violets from the king, but the correspondence continued on affectionate terms.

Jane spent a rather depressing summer in the company of Karl and his dying brother, and apparently had difficulty keeping herself occupied. She wrote Ludwig that to pass the time she had sat for a new portrait by a "Mr. Heiss," and that it had turned out "more like me even than Stieler's." That was the only comment Jane was known to make on the portrait Ludwig's court painter made of her, but it is quite possible that she had not been pleased with it. (By the time Stieler painted Jane in 1831, he was apparently tired of the king's beauties, and most of his women had begun to look alike—the same curls, the same soulful eyes, the same rather vapid expression.) Mr. Heiss, according to Jane's letter, had recently returned from Italy, where he had painted the Marchesa Florenzi at Columbella. Undoubtedly Heiss had heard the rumors that Jane and Marianna were rivals for Ludwig's affections, and he was probably astute enough to guess that the Baroness von Venningen would not wish to be outdone in any way by the marchesa. (The whereabouts of the Heiss portrait of Jane is unknown today.)

Early in September, when the first frost came to the Bavarian Alps, Ludwig and his court returned to Munich, and the capital literally burst into life to the rousing sound of brass bands. Unlike London, where the high season was in the summer months, Munich's social life was at its gayest from mid-September until the beginning of Lent. Things got underway with the reopening of Parliament, observed in true German style with a grand parade. King Ludwig and Queen Theresa rode through the streets in one of their ornate gilded carriages, followed by marching bands and nearly half of Munich: infantry, cavalry and artillery units in brilliant uniforms; the Bavarian nobility handsomely arrayed with all their decorations; trade guild members and university students in *lederhosen* and jaunty feathered hats. Even the Archbishop took part, splendid in his red clerical habit, bestowing his blessings on the crowds that lined the parade route.

This colorful parade was followed almost immediately by another one, a great deal more boisterous, to open the famous harvest beer festival, the *Oktoberfest*, which despite its name was held the last two weeks of September to take advantage of the good weather.

During Ludwig's reign, the *Oktoberfest* included such cultural attractions as art expositions, and in the fair of 1835 Jane's portrait by Mr. Heiss was shown. The artist was very unhappy, however, about where his painting was hung, and Jane dropped a note "*À Sa Majestie, Le Roi de Bavière*" to see what her royal best-beloved friend could do:

I am sorry to trouble you with these lines on a subject with which perhaps you have nothing to do, but Mr. Heiss was here this morning to tell me he must take his portrait from the Exposition as they had hung it in so unfavorable a light and so high that it could not be seen. I thought perhaps you could make it have a better place, as he says the walls are far from filled. Tomorrow I hope to have the happiness of seeing you in the tent, and probably tonight *at a distance* in the masked ball.

The people of Munich scarcely had time to clean up the debris from the *Oktoberfest* before the holiday season, known as *Fasching*, was upon them. Every evening the streets of the Bavarian capital were thronged with costumed merrymakers going to and from a continuous round of masked balls. In the Wittelsbach Archives there are only two notes from Jane to Ludwig that appear to have been written during the late autumn of 1835, and this unusually small number suggests that the baroness and the king were seeing each other so frequently at the *Fasching* carnivals that there was no need to write.

Then, at the height of all the gaiety, Karl Venningen quite suddenly took his wife away from Munich once more, and this time the puzzling "friendly romance" of Jane and Ludwig came to an abrupt end. She continued to write the king for two more years, but things were no longer the same between them. The circumstances of the Venningens' departure from the Bavarian capital are not clear, but the ensuing coolness of Ludwig toward Jane was unquestionably caused by a dashing Greek count named Spiridion Theotoky.

How a titled Greek came to be at the Bavarian court in 1835 was a story that began fourteen years earlier, on March 25, 1821, when a Greek bishop named Germanos and a band of his followers raised the standard of rebellion against the Ottoman Empire at the monastery of Aghia Lavra in the northern Peloponnese. When news of the Greek independence movement spread, romantics like Byron and Shelley took up the cause, and misty-eyed ladies in Paris and London made silk banners for the freedom fighters. The statesmen of the major powers, however, who tended to be nervous about rebellion in any form, were unmoved by this wave of philhellene sentiment. It was only in August of 1829, when Russia was at war with Turkey and appeared on the verge of taking Constantinople, that Wellington suddenly became anxious to see a fully independent Greece. After much maneuvering, Russia, France, and Great Britain settled upon the establishment of a Greek monarchy under their joint protection, and the search for someone to sit on the throne dragged on for two years. In 1832 Otto, a younger son of King Ludwig of Bavaria, was finally chosen, largely because he was the only candidate acceptable to all the major powers. Ludwig, who worshiped everything Greek, was delighted.

The bleak little war-ravaged kingdom that Otto first saw when he landed at the Peloponnesian port of Nauplia on a cold, gray February day in 1833 bore little resemblance to the "golden Greece" of Byron's poetry or the classical Greece of Ludwig's imagination. It was bounded on the north by the Thessalonian frontier and included neither Crete nor the Ionian islands. Otto was undaunted by the shrunken size of his new country; he was very young (seventeen), fired with his father's enthusiasm, and temporarily financed by the Bavarian treasury. His first project was to move the capital from Nauplia, where it had been established by the freedom fighters, to Athens, so the kings of modern Greece might bask in the ancient glory of the Acropolis.

In the early 1830s, however, Athens was little more than a few shepherds' huts clustered at the base of the Acropolis. To help make the dream of a new Athens come true, an army of architects, sculptors, artists and artisans poured into Greece from Bavaria. While the Bavarians were invading Greece, a considerable number of Greeks were invading Bavaria. Ambitious young men of good Greek families, anxious to ingratiate themselves with their new king, came to Ludwig's court to learn Bavarian customs and the German language. The dark-eyed Greeks in their colorful native costume, the fustanella, created a sensation in Munich. The rotund burghers may have thought that men looked foolish and feminine in stiff white pleated skirts, but the local ladies thought otherwise. The Greeks were lionized much as foreigners had been in the London society of post-Napoleonic years.

No one in Munich in that fall of 1835 could have been more vulnerable to a foreign coup than the Baroness von Venningen. Jane's ideas of Greece and the Greeks had been formed by some very potent influences: the highly romantic impressions in Byron's poetry, the magnificent traces of ancient Greek civilization in Sicily, and the overwhelming enthusiasm of Ludwig the classicist. Time and distance had apparently finally eroded Jane's passionate longing for Felix Schwarzenberg, and she must have felt a hunger for romance which neither her nebulous relationship with the king of Bavaria nor her marriage to Karl Venningen had assuaged. There is no record of Jane's first meeting with Count Spiridion Theotoky, but from one of her notes to Ludwig, it appears that they were introduced at a carnival ball.

Count Theotoky in his white fustanella and red velvet vest encrusted with gold was dazzling. His portrait by an unknown Italian artist attests to the extraordinary handsomeness of his face and his Phidian figure. This new Prince Charming came from one of the most aristocratic families on the island of Corfu. His title, one not usually borne by Greeks, dated from the time when Corfu had been under the reign of the Venetian doges. Spiro's father was Count Johannes Theotoky, a former freedom fighter in the Greek independence movement and minister of justice at Epidaurus. The Corfiote Theotokys would later give Greece a prime minister (George), a famous writer (Dinos), and a cabinet minister (John). While Spiro turned out to be a bit short on the qualities that distinguished other Theotokys, he was long on *joie-de-vivre*.

The count from Corfu was only twenty-four—four years Jane's junior—gay, impetuous, and carefree, the antithesis of the sober, conservative Karl Venningen. Jane's beauty must have stunned the Greek nobleman and what Theotoky heard of her scandalous background undoubtedly enchanted him all the more. Such reckless disdain for convention was enormously appealing to a fiery young man like Spiro. Here was a kindred spirit; here was adventure calling. Neither the count nor the baroness knew that night in Munich where the adventure would lead, but the excitement of the moment was all that mattered.

In the beginning Jane told Ludwig that she was having a harmless flirtation, but her description of Spiro, which she underlined, is prophetic and revealing: "I find the *dangerous* Ct. Theotoky is not invited, but that will not prevent me amusing myself as I did the first carnival." This is the first time Spiro's name appears in Jane's notes to the king (it appears only once more), and it is obvious that she had already discussed the Greek nobleman with Ludwig. This was apparently the last time that Jane wrote to the king from Munich, but she gave no hint that she expected to be leaving the capital any time soon. Whether the baron had a premonition of danger, whether business summoned him home, or whether Phila's condition prompted him to leave Munich, taking Jane with him, is not known. At any rate, the Venningens arrived once again in Weinheim late in November.

A very short time afterward, Spiro Theotoky arrived in Heidelberg, only eleven miles away. The distance was an easy ride, but there was a formidable obstacle to a rendezvous. The baron was not occupied with politics as had been Lord Ellenborough, nor was there in the small town of Weinheim a gentlemen's club in which he could pass his leisure hours as had Edward in London. Karl was very much in residence with his family, and the baroness did not have the freedom of movement that had been hers in her first marriage. But when romance and adventure called, Jane was compelled to answer, and a solution was not long in coming.

At Schwetzingen, only five miles from Heidelberg, was the magnificent baroque palace that had been one of the residences of the elector of the Palatinate until that state had been dissolved in 1801. It now belonged to the state of Baden, and it was a place to which Jane could go without arousing suspicion at home. The Schwetzingen gardens, with their exquisite neoclassical temples of Apollo, Minerva and Mercury, a Turkish mosque and an elaborate Chinese bathhouse, were renowned throughout Europe. The gardens were hardly at their best in November, but the waters of Schwetzingen were highly recommended for *crises des nerfs*, from which the Baroness von Venningen was obviously suffering.

What happened at Schwetzingen belongs more in the realm of legend than recorded fact. There is no firsthand account by any of the three persons most closely involved, but there is no question that the ensuing scandal stemmed from actual events. As the story goes, Jane behaved at Schwetzingen with decorum during the day, but when the palace was asleep, she mounted her thoroughbred mare and rode through the night to meet Theotoky in Heidelberg, returning each morning before dawn. A German writer, Hans Arthur Thies, claimed that Jane, in a spectacular feat of horsemanship during one of these midnight dashes, jumped her mare over a fruit wagon and its owner sleeping beside it. (Thies also says that the mare's name was "Indefatigable.") Whether or not this story was true, neither the count nor the baroness was noted for caution, and neither was exactly inconspicuous, so it is hardly surprising that rumors of these nocturnal adventures should reach Karl Venningen.

There are varying versions of what actually precipitated the spectacular climax to the affair. One story was that Jane's horse stumbled and broke its leg as she was returning from a late rendezvous with the count. According to this version, she went back to Spiro, who pressed his advantage for an immediate elopement. The more likely story, and the one most often repeated, places the rising action at a ball in Schwetzingen Palace. During the evening Karl confronted his wife with the rumors he had heard of her romance with Theotoky. They quarreled; Jane, impulsively, fled to Spiro; and the two lovers rode off together. Balzac wrote to Eve Hanska an abbreviated version he had heard from his Paris neighbor, Princess Schönburg: "...she informed me that Lady E. has just escaped again with a Greek, and that Prince Alfred had stopped her from going farther than Stuttgart. The husband came, fought with the Greek and brought back his wife. What an extraordinary woman!" Balzac's story undoubtedly originated with Prince Alfred Schönburg himself, who liked to star in his own anecdotes. Alfred could well have been at the Schwetzingen ball, but it is not likely that the lovers got as far as Stuttgart, since subsequent events indicate that Karl Venningen caught up with their carriage in the neighborhood of Weinheim.

The only account of what happened next was recorded by Count Apponyi, the gossipy Austrian ambassador to Paris, who was not always accurate. Apponyi wrote that Count Theotoky was hauled out of the post chaise by the irate husband, who demanded that a duel be fought on the spot. The postillions were forced to act as seconds and Jane, according to Apponyi, had to look on, realizing that whichever man fell, the blame would be hers. Only one shot was fired, and Spiro Theotoky dropped to the ground, blood staining his shirt just above his heart. The Greek believed, so the story goes, that he was dying, and tried with his last breath to save Jane from her husband's wrath. He swore to Karl that although he loved the baroness, they had not behaved dishonorably, and claimed that their flight had been totally unpremeditated, not the result of a long liaison behind Karl's back. The baron, a man of honor and stern principles, could not believe a dying man would speak falsely and wondered if he had killed an innocent man. According to Apponyi's account, Karl Venningen actually considered killing himself for his error. If that was indeed the case, it is fortunate that he waited.

There is little doubt that such a duel did, in fact, take place, and that Theotoky was wounded. From that point, however, what had looked like a Greek tragedy begins to take on the air of opera bouffe. Theotoky, Apponyi related, took so long in breathing his last that the four mourners, who did not want to wait forever by the roadside on a frosty winter night, carried him back to the post chaise in which he had, such a short time before, been gaily eloping. No one, it seemed, expected him to recover, but it was only Christian to allow him to die in bed at the nearby Schloss Venningen.

Instead of dying, Spiro began to recover, and Karl Venningen, who had been so distressed believing he had killed the Greek, was surely equally distressed to see him alive and well. How, precisely, he resolved this dilemma is still a matter of conjecture, but he did not, as earlier biographers have been led to believe, give the couple his blessings and send them on their way. Jane's last letters to Ludwig in the Wittelsbach Archives reveal that she remained with Karl for more than two years following the duel. Where Count Theotoky bided his time during their long enforced separation is not known, but it appears likely that he and Jane maintained some kind of clandestine communication.

In her first letter to the king after the Theotoky scandal broke, Jane asked Ludwig if he would like to know her own story of what happened:

> I truly confess the circumstances which quickly followed our departure (and of which you have doubtless heard) left me little courage to incur the displeasure and reproaches of Him whom I have for years regarded as my best friend, the *only* one to whom on all occasions I dared lay open my whole heart. If such an explanation can have any interest for you, in your asking for it, I will state the facts that followed my acquaintance with Theotoky as they *really* occurred, and not as probably the gossips of Munich have set them forth.

Ludwig does not appear to have asked for Jane's version, and without an accurate account available, biographers have depended upon the rendition offered by Count Apponyi, whom Jane had the misfortune to encounter once more when she and Karl were in Paris during the winter of 1836. The Austrian ambassador added a bizarre and completely false touch to the story, which has caused confusion ever since. He wrote in his journal for February 24, 1836: "I could hardly believe my eyes upon seeing Lady E——. I met her recently on the Place Louis XV giving her arm to a very handsome young man." Apponyi had already heard of the duel, and he decided that the handsome young man he met with Jane was Theotoky, not Karl Venningen. When he heard from other sources that Jane's husband was in Paris with her, he jumped to the ridiculous conclusion that the Venningens and the Greek nobleman were traveling together! "And here are the three of them who instead of returning to Munich, take the road to Paris under false names, but not with false hair and mustaches, which means that one did not have trouble in recognizing them on the streets or on the public squares as happened to me."

Karl might have taken Spiro's word that Jane's honor was still intact, as reported by Apponyi, but a man who fought a duel over his wife would hardly be inclined to share a Parisian *ménage à trois* with his rival. Jane gave Ludwig an explanation for being in Paris which there is no reason to doubt. "We are on our way to fetch Heribay who must be now at Marseilles," she wrote on February

27, 1836, "and shall probably return to Weinheim in the beginning of April. My father and mother intend spending the summer there with us." This is the first and only mention in the correspondence of the son born in Palermo who was to inherit Karl Venningen's title. The *Almanach de Gotha* listing agrees with the Sicilian birth registration, but where little Heribert (Jane's spelling was a nickname) spent his first three years remains a mystery.

Ludwig was dismayed by the new scandal that enveloped his "ever affectionate and devotedly attached Ianthe," but he did not cut off their correspondence immediately. In June of 1836 Jane sent him a chatty letter from Weinheim telling him that the Countess of Westmorland ("one of the cleverest talking women I know and high Tory in her principles") had visited Schloss Venningen on her way to Munich, and that Jane herself was accompanying her mother to a German spa during July. "I am much flattered that you still have my cap, but it must be now quite old and faded," she wrote. "I will work you another with the greatest pleasure, although you will probably have stores of Turkish embroidery with which there is no comparison."

For reasons unknown Ludwig chose not to reply to this letter, and when Jane finally wrote again on December 22, 1836, it was in a very formal tone, and "Dearest Lewis" became "Sire":

> Your Majesty will doubtlessly be surprised if not displeased at receiving these lines; you will say, "My silence ought to make her understand my wish is that all correspondence should end," and I had thus interpreted it, if the Baron's last letter had not mentioned having seen you, and that you had charged him with your remembrance to me, and that you regretted you could see me no more at Munich. At thus seeing myself not entirely forgotten, how can I resist seizing the opportunity of his being still near you to thank you ten thousand times for this mark of your remembrance.
>
> Much as the idea of never seeing your Majesty again pains me more deeply than I can ever express, still I would not for worlds that you should think that in Munich I regret aught else than that attachment I so highly prized and which I have now lost. It was to *you* I owed my position in society, for of this I was always convinced that those who called themselves my friends depended upon the degree of protection *you* bestowed upon me; events have proved I was right in any conjecture.
>
> Notwithstanding the many real errors which I have been guilty of, and with which you were acquainted by *my own lips*, I still think it possible that your Majesty may have heard much that was *untrue*. It is not for me to justify myself, and in writing it is impossible to enter into details on such a subject; but upon *my word of honor*, which hitherto you have always believed, I have reason to think that my conduct has been much exaggerated in this circumstance. I repeat and beseech you, my still, and *ever beloved* Sovereign to *believe* that the world and its amusements have no longer any attraction for me. I am not happy, but more upon the account of others than my own, and in Bavaria I have but one tie, one regret, and that is *yourself*. The Nuncio and Mme. de Cetto still write to me

and press me to return to Munich, and the Baron's affairs would now permit him to do so, but being estranged from you, who are the *only* being I there care about, I always try to dissuade him. There are some sentiments no time, no circumstances can efface, and such are those which must forever bind my heart in deepest attachment to your Majesty and make it impossible for me to be in a place where I should daily see you pass me by with indifference, if not aversion. I have now but to entreat you to forgive my having written, and to accept the sincerest, warmest wishes for your next year's happiness from her who for years has never ceased to love and revere you.

> Your Majesty's most devotedly
> attached & truly affectionate
> Ianthe

If this plaintive letter touched the heart of the King of Bavaria, it took many months for him to reveal its effect to his devoted Ianthe. In July of 1837 he finally broke his silence, and Jane was overjoyed. "You can imagine with what surprise and delight I received your letter! I could scarcely believe my eyes, so entirely had I given up the hope of ever hearing from you again." She immediately availed herself of his permission to write as formerly "to one who for six years I have considered as my Best and Dearest Friend." Ludwig asked Jane the status of her marriage to Karl, and in her frank answer lies an important clue to this extraordinary woman:

> The Baron and I go on what the world may call "well" together; the difference that exists in our characters cannot be changed. His *really* noble qualities are justly appreciated and esteemed by me. I am attached to him from affection and habit, but between ourselves, his want of *demonstration* and *warmth* of feeling stifles a passion I fain would feel, and which, once felt, and *returned*, would prevent my wandering even in thought to other objects. The misfortune of my nature is to consider "Love" as *All in All*, without this feeling life is a dreary void—no earthly blessing can compensate its loss, and having at first setting out in life sacrificed *all* without regret to one great and absorbing passion, the necessity of loving and *being loved* is to me as the air I breathe and the sole cause of all I have to reproach myself with.

This fascinating passage could serve as a blanket apology for all of Jane's scandalous behavior. If her assessment of her own nature was accurate, she was neither the nymphomaniac nor the heartless wanton that she has often been painted, but instead a romantic child-woman, trying desperately to recapture the "one great and absorbing passion" of her life.

Jane's letter also contained the news that she was going to England to spend the summer with her family, and she told Ludwig that she hoped to have an interview with her first husband: "I wish if possible to induce Lord Ellenborough to enter into another arrangement with me by which means I should possess a capital which I could employ in buying an estate in Bavaria instead of the pension he gives. With his great fortune and no children it cannot to him make much difference." (There is no record that this meeting took place, and if it did, Edward apparently rejected her proposal.) In a lighter vein, Jane repeated to Ludwig a story she had heard about a mutual acquaintance, Princess Esterhazy, the formidable and notorious patroness of Almack's. The princess, Jane said, had recently undergone a beauty treatment at some European spa, where she had been "wrapped like a mummy in linen and doused with ice cold water. This must have been a cooling expedition even for her fiery temperament!"

When Jane returned as planned to England in the summer of 1837, she gave no evidence of being "heavy with shame and sorrow," as the reviewer of Lady Blessington's novel had predicted the previous year in *Fraser's Magazine*. Quite the contrary. Accompanied by her handsome, aristocratic husband and two children, the Baroness von Venningen came back to her homeland in rather elegant, and certainly respectable, style. "I was perfectly well received by my family and almost all my old friends and acquaintances—notwithstanding which, England has too many painful associations for me to be sorry to quit it," she wrote Ludwig. Her use of the word "almost" suggests that Jane may have received a few slights, but nothing else is known of her summer in England. There is no evidence that she went to Holkham Hall to visit her eighty-three-year-old grandfather, Tom Coke, who had left his London home for Norfolk by the time Jane arrived, and she made no mention in her letter to Ludwig of the news that Coke had just been created Earl of Leicester. After serving in the House of Commons for fifty-six years and refusing a peerage seven times, the famous Coke of Norfolk decided to try out the House of Lords; he had requested and received the title that had once been borne by his great-uncle, the builder of Holkham.

Jane undoubtedly found much changed in the eight years since she had fled England to be with her Austrian lover. Her younger brother, Kenelm, a schoolboy when Jane last saw him, was now an Anglican minister, married to the former Caroline Sheppard, and the father of a son. (Kenelm and Caroline eventually had a total of nine children.) Jane just missed the June wedding of her elder brother, Edward St. Vincent, and Lady Theresa Anna Maria Fox-Strangways, daughter of the Earl of Ilchester. (They would become parents of seven.) These were both proper and permanent unions, and they fit gracefully into the mold of the new English morality whose emergence began that same summer of 1837 when the young Victoria came to the throne. It was up to Jane, apparently, to be the family's black sheep, and in that one respect she never failed them.

The last surviving letter of Ianthe to Ludwig was written from Mannheim on January 19, 1838. Karl had sold the estate at Weinheim, and even though Jane had not been happy there, Mannheim was a step in the wrong direction: "We returned here in November, where unfortunately the Baron's affairs oblige him to remain till the spring. What a difference from Munich! In my life I never met with a town more stupid." There is no hint in this letter that Jane was considering abandoning another husband, two more children and her newly restored though shaky respectability. She told the king she and Karl would be passing through Munich in May on their way to Austria to settle some business affairs, and she hoped Ludwig would permit her to see him once more. ("Two long years have now elapsed since I last had that happiness. To me they appear long indeed!") Jane chatted about the weather ("18 to 20 degrees, excellent for sledge parties...") , and she asked Ludwig what it was like in Munich. "But I believe you do not suffer from wintry weather, only the dull, cold fogs which depress the spirits." In closing the letter, Jane appeared uncertain as to how the king would receive it:

> Forgive me, my best friend, if I have done wrong in writing, in intruding on your time, but if you knew how painful it is to me to be months and months without any tidings from the one who, though highly placed, is so sincerely loved, you will excuse my reminding you again of your ever affectionate and devotedly attached
>
> Ianthe

This time Jane did not hesitate to use the word "loved," but there seem to be no romantic overtones here.

There is no evidence that the hoped-for meeting with Ludwig ever, in fact, took place, and it is unlikely that the King of Bavaria ever set eyes on his devoted Ianthe after the autumn of 1835, when she first met Theotoky. Although Jane's letters to Ludwig cover a period of seven years, the two were actually very seldom in the same place at the same time: for seven or eight months after her first arrival in Munich, followed by a separation of two years; four months in Munich immediately after her marriage to Karl, followed by a separation of a year and a half; six weeks in 1835, and then it ended. Ludwig was left with only her letters and the Stieler portrait to remind him of his lovely English lady.

For two years after Jane wrote what was evidently her last letter to Ludwig in January of 1838, little is known of her life, but legal documents now in the possession of the Digby family indicate that in the spring of 1839 she abandoned respectability once more and took up residence in Paris with Count Spiridion Theotoky. If anyone would be justified in vilifying Jane Digby, it was Karl Venningen. He never once did so. He is reported to have said of the woman who deserted him and their two children that "she could not be accused of an unworthy mind or of a depraved will, or of inconstant affection. It was the injustice of fortune, or at worst a little indulgency of a gentle nature which sprang from some indiscretion or rather want of experience that made her liable to censure." It was painfully obvious to Baron von Venningen that he could not hold his enchanting will-o'-the-wisp, that she was simply not constituted to be happy in any life that he could offer. The gentle, gallant Karl had won the duel but lost the prize.

When Jane left to join Count Theotoky, she was once more on the trail of that elusive grand passion, and the fiery Greek was elected to fill that "dreary void," to provide that happy state of delirium that was the breath of life for her. Sustaining the delirium was a tall order for any man, but the count from Corfu was willing to try. She was, after all, an extraordinary woman.

11

The Isles of Greece

Here great trees cool-shaded grow, pear,

pomegranate, red apple, honey-sweet fig and

blossoming olive, forever bearing fruit.

—HOMER ON CORFU

On March 27, 1839, the Baroness von Venningen arrived in Paris, accompanied by her Greek lover. The date was noted in an unusual legal document from the Archducal Court of Baden, which states somewhat euphemistically that the baroness "did not have her husband's permission" to make this trip. According to the German document, Jane spent several months in Paris "in intimate relationship with Count Spiridion Theotoky," posing as the niece of the Greek nobleman. Then on August 7, 1839, the couple went to Honfleur (near Deauville), returning to Paris on September 15 to take a house at 83 Place Bourbon, where they masqueraded as man and wife. The document further reveals that on March 21, 1840, the lady who called herself Madame Theotoky gave birth to a son, who was baptised "Jean Henry, Comte Theotoky." (There is some confusion about this baptismal name, as the child was always called Leonidas by his parents.) The birth was recorded not in the customary place—the Paris birth registry—but at the Greek Embassy, where the father was listed as Count Spiridion Theotoky.

In the skeletal chronology made by one of the nineteenth-century Digbys to trace Jane's activities, it was noted that Count Theotoky came to London in the late spring of 1840, after Leonidas was born, to see Jane's parents. This bare fact is all; there is no hint of how Spiro was received by Lady Andover and Admiral Digby or what the purpose of his visit was, but it appears that the count from Corfu had his share of courage. At about the time that Jane's Greek lover went to England, Jane's German husband came to Paris, hoping to persuade her to return to him. He failed dismally. Karl did not know that since he had last seen his wife she had given birth to another man's child, and, according to the Baden document, Jane neglected to tell him. He found out more than a year later when he sought a divorce. In June of 1840, however, Karl wrote a poignant and rather astonishing farewell letter, addressed to "Madame Theotoky," in which he forgave Jane completely for deserting him and their two children:

Chère amie,
    When you receive these lines, I shall be far away from Paris. But my last word

must be for you, to tell you once more that which I told you so many times in person—that my friendship and my attachment to you will end only with my life, and that each time I shall have to prove it to you will be a source of great satisfaction to me. May you find in those faraway lands where you will live the happiness I tried in vain to give you and which I regret so deeply is now forever lost to me. It is the only true happiness, the kind which lasts until the grave—of this I am convinced. May God give it to you. This is the only thought which in part, with time—and *perhaps*—will console me in my own misfortune.

May I learn some day soon that you are completely happy. Think then, under that beautiful sky of the Orient, that in cold and sad Germany a warm and faithful heart is beating for you, a heart which will *never* forget the happiness and the heavenly bliss you gave him during several years. If the Almighty should decide otherwise about our fate, remember me still—my house will be a secure haven for an unhappy Jane.

Again, farewell, my dear one. When I have seen the children to whom I shall give your love and your gifts, I shall let you hear from me again. Write me soon and tell me your final plans.

Everything always to you,
Karl

It is not surprising that this letter was the only one kept by the Digby family out of several hundred Jane received from husbands, lovers and friends during her lifetime. Not only is Baron von Venningen's true nobility revealed here, but a suggestion of Jane's unique personality comes through as well. Karl's wife had betrayed and abandoned him to live openly in adultery with Theotoky; she had left their two children with little expectation of ever seeing them again. And yet Karl showed not a trace of bitterness. There had to be something utterly irresistible about this woman—that curious air of innocence, that soft, sweet voice, perhaps—that compelled those who loved her to forgive her almost anything.

The Digby chronology states that as early as June of 1839, a year before Karl came to see Jane in Paris, she had written him, asking him to divorce her, but he had at first refused. Finally, at her repeated urging, the baron initiated divorce proceedings sometime in 1841. The scandal was somehow kept out of the German press, and there was none of the unpleasant notoriety that had accompanied the Ellenborough divorce. The Digby notes indicate, however, that Baron von Venningen wrote Jane's parents that he was surprised and dismayed when an order was issued (by whose authority is not revealed) prohibiting Jane from ever setting foot in Bavaria or any of the German states again.

The divorce decree, which was handed down in 1842, is not among the Digby papers, but there are references to it in the Baden document of July 22, 1844, which is preserved in the Muniments Room of the Digby estate at Minterne in Dorset. A translation of the later document's spidery Gothic script revealed it to be the verdict in a suit brought by Karl Venningen to disclaim paternity of Leonidas:

Concerning marital birth, it is legally decreed after lawful trial: The child born March 21, 1840, in Paris to J. E. née Digby, the divorced wife of the plaintiff, who by baptism was given the name of Jean Henry, Comte Theotoky, is to be declared as not fathered by the plaintiff, Baron K. Th. H. v. V. U. and illegitimate...

According to the document, Karl first learned of the child's existence from evidence presented at the divorce hearing by a witness named Nathaniel Nicolas Friedmann. (Friedmann was probably an investigator engaged by Karl's family.) As Jane and Spiro had already left Paris when the divorce hearing began, it took Karl several months to trace his wife to ask her about this unexpected development. Jane eventually confirmed Friedmann's testimony. Karl had been legally married to Jane when the child was born, and he was now forced to go to court again to establish the fact that he was not the father of this child, "because of his duties toward himself, his legitimate children and his family." The divorce evidence of his wife's adultery had to be re-examined, and the long-suffering Baron von Venningen had to prove that he could not possibly have cohabited with his wife during the legal period of from 300 to 180 days preceding the birth. These intimate details, couched in legal terms, must have given Jane's mortified family an unpleasant sense of déjà-vu.

Karl Venningen never remarried, and despite all the hurt and humiliation he had suffered, he remained, as he had promised, a faithful friend to Jane. He corresponded with her and kept her informed of their children's lives for more than thirty years, until one July day in 1874, riding in Munich's Hofgarten, where he had first seen the beautiful Lady Ellenborough, the gallant Baron von Venningen dropped dead in his saddle.

By the time that Jane had given birth to Leonidas in March of 1840, she had as poor a record for maternal devotion as a good one for fertility. She had exhibited very little interest in her firstborn, the delicate Arthur Dudley Law, who had died at the age of two. She had given up Didi, her daughter by Schwarzenberg, to Felix's sister, apparently without a struggle. Her son by Felix had died in infancy before he had a chance to become a burden. Heribert, the son she had borne in Palermo before she became Karl Venningen's wife, seems to have been left in the care of a Sicilian nurse for three years before he was reintroduced to his mother. When Jane ran away to Paris with Count Theotoky, she abandoned not only Heribert but his four-year-old sister, Bertha. On the surface, such behavior looks shockingly callous, but it should be viewed against the background of the times. Among the wealthy, children were entrusted so completely to the care of nurses and governesses that they scarcely saw their parents. When they did, it was from a respectful distance. Among fashionable French women, according to Charles Dickens, there was

...scarcely anyone, who in her manners and appearance owned to being a mother. Indeed, except for the mere act of bringing a troublesome creature into this world, there was no such thing [as motherhood] known to the world of fashion. Peasant women kept the unfashionable babies close and brought them up, and charming grandmammas of sixty dressed and supped as [they had] at twenty.

That was hardly the entire story, of course. In the cases of Arthur Law and Heribert Venningen, succession to title was involved, and their mother could not have taken these important male heirs from their fathers' custody even had she desperately wanted to do so. Jane almost never mentioned her children in those letters that still exist, so there is no way of knowing what her true feelings were. There is a good deal of evidence to suggest that the notorious woman who left her children behind when she went to seek new adventures never entirely grew up herself.

No account remains of the Digbys' reaction to the news that their daughter had deserted her German family for a Greek, but a story in E. M. Oddie's biography of Jane Digby indicates that they were not at all happy about it. According to Oddie, a young boy who came to spend the summer of 1839 at Minterne, the Dorset estate of Jane's parents, unintentionally poured salt in the Digbys' fresh wounds, and it was an experience the boy would remember all his life. The visitor was the Honourable Henry Coke, a son of Jane's grandfather by his second wife. (This was the child whose birth had brought Jane to Holkham in 1827 to pay her respects and to find, quite unexpectedly, a brief romance with a librarian named Frederick Madden.) The twelve-year-old Henry was having breakfast one morning with Lady Andover and Admiral Digby when he noticed on the dining room wall the portrait of a strikingly lovely girl with tumbling ringlets and a sweet expression. He asked who this beautiful creature was, and after an uncomfortable silence that frightened him, he was told gruffly to get on with his breakfast, and mind his own affairs. The next time he came to the table, the picture was gone, and he later discovered it tucked away in the housekeeper's room. The fact that Henry at that time had no idea who Jane was suggests that Tom Coke did not allow any mention of his scandalous granddaughter in the presence of his young children. Jane and her mother were eventually reconciled and were together on several later occasions, but the estrangement between Jane and her father caused by her elopement with Theotoky was apparently permanent, and Admiral Digby never saw his daughter again.

In 1840 Jane was living with Spiro in a Paris mansion only a few doors away from the one she had shared with Felix Schwarzenberg nine years earlier. This location had undoubtedly been chosen by Jane, who knew Paris as Theotoky did not, and it suggests that she was trying hard, consciously or not, to recapture with a different man the passionate interlude she had once had with the prince. Place du Palais des Députés had been renamed Place Bourbon; the Austrian lover had been replaced by a Greek, and this time the baby in the nursery was a boy, but little else was changed. France was still ruled by Louis Philippe, the "king of the barricades," who had come to the throne in the turbulent August days of 1830, when the romance of Lady Ellenborough and Prince Schwarzenberg was in its yellow leaf. Louis Philippe was still trying to ingratiate himself with the Bonapartists, and in 1840 he became, at least temporarily, their hero. After seven years of negotiation with Great Britain, the king had finally obtained permission to bring Napoleon's body from St. Helena to the French capital for re-burial, and when the controversial corpse arrived, most of Paris turned out for the parade. More than 100,000 spectators braved a heavy snowstorm on December 15, 1840, to watch the conqueror's funeral cortège pass.

Aside from the few facts noted in the Baden document and the Digby chronology, nothing is known of the two years from 1839 to 1841 that Jane spent in France with Theotoky, but it must have taken longer than she had expected to get to Byron's "Isles of Greece." Early in 1841, when Jane and Spiro learned that Baron von Venningen had not even taken the first step toward a divorce, they apparently became impatient and decided to have Jane's marriage dissolved through the Greek Orthodox Church. Where and when this was done is not known, but the process necessitated Jane's conversion to Greek Orthodoxy. In the Theotoky family it is believed that Jane and Spiro were married in a Greek Orthodox ceremony in Marseilles before embarking for the Aegean island of Tinos, where Spiro's father was serving as governor. It is known that the Theotokys left for Greece in March of 1841 and that they were accompanied by a French maid named Eugènie, who was to figure prominently in Jane's life for many years.

A French historian, Alexandre Buchon, in a book about his travels in Greece, described the warm reception that awaited Jane, arriving on the small island in the Cyclades. After Bouchon and his party dropped anchor at the port of Tinos on April 2, 1841, they walked along the coast to what was then known as St. Nicholas and is now the town of Tinos to pay a call on the island's governor, Count Johannes Theotoky. When Buchon arrived, Spiro's father and the house servants were busily unwrapping furniture, books and handsome leather saddles. These things, the count explained, had just arrived from Paris, shipped by his son and new daughter-in-law, whom he was expecting any day. In his isolated location the elder Theotoky had heard nothing of Spiro's wife except what his son had written him, and Spiro had wisely left out a few critical details. The governor was under the impression that his son had eloped with one Lady Ellenborough, whose much older husband had sadly neglected her. Count Johannes thought it a very romantic story, and Buchon, who was somewhat better informed about Jane's career in the more than eleven years since she had left Lord Ellenborough, kindly kept his own counsel. He made, however, a few observations about this new chapter in the life of the colorful Mademoiselle Digby:

> M. Theotoky told us his son and bride...were coming to spend at least six
> months and probably a year in his house. I asked him if he had not chosen for

them a house with a view on the ocean, and he assured me that it would be impossible to find a larger and more comfortable house than the one he was living in today, a house situated in a tiny inclined street, narrow, tortuous and without a view of the country, the rocks or the ocean. I don't know what story Theotoky could have made up for Lady Ellenborough to convince her to come and settle in a country devoid of all comfort, of all attractions, of all beautiful countryside and of all conversation. To send saddles for horses to a country where one cannot walk a horse and where even mules have difficulty in standing erect on the slopes of slippery rocks shows a complete ignorance of the country where she will have to live, and she will be sadly disappointed when she sees what there is of Tinos: the governor's house, a garrison, a harbor, a town, a rugged landscape and a goat trail into the country! It will be a hard penance for the follies of her youth, terminating in the greatest of all follies.

Buchon may have known something of Jane's past, but he knew nothing of her temperament. The very inconveniences he deplored made Tinos all the more exciting and appealing to the new Countess Theotoky.

Perhaps those inconveniences were partly responsible for a metamorphosis that no one familiar with Jane's past would have anticipated. According to biographer E. M. Oddie, who had access to personal papers now lost, Jane lavished on Leonidas Theotoky all the affection she had denied her other children. The small house of Count Johannes, which could not accommodate a staff of servants, and the informality of family life there apparently brought out the maternal in Jane, and Leonidas, who was little more than a year old when he was brought to Tinos, reaped the benefits. For the first time Jane became a devoted and conscientious mother. A portrait of Leonidas at age six reveals a strong resemblance to his mother. His hair was darker, but he had Jane's magnificent complexion and the same large, wide-spaced violet eyes; it is not unlikely that he inherited some waywardness from both his parents. As the governor's grandson, Leonidas was undoubtedly pampered by everyone on the island.

Buchon's description notwithstanding, Tinos was not without charm. The capital had long been a center of Venetian influence in the Aegean, and Jane discovered lovely traces of Venetian architecture alongside the simple stone houses common in the Cyclades. All the buildings were stacked one against the other in the twisting, climbing, narrow lanes, and their dazzling whitewashed walls almost blinded the eye against the unbelievably blue water of the Aegean. The entire island was dotted with picturesque dovecote towers, and the mountain heights in the center of the island commanded an unparalleled view of the sea and nearby Siros, Mykonos, Delos and Andros.

Tinos and the neighboring islands, which Jane and Spiro visited frequently, were treasure troves of ancient Greek civilization, and Jane developed an enthusiasm for archaeology which she never lost. Not far from the Theotoky house, where excavations had been made for the island's famous shrine, the Church of Our Lady, fragments of many marble statues were found, and several tombs and ancient inscriptions were uncovered. While Jane was living on Tinos, a small alabaster statue of a man and woman leaning against each other was found by a young islander. The finder offered the piece, which was in perfect condition, to the English consul on Siros, a Mr. Wilkinson, before the Theotokys had a chance to buy it.

There was little social life on the island, but there were occasional dinners with an Italian doctor-historian named Zallony, who lived with his sister near the port, and a group of foreigners who lived on the nearby island of Siros: Mr. Wilkinson, two French families named Devoize and Sartiges, and the Russian consul, M. Curzer. Jane seems never to have been bored, because she was with the man she loved, and the simplest pleasures of Tinos had an exotic novelty for her.

By the time Jane and Spiro ended their several months' visit on Tinos, the countess was speaking fluent Greek and had acquired a taste for the local delicacies: pigeons preserved in casks of vinegar; octopus marinated in olive oil; exotic herbs like thyme, oregano, rosemary, bay leaves and basil, which grew in wild abundance throughout the island. Basil was thought of so highly on Tinos that strangers were often welcomed with a sprig of it, and the natives sometimes wore a sprig behind their ear. Jane, who was always interested in plants, was fascinated by the delicate pinkish-white blossoms of the caper shrubs on Siros, which, when nipped in the bud and pickled, added such a pleasant tang to the salads and seafoods. From another island in the Cyclades group, Santorini (now called Thera), the Theotokys imported the very special Santorinis wine, which Edmond About said "would have been appreciated at a king's table. It is as yellow as gold, transparent as the topaz; it shines upon you like the sun, and beams upon you with the smile of a child. It absolutely lights up the table."

In the spring of 1842 the young Theotokys left Tinos for Corfu, where Spiro was to manage his family's estate. On Corfu, the enchanted isle of Shakespeare's *Tempest*, Jane discovered an entirely different Greek flavor. The Ionian island has none of the barren harshness of the Cyclades. Here all is lush and green, soft and yielding; here fruits and flowers grow in rich and careless profusion. Corfu's location and its unique history have given it an air more European than Levantine. In the fourteenth century, when the Turks were expanding their frontiers, the citizens of Corfu wisely put themselves under the protection of Venice and, despite several bitter assaults, never became part of the Ottoman Empire. After the fall of Venice in 1797, Corfu was involved in a strange game of musical chairs played by the major powers. Under the treaty of Campo Formio, the French occupied all Venetian territories, but the occupational armies were stretched a bit too thin. In 1800 the French were ousted by Russo-Turkish forces, who established the Septinsular Republic in the Ionian islands. Russia took over Corfu completely in 1802, only to be dispossessed five years later by the French. Britain joined the game in 1810, but the French garrison on Corfu held out against the British blockade until 1815, when the treaty of Paris reestablished the Ionian Republic under British protection.

When Jane arrived on Corfu in 1842, Lord Nugent was the British High Commissioner of the islands, and the administration of Corfu was directed from the magnificent Palace of St. Michael and St. George. It must have been a shock to Jane, coming from the modest house of the governor of Tinos, to see the British government house, designed by the talented Sir George Whitmore, as fine an example of Regency architecture as could be found outside London. She found she could step from the English palace to an elegant, tree-lined French boulevard with Parisian-style arcades; turn into a Neapolitan backstreet, where a colorful array of the day's laundry fluttered from lines strung overhead, linking one tall house to another; then find just around the corner a Byzantine church, hung with icons and fragrant with incense. The scenes that captivated Jane in 1842 remained for Lawrence Durrell to describe so lovingly a century later:

> ...the Venetian houses above the old port are built up elegantly into slim tiers with narrow alleys and colonnades running between them; red, yellow, pink, amber—a jumble of pastels which the moonlight transforms into a dazzling white city built for a wedding cake. There are other curiosities. The remains of a Venetian aristocracy living in overgrown baronial mansions deep in the country, surrounded by cypresses; a patron saint who lay (a cured mummy) in a silver casket in the church of his name, and who performed terrific miracles; festivals, dances, olive pickings, holidays, storms, births, deaths and magnificent murders.

The patron saint Durrell speaks of is St. Spiridion, for whom the young Count Theotoky was named, as is one out of every two Corfiote males. This formidable figure, around whom much of Corfu's religious life revolves, is credited with saving the island from plague in the seventeenth century and from conquest by the Turks in the eighteenth. The body of St. Spiridion is still carried through the streets of the town in colorful processions on Palm Sunday, Holy Saturday, August 11 and the first Sunday in November.

There was a Theotoky town house, one of those tall, narrow Venetian residences, on the esplanade, but Jane and Spiro made their home at Dukades, the family estate, some twenty miles from the capital. The house at Dukades was a modest Italian-style villa, but the grounds were enormous, and the surrounding country with its seven hills, its luxuriant shrubs and flowers, orange groves, and gnarled olive trees, was Corfu at its best. Jane planted a cypress tree to celebrate her arrival and immediately began laying out gardens.

In true feudal style the life of the small village was completely a Theotoky operation; the small chapel, the olive press, the crops—in effect, even the peasants themselves—all belonged to Spiro's family. Despite their lofty position, the Theotokys were not people of great wealth, but Jane's income was sufficient to make her new home as elegant as any on Corfu. The time she and Spiro spent in Paris waiting to legalize their union had given Jane an opportunity to collect some treasures to refurbish Dukades. With these she made a Parisian drawing room with gilt cornices, mirrors and chairs. For Spiro, who had literary leanings and whose hobby was bookbinding, she created an English library in the style of the one at Holkham, but on a smaller scale. Her magnificent silver and crystal and the elaborate dinner service for one hundred she had ordered in Paris (emblazoned with gold bands and the gold Theotoky crest—a lion rampant within a crown of laurels) all were brought to Dukades by mule pack from the harbor at Corfu. By this time Jane had become expert in the art of moving.

Now the saddles Buchon had rightly thought so inappropriate for Tinos could be put to use, and Jane and Spiro spent many days on horseback exploring the island. At other times they drove about in an ornate carriage displaying the family banner. Theotoky took his wife to see the celebrated frescoes in the church of Our Lady at Cassiopi, a small fishing village on the northeast coast of Corfu. Cassiopi had been a flourishing port when Cicero spent several days there on his way back to Rome from the East. Only five miles across the channel from the town is Albania, where rugged, snowcapped mountains rim the horizon. In the narrow stretch of water between Corfu and the mainland the first sea battle in Greek history was fought around 644 B.C., and here a later clash between Spartan and Athenian ships triggered the Peloponnesian Wars, which ended the Golden Age of Athens. Less than five miles away from Dukades on the western coast of the island was the Theotokys' favorite bathing beach, the breathtakingly beautiful Bay of Paleokastritsa. Legend claims that Ulysses was washed ashore from a shipwreck here and rescued by Nausicaa, daughter of the king of ancient Corcyra. High on a promontory overlooking the peacock-blue waters of the bay stands a thirteenth-century monastery, whose gate is guarded by a rusting cannon, a legacy from the brief Russian occupation of the island.

While England was going drably Victorian, the Count and Countess Theotoky were living in the grand eighteenth-century manner. There were balls, levees, and concerts in town, and Jane and Spiro kept continuous open house at Dukades, where they entertained lavishly. At one gay party the guests enjoyed themselves so much that, following numerous toasts, they smashed not only their glasses but almost the entire gold and white dinner service. Jane discovered that a combination of the excellent Theotoky wine, *ouzo*, and Corfu's potent kumquat liqueur could make Greeks and even Englishmen behave in a most uninhibited manner. The Theotoky family treasured for years a marble-topped table which "Uncle Spiro" is said to have cracked the night of the famous dinner.

The customs of Corfu delighted Jane, and she was quick to adopt them. The first day of May was Flower Day, when everyone on the island decorated their houses with wreaths of fresh flowers. On New Year's Day a special fire was laid—olive wood for peace, cypress for many children, oak for long life—and they were all burned together. The mistress of Dukades learned to relish the lamb dishes of *souvlakia* and *moussaka*, and the stuffed grape leaves called *dolmades*. Spiro introduced his wife to *melamacarona* (honey cakes), *kurabiedes* (almond cakes) and the delicious Greek pastry, *baklava*, and he bought her a Corfiote wedding costume—the simple dark cotton skirt, vividly embroidered velvet blouse and elaborate headdress of red ribbons, flowers, lace, peacock feathers and tiny mirrors.

What contact Jane had with her English family during her first years with Spiro is not certain, but it must have taken several months for the news to reach her at Dukades that her grandfather and father had died within six weeks of each other in the summer of 1842—the Earl of Leicester on June 30, and Admiral Sir Henry Digby on August 19. Lady Andover, who had lost her first husband and her mother almost simultaneously in 1800, was in double mourning again.

From what can be pieced together of Jane's two years on Corfu, this seems to have been a time of happiness and rare contentment for her. Unfortunately it could not last. The chain of events that would eventually take her away from Dukades began in Athens, where the Bavarian king of Greece had been neglecting his political fences. There were many reasons for the coup d'état staged in the Greek capital in the fall of 1843, but the major one was the discontent of those Greeks who had played leading roles in their country's affairs during the War of Independence. Since Otto had become king in 1833, the government of Greece had been in the hands of Bavarian officials, and the few subordinate positions offered to Greeks wounded the pride and thwarted the ambitions of the men who had fought to free their country from the Turks. Finally, on September 15, 1843, the Athens garrison, under Colonel Kallergis, surrounded Otto's palace and refused to allow the ministers of Britain, France and Russia to enter until the king agreed to grant a constitution, and to replace his Bavarian officials with Greeks. Perhaps it was at Ludwig's suggestions that in 1844 Otto named Count Spiridion Theotoky as one of his new aides-de-camp. The opportunity to hold an important post at Otto's court appealed to Spiro, and a move to Athens was, of course, mandatory. With it came the end of Jane's three-year Greek island idyll and the twilight of wedded bliss for the Theotokys.

12

◇————◇

A King of the Mountains

Land of Albania! let me bend mine eyes
On thee! thou rugged nurse of savage men!

The "glory that was Greece" was not much in evidence at the port of Piraeus in the summer of 1844. Those who came to Athens by boat were first greeted by a few ramshackle tavernas and warehouses, and the road leading inland to the capital five miles away was not much more inviting. During the dry season (from May through October) the slightest breeze or movement raised thick, penetrating clouds of dust that stung the eyes, irritated the nose and covered every bit of the sparse greenery with a monotonous dun color. Travelers usually forgot these minor disappointments when they caught their first glimpse of the Acropolis rising from the plain of Attica, crowned by its majestic ruins, but when they reached the town itself, it was quickly apparent that the ruins were by far its most attractive feature. Athens in 1844, according to all contemporary accounts, was a civic disaster.

Turning a sleepy Turkish village into a royal capital had created a population that could not have been given adequate housing had every builder in Bavaria come to help. There were fewer than 1000 residences for more than 15,000 inhabitants, and many Athenians with no place to sleep lay about in doorways at night like bundles of discarded clothing. The only accommodations considered "respectable" for foreigners were at the Hôtel d'Europe in Aeolus Street over the shop of a German bookseller named Herr Nast. Far from luxurious, the Europe at least provided entertainment when the French landlord periodically beat his Maltese wife, who invariably called on the hotel guests for protection.

The town was divided into four quarters by the two main streets that intersected in the center: Hermes Street, which was the continuation of the road from Piraeus, running in a straight line to the royal palace of King Otto; and Aeolus Street, which began at the base of the Acropolis and became the road to the village of Patissia, a mile away from Athens. The old Turkish part of town, composed of rude huts clustered on the eastern and northern slopes of the Acropolis, formed one quarter. There children, chickens and pigs played among the dunghills, and the lanes were narrow and crooked.

In the triangle formed by the palace and Hermes and Aeolus streets was the *Neapolis*, or new town. This quarter had been laid out by a German architect named Schaubert, who failed to take into account the Athens climate; in his

144

broad, treeless avenues the summer sun and dust (and winter winds) were merciless. Friedrich von Gärtner had come from Munich to design King Otto's palace, but Otto did not have his father's good taste, and the royal residence was a box-like structure, built of magnificent Pentelicus marble, carefully plastered over. The private residences in *Neapolis* were considerably more attractive than the palace. Most had pale yellow stucco facades, heavy wrought iron balconies, ornamental balustrades, little porches of Ionic columns and small gardens in back. Their most obvious drawback, however, was a series of large drainage ditches, little more than open sewers, which ran down the center of each street.

The residents of *Neapolis* were a group who called themselves "Athens society"—foreign diplomats, teachers, generals, retired European philhellenes and a few select Greeks with aristocratic names such as Botzaris, Soutsos, Metaxas, Mavromichalis, and Mavrokordatos. Despite their somewhat primitive surroundings, these socialites tried to live *la vie parisienne.* They spoke French. The men wore black frock coats in the European style and turned up at the court balls in a bizarre assortment of outdated uniforms. The ladies bleached their complexions with copious amounts of *poudre de riz* and wore pink or white watered silk gowns, which they trailed in the dust (or mud, depending upon the season) at the weekly band concerts. Every Sunday anybody who was anybody promenaded along the muddy (or dusty) Patissia Road as if they were in the Bois de Boulogne. For these promenades every Greek shopkeeper, shoemaker and hairdresser who could borrow three hundred drachmas bought a horse, and those who could not hired one for three drachmas. A visitor from Paris during the Othonian period commented that "in Athens good manners are as rare in society as fleas are common in the hotels."

The lower classes held their promenades in coffee houses such as "The Beautiful Greece," or in the Turkish markets or the middle of the streets, and their gatherings were far more colorful than those of the frock-coated, watered silk aristocracy. Sailors from Crete and other islands of the Levant anchored their gaudily painted boats at Piraeus and swaggered (usually full of the anise-flavored liquor called *raki*) down Hermes Street in baggy blue Turkish trousers, black vests and crimson caps and sashes. Peasants in shaggy, goathair capes drove flocks of goats and turkeys to the market. The mountain men (or Pallikari) wore the traditional fustanella—the pleated skirt—and gaiters or stockings, none of which were the snowy white they had originally been, and they twisted cloths around their heads in the fashion of the turban.

Much of the male population of the city sat far into the night drinking countless miniature cups of thick Turkish coffee and smoking *narghiles* in the numerous cafes. Their only other diversions were incessant card games, gossip and the puppet theater starring *Karaghiosis*, the impoverished but cunning hero whose lewd antics are still popular in the Levant. The streets were only dimly illuminated at night by olive oil lamps, which were not lighted at all when the moon was full. Anyone who ventured out after dark needed a lantern to light the way and a stick to ward off the dogs.

In the eleven years since Ludwig's son had landed at Nauplia, there were few who had been pleased with his rule. The disgruntled Greeks found they were far more heavily taxed under the Bavarian monarch than they had been under the Turks. They had exchanged government by the sword, which they at least understood, for government by official regulations, which they despised. There is no doubt that Otto loved his adopted country and that his intentions were the best, but he was faced with staggering economic problems from the outset of his reign, and the fiercely independent Greeks would likely have sabotaged any program, no matter how brilliant, that required cooperation on their part. Ludwig himself came to Athens in 1836 to see what could be done to shore up Otto's shaky throne, and he recommended a royal marriage with an eye to a Greek-born heir. Of course, it never occurred to Ludwig that a Greek wife might enhance Otto's popularity. In any case, there were no princesses in Greece, and since the German states were full of them, a marriage was quickly arranged with the pretty nineteen-year-old Princess Maria Frederica Amalia, daughter of Grand Duke Augustus of Oldenburg. When Otto brought his bride back to Athens in 1837, Amalia, barely out of the schoolroom, very quickly proved to be domineering and capricious. As the years passed, it became apparent that there would be no heir. Otto's health was wrecked by malaria, and the childless Amalia directed her boundless energies into other channels. Edmond About, the brilliant French satirist, taught at the *Ecole Française* in Athens during the Othonian period, and in a book about his experiences, *La Grèce Contemporaine,* he described the royal couple:

> The King appears older than he is. [Otto was then about thirty.] He is tall, thin, feeble and worn out with fever; his face is pale and worn, his eyes dim; his appearance is sad and suffering, and his look anxious. The use of sulphate of quinine has made him deaf.... His tall figure...and a vague air of wearied majesty have impressed foreigners who have seen him from a distance. His mind, according to all those who have worked with him, is timid, hesitating and minute. His last word in every business is always, "We will see."

About had even less admiration for Amalia:

> The Queen is a woman who will not grow old for a long time; her *embonpoint* will preserve her. She is of a powerful and vigorous constitution, backed by iron health.... Her face is full and smiling, but somewhat stiff and prim.... it seems as if she smiles provisionally and that anger is not far off. . . . Nature has provided her with a remarkable appetite, and she takes four meals every day, not to mention various intermediate refreshments. One part of her day is spent gaining strength, the other expending it. In the morning the Queen goes out into her

garden either on foot or in a little carriage which she drives herself. She talks to her gardeners, she has trees cut down, branches pruned, earth levelled; she takes almost as much pleasure in making others move as in moving herself, and she never has so good an appetite as when the gardeners are hungry. After the mid-day repast and the following siesta, the Queen goes out riding and takes more than three leagues at a gallop. In the summer she gets up at three in the morning to bathe in the sea at Faliron, where she swims for an hour without a rest. In the evening after supper she walks in her garden. In the ball season she never misses a waltz or a quadrille, and she never seems either tired or satisfied.

Amalia's dissatisfaction was often expressed in pettiness. Nothing was easier than to offend her; nothing more difficult than to get back into her favor. According to About, the queen never forgave one unnamed foreign diplomat for not having a good appetite when he dined at the palace. Amalia was certain that the man was deliberately insulting the royal cuisine. Amalia once had as a lady-in-waiting Photini Mavromichalis, said to be the wittiest and loveliest young woman in Greek society. Photini's uncle was an aide-de-camp to Otto, her father a senator. When someone whispered in the queen's ear that Photini was being clever, beautiful and virtuous so the king would fall in love with her, the entire Mavromichalis family was forthwith sentenced to social oblivion. "The Queen," About said, "is a jealous divinity who punishes the guilty unto the seventh generation."

In the summer of 1844 Count Spiridion Theotoky, Otto's new aide-de-camp, brought his stunningly beautiful English wife to the Athens court, and it was hardly surprising that Queen Amalia soon found a fresh cause for dissatisfaction. Jane's income, which would have been modest in England, was great wealth in Greece, where the highest government officials were paid a bare living. The Theotokys lost no time in engaging Athens' most famous builder, Kleanthes (sometimes written Cleantis), to construct an imposing mansion for them in *Neapolis*, and Jane was soon a familiar, and apparently sensational, figure at the promenades on Patissia Road.

It was not long, according to About, that she first incurred Amalia's displeasure:

> I have often met Ianthe, who used to leap the ditches on a splendid white horse. She was the best rider in town; when she went out, followed by a large company of friends, she made such a grand appearance that the little boys always ran to salute her as she passed; they thought she must be the Queen. The Queen will never forgive those mistakes.

Amalia considered herself the most accomplished equestrienne, and of such things close friendships are seldom formed. This, however, was a minor irritation compared to Amalia's rage when it became obvious that Otto shared his father's taste in women. The king loved the polka, which the queen despised and refused to dance. Ianthe Theotoky, though, was an excellent polka partner, and her conversation made Otto laugh in a more relaxed manner than the court had seen before. Jane was eleven years older than the queen, but according to About, she looked as young as Amalia and was considerably more youthful in spirit.

Some years later Jane referred to Amalia in her diary as "my rival," leading one of her biographers to believe that Otto had been Jane's lover. This is highly unlikely. About, who heard all the court gossip, wrote that "The King and Queen lead an irreproachable private life . . . and their most mortal enemies do justice to their morals." Otto might, in fact, have been more popular with his subjects had he exhibited a few weaknesses of the flesh, but he was not a womanizer, he drank little and was said to be the only man in Greece who did not smoke. There is little doubt, however, that the king did enjoy the company of the beautiful Jane Theotoky, and he knew her background well enough before he ever met her to suspect that she was not unattainable. While Spiro and Jane were still on Tinos, Otto had answered an inquiry, forwarded to him by Ludwig, from Karl Venningen, who had lost touch with his ex-wife and wanted to know where he could write to her. From contemporary accounts, however, the king of Greece was not the attractive man his father was, and it is improbable that Jane carried on more than a mild flirtation with Otto.

Regardless of Amalia's dislike of Jane, Spiro was Otto's aide-de-camp, and protocol demanded the Theotokys' presence at all court functions including, of course, the balls. About wrote that the only really handsome room in the palace was the ballroom, decorated with beautiful arabesques in the style of Pompeii, but the French author felt that the whole effect was spoiled by "an Italian dauber who has painted large ridiculous figures such as Tyrtaeus wearing a helmet and playing a lyre." The description About gives of a court ball suggests that these occasions were less than lively:

> At nine o'clock exactly the grand-master of the palace and the grand-mistress, the aides-de-camp, the orderly officers and the maids of honor enter with measured step, followed by the King and Queen.... A great circle is formed around their Majesties—everybody, men and women, remain standing—etiquette requires it.... The King speaks to all the diplomats, one after another, and the Queen speaks to their wives. Then the King goes and speaks to the ladies while the Queen speaks to their husbands. These conversations, as it may be supposed, are neither animated nor varied.... After about half an hour of this, the King allows newcomers to be presented. When all the presentations are finished, the Marshal of the palace, receiving an order from the Queen, gives the signal for dancing. Then the ball begins by a majestic promenade of the court and the diplomatic corps. The King gives his hand to an ambassador's wife, the Queen hers to an ambassador, and all the rest of the important people follow behind, holding hands. At each turn around the room the couples separate and form again. This dignified procession lasts a quarter of an hour.... At the close of the

ball, the grand diplomatic circle reconvenes.... The balls end at three in the morning; they last therefore six hours, two of which are taken up with conversation. The lighting of the ballroom is very brilliant, the refreshments are very much less so; the cakes which are handed round are almost always gingerbread in disguise. At the end, there is some fighting to get at the soup.

There is no surviving personal record of Jane's life in Athens. However, in later entries in her journal, she complained that her maid, Eugènie, had known of several extramarital affairs carried on by Count Theotoky during the period from 1844 to 1846, but had waited some time before revealing this knowledge to her mistress. From a portrait painted in 1846, it is clear that Spiro was still extraordinarily handsome. By the time the Theotokys arrived in Athens, Spiro's passion for Jane had had several years to cool off, and he did not appear to be a man addicted to monogamy. At any rate, subsequent events indicate that sometime during their first three years in the Greek capital, the Theotokys' romance turned to ashes, and only their mutual adoration for their son Leonidas held them together.

When summer came to Athens, the hot sun made the poor sanitation of this overcrowded city unpleasantly obvious, and many Greek children died of fever. Families who could afford it always fled to healthier climates. In late spring of 1846 the Theotokys left Greece for an Italian spa, Bagni di Lucca, where they planned to pass the hot months in cool comfort. Lady Andover, accompanied by Steely and Steely's sister, came from England to spend the summer in Italy with the Theotokys, according to a note in the Digby chronology of Jane.

The Theotokys arrived by boat at Naples, where Jane was probably surprised to learn that Prince Felix Schwarzenberg, of all people, was in residence, representing Austria at the Neapolitan court. There is no evidence, however, that the former lovers met face to face in 1846. The only account of what may have happened in Naples is one that has passed by word of mouth through several generations of the descendants of Mathilde Selden (Didi). According to this story (which is said to have been told by Felix or his sister to Didi sometime afterward), Jane made a request through an intermediary that she be permitted to visit her daughter, who was living in Naples with the Schwarzenbergs. The elder Mathilde was opposed to granting this request, but an arrangement was finally made for Jane to come to the Schwarzenberg villa one evening while Felix and his sister were out. Jane was allowed one brief glimpse of Didi, but the seventeen-year-old girl was not told the lady's identity. Jane saw Didi only once more, according to the same story, and that was in Rome later that year when she was permitted to observe her daughter during her afternoon walk on condition that she would not attempt to speak to her.

Despite the unexpected presence in Naples of Prince Schwarzenberg the Theotokys remained there long enough for Jane, Spiro and Leonidas to have miniature portraits painted by an unknown Italian artist. Jane was forty years old when she sat for this, her last known portrait, and while her beauty is still evident, she does not appear happy.

To travelers from the parched and almost treeless capital of Greece the Tuscan village of Bagni di Lucca in a green valley at the base of the Apennines must have looked like paradise. The streets leading from the picturesque Ponte del Diavolo, an ancient arched stone bridge, were shaded by magnificent trees, and the air was cool. The Theotokys had taken for the season a house belonging to a Colonel and Mrs. Stisted, long-time leaders of a flourishing English colony which later included the Brownings and the novelist Ouida. Mrs. Stisted was a formidable lady known among her fellow expatriates as "Queen of the Baths." She and the colonel owned two houses in Bagni di Lucca, one which they occupied themselves and another which they leased to people who came for the climate and the warm springs. The Theotokys' summer residence was a tall, square building with a facade of egg yolk–yellow stucco and dark green shutters typical of Florentine villas. The reception hall was three stories high, and inside balconies ran around three sides of the upper stories. It was a house that would have delighted an adventurous six-year-old boy. One day shortly after the Theotokys had settled into their villa with Lady Andover and the Misses Steele, some members of the foreign colony came to call. Leonidas was supposed to be taking his nap in the nursery on the top floor when he heard voices in the hall below. The child either leaned over the balcony railing to see who was talking, or he climbed on the railing to attract attention. He lost his balance and fell to his death on the marble floor before his mother's horrified eyes.

This was a tragedy from which Jane never fully recovered. Shattered with grief, she believed that her beloved Leonidas was taken from her in retribution for the neglect of her other children. People who knew her in later years said that she kept a locket with one of her Greek son's curls in it and often cried when she spoke of him. Nothing is known of this dark period in Jane's life, from 1846 to 1849, but it is apparent that she could not bear to remain in Bagni di Lucca, and shortly after Leonidas's death she and Count Theotoky went off in different directions. Long afterward a myth sprang up that during the 1840s Jane had "six Italian husbands," a story that infuriated her and one she categorically denied. Jane's wealth and beauty, combined with her frantic search for forgetfulness and consolation, undoubtedly did make her an easy target for adventurers, and it might be assumed that there were some nonfiction episodes that contributed to the myth. At any rate, she never saw Bagni di Lucca again, and the house where Leonidas died became in time *La Chièsa Inglese*, where services of the Church of England were held.

In 1849, Jane was back in Athens, and her house on Hodos Sokratous was soon the meeting place for the liveliest society of the capital, including the British minister, Sir Thomas Wyse; the French minister, M. Edouard Thouvenal; the Austrian minister, Baron von Prokesch-Osten; and a dashing young French attaché, Baron Roger de la Tour-du-Pin, who represented the Paris Jockey Club at the Patissia Road promenades. Politics were rarely discussed in Ianthe's salon, but the weather was undoubtedly a major topic of conversation during the winter of 1849 to 1850, one of the bitterest ever known in Athens. Snow fell, and the temperature dropped below zero; in one night hundreds of animals, not accustomed to such cold, died, and Amalia lost many of the precious trees and plants in her garden.

The Royal Gardens, for which a large percentage of the capital's scarce water conduits had been allocated, were partly responsible for a grave confrontation between the governments of Britain and Greece in the frozen January of 1850. Twenty years earlier George Finlay, a Scot who had been with Lord Byron at Missolonghi in 1824, had bought a plot of ground from a Turkish official. The plot was incorporated into the Royal Gardens in 1837 without so much as a by-your-leave, and the Scot's unpaid claim against the Greek monarchy, as well as another by a British citizen named Pacifico, became the subject of many angry dispatches between London and Athens. The British foreign minister at the time was Lord Palmerston, Jane's old friend from the heydays of Almack's. Palmerston, who was no admirer of King Otto, decided to wrap the claims of Finlay and Pacifico in a parcel with some minor disputes between Britain and Greece over the Ionian islands and engage in a little gunboat diplomacy. In January the British fleet under Sir William Parker blockaded the port of Piraeus and impounded the tiny Greek navy. Otto refused to be intimidated by this show of force, and his stubborn courage won him the respect of many Greeks. Palmerston's militancy eventually forced Otto's government to pay £8000 in claims, but his conduct was condemned in the House of Lords and aroused angry comment throughout Europe. During the six months that the blockade lasted, Jane's house was frequently filled with high-ranking British naval officers. One of these was a Captain Drummond, who later became Admiral Sir James Robert Drummond, Naval aide-de-camp to Queen Victoria. Drummond's friendship with Jane, which was apparently platonic, lasted many years.

In 1851 Jane was traveling again. According to Digby family records, she met her mother in Switzerland during this trip. Lady Andover was then seventy-four, and such a trip was obviously not easy for her, but she still loved her black sheep. How she felt about the dissolution of Jane's third marriage is not known, but the times when she could have approved of her daughter's actions had been few and far between since Jane first left England twenty-two years earlier. The former Lady Ellenborough was now persona non grata in the royal circles of London, Munich and Athens.

A large portfolio of Swiss sketches which Jane bequeathed to her brother Kenelm bears the date 1851, and is signed J. E. D., indicating that she no longer used the name Theotoky. When About wrote of meeting her, he remarked on this:

First of all I must confess that I have no right to speak of Ianthe by her Christian name. If I speak of her so familiarly, it is because this name is the only one that remains of the many she has borne. She has taken and lost successively the names of Lady E——, the Baroness F—— [About had trouble spelling Venningen] and the Countess T——. And though the Count T——, the Baron F—— and Lord E—— are all living, Ianthe today calls herself Ianthe and nothing more.

Jane returned to Athens later that year, and struck up a friendship with an older woman who was quite extraordinary in her own way. In 1851, according to About, the two most famous ladies in the Greek capital were Ianthe and Sophie, the Duchess of Plaisance, both of whom had graced the most elegant courts of Europe before committing themselves to "oblivion" in Greece. The duchess was the daughter of the Marquis de Barbe-Marbois and had married one of Napoleon's generals, Lebrun, who was later made a duke. The Duchess of Plaisance had been one of the ladies-in-waiting to the Empress Marie-Louise, and after the fall of the empire, had left her husband to roam Europe with her adored daughter Louise, hoping to find a prince for a son-in-law. The search was unsuccessful, and Louise's early death had left the duchess lonely and, most thought, slightly deranged. At one point during Jane's years in the Greek capital, she lived with the duchess in a magnificent Florentine villa with arch-fronted loggias, which is today the Byzantine Museum of Athens. Sophie liked an occasional new face to enliven her mansion but usually preferred the company of her dozens of dogs, including five enormous wolfhounds capable of devouring trespassers.

Sophie's background, according to About's account, was as solidly virtuous as Jane's was otherwise, but the bizarre side of her personality was expressed in the unique religion she created for herself, a religion in which she was both priestess and prophet. The duchess believed that God, with whom she claimed to be in constant personal contact, had commissioned her to build on Mount Pentelicus an enormous altar, which would win her eternal life, and she was waiting for a plan for the altar that would be worthy of God and herself. She spent a good part of her large fortune on other unusual constructions, which she always left unfinished out of a superstitious fear of dying when any was completed. Despite these peculiarities, Sophie was intelligent and witty, and she found in Jane one of the rare women who, like herself, had the courage to let public opinion be damned.

No two women could have been more unlike in appearance. The striking contrast was noted by About, who often saw them together when Jane was living with Sophie. He described the duchess as "a little woman, extremely thin, who seems to be barely alive." Both summer and winter Sophie wore a white cotton dress and a white veil in the Jewish style covering her white hair. The whole effect was ghostly. The forty-four-year-old former Countess Theotoky impressed About as anything but ghostly:

Ianthe is an admirable incarnation of vitality and health. She is tall and slim, without being thin; if she had a longer waist, it would be impossible to find a woman better proportioned. Her feet and her hands reveal an aristocratic origin; the lines of her face are of incredible purity. She has great blue eyes, as deep as the sea; beautiful chestnut hair, highlighted here and there by golden tones; as for her teeth, she belongs to that elite of the English nation who have pearls in their mouths instead of piano keys. Her complexion has kept that milky white-ness that only flourishes in English fogs, but at the slightest emotion becomes flushed. You might say that this fine and transparent skin is only a container for the passions it encloses; they can be seen stirring beneath the surface, all trem-bling and rosy.

About, who came to know Jane and the duchess rather well, would have been astonished at the distorted presentation of the two women that appeared in a twentieth-century Greek novel, *Jenny Theotoky*, written by Polzbias Demetra-kopoulos. The Greek author fictionalized a rivalry between the two friends and was strongly biased in favor of the duchess. He portrays Sophie as the virtuous beauty, trying to save innocent young men from the clutches of Jane, who is struggling fiercely to retain her fleeting youth and consulting with a faithful maid named Anna as to the best methods of seduction. Anna may have been drawn from Eugènie, who was with Jane for thirty years, and the aged Duchess of Plaisance was indeed virtuous, but there all similarity to known facts ends, and the string of lovers Demetrakopoulos attaches to Jane during this period appears to be without any basis in fact.

Two anecdotes involving Jane recorded by her contemporary About sound more probable. In one of his stories, About seems to have tried deliberately to conceal her identity:

> A traveller of adventurous spirit, who called herself Mme. D., painted landscapes and lived with the Duchess, was robbed a few steps from town on Mount Lycabettus by a young Greek, well-dressed and handsome, who snatched a gold chain from her. She told the story all over Athens that she was busy painting when this enterprising young man came up. "But why," someone asked, "why did you let him come so near?" "How could I guess," she answered candidly, "that he was only interested in my chain?"

One of Jane's sketchbooks now in the possession of the Digby family is filled with Greek scenes. A sketch of the Acropolis is dated May 1849, and there are several drawings of men in Greek and Turkish costumes, as well as Athens landscapes.

Another About anecdote was a fascinating conversation with Jane which the French author recorded verbatim:

> Ianthe: "A long time ago I consulted Mlle. LeNormand; she predicted that I would turn many heads—"

About: "One would not have to be a fortune teller to know that."
Ianthe: "—and amongst others, three crowned heads. Although I've been searching, I can only find two."
About: "That's because the third one is in the future."

The woman Jane referred to was a Madame (not Mlle.) LeNormand, a fortune-teller much in vogue in Paris when Jane and Felix Schwarzenberg were together there. She had been a favorite with Napoleon before she tactlessly predicted the emperor's defeat by Wellington. About did not comment on the royal lovers—if Jane had Ludwig and Otto in mind, she chose not to elaborate. At any rate, a third king, whose only crown was a red Greek cap and whose title was purely honorary, was ready to complete Madame LeNormand's trio.

With the rise and fall of political parties in Athens, Otto's aides-de-camp changed continuously, and in 1851 the post Spiro had once held was given to the most colorful man in Greece, the brigand chief General Cristodoulos Hadji-Petros. The origins of Cristos Hadji-Petros are shrouded in legend. Some say that he came originally from the island of Tinos, others that he belonged to a Moldavian colony which for centuries had been settled in Aetolia on the Achelous River. In his youth he made a pilgrimage to Jerusalem, after which he added the "Hadji" ("pilgrim") to his name in the Muslim fashion. According to Edmond About's version, Hadji-Petros, after a stint of piracy at sea, decided that this pleasant and profitable pursuit would be his life's calling, but as he could not afford his own boat, he would have to settle on piracy by land.

In the 1820s he joined the fierce band of mountain men who initiated the Greek war of independence from Turkey. About claimed that toward the end of the war Hadji-Petros was on the Acropolis with a group of chiefs who were besieged by the Turks, when suddenly the roof of their headquarters collapsed, killing all but one. Through this "suspiciously fortuitous" accident, Christos, who was outside smoking at the time, became the leader of all the brigands.

When independence was finally won in 1828, the freedom fighters were dismayed to discover that most of their native land had been left by diplomatic expedience in the hands of the Turks, and they were forced to come down from the hills to the new kingdom they had helped to found. With them they brought their unique brand of mountain morality. Many nineteenth-century writers referred to these highwaymen-soldiers as Albanians because their territory bordered Albania and many had, in fact, Albanian origins. They were also called "Klephts" (Greek for "brigands"), but they gave themselves the title of "Pallikari" ("the brave ones").

Most Pallikari were descended from Greeks who had retreated to the mountains during the three centuries of Turkish occupation and conducted guerrilla warfare against the conquerors. Unable to defeat these shadowy fighters, the Turkish pashas finally came to uneasy terms with them and granted them possession of certain districts and the custody of the highroads. The mountain men made these pay very well. Hadji-Petros had been an armatole, or local governor, under the Turks before the war of independence broke out in 1821. When he turned his talents against the Ottoman Empire, the robber chief became a heroic Greek freedom fighter, an inspirational figure to Byron and other Europeans who espoused the Greek cause.

The Pallikari, who never really decided themselves whether they were patriots or thieves, had about them the same romantic aura of adventure and danger that was associated with the Scottish border raiders. Their ballads, like those of the Scots, told of family loyalty, fighting, love and death—but the villains were Turks instead of Englishmen. One of the ballads Jane heard often in Greece began:

> *Down to the plain came the black-eyed Klepht,*
> *His burnished gun hung by his side;*
> *To the vultures he cried, "Oh stay with me,*
> *For a pasha of Athens your feast soon shall be!"*

The Turks taught the Pallikari some lessons in the fine art of cruelty, and the Pallikari were apt students. When there was plunder to be had, it was immaterial whether the village to be burned or the victim to be tortured was Turk or Greek. But these ruthless fighters were devout in their religion; they never failed to give a tenth of their earnings, no matter how brutally obtained, to the monks, and though human life had little value to them, they thought their souls would be lost if they ate meat on a fast day.

Despite the fear and thinly veiled contempt that the Pallikari inspired in many of their more civilized countrymen, there was no getting around the fact that without them the Turks could never have been defeated, and King Otto was obliged to try to placate these brigand-heroes. For this reason, and in the hope that there might be fewer throats cut on the roads outside Athens, Hadji-Petros, the "King of the Mountains," was brought to Otto's court. By coincidence he and a group of his loyal followers took a house opposite Jane's on Hodos Sokrotous.

The white-haired, mustachioed chieftain carried his more than sixty years very lightly and made a handsome, imposing figure in his native dress—white cotton shirt with large open collar, white pleated skirt cinched tightly at the waist, white stockings, gold-embroidered vest of red silk, embroidered gaiters buttoned to the knee in the manner of Homer's warriors, red slippers, red cap with blue tassel, and a large leather belt from which hung weapons (two pistols and a yataghan, or scimitar), embroidered handkerchief, money bag and tobacco pouch.

The women of Hadji-Petros's mountain band were for the most part as plain as the men were dashing; their waistlines were free to wander at will, and they were generally as free of coquetry as they were of a drachma to call their own. Their shortcomings were reason enough for the Pallikar general, who was a widower, to show a lively interest in his wealthy, beautiful and elegantly groomed English neighbor. It is harder to explain how the well-bred Ianthe could fall in love with this rough brigand who had little education and who, if one is to believe About, smelled of too much garlic and too few baths. He must have represented the ultimate in freedom, romance and adventure for Jane, a refreshing change from the stilted and artificial court life. Also, Hadji-Petros had a son named Eirini, a delicate child whom Jane immediately adored and whom she thought might fill the place of her beloved Leonidas.

Soon after this unusual love affair began in 1852, but before it became common knowledge, Cristos received a change of assignment. He and his followers were uncomfortable at court, and the feeling was surely mutual. Otto resolved the problem by putting Hadji-Petros in command of the garrison at Lamia, a small town in the north where the Pallikari felt at home and where their life style would not be cramped. There were no ties to keep Jane in Athens, and without a moment's hesitation, she sold her house on Hodos Sokrotous and accompanied her lover to this rugged outpost. In his true element Cristos was more attractive to her than ever. Edmond About wrote that:

> When she saw Hadji-Petros in his glory, Ianthe imagined that she was born Pallikar; the next day she was reigning over Lamia. All the town was at her feet, and when she came out to go for a walk, the drums were beating in the fields. This delicate woman lived with drunkards, galloped on horseback in the mountains, ate literally standing up on the run, drank retsina, slept in the open air, next to a big fire, and found herself in excellent health.

Jane was happier than she had been in years, and the brigand was beside himself with joy and pride to think that he had won the heart of this lovely foreigner, twenty years younger and twenty times wealthier than he. Hardships notwithstanding, there was a certain grandeur to Pallikar life when one had Hadji-Petros's lofty position. This grandeur impressed even the critical About when he paid a call on a wealthy young Pallikar deputy at home in his native province:

> His mother received me with the cordial dignity of Penelope doing the honors of her palace to one of Ulysses' guests. She had surrounding her five or six servants to whom she was assigning their tasks. Under the porch some twenty young men, some armed and some not, were playing cards, talking or sleeping; these were the friends or relatives of the owners of the house. I thought I had found myself in the middle of the Odyssey and into the heroic life of which Homer has given us a description so precise that one can verify it every day.

In the midst of this grand Homeric adventure, it bothered Jane not at all that her lover's small government salary was well supplemented by highway robbery. She had become sufficiently Hellenized that brigandage neither shocked nor dismayed her, and Cristos was careful to shield her from its more cruel and bloody aspects, which she would not have tolerated. Jane, in any case, always saw what she wished to see. If, as About reported, the men of Hadji-Petros's band referred to her as "the queen of love and beauty," how could she possibly judge them harshly? In a conversation with About about a famous brigand named Bibichi, Jane said disarmingly, "Ah, that poor man who became a brigand because he had been deceived! If all men were of the same temperament, one-half of humanity would be robbing the other half." In Greece brigands were not separated from the society; often peasants, when something tempting turned up, became bandits for a few weeks and then returned peacefully to their fields. There was no question that the brigands had their representatives in all levels of government, and the army, which was supposed to destroy them, was thoroughly infiltrated.

After About left Greece in 1853, he put down his unflattering impressions of Otto's country in *La Grèce Contemporaine*, which outraged the Greeks when it was published in 1855, and he followed it the next year with a satirical novel, *Le Roi des Montagnes* ("The King of the Mountains"), in which Hadji-Petros is scarcely disguised as one "Hadji-Stavros." The book is fiction, but About knew the facts about brigandage in Greece and he knew Hadji-Petros. If one-tenth of the cruelty and cunning he attributes to the Pallikar chief is not exaggerated, Jane was fortunate to have come out of this ill-advised love affair with her head still attached to her shoulders. In the About novel the brigands boast of committing unspeakable acts of torture, murdering men, women and children with complete equanimity if the ransoms demanded for their release were not paid. Despite these horrors, the book is hilariously funny when it describes the elaborate corporate structure of the mountain king's brigandage business, in which half the officials of Greece are shareholders. Hadji-Stavros, who cannot read or write but who has a phenomenal memory for figures, dictates to his secretary the annual report to the shareholders, complaining of the lack of foreign travelers: "A spirit of distrust, originated by some French and English newspaper correspondents, keeps out of our reach many people whose capture would be most profitable. Yet, gentlemen, such is the vitality of our Institution that it has more successfully resisted this crisis than either agriculture, trade or commerce." The expenses of the brigand's operation are itemized on page 158.

For a few months in Lamia in 1852 Jane found no reason to regret having cast her lot with the real-life King of the Mountains, who was on his best behavior. Copies of the *Minerva* and the *Mandora*, popular Athens newspapers, seldom penetrated this far beyond the capital, and Jane had no way of knowing that the first great passion of her life, Prince Felix Schwarzenberg, had died suddenly of coronary thrombosis in Vienna. (The papers did not say, however, what intimates of Felix knew: that death came to Austria's prime minister while he was dressing for a rendezvous with the young wife of a Polish officer.)

The mistress of Hadji-Petros was perfectly happy to discard her Paris gowns

	Francs
A tenth paid to churches and monasteries	26,148
Interest on capital at the rate of 10%	12,000
Pay and food of 80 men, 650 francs per annum	52,000
Material, arms, etc.	7,056
Repairs of the road to Thebes, which had become impassable, and where therefore we found no travellers to stop	2,540
Expenses for watching the high roads	5,835
Stationery	3
Paid to journalists	11,900
Sums given in rewards to sundry employees, attached to various administrative and judicial offices of the State	18,000
Total	135,482

for the costume of the Pallikar women: a coarse cotton chemise embroidered on the hem, collar and sleeves with bright colors of silk thread, a wide black wool belt and an embroidered head scarf, a peasant costume to which she gave uncommon style and grace. The simple diet of spitted kid, crusty fresh bread, olives, onions and cheese with a liberal seasoning of garlic and oregano agreed with her, and she learned to make the native feta cheese in a cradle of cloth suspended over a bucket, allowing the curds to drip whey and dry into crumbly form. She slept on rough goathair blankets and was awakened in the morning by the tinkling of goat bells. With her remarkable gift for languages she quickly mastered the Romaic tongue of the mountain Greeks and could sing to little Eirini in her sweet, soft voice the familiar lullaby of his people:

> *My dear son, my dear little Pallikar,*
> *Sleep well, my dear child.*
> *I shall give you something beautiful—*
> *Alexandria for your sugar, Cairo for your rice*
> *And Constantinople for you to reign over three years.*
> *And then three villages and three monasteries.*
> *The towns and the villages for you to walk in*
> *And the three monasteries so that you may pray.*

This blissful mountain adventure might have gone on indefinitely had it not been for a volatile mixture of politics and jealousy. When Athens society learned the shocking news that Ianthe Theotoky was playing blue-eyed banditti queen with Hadji-Petros in Lamia, there were screams of outrage on all sides. Most outraged was Queen Amalia, who had already destroyed the careers of several officers for openly keeping mistresses. Finally, Amalia saw a beautiful opportunity to avenge all the slights she imagined she had suffered from Ianthe Theotoky. Hadji-Petros received an abrupt dismissal from government service.

Not one to accept defeat easily nor, obviously, overburdened with loyalty to anyone but himself, Cristos sent an urgent letter to the queen. The fact that he addressed his petition to Amalia rather than Otto was a good indication of who was in fact governing Greece. The letter, which the triumphant Amalia promptly had printed in the official court newspaper for all of Athens to read, spoke volumes about the character of the man Jane was ready to marry:

> Your Majesty had me removed; this is without doubt because I lived with Countess T; but whatever my enemies have said to you, I declare upon my soldier's honor that if I am the lover of this woman, it is not for love but for profit. She is rich and I am poor. I have a rank to live up to, children to educate. I trust therefore...

Even with this remarkably ungallant declaration, Hadji-Petros got nowhere with Amalia, who was thoroughly enjoying the humiliation she had heaped on Ianthe Theotoky. If, however, the queen had expected to break up the love affair between Jane and Cristos by making the Pallikar's letter public, she was disappointed. With her astonishing faculty for overlooking defects in the men she loved, Jane acted as if nothing whatever had been said. She returned from Lamia with the sacked general and immediately rented two identical small houses sharing a garden on the outskirts of Athens. Cristos and a group of his followers were installed in one, and Jane and her servants occupied the other. This small concession to public opinion was, however, too little and too late. All the doors of her former Athens friends were closed to her—except for that of the Duchess of Plaisance, who loved to go against the prevailing wind. Sophie had no fear of being compromised and took pleasure in excusing her friend's affair, which she termed a "free union." The only thing she criticized Jane for was the allowance Spiro Theotoky continued to receive from his estranged wife. This the parsimonious Sophie found utterly indecent.

There were new drains on Jane's seemingly limitless purse. The Pallikari practiced a ruinous hospitality, which dictated that anyone from their region who came to Athens had to be given food and a place to sleep. The mountain men imitated the reserved silence of the Turks, smoked incessantly and drank enormous quantities of coffee, retsina and *raki*. Jane was wise enough to keep Cristos and his men out of the drawing room on the rare occasions when she had callers, but Edmond About felt that Ianthe Theotoky was as out of place in this existence as "a Lawrence portrait in the kitchen." It was certainly not Jane's style to be the cloistered Pallikar wife, who was usually ignorant, shy in society and always trembling in front of the man she called her lord.

None of these incongruities had any effect on Jane's decision to marry Hadji-Petros, and she decided it was time to make a formal ending to Spiro's claim on her. Instead of a divorce, which could have been refuted by the courts, Jane sought an annulment from the Church. The Greek priests were pitifully poor and not incorruptible. According to About, for the right sum the Greek Church could discover "in the most legal union five or six points by which it could be decreed that two people who had had eight children together were no more than strangers to each other." Jane's annulment was quickly granted, and it was declared that she and Spiro had never been married at all.

All of Athens expected the erstwhile Countess Theotoky to wed Hadji-Petros, and stories circulated throughout the capital of the mansion Jane had begun to build at Piraeus with a bedroom that resembled a throne room, a magnificent apartment for Cristos, and a garrison for his brigand followers. Then, suddenly, and without notice to anyone, Ianthe vanished from Athens, leaving Hadji-Petros behind.

A rumor spread that the bride-to-be had decided on the spur of the moment that only the best Arabian horses would do for her fine stables, and she had gone to Syria to purchase them herself. But why had she not taken her lover along? Other rumors circulated that Cristos had reverted to type and had begun to abuse his mistress physically. The facts were quite different. Later entries in her diary reveal the real reason why she so abruptly abandoned her Pallikar chief: Eugènie, her faithful *femme de chambre*, complained that she was tired of fending off the amorous advances of Hadji-Petros. Jane was thunderstruck to learn that the man she planned to marry had repeatedly tried to seduce her maid! After a furious "fall-out," as she herself described it, with Eugènie, the shocked Jane weighed the story against her own intimate knowledge of Cristos and came to the depressing conclusion that her maid was telling the truth. Jane had been willing to accept the Pallikar's fawning letter to Amalia on the grounds that the practical brigand would have told any lie to have his position restored, but this matter with Eugènie raised the unpleasant possibility that a lie had not been necessary, that Cristos really did care only for her money. Despite her grief and anger at this ultimate betrayal, Jane had sense enough not to confront her lover with an accusation. She knew Hadji-Petros well enough to realize that he would have a reasonable explanation for everything, and she would be tempted to listen and forgive him. This she could not allow. She had, in fact, been planning a trip to Syria to buy horses, and she seized upon this journey as an escape from a situation she did not care to face. In April 1853, three days after her forty-sixth birthday, Jane sailed with Eugènie out of Piraeus to the east. If she hoped that the strangeness and excitement of the Syrian desert would help her forget her broken heart, she little dreamed that she was only on the threshold of her greatest adventure.

13

Pilgrimage to Palmyra

Slender is her waist, her neck like that of a glass vessel,

And her hips, Allah be thanked, how shapely!

She walks toward me like the daughter of the kbejse mare,

And sweet she looks when her step comes near.

—BEDOUIN LOVE SONG

The voyage to Syria was undoubtedly a time of bitter reflection for Jane, who was once more a fugitive from her own impetuous and ill-advised actions. She was no longer young, and she was farther than ever from her family and her native England. After having borne six children, she was, largely through her own fault, childless. There was nothing to return to in Greece, there was no place to call home, and the future was a bleak and unpromising question mark.

No record remains of Jane's impressions when her boat anchored outside Beirut, but the first glimpse of a new continent and the exhilarating scent of Lebanon pine, which sailors claimed they could smell several miles offshore, must have lifted her irrepressible spirits. Beirut, the major port for travelers to Syria, spread out along the coastline and climbed haphazardly up the mountain slopes. The bright yellow sand, the deep green pine forests and the cobalt Mediterranean made a far more inviting picture than the dun-colored port of Piraeus she had left a few days earlier. The splendid Lebanon mountain range was dotted with small villages, which in some places appeared to overhang the sea, and the early morning sun tinted them with delicate lights and shadows. In 1853 most of Beirut's ancient city walls were still intact, and the great aqueduct towered over the port as it had in the time of Herod the Great, when it brought fresh water from Lebanon to the city. Beirut, like Athens of ten years earlier, had only one hotel that catered to European travelers—the Bellevue, overlooking the sea. It was not luxurious, but the Greek owner, Andreas Boucopoulos, provided clean and comfortable quarters.

During the voyage from Piraeus to Beirut, Jane had decided to make an extended sightseeing tour of Syria. She was certainly not anxious to get back to Greece, and the idea of a desert caravan undoubtedly appealed to her sense of adventure. The deserts of Syria and Arabia had a strong fascination for Westerners in the nineteenth century. In 1845 J. W. Burgon had won the Newdigate Prize at Oxford for his poem about the ancient city of Petra and had stirred the imagination of the English-speaking world with his lines,

161

> *The hue of youth upon a brow of woe,*
> *Which men called old two thousand years ago!*
> *Match me such marvel, save in Eastern clime—*
> *A rose-red city,—half as old as Time!*

Jane had read a romantic account of desert travel, *Eothen*, by William Kinglake, which created a sensation when it was published in England in 1847. "I can hardly tell why it should be," Kinglake wrote, "but there is a longing for the East, very commonly felt by proud people, when goaded by sorrow." Jane seems to have taken her itinerary from Kinglake: south to Jerusalem and a tour of Palestine; then north to Damascus en route to her primary goal, the fabled city of Palmyra, said to have been built by Solomon centuries before Christ. (Palmyra was known to the Arabs as Tadmor, from its biblical name.)

Before Jane's desert journey could begin, however, there were many financial arrangements to be made at the Imperial Ottoman Bank. There were no established relay stations for horses, and Jane was obliged to hire animals in Beirut for the entire trip. From about the time she left Beirut she began to keep a personal journal, which she continued for the rest of her life. These notebooks came into the possession of her English biographer, the late E. M. Oddie, who quoted from them in *The Odyssey of a Loving Woman*, but when the author died, all trace of the notebooks vanished. Only in Oddie's book has a fairly complete chronology of Jane's later years been preserved, along with a few—far too few—of Jane's own words.

Almost before the pilgrimage to Palmyra got underway, Jane's passion for antiquities was overshadowed by a stronger passion for a young Bedouin named Saleh. Little is known about Saleh aside from his physical charms, which were sufficient to make the broken-hearted lady forget Cristos and feel young and desirable once more. If Jane recognized her old symptoms of infatuation, she did not act to stifle them. The past offered her no lesson she was willing to heed; the future was a mystery she never really attempted to penetrate. Only the present seemed to matter. Jane did not have to buy Saleh's affection. Despite their age difference, he apparently found her every bit as attractive as she found him. Although their affair was destined to be a brief one with an unhappy ending, meeting Saleh gave Jane's life a new direction. If it had not been for him, she would never have thought of making her home in Syria.

Unlike the majority of her English contemporaries, Jane exhibited no racial prejudice. Her initial impressions of the desert migrants were recorded in a letter to her mother in 1853:

> My heart warms towards these wild Arabs. They have many qualities we want in civilized life, unbounded hospitality, respect for strangers or guests, good faith and simplicity of dealing amongst themselves, and a certain high-bred innate politeness, quite unlike the coarse vulgar Fellah. But the children are wholly

untrained in duty to father and mother who spoil them dreadfully and their habit of taking the Lord's name in vain is almost as shocking as the Italians. Still there is much to like in them; a vast difference of character which enables one to make a selection of particular cronies.

Jane met Saleh while riding down to the Jordan River on May 4, 1853, less than a month after she had left Athens. Their first encounter took place against the romantic background of an encampment of low, black Bedouin tents, as Jane was bargaining for a horse that had caught her fancy. A highly colored version of this episode appeared in Edmond About's *La Grèce Contemporaine*, and was completely deleted when the book was published in England. About heard the story from the Duchess de Plaisance, who must have heard it from Jane herself, but it is obvious that he added a few of his own touches; he was under the erroneous impression that Jane had married the hero of the story, confusing Saleh with the man who was to become her fourth and final husband.

Ianthe found in an Arab tribe the thoroughbred horse she was looking for. The animal belonged to a sheik, who was young and strikingly handsome. He said to Ianthe, "This horse unfortunately cannot be broken. If she were broken, she would be priceless, and I would prefer her to everything, even to my three wives." Ianthe replied, "A beautiful horse is a treasure, but three wives are not to be frowned upon when they are beautiful. Have your horse brought here so that I may see if she cannot be broken." Two Arabs brought the horse to Ianthe, who with little difficulty was able to saddle and mount it. While she was fearlessly galloping on the "unbreakable" horse, the sheik found her more exciting than his three wives put together. He said to her, "Woman sometimes succeeds where man fails, because she knows how to bend. This animal is now priceless, but since you were able to dominate her, it is not with your money that you will pay for her if you want her." Ianthe, who had been admiring the sheik, replied, "I will pay what you wish for your horse. I did not come from such a great distance to bargain, but women of my country are too proud to share the heart of a man. They only enter a tent where they reign alone, and I will pay for your horse only if you dismiss your harem." The sheik said heatedly, "The men of my country take as many wives as they can feed. If I dismiss my harem to live with one woman alone, I will look like a 1200 franc clerk. Besides, I must follow my religion, set an example to my people and stand up to the Turks." After a lengthy discussion, an agreement was reached, and at this very moment Ianthe is the wife of the sheik. She has a three-year lease, and when the lease is up, the sheik can take back his harem if he wishes. The lease can be renewed. But will it be? I doubt it. Woman is a fruit which ripens rapidly under the Syrian sun.

Whatever the negotiations may have been, Jane did apparently enter Saleh's tent and came out determined to marry him. Once again she was wholeheartedly in love. Despite her forty-six years, she retained not only her youthful beauty and vivacity, but her youthful capacity for self-deception and illusion. She was probably twenty years older than Saleh, but if he didn't let that come between them, why should she?

Passionate as was this new romance, Jane did not let it change her plans to see Palmyra. She had contracted for the whole journey, and she saw no reason why she shouldn't complete it before returning to Greece to clear the way for her new life. Saleh did not accompany her to Damascus because the route lay outside his tribe's territory. They had a tearful separation, each one vowing that it would be only temporary, but only one of them sincere. Saleh, like so many other men in Jane's life, underestimated the singlemindedness of Jane in love. He did not really expect her to come back. He had pleased her, she had pleased him; it had been a fair exchange.

All the way to Damascus, Jane was in her favorite state of delirium, making the wildest, most impractical plans. Her first view of the fabled "earthly paradise of the Prophet" was a moving experience shared by travelers of countless centuries, who crossed a torrid wasteland and saw in the distance a long, low line of deepest green stretching across the horizon from east to west. At first only the glistening white minarets could be distinguished, then the city itself came into misty focus, seven miles of rustling boughs and cool shade, following the ice-cold torrent of the Barada River, which tumbles from the snowy sides of Anti-Lebanon. When Jane entered this oasis of hidden palaces, fertile gardens, whispering fountains and bubbling streams, she apparently was so enraptured that she was ready to put the West aside forever. The homeless wanderer had come home at last.

Even Damascus's one hotel enchanted her. The establishment, owned by a man named Dimitri, was a handsome Arab house built around a lush courtyard, where orange and lemon trees surrounded a sparkling fountain filled with goldfish. There were tiled stairs and a covered gallery looking down on the patio. Near the fountain was a *liwan*, a raised indoor-outdoor salon with a divan, oriental carpets and tables for visitors to recline, drink the thick black coffee seasoned with cardamon, and smoke *narghiles* or *chibouques.* The reception room was in pure Damascus style: an oblong, high-ceilinged hall, the middle of which was set off by Moorish columns, creating a marble passage with a fountain in the center. The food and wine were only passable, but the atmosphere and Dimitri's attention to important guests more than compensated.

The impact Damascus made on Jane was scarcely more striking than the impact Jane made on Damascus. When news circulated in the bazaars and cafés of the city that the beautiful English lady who traveled with a mountain of luggage and no husband planned to attempt the dangerous journey across the desert to Tadmor, everyone decided that she was demented. The British consul, Richard Wood, to whom Jane applied for information about hiring an escort for her trip, was nearly apoplectic in his denunciation of her foolhardy venture. He told her that Tadmor was eight or ten days away on horseback, more by camel, across a desert infested with tribes who looked upon wealthy travelers as a gift from Allah. It was necessary to engage a large band of local Arabs who knew the location of the few wells en route. Although this expensive escort was supposed to be protection against bandits, there was a time-honored trick among some Bedouins to provide half the tribe as escort while the other half staged a raid along the way. After a very realistic mock battle, there was a choice of two procedures: either the raiders would "win," relieving the unfortunate travelers of all possessions and sometimes holding them for ransom as well; or the escort would "win" and claim a heavy reward from their frightened and grateful employers for "saving" them from the marauders. Even a legitimate escort group was no guarantee of safety.

Nothing the consul told her frightened Jane, who had lived among Greek brigands in Lamia and almost married their chief. Fear of consequences had never before stopped her from doing what she set her heart on; a formidable obstacle course only added zest to the adventure. Consul Wood finally threw up his hands, disclaiming all responsibility, and told her to contact the Mesrab Arabs, who for centuries had controlled the stretch of desert on the way to Palmyra.

The Mesrabs, under whose protection the eccentric Lady Hester Stanhope had made a similar pilgrimage years earlier, were the least wealthy band of the great Anazeh Bedouins, but their Sheik, Mohammed, came from one of the oldest and noblest families of the Saba tribe. Mohammed was the eldest of nine sons of an unusual Bedouin chief, who had high ambitions for his children and gave them educational advantages unique among the Bedouin. It was not Mohammed, however, who was chosen to negotiate with the celebrated Madame Digby, but his younger brother Medjuel. Medjuel could not only read and write but spoke several languages and was an authority on desert history. At the time Jane met Medjuel, he did not carry the title of Sheik, which implies chief of the tribe, but the childless Mohammed later abdicated his leadership to him. Medjuel's age in 1853 has never been definitely established, but he had nearly grown sons, so he could hardly have been the youthful twenty-five often suggested by chroniclers who, like About, confused him with Saleh. Lady Anne Blunt, Byron's granddaughter, who met Medjuel many years later in Damascus, described him as "a very well bred and agreeable man.... In appearance he shews all the characteristics of good Bedouin blood. He is short and slight in stature, with exceedingly small hands and feet, a dark olive complexion, beard originally black, but now turning grey, and dark eyes and eyebrows." The most vivid portrait of Medjuel come from Emily Beaufort, Viscountess Strangford, whom the Arab Sheik guided to Palmyra six years after Jane's first trip:

He is like *all true* Bedoueens, a small man, about five feet, three inches in height, slightly made, but erect, very graceful in all his motions, and with a light, easy step. His face is really beautiful—of a perfect oval; a long aquiline nose, delicately-formed mouth, small regular teeth of dazzling whiteness, and large black eyes that could be soft and sweet as any woman's, or flash with a fierce, wild eagle glance that really made one start. He wore a short black beard, and long crisp ringlets under his *kefiyeh*, which was of the very finest and brightest Damascus silk, bound round his head with the pretty *akgal*—a double wreath of camels' hair tied and tasselled with coloured silks. His dress was a *kumbaz* or long tight gown of striped and flowered silk, with wide, open sleeves hanging down to the knee; then his sheikh's cloak or pelisse of bright scarlet cloth bound with black braid, and with three bars of broad black braid across the chest,— this, with the scarlet leather boots worn over stockingless feet and reaching to the knee, is the distinguishing dress of the sheikh. Over all came a *mash'lah*—a shapeless but very comfortable cloak—sometimes of thin white cloth edged with color, sometimes of coarse, thick brown and white camel's-hair cloth, sometimes of the same material in black, violet or brown, with a handsome pattern in gold thread woven in up to the shoulders—this latter kind comes from Mekka and are costly, but very beautiful. A silk scarf wound many times round the waist, into which a couple of revolvers and a big knife were stuck, and a sword hung round the neck by a crimson cord, completed the costume. As to his manners, the "best-bred" English gentleman is not more polished than he, and the Bedoueen chief joins an easy chivalrous grace to his quiet dignified demeanour, which has a double charm.

Judging from Lady Strangford's description, Medjuel was a far better choice than Saleh for Jane, but it would take her some time to discover that.

Before this aristocratic Arab met the aristocratic English lady to discuss terms for the escort to Palmyra, a number of plans were already being discussed in various Bedouin tents to relieve the lady of her valuables. The Mesrabs were generally considered to be above this kind of banditry. They were a small band, numbering no more than a hundred tents, and for safety they were obliged to travel with the Gomussa, who had a thousand tents, or the Resallin, who had five hundred. All three of these groups belonged to the Saba tribe, the most important branch of the great Anazeh, numbering some 23,000 tents. The two major Bedouin groups of the Syrian desert were the Anazeh and the Shammar, whose territories were divided by the Euphrates River. From time immemorial the Shammar had extracted tribute from everyone on the east bank, and the Anazeh had the same privilege on the west. As one or the other group was continually crossing the Euphrates, a perpetual state of war existed between these sworn enemies. This hostility did little to unify the many groups who made up the Anazeh, and their smaller feuds, which resulted in frequent intertribal skirmishes, were often deliberately provoked by the Turkish authorities to keep the individual sheiks from consolidating too much power. Considering the tenuous nature of Bedouin protective alliances, it is conceivable that Medjuel was not informed of the planned raid on Jane's caravan. Normally the Saba Bedouins were honorable, courteous and hospitable. Possessing the best horses and camels in Arabia, they fought only in self-defense, almost never for plunder, but there were those among them who regarded European travelers with contempt, trespassers who were lawful prey.

If Medjuel was unprepared for the raid, he was equally unprepared for the fascination of his traveling companion. In the very beginning he was nonplused by her beauty, her total lack of condescension, her friendliness and her unique refusal to haggle over money. When a price of 8000 francs for the journey to Tadmor and back was agreed upon and all the arrangements made, the caravan was ready to set out from Damascus. Jane passed with flying colors the ordeal that confronts anyone mounting a camel for the first time, winning the admiration of Medjuel and his Bedouins, who believed that this initial encounter determines whether or not someone will be a good rider and worthy of the animal. She apparently made a better impression than had Lady Strangford, a younger Englishwoman, who made the same journey six years later and described her experience in *Egyptian Sepulchres and Syrian Shrines*:

> A couple of men held down each dromedary by standing on its fore-knees, while the Sheikh himself [Medjuel] lifted us ladies, each with a sort of flying jump, into the middle of the seat, hastily settling our shawls, etc.; and while directions were shouted on all sides, with such earnest vociferation that it was impossible to understand one syllable of them except to "hold fast!" up jumped the animal, raising his hind legs first, when you go nearly over his nose, then his forelegs, jerking you as unexpectedly backwards, against the hinder pommel of your saddle, and affording you a knock on your spine that you remember against all future occasions.

In her book, Lady Strangford also gave a colorful picture of her caravan's departure from Damascus with Medjuel and his tribesmen:

> By four o'clock we had all streamed in procession out of the gate—a goodly cavalcade of eleven dromedaries, besides the Argeels, their owners, who always accompany the camels, sometimes on foot, sometimes mounted behind the riders. The dromedaries carried our party, including the servants, the Sheikh, and the escort of the armed Bedoueens, Anazehs and others—thirteen men in all; while several Damascus acquaintances accompanied us for a mile or two, after the kindly Arab fashion of leave-taking. Such a noise as we made altogether! For the Bedoueens had a darabouka (a drum) to which they sang lustily, shouting their goodbyes on all sides, the whole way through the delightful gardens and green lanes that encompass the city! In two hours and a half we reached the village of Doumah, which stands on the edge of the gardens; it was all alive with men and women gathering the grapes, and spreading them out so thickly on the ground to dry into raisins that we took them for red carpets; while many were crowding round the fires, by the aid of which they were turning the juice into *dibs*—a luscious sweet in which the Arabs delight, and which is so often mentioned in the Bible, rendered in our translation, as honey. From this we passed out upon the

great plain, and presently met the Baghdad postman galloping in at the end of his nine days' journey.

These scenes were undoubtedly the same ones which so delighted Jane when she set out for Palmyra with the Bedouins in 1853.

Traditionally the first day out in caravan was a short one, beginning in the afternoon, to break the camels gently into their loads. Just at sundown Medjuel struck his lance into the sand and shouted a command. The camels, as if choreographed, halted in their tracks and dropped to their knees. In an astonishingly short time the women of the tribe had driven the tent pins with their heavy wooden mallets, the black goathair tents were raised and the oriental rugs spread inside. Soon a kettle was boiling over a fire made from the dry desert thorn plants, and a supper of hot tea and cold fowl was ready. The camels, who each had one leg tied close underneath to prevent their wandering away during the night, were arranged in a circle surrounding the camp; the saddle frames were built up into a protective wall; and the hunting falcon which always accompanied Medjuel was unhooded and placed on his perch. While these tasks were being performed, the chief and the lady lingered before the fire.

Conversation was not difficult for these two linguists, who spoke to each other in a mixture of Turkish and French. Medjuel was an authority on Arab horses, and he was full of fascinating stories about Palmyra, whose legends were interwoven with those of his own people and whose ruins were genuinely loved and treasured by his tribe. Jane, never known for keeping her love affairs secret, told her Bedouin escort about Saleh and her plans to make her home in Syria. Far from being discouraged by this disclosure, Medjuel was overjoyed to learn that this fascinating, blue-eyed, golden-haired *Engleysi* would consider marrying a man of the desert.

Every morning at sunrise the camp came noisily to life. Jane found that her preparations for the day consisted merely of shaking out the riding costume she had slept in. Breakfast was a hasty duplicate of supper. During the journey she learned much about desert protocol. Medjuel's men talked and joked freely with their chief, sometimes addressing him as "Sheik" but more often simply as "Medjuel," pronounced "Midgewell." When the Sheik entered a tent, everyone rose and remained standing until told to sit. Medjuel was not allowed to do any of the menial camp work, but during the caravan he was expected to attend to his own camel and eat the same food as the others. There were rigid rules of privacy pertaining to the long narrow tents, which were closed in back but partially open in front. To look into someone else's tent or even pass too near the front was to give the deepest offense.

About midway between Damascus and Tadmor the caravan passed the village of El Qaryatein, whose squalor was in marked contrast to the nearby ruins of a Roman spa. Still standing at the Roman site was a vaulted chamber known as the "Bath of Balkis," from the traditional name of the Queen of Sheba. In the center of the tiled floor an opening about a foot in diameter poured forth a continuous current of moist, hot, sulphurous air. Since Roman times the air was believed to possess healing qualities, but the heat was so suffocating that it could be endured only for a moment.

Then, a short distance out of El Qaryatein the raiders appeared. Even with Medjuel at her side the usually unflappable Jane Digby was terrified by the sight of a wild band of Arabs, who came racing across the sands, yelling blood-curdling threats and brandishing their fierce-looking pointed lances. After token resistance, the Bedouins of the escort group seemed to melt into the desert. Only Medjuel was left to protect the Englishwoman, and he turned on the attackers with the fury of a madman, refusing to be captured. This unexpected development caused utter chaos among the raiders, who could not afford to harm a brother tribesman and who could not understand how Medjuel's loyalty to a foreigner could come before his tribal bonds. They finally retired in confusion, the members of the escort party sheepishly reappeared, and the caravan continued on its way to Tadmor.

It is a matter of conjecture whether Medjuel had been a party to the raid. Apparently it never occurred to Jane that he might have been. Oddie, who had access to Jane's own account, wrote: "She believed that he had saved her life. The slight insignificant little man who was as brave as a lion was a man after her own heart. She was passionately grateful." Certainly such behavior on the Sheik's part was not that unusual, as an old Bedouin poem reveals:

> *O sweetheart mine, who gives forth a fragrance of*
> *ground cardamom!*
> *Stop thy camel at the raiders' assault,*
> *For I will betray my kin to guarantee thy safety.*

A colorful episode like the Bedouin raid did not escape the notice of Jane Digby's other chroniclers, who created various versions of it. One has Medjuel leading the raiding party when he is struck by love at first sight. Another has Jane agreeing out of gratitude to marry her hero immediately. Still another insists that they agreed to wait two years to marry, giving Jane time to learn Arabic and overcome her family's objections. None of these versions was the story Jane told Damascus friends.

Medjuel did ask Jane to marry him when the caravan was encamped at the ruins of Palmyra, and it was his own idea to offer to give up his wife, the mother of his two sons. Jane refused him for two reasons: she was still infatuated with the youthful Saleh, and she had a quaint sense of honor that made the idea of taking another woman's husband repugnant to her. In her journal Jane claimed that she and Medjuel never exchanged so much as a kiss on their first journey together, and there is no reason to doubt a woman who was always so candid about her amorous escapades.

The last lap of the journey to Palmyra was immensely demanding, but the hardships were of little consequence to someone of Jane's incredible stamina, and they were completely forgotten the moment she saw a hundred rose-colored limestone columns rising more than fifty feet out of an endless sea of sand. Palmyra's principal thoroughfare, the great avenue of columns, led to a magnificent triumphal arch flanked by two smaller arches, which served as a triple gateway to the mammoth Temple of the Sun. Although earthquakes and the vandalism of Muslim fanatics had taken their toll, eight of the temple's tall fluted columns and practically all of one side wall remained so that Jane might imagine how beautiful this sanctuary must have been in the third century during the reign of Zenobia.

At the time when Palmyra was the queen city of Rome's eastern empire—a polyglot settlement of Arabic, Aramaic, Greek and Roman elements—more than 750 of the imposing limestone columns with elaborately carved capitals stood as monuments to the brave men who led caravans across the desert. Caravans were the reasons for Palmyra's existence; this oasis was the spot where in ancient times the two great desert trade routes met: one crossing from Phoenician ports to the Persian Gulf and the other coming from Petra and southern Arabia.

From later trips to Palmyra, when large Bedouin encampments near the ruins made longer exploration safe, Jane painted many watercolors of this area and became a respected authority on the history of the once-flourishing desert city. Her invaluable help was acknowledged by a missionary friend, Dr. William Wright, in his book about Zenobia's empire:

> For much of the traditions to which I attach weight, I am indebted to the Lady Ellenborough, who spent a great deal of time at Palmyra and busied herself in weaving together the local stories regarding the great desert queen. Chiefly from this source I derived my information regarding Zenobia's military camps and the routes by which her armies marched to meet Aurelian. Lady Ellenborough's identifications were confirmed by an intelligent young sheikh who accompanied me to traditional camping grounds.

Some thirty years before Jane came to Palmyra for the first time, one of the great eccentrics of the nineteenth century, Lady Hester Stanhope, had visited the ruins and claimed later that the Bedouins encamped there had crowned her queen. Lady Hester did indeed wield absolute authority for many years over several hundred members of the Druse sect in the area around Sidon, but her claim about Palmyra is suspect.

If Medjuel had heard stories from his tribe about Lady Hester's visit to Palmyra, he does not seem to have mentioned them to Madame Digby. According to Oddie, however, the Bedouin sheik told his bewitching client that she was another Zenobia, a woman worthy of ruling a desert empire. She may have been flattered by the comparison, but it was still Saleh who interested her romantically. For Medjuel she felt a strong bond of friendship, nothing more.

The grand entry of the caravan into Damascus made a vivid impression on Jane. About two hours from the city the travelers met the beautiful Mesrab horses out exercising. In a flash Medjuel was off his camel and mounted on his favorite mare, galloping wildly all around the caravan. The camels, who knew they were near home, stepped up their pace, and the Bedouins of the escort group burst into song, some of them standing up and dancing on the camels' backs amid peals of laughter and the ceaseless throb of the *daraboukas*. The road was suddenly full of people shouting greetings to Medjuel and demanding a hundred repetitions of the caravan's adventures. After Jane's long journey, the refreshing sight of green trees overhanging the path and sparkling streams along-side, combined with the tumultuous welcome, could only have persuaded her, if she needed persuasion, that this was home.

Before she could put down new roots in Damascus, however, there were old ties to be disposed of in Athens, and Jane made hasty arrangements for the journey. Little is known of her brief return to Greece in 1853. She avoided Hadji-Petros for obvious reasons, and she stayed clear of Otto's court. When she told the Duchess de Plaisance that she planned to settle in Syria because she had fallen in love with a young Arab, that crusty old lady lost all patience with her beloved Ianthe. Sophie realized that nothing she could say would prevent this madness, and she quarreled violently with Jane, so that, as she later told Edmond About, she would "not miss her so much." Ianthe and Sophie never saw each other again; the duchess died the following year.

By mid-November, having made arrangements for the disposition of her Athens property, put her jewelry in safekeeping and said her goodbyes, Jane was back in Syria. Two drawings from her sketchbook, one of the "Schick Selamé" and another of an Arab named "Chifouk" dated November 25, 1853, are evidence that she had by then returned to the desert. Her faithful and long-suffering maid, Eugènie, who spent a good many years of her life packing and unpacking for her peripatetic mistress, accompanied Jane uncomplainingly on this new adventure. Eugènie, who had concealed from Jane many of Spiro's infidelities while the Theotokys were still living together, must have wished she had been as discreet about Cristos. Had it not been for her revelation, she could have remained in a halfway civilized country, where she had finally become accustomed to Madame Digby's unusual companions, instead of setting out for this God-forsaken desert. And for an unhappy period following Jane's return to Syria, it looked as if Eugènie's devotion was all that was left.

Blindly trusting as always, believing as always that her infatuations would be reciprocated, the archromantic raced across the desert for a reunion with her adored Saleh, only to find that her place in his tent had been taken by a beautiful, dark-eyed girl named Sabla, scarcely more than a child. It was plain from Sabla's triumphant glance that she knew all about this foreign woman and had no fear of being cast aside. Confronted with this crushing humiliation, Jane could do nothing but make a hasty and not very dignified exit. At the time it apparently never occurred to her that she might recover from this heartbreak and betrayal as quickly as she had from her disillusion with Cristos and others before him. Once more life was unbearable, and the land that was to have been her paradise became instead a fiery purgatory.

As she turned back toward Damascus, Jane recorded her firm decision to eliminate men from her life altogether. She would find a little house in an out-of-the-way section of the city, where she and Eugènie would spent their sunset years in quiet seclusion. But before she would settle down to this cheerless existence she decided another trip might be the balm she needed to soothe her aching heart. Her bags were not unpacked in Damascus before Jane, forty-six, joined a caravan to Baghdad. On New Year's Day, 1854, she was crossing the Euphrates into Shammar territory.

14

A Bedouin Sheik

If I had neither mirror nor memory, I would
believe myself fifteen-years-old.
—JANE DIGBY, AGE FORTY-SEVEN

When Jane was happy, she seldom looked back, but when she was in "an *abîme* of misery," as she described herself during the journey to Baghdad, the past had a way of crowding in on her. January 4 was the Greek Christmas, an occasion Ludwig had always celebrated; on this particular day in the middle of the desert memories of Ludwig came flooding back. That gentle monarch had lost his throne in 1848, owing mainly to his infatuation for the ambitious courtesan Lola Montez, and Jane saw an uncomfortable similarity between Ludwig's and her own unhappy state. Both were exiles; both had been brought to grief by foolish romantic dreams. In the midst of these reflections in her journal, Jane was surprised to find her thoughts had strayed from Ludwig to Medjuel, and for the first time she realized that the Bavarian and the Bedouin had many similar endearing qualities. It suddenly occurred to her that she was anxious to see her desert defender again.

Jane's escort on the Baghdad Caravan, Sheik El Barrak, was a very different kind of Bedouin from Medjuel, but he was no less attracted to his fascinating English client. El Barrak's intentions, however, were considerably less honorable than Medjuel's. With her usual lack of caution, Jane was unable to keep from talking about Saleh, and her present guide saw a possibility of becoming the young Arab's successor.

It is unlikely that the sheik was able to make much headway in Baghdad, however, where the only fitting accommodations for an aristocratic English lady were at the British Consulate. Jane did not record her stay there, but she could hardly have missed meeting the British consul-general, Lt. Col. Henry Creswick Rawlinson, who was as famous a sight in Baghdad as the city's tiled mosques. Rawlinson was noted not only for his knowledge of ancient civilizations but for the ingenious manner in which he combatted the 120-degree heat to work on his translations. The colonel sat in a kiosk at the foot of the residency garden, where a waterwheel was set up to pour a continuous stream over the roof. A lion cub that he had found abandoned in the rushes of the Tigris lay under his chair as he wrote, ate out of his hand, followed him like a dog and made his visitors extremely wary. Rawlinson lived like a monarch, with a guard of sepoys, who gave an impressive roll of drums when he entered or left the residence. His lavish banquets of Indian food followed by desserts and cheeses, a great tureen of hot punch and finally deviled herring and turkey legs, were renowned throughout the Middle East.

Neither the colorful colonel nor the city of the *Arabian Nights*, however, was enough to make Jane forget Saleh. On the return journey she tried to distract herself with her pencils and brushes. Her sketchbook contains a scene along the Tigris dated March, 1854, and one of Kurdistan dated April, 1854, but sketching proved to be thin therapy for a broken heart. Jane was still bemoaning her loveless condition in her diary when the caravan passed through the valley of the Jordan, where she and Saleh had first met and become lovers. She saw herself "Alone, always alone!" and she fretted over the loss of an inexpensive ring Saleh had given her as if it were worth a fortune. "Why, why," she lamented in her diary, "do I still love Saleh? Still cling to his remembrance as if that love were requited? Why? . . . I must see him again! If Heaven permit it!"

It was at this point that El Barrak decided to make his move. The overtures from the guide to whom she had paid so little attention astonished Jane, but she was too lonely and too much in need of someone to love to refuse him. At first El Barrak was surprisingly tender and affectionate, but within two days Jane and the sheik quarreled violently over a stray camel that had appeared at Jane's tent on the verge of starvation. The soft-hearted lady, who could not bear to see an animal suffer, fed it flour from her own hands. When the sheik happened upon this scene, he filled the air with curses for what to him was a shocking waste of food. Then Jane lost her temper too. She could never understand the Arabs' indifference to their camels, which she called those "dear, useful animals."

Angered by the argument, the sheik set out to avenge his wounded pride by making the next few days as uncomfortable as possible for Jane. He put the caravan on the move at three in the morning; he overworked all the camels, making them travel a hard ten hours at a stretch; and he assigned some women of the tribe to share Jane's tent, an invasion of her privacy that she felt was a great insult.

Eventually, El Barrak and Jane made a truce of sorts, and she wrote that he accompanied her willingly on several side expeditions to places that interested her. The Sheik had apparently decided that since he could not regain the lady's affection, he might as well try to regain her good graces in order to receive a generous bonus at the end of the journey. He halted the caravan long enough to climb a mountain with Jane, where she could get a better view for her sketchbook; he accompanied her on a shopping expedition through a village *souk* (market); and he guided her to some ruins where Jane found an ancient Greek inscription carved in a rock and saw cliff-hanging tombs like those at Palmyra. There was a magnificent old mosque at Mardin Diabeh and some well-preserved Grecian columns. "What a journey would this be," Jane wrote, "with one I really loved with enthusiasm, and who could understand and return my attachment. But what folly! And yet! There are moments in which—*si je n'avais, ni*

King Ludwig I of Bavaria, protector and confidant of Jane, believed by some to be her lover. Jane called him "my best beloved friend."

Josef Stieler portrait of Jane, commissioned by Ludwig for his "Gallery of Beauties" at the royal *Residenz*. The background letter is one of more than seventy that were written by Jane to the Bavarian King, who called her "Ianthe."

Baron Karl von Venningen, Jane's second
husband, who fought a duel over her.

Schloss Venningen in Weinheim, where
Jane and Karl spent several years.

Portraits of the Theotoky family, Jane, Spiro and their son Leonidas, painted in Naples, shortly before Leonidas died in a tragic accident. Spiro was Jane's third husband.

King Otto and Queen Amalia of Greece, whose
court Jane scandalized in 1852.

The house in Bagni di Lucca, Italy, scene of Leonidas Theotoky's fatal fall.

Watercolors painted by Jane at Palmyra and on caravan in Syria during the 1860s.

Portrait by Jane of Sheik Medjuel el Mesrab, her fourth
and last husband, drawn while Medjuel was asleep.

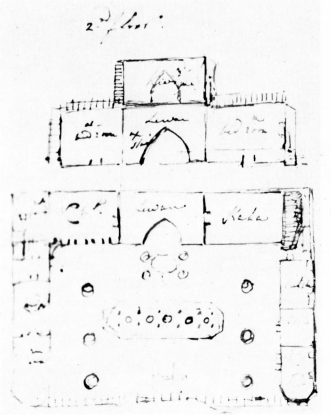

Floorplan sketched by
Jane of her house outside
the walls of Damascus.

Isabel Burton and her husband, Captain Richard
F. Burton, close friends of Jane in Syria.

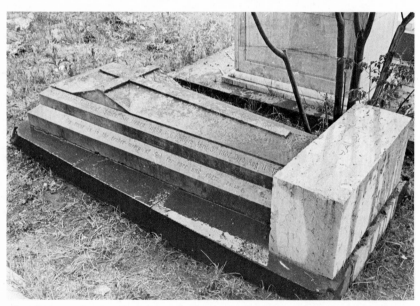

Jane's grave in the Protestant Cemetery in Damascus. The footstone with
Jane's name in Arabic was placed there by her Bedouin husband after the main
stone had been erected.

miroir, ni mémoire, je me croirais quinze ans." If she had neither mirror nor memories, Jane would believe herself to be fifteen years old. She was the first to admit that emotionally she was still an adolescent.

When the caravan arrived at Aleppo, Jane visited the grave of her cousin and childhood playmate, Henry Anson, who had died there so tragically nearly thirty years before. In a chance encounter with a Mr. Kopini, a Greek she had known in Pisa, Jane heard that King Otto and Queen Amalia had been forced by political unrest to flee their adopted country. (The exile turned out to be only temporary, however; Otto did not actually lose his throne until 1862, eight years later.) Jane was unashamedly pleased to think that Amalia had been deposed, but in her diary she worried about how this would affect Hadji-Petros. "So then my wish is granted and my rival the Queen is annihilated. And Greece? My friends? Cristodoulos! Can I be so indifferent to his fate? And yet, why was he so infamous with Eugènie—Eugènie whom he could never love...While I?..." Jane had long since gotten over her infatuation with Cristos, but with the defection of Saleh she briefly considered the possibility of returning to Greece. Then she abruptly rejected the idea. "No...I dream of staying at Damascus, *triste* as I shall be.... Alone...Quite alone..." More melancholy thoughts engulfed her when the caravan reached Riha. "Riha! Oh, that name! What memories does it not call up? Saleh! It was at Riha I fondly dreamed that you loved me, loved as I did!"

Jane's depression did not lift until she arrived at Hama, the ancient Hittite city that had become a center of Bedouin commerce. This was Mesrab territory, and it was associated with Medjuel, not Saleh. Although the town was unbearably hot, the vast water wheels that since the Middle Ages had carried water to the high ground for irrigation were a familiar and comforting sight to her, and she felt she was back among friends. As she strolled through the *souk* with its tiny, cluttered stalls, she imagined she saw the face of Medjuel on every Bedouin who passed by. And for once the man on her mind reciprocated with wholehearted enthusiasm. Medjuel had not forgotten for a moment the beautiful English lady. Through the desert grapevine he was kept informed of the caravan's progress, and when it approached Damascus, he rode out to meet it, bringing to Madame Digby a valuable Arab mare as a gift of welcome. For Jane this warm gesture was a miracle. The pleasure of seeing Medjuel and the excitement of coming home to the enchanting city that had cast its spell on her the first time she saw it put an end to all thoughts of Saleh.

Jane admitted later that in the light of all her past errors of judgment, she had a few misgivings about this new romance. In a brief and uncharacteristic moment of caution she wondered if Medjuel were interested more in her wealth than anything else. It never occurred to Jane to question her own feelings even though just a short time before she had been declaring her undying love for Saleh. As always the present was what counted, and she brushed aside all doubts as she and Medjuel rode into Damascus together.

Although he was obviously delighted to see Jane again, Medjuel did not renew his proposal of marriage during the ride. The next day Jane waited all morning at Dimitri's Hotel, pacing the corridors and the garden in a feverish state of excitement. At noon Medjuel appeared, and they went for a ride in the desert. Still he refrained from mentioning love or marriage, and Jane began to wonder if she had been too forceful at Palmyra when she told him they could be no more than friends. Perhaps he was waiting for a sign from her that she had changed her mind, but how could she let him know?

She need not have worried. Medjuel had never given up hope of marrying Jane. He had already sent his wife back to her people with the dowry she had brought him. This was the Arab manner of divorce, but there were other formidable obstacles in Medjuel's way. His family was firmly opposed to his marrying the foreign woman. Their hostility to Jane was painfully obvious on one occasion when she dropped a flower, and one of Medjuel's relatives trampled it, muttering furiously that it was "hers." The Mesrabs cared nothing for Jane's wealth; they were extremely proud of being one of the first four noble families of the desert, and Madame Digby, despite her aristocratic lineage, was not *asil* (noble) in their eyes. It was not wise, they felt, to mix races. Medjuel, however, happened to be that rare Arab, that rare man, for whom love was "all in all" as it was for Jane, and he was just as determined to follow the dictates of his heart now as she had been on several previous occasions.

On the second day after her return to Damascus, Medjuel told Jane that he was a free man, and he begged her to marry him. The suspense he had created by biding his time had the desired effect, and Jane accepted him with enthusiasm. As if she were truly a girl of fifteen caught up in her first romance, Jane recorded in her diary the time and place of Medjuel's first kiss. A marriage that by all odds should have been a disaster was destined to be a triumph.

What turned out to be the most important day of Jane's life had a singularly appropriate climax. She and Medjuel were invited by El Barrak, who wisely had decided to bow to the inevitable, to a grand "fantasia" to welcome home the Baghdad travelers. This Arab fiesta had all the color and excitement that even Jane could ask for. El Barrak's encampment outside Damascus blazed with brilliant silk banners, and the throb of *daraboukas* and the wail of flutes could be heard for miles. It was a medieval jousting tournament Bedouin style—people and horses were arrayed in their gaudiest trappings for this rare entertainment. The best horsemen of Barrak's tribe were lined up in two teams a hundred yards apart, and they each carried a long feathered lance called a *djerid*. When a signal was given, the teams rode at full speed toward each other, and as they passed, each hurled his *djerid* at the nearest opponent. The riders exhibited every trick of horsemanship to avoid the flying missiles or to catch them in midair and throw them back. They rode hanging by one stirrup on the side of their horses, wheeling and turning, guiding their animals only by the pressure of a knee. Watching this centuries-old pageant for the first time, Jane Digby seemed to have realized more than ever that she belonged to the desert, "the dear desert that I am so fond of." Like El Barrak and the rest of the caravan, she had come home.

These warm feelings did not evoke much sympathetic reaction from Richard Wood, the British consul in Damascus, when Jane consulted him on the steps necessary to marry Medjuel. If he had earlier thought her demented when she undertook the dangerous journey to Tadmor, the cautious British representative was now certain of it. The consul reminded Madame Digby that Bedouin women were often mistreated and that while Muslim law permitted men as many as four wives, infidelity in a wife of the Anazeh tribe was punished by decapitation. He was too delicate to point out that Jane's record tended to make her a rather poor risk, but he considered putting her under some form of restraint while he waited for instructions from England. This kind of treatment came as no surprise to Jane, who was no novice at shaking up British legations.

The wedding had to be postponed, but it was not due to the intransigence of Queen Victoria's representative. Jane received word that some of the jewelry she had left in "safekeeping" in Athens had been stolen, and this necessitated a trip to Greece. Medjuel was understandably reluctant to turn loose his betrothed, for whom he had waited so long. He was afraid the difficulties involved in arranging their marriage and his kinsmen's disapproval would cause Jane to change her mind. (And who could guess what new adventures might befall the romantic lady on the way to Greece and back?) Jane put the sheik's fears to rest by leaving nearly all of her possessions with him as a guarantee of her return. In less than a month she was back.

Jane and Medjuel were married at Homs by a Turkish official in a ceremony quite unlike the Anglican, Roman Catholic and Greek Orthodox ones in which the bride had taken part previously. The ceremony was performed according to Muslim tradition, but there was nothing Muslim about the curious pact the couple made between themselves. Medjuel agreed to live in the monogamous fashion of the West, but as a safeguard he reserved the right to take a Bedouin wife at some future date if he so desired. In that event, he promised to spare Jane all knowledge of her rival. This unique arrangement, which satisfied Jane at the time, caused her much anxiety later on. This version of the marriage agreement is Jane's own and differs from the one Isabel Burton claimed to have heard firsthand when she met Jane sixteen years later:

> Gossip said that he had other wives, but she assured me that he had not, and that both her brother Lord Digby and the British Consul required a legal and official statement to that effect before they were married.

Mrs. Burton was notoriously inaccurate in matters concerning Jane Digby, and the kindest assumption is that her active imagination assisted her in filling in facts when they were unavailable. For one thing, Jane and her brother Edward were not even on good enough terms at this time to exchange letters. Consul

Wood took no part in the ceremony and had, in fact, written to the Queen's Advocate for an opinion on the legality of the marriage; he was notified that the marriage would not be recognized in any Christian country.

For the first few months following their wedding, the couple whose union created shock waves in Syria made their home at Homs. With her easy adaptability, Jane quickly picked up the patterns of Bedouin life. She had thoughtfully arranged her trousseau to include Bedouin garments and the traditional possessions of the wealthy Arab bride: a heavy marquetry "hope chest" inlaid with mother-of-pearl, matching marquetry clogs a foot high for walking about the courtyard, and yellow kid slippers with curved toes for household wear. Gestures like this, her facility for language and her gentle manner gradually overcame the initial hostility of her adopted people. Before long the Mesrab Bedouins and even Medjuel's two sons, Schebibb and Japhet, who had resented Jane bitterly in the beginning, began to treat her with affection and respect. They gave her the name *Umm-el-Laban* or Mother of Milk, because her beautiful fair skin was the color of Bedouin yogurt. As Medjuel's wife, her official Arabic title was the Sitt Mesrab.

The first winter of their life together Medjuel dispelled any lingering doubt Jane might have had that he was interested in her wealth when he insisted upon going off into the desert with his tribe to arrange winter pasturage for the Mesrab flocks. Jane was not happy over the idea of being separated from him, but she was surprised and impressed by his reasons. She wrote in her journal that her husband was *"trister* than *triste"* at having to leave her even for two short months, "but the wish to send money to his brother, not from my purse, spurs him on!"

For longer than she could remember, Jane's purse had been at the disposal of the men she loved, and Medjuel's reluctance to live off his wife was for her further proof that she had finally found the man she had sought so very long. "Ah, his is the character I would like to have met earlier in life, so upright, so truthful, so true. Such a companion might have saved me much. Heaven's will be done! I have met with the sorrows that were no more than my just reward!"

Unlike most Bedouins, Medjuel was a devout Muslim, who prayed to Allah at sunrise and sunset with a simple faith that Jane found moving, but his piety did not incline her toward a Muslim conversion. Instead, she often found herself longing to return to the religion of her childhood. She was afraid, however, that the Church of England would look with horror upon her Muslim marriage and insist that she give up Medjuel before she could be given absolution. That was a risk she did not care to take. Her lack of formal church ties did not prevent her from praying to an Anglican God fervently and often, each time Medjuel was away from her, for his safe return.

Jane never lost the fear that she would be punished for marrying a nonbeliever by losing Medjuel in some manner, and her anxiety was heightened by a cholera outbreak in Beirut in 1855. She worried about what would happen to Medjuel should anything happen to her, and she wrote in her journal: "I fain would put my affairs in order to assure him at least of a token of my affection and gratitude and the happiness he gives me. I am happy with Medjuel whose equal I never met but once—BASILY."

Once more she noted the similarity between Basily (her nickname for Ludwig) and her Bedouin, the two large-hearted romantics who came from such disparate cultures. Unfortunately Jane's English family was unable to appreciate this comparison. The Digbys could not dissociate Medjuel from his race and could not think of him as anything but an Arab and—even worse—a heathen. Stiff-necked Steely, who was now the widowed Lady Andover's companion, refused even to recognize Jane's new name and addressed a letter to her as "Madame Theotoky," a gesture that was not lost on the recipient. "That hated name!" Jane wrote in her diary, "The cause of so much evil to me." It did not help matters when a report reached the Digbys that Jane was in a Sheik's harem, although Edward Digby's wife, Lady Theresa, assured Jane in a letter that Edward had refused to believe such a thing of his sister. In her answer, dated June 22, 1856, Jane said she was very glad that her brother had thought better of her than that, showing he still loved his "Jenny" of childhood days despite their long estrangement. She admonished Theresa not to confuse the Bedouin character with the "kind of Mohammedanism practiced in Istanbul by the Turks." "Believe me," she wrote, "when I say that had I even in early life married the Sheik, or a man with a character resembling his, for high morality, justice, truth and many other qualities I set store by, I *could* not have caused so much grief to him, or to my family." Theresa had evidently mentioned the garden at Minterne, for Jane told her, "I too have a garden, which I am trying to turn into something *English looking*, as far as serpentine walks and magnificent walnut trees can make it."

Theresa's letter contained the news that the aged Lord Digby, Admiral Digby's cousin, had died childless in May of 1856, making Jane's brother Edward heir to the title, but not, unhappily, to the old peer's fortune. There were estate matters to be settled, some of them apparently involving Jane herself. For this reason, and also because she very much desired a complete reconciliation with her family, Jane decided to make her first visit to England in nearly twenty years. In the fall of 1856, when it was time for Medjuel to join his tribe for the annual winter migration, Jane sailed from Beirut on a ship of the Pappayani line.

15

Family Reunion

All the romance and poetry in life
ought to be long past and over, and
here am I still with a beating and
burning heart.

—JANE DIGBY, AGE FIFTY

When the Greek ship arrived at Piraeus on November 25, 1856, Jane was dumbfounded to see, waiting on the dock, General Hadji-Petros, resplendent in crimson, white and gold. She had written to several Athens friends, including Cristos, that she would spend a few days in Greece on her way to England, but she hardly expected that the Pallikar she had abandoned so suddenly would come to meet her. Seeing the tears in his eyes and listening to his reproaches unnerved her completely. Their tears mingled as they embraced. All the way into Athens their conversation dwelled on how much each had made the other suffer. Oddie's description of Jane's reunion is based on a letter of hers that has since been lost:

> Cristodoulos struck a heroic attitude at once. Forget her? How could he forget her? Betray her love by making overtures to a common graceless creature like Eugènie? How could Ianthe believe such things of him? There was not a word of truth in the story. It was an infamous fabrication of Eugènie's own. Could any man who had loved Ianthe—who had been privileged to enjoy Ianthe's love and tenderness—give anyone like Eugènie a thought? He went on weeping as he assured her that she had broken his heart, ruined his life, and at seventy, wrecked his career. Still more distressing was his news of Eirini [his son] who was at the moment so seriously ill that there was little hope of his recovery. Jane's high spirits were dampened down with depression. Had she misjudged him? Had she too readily accepted Eugènie's word and done her once so dear Cristodoulos a serious injustice? She was full of remorse when he continued to shed emotional tears; tears for his dying child; tears for the loss of his lovely, loving Ianthe; tears for the loss of the fortune she had shared so generously when she had lived with him; tears of wounded vanity that he had been supplanted so easily by an obscure Arab sheikh.

Hadji-Petros was a hard loser. He tried every trick in his ample repertoire to woo Jane back, not even hesitating to remind her of Eirini's illness. When she saw the child, Jane knew he had not long to live, and her heart went out to Cristos. She knew what it meant to lose a beloved child, and there was no question that the old Pallikar's love for his son was genuine. But she did not allow her sympathy to overcome her judgment, and much to the disappointment of Hadji-Petros, she refused to stay under his roof. In the days that followed, Cristos tried desperately to persuade Jane that her Muslim vows meant nothing, that she would be far happier married to him than returning to a savage Bedouin in the desert. His arguments were artful, but they fell on deaf ears.

Athens had little attraction for Jane now. She missed the duchess, who lay buried in her elaborate tomb on Pentelicus with two of her favorite white wolf-hounds beside her. Sophie's lovely house, where Jane had once found refuge, was now a barracks, and the strange villa on Pentelicus stood empty and unfin-ished. There was no gaiety at the court of Otto, whose popularity had reached a new low. His small kingdom was still smarting from having picked the wrong side in the Crimean War. The Greeks, who could never find much charity in their hearts for the Turks, had shown a militant enthusiasm for Russia, and their ill-advised activities had brought about a two-year military occupation of Piraeus by England and France, Turkey's allies in the strange conflict.

Jane was not sorry to leave Greece, although she did weep when she told Cristos goodbye, knowing she would probably never see him again. There was another emotional scene at the dock before her boat sailed on December 3. Cristos' parting words were another reproach that she had not given him a chance to defend himself against Eugènie's charge. An ironic footnote to the love affair of Jane and her brigand chief appears in the journal of an English economist, N. W. Senior, who visited Athens in 1857. At a court ball Senior saw a tall, handsome man in a splendid, gold-trimmed Albanian uniform, and he was told that this was the famous General Hadji-Petros. Apparently Senior's infor-mant did not bother to point out the Pallikar's brilliant role in the Greek war of independence or his bold maneuvers on the Thessalonian frontier in 1854. "He is chiefly famous," Senior wrote, "for having lived for some time with the lady who was once Lady Ellenborough."

There was a different kind of reunion at Folkestone dock on December 19 when Jane Digby stepped ashore in England for the first time since she had come with Karl in 1837. Miss Jane Steele, sister of the Digby children's old governess, had been sent by Lady Andover to meet the boat. Upper-class ladies, even middle-aged ones, did not travel unchaperoned. Jane's former painting teacher gave her the warmest and most loving of welcomes. Nevertheless, all the way to Tunbridge Wells, where Lady Andover lived in retirement at Ernstein Villa with the two Steele sisters as companions, Jane's emotions were in turmoil.

The greeting was as good as could have been expected. However, nothing Miss Steele told her prepared Jane for the altered appearances of her mother and her former governess. Steely looked very old, wrinkled and frail; Lady Andover, who had been a stout but still handsome woman when Jane last saw her, was now eighty, enormously fat, and fretful. Still, the prodigal daughter had come home, and there were sweet reconciliations all around. It all seemed unreal to Jane. "*I* in England!" she wrote in her journal that night, astounded that the land of her birth should seem more foreign to her than the desert she had adopted.

After a few uneasy days of getting used to one another again, Lady Andover and her daughter began to slip into a more comfortable pattern, and even the tight-lipped Steely loosened up a bit. There were, however, certain topics of conversation that Jane very quickly learned to avoid. Any mention of Medjuel or her life in the desert brought a profound chill to the atmosphere, and at the first opportunity Steely firmly stated her belief that Arabs were "lesser creatures, their skin especially pigmented by the Almighty that one might recognize them as inferiors." Jane confessed in her journal that she was "angry with Steely's as I thought dictatorial manner about Arabs.... Is this right?" On another occasion she wrote, "Many are the scenes I could and would wish to note, had I a motive, about things assuredly curious and peculiar in Bedouin life, but after Steely's remarks, what is the use of my noting anything?" She was aching to describe the color and excitement of Syria, but no one wanted to listen.

When her brother Edward and his wife, Theresa, came to visit her in January, Jane hoped that someone of her own generation might be a little more open-minded, but she was quickly disillusioned. Jane was dismayed to observe their tenseness when she showed her sketches of Palmyra and other desert scenes. Neither Edward nor Theresa would mention the name of Jane's Arab husband; it was as if they had willed Medjuel out of existence. Much as their attitude disturbed and hurt Jane, she understood it. Her brother had been an army officer and was still active with his Dorset Yeomanry. To Queen Victoria's soldiers, as to Steely, dark skin and un-British customs spelled inferiority.

In 1837, when Jane made her first return visit to England, the rules of personal behavior among the upper classes still retained some of their Regency flexibility. Now, after two decades of Victoria's reign, respectability had become the religion of the country, and every aspect of English life was measured by the yardstick of "What will people say?" Against such a yardstick Jane Digby could only be a social disaster. Almost none of her activities during the past twenty years provided appropriate parlor conversation, so Lord and Lady Digby filled the void with endless details of their seven children. Returning from a walk with them on Rusthell Common, Jane was plunged into a state of depression that she could reveal only to her journal. "My family ties burst asunder; no children; no English home! And oh, the grief I have brought upon others, on my dear kind parent, by my fatal misconduct. And here I am, sitting almost a stranger when I hear of my own family whom I hardly know. I am not gay as I gaze around and think of what might have been and what is." The fact that she had not heard from Medjuel since she left Syria did not help her sagging morale.

Before the three-day visit of Edward and Theresa ended, however, relations eased somewhat. Brother and sister parted on terms of affection, and Edward gave his sister a seal as a token of his love.

The visit of Jane's younger brother Kenelm, following that of Edward and Theresa, was an unqualified success. This warm-hearted clergyman, who was said to be as strikingly ugly as his brother and sister were handsome, was a rare breed of churchman for Victorian England. With the same uncritical nature he had exhibited in his childhood, Kenelm was the sympathetic listener Jane had been waiting for. Of all her family the Anglican minister, who should have been most distressed by his sister's marriage to a Muslim, was by far the most tolerant. To Kenelm Jane could unburden herself of all that she had been forced to keep bottled up: her love for Medjuel, his noble character and her fascinating life among the Bedouins. Kenelm made all the right responses, and these were the most comforting few days Jane spent in Ernstein Villa.

As soon as Kenelm left Tunbridge Wells the gloom descended again. Steely's bigotry and Lady Andover's martyrdom were minor worries compared to those that beset Jane from abroad. There was still no word from Medjuel, and what mail did arrive was extremely depressing. Baron von Venningen wrote that their daughter Bertha, who had been showing signs of mental illness for several years, was steadily growing worse. The day after she received this report from Karl two more disturbing letters arrived: a pathetic one from Bertha herself, begging her mother to come take her to Syria to live, and a message from Cristos that Eirini had died. Jane's reaction to these letters revealed that she was not unaware of her shortcomings as a mother:

> I received the melancholy news that poor Eirini expired the day after I left Athens.... May the Lord have mercy on the poor child's soul. Where I do take an interest in children I have been unfortunate, witness my own Leonidas and poor Eirini.... Read Bertha's letter which made me most uncomfortable thinking my own early neglect of her is in part the cause of her unhappy state of mind. The scorpion's sting is like the sting of conscience.

Jane was willing to shoulder part of the blame for Bertha's mental state, but she attributed some of her daughter's problems to what she considered the unhealthy influences of Karl's implacable mother and sister Mimi:

> Wrote to poor Bertha and the Baron on her subject. To her I wrote to say that I was married and that the East was no place for her, and to him I wrote at length about her, advising him to see Dr. C., and if necessary suggesting that she should come to England. I would help in the arrangements. Her last letter grieved me, for I see all old Madame de V.'s spirit breathing in it and Mimi Waldkirchen's strange and wrong ideas.

"Poor Bertha," barely in her twenties, never got to England; she died soon after in a Munich asylum. Her brother Heribert, however, was from all accounts a normal, well-adjusted young man, serving in 1857 as an officer in the Austrian army. From this period until Jane's death he kept up a loving correspondence with the elusive mother he had not seen since he was a very small boy.

Overwhelmed by all the bad news, Jane was not reluctant to leave Tunbridge Wells for London, where she planned to spend several weeks. The altered appearance of the city she had once found so gay and exciting shocked her nearly as much as had the changes in her mother and Steely. In the mid-nineteenth century Great Britain was queen of the seas, and London was the world's financial capital, but the industrial revolution had spawned a cruel new kind of poverty. Jane was horrified by the slums, especially Wapping, a seething mass of human misery that stretched back from the London docks. She had seen plenty of poverty in Damascus, but there was something infinitely sadder about this grim, grey existence, which the novels of Charles Dickens were beginning to bring to the attention of the English upper classes. London was not made more appealing by the chilly dampness of late February, and Jane longed for the warmth of the desert sun. Occasionally, over the traffic sounds of the city she found herself listening for the muezzin's call to prayer from a distant mosque. How could she have once believed that this drab and dreary place was the center of the universe?

London society as Jane had known it no longer existed, but that was of little consequence now to the former belle of Almack's. Her presence in England was a secret well kept from all but her family and a few close friends, as no one wished to have the nearly forgotten scandals revived in the press. Jane's first husband was now Earl Ellenborough, a respected senior statesman who had served Queen Victoria as governor-general of India and First Lord of the Admiralty. It would have been unkind to Edward to open old wounds, and Jane was determined to avoid attracting any undue attention.

Only once during her stay did she attend a public function. A trip to London in 1857 would have been incomplete without seeing Louis Antoine Jullien, the French conductor who brought a touch of P. T. Barnum to concert music. Friends assured Jane that she could be perfectly anonymous at a Jullien concert, where all eyes would be glued to the star performer. Jullien was famous for his imposing side whiskers, his gaudy waistcoats and cravats, for the crimson and gold platform from which he conducted and the gold and white armchair into which he would sink exhausted after each performance. When a Beethoven composition was played, the great showman used a special jeweled baton brought to him ceremoniously on a silver tray. During his "Fireman's Quadrille" the ceiling seemed to burst into flames, and real firemen in full regalia came charging down the aisles while women fainted. It was no wonder that the presence in the audience of the notorious former Lady Ellenborough went unnoticed.

Most of Jane's time in London was spent taking care of business affairs, stocking up on items that were unavailable in Damascus, and receiving the few visitors who knew she was in the city. She was delighted to see Captain Drummond, her old friend from Athens days, who had just been named Naval aide-de-camp to Queen Victoria for his distinguished service in the Black Sea during the Crimean War. They reminisced over the gay parties in Jane's house on Hodos

Sokrotous, and Drummond was enthusiastic about Jane's new life in Syria. He promised to come to Damascus to meet Medjuel the next time he was on duty with the Mediterranean fleet, a promise he later kept.

Another welcome visitor in London was Jane's cousin, Fanny Anson Isted. "Dear, kind, warm-hearted Fanny," as Jane described her, was as uncritical of Jane's unusual marriage as Kenelm and Captain Drummond had been. Fanny knew well what it meant to have a family firmly opposed to the man of one's choice. In her teens she had fallen in love with a childhood friend, Ambrose Isted, who was deaf and dumb. The Ansons objected to the match, and Fanny, considerably more docile than Jane, had given up Ambrose to marry a man her family selected for her. One sacrifice led to another, for her husband soon became a chronic invalid, and Fanny had spent years nursing him. After his death she was finally free to marry her real love. From Fanny Jane heard news of Gen. George Anson, who was then commander-general of the Army in India. Months later Jane learned that her handsome Almack's dancing partner died of cholera on May 27, on his way to retake Delhi from the Indian mutineers.

Both Kenelm and Edward Digby came to London to see their sister again. This time Kenelm brought Caroline, who had been unable to make the earlier trip to Tunbridge Wells. Jane and Caroline formed a close friendship immediately. Despite their vastly different personalities and situations, the two women discovered they had many common interests. Caroline was as avid a reader as Jane, and she was able to bring her sister-in-law up to date on the contemporary London literary scene. They had lengthy discussions about the Brownings, the Carlyles, Dickens, Thackeray, Trollope and Tennyson. Throughout their long and intimate correspondence, which began with this meeting, Caroline recommended books, which Jane would order from Mudie's lending library.

By April 1, all the shopping had been done and business taken care of, and Jane left London for Tunbridge Wells to spend her last few days in England with her mother. Jane's fiftieth birthday arrived on April 3. "Fifty! *Triste* and melancholy anniversary," she wrote. "All the romance and poetry in life ought to be long since past and over, and here I am still with a beating and burning heart. . . ." Victorian England was a stifling place for Jane, who was more than ready to leave for the desert when finally she kissed Lady Andover goodbye. To her mother's parting words that it was a shame to miss the Varsity Boat Race, Jane felt totally incapable of a reply.

On April 6 Jane embarked for Calais, accompanied by a staggering amount of luggage, including a flock of Norfolk turkeys for Medjuel. In a few, frenzied shopping days in Paris she accumulated a piano, numerous bolts of fabric, painting and sketching materials, a copy of Flaubert's just-published *Madame Bovary*, and a small arsenal of arms for her Bedouins. The piano could not be crated in time to take with her, and she arranged for it to be shipped on a later boat. Before Jane sailed from Marseilles on April 13, 1857, she wrote a brief note to her mother that was both a farewell and a benediction:

I would gladly be as you are, but I cannot change my nature. I am different. How different I had hardly realized.... I regret much of the past, but over the future I feel sanguine.

Jane had made her peace. She was certain she would never see her mother or England again. She was aching for Medjuel and the desert, where now more than ever she knew she belonged.

16

The Sitt Mesrab at Home

*Then a horror of the common groove, of the
cab-shafts of civilization, of the contamination
of cities, of the vulgarities of life, takes hold of
me, and I yearn for the desert to recover the
purity of my mind and the dignity of human
nature . . . to be regenerated amongst the
Arabs.*

—ISABEL BURTON

Beirut with its apricot-colored shoreline had never looked so beautiful to Jane as
it did at the end of April 1857. Its particular enchantment this time had little to
do with the season or the landscape—it was close to home and to her husband.
Before Jane could leave Beirut, however, there were the usual financial matters
to be taken care of with Mr. Heald at the Imperial Ottoman Bank, and arrangements to be made for the overland journey. These delays made her all the more
impatient for her reunion with Medjuel, and it was small comfort that waiting in
Beirut was far more comfortable than it had been when Jane first came to Syria.
Nicholas Bassoul, who had served as dragoman to the English traveler writer
Eliot Warburton, had recently opened the Grand Hotel Bassoul, a handsome
nineteenth-century example of Turkish architecture with gardens stretching
down to the sea. (Its gardens have long since been amputated, but the hotel is
still operating today.) One of Bassoul's guests in 1857 was Herman Melville,
but if his visit coincided with Jane's that April, she was too preoccupied to meet
the American author.

The moment that her business in the port city was completed, Jane took off as
if pursued by demons. The drivers of her hired omnibus were promised a bonus
for a fast ride, and they took the winding steep ascent to the top of the Lebanon
range at a reckless speed. For several hours every turn of the road gave a
magnificent and ever-diminishing view of Beirut and the sea, but Jane was not
interested in looking back. She rode through the darkness without a halt—over
the Lebanon peaks and across the valley of Beka'a, ignoring the usual halfway
stop at Chtaura. There was another winding ascent in the Anti-Lebanon range to
the plain called in Arabic El Sahara. Then the party passed through a gorge cleft

187

by the sparkling Barada River, and finally the gleaming gold and white city in its green jewel case spread out at her feet. This was one reunion that lived up to all Jane's romantic expectations. "With beating heart I arrived at Damascus," she recorded. "He arrived, Medjuel, the dear, the adored one, and in that moment of happiness I forgot all else."

Assured now of Medjuel's affection and certain that the West held no more attraction to her, Jane began to pour all her energy and financial resources into her new life. She and Medjuel agreed that they would spend part of each year in the desert with his tribe and the rest in semi-European style in Damascus. Creating a house that would accommodate both their tastes was a labor of love for Jane. Descriptions of her Damascus residence suggest that, rather than building from the ground up, she took an existing structure and added a second story. The ground floor of the house was pure Arabic with three wings enclosing a large courtyard. In the middle of the center wing was a *liwan*, or indoor-outdoor sitting room with one side open to the courtyard, furnished with traditional divans and oriental carpets. The windows of the house were masked with the magnificently carved wooden screens known as *mashrabiyas*, which created fascinating patterns of light and shadow on the walls and floors. Over the center wing were two bedrooms, another *liwan* and, overlooking the English garden behind the house, a very non-Arabic drawing room furnished in the expensively cluttered style of the great houses of Europe with gilt cornices and ceiling, walls inlaid with mirrors, and windows draped with heavy damask. Into this room went Jane's precious piano, when it arrived from Paris. Here also were her crowded bookshelves, her easel and her writing desk.

The walls were hung with Jane's paintings from her travels, which, like her books, multiplied year by year. A young English traveler, Barty Mitford (later Lord Redesdale), who called on Jane in 1871, noticed that "her tables were covered with miniatures, knick-knacks and ornaments indigenous to Mayfair— quite out of tune with Damascus." One of the most valuable ornaments in Jane's drawing room, however, was Arab—and priceless. This was a lamp from the Great Mosque at Mecca, on a pane of which the sultan had scratched his seal—the symbol of Allah—as a token of his esteem. The entire house had a fascinating duality reflecting its unusual occupants—half English, half Arab.

Isabel Burton gave her English readers a picture of Jane's home as it appeared in 1870:

The house is made noticeable by its projecting balcony-like windows and coloured glass. We come to a large wooden gateway, and are received by twenty or thirty Bedawin of the tribe of Mesrab, lounging in the archway, and a large Kurdish dog, which knows his friends and will let me pass. This tenement is in the form of a three-sided square. Downstairs a reception-room is hung with arms and trophies; on the right hand are the stables. The court presents a picturesque appearance, with the thoroughbreds tethered here and there to the trees, eating piles of cut grass. A fountain plays in the middle. On the other side is the reception-house for any of the tribe who happen to come into town; also the bath-house, the conservatory, and the house and play-ground for the fowls, amongst which we find curious snow-white geese with curling feathers, turkeys, ducks, poultry, pigeons, guinea hens, and other pets. The whole is fronted and sur-rounded by a choice flower-garden. Upstairs is a suite of apartments which is elegance itself. Family and home treasures, and little reminiscences of European life, old china and paintings, are mingled with Oriental luxury, whose very atmosphere bespeaks refinement.

The Mesrab menagerie was unequaled in Damascus. Lady Burton did not enumerate among Jane's "other pets" her countless dogs and cats, gazelles, partridges, turtle-doves, falcons, and a tame pelican, which was as famous in Damascus as its owner. Medjuel bred Arab horses, and for these Jane built magnificent stables on the order of those at Holkham Hall. The "Babelar confu-sion" all these animals created in the courtyard when a caravan was preparing to set out from the Mesrab house was described by Emily Beaufort (Viscountess Strangford), whose party Medjuel escorted to Palmyra:

Eleven dromedaries were on their knees, all roaring and growling and groaning, as if they were being killed, after the manner of dromedaries the moment they are requested to kneel and the whole time they are kneeling; all the camel-drivers and armed escort rushing about screaming and shouting—flocks of poultry at one side shrieking, gabbling and cackling—pet gazelles were hiding in a corner—and a number of beautiful Arab mares were standing transfixed with astonish-ment at the unwonted crowd and noise.

Jane also managed to create one of the most beautiful gardens in a city famous for its gardens. This hobby of Jane's bewildered Medjuel, to whom plants and shrubs were merely fodder. But it was her money, and he was uncon-cerned if she wanted to throw it away importing rare plants from all over the world and fruit trees that bore fruit never seen before in Syria. Medjuel was willing to concede that the tall trees and flowering shrubs screening their house from the outside world served a useful purpose, but he was amused that his wife could devote so much time and thought to designing a lily pond, and the English-style gardens with their herbaceous borders, dahlias, Sweet William and candy-tuft were beyond his comprehension. Undaunted, Jane continued to make such entries in her detailed household account book as the following:

1 pot yellow narcissus
40 poles for dahlias
repairing garden drains
6 *jours travail* in garden
nails and wood for trellises

roots and seeds for garden
wire frames for dahlias
stocks and carnations
tulips (white and gold)
4 pots *fleurs très grandes*
10 wire frames for greenhouse

Although everyone in Damascus was familiar with Jane and Medjuel's house during the years it served as headquarters for the Mesrab tribe, its exact location is a puzzle. All that is known is that it was a short distance outside the Damascus walls and that it is no longer standing. In Jane's will the house is described as "situated near the Bab Menzel Khassabb." Lady Strangford placed it "outside one of the gates of the city—the Bab Tuma," and Lady Burton wrote of approaching it from yet another gate—the Bab Faradis.

Jane's drawing room, stables and gardens were among the few concessions she made to her English heritage once she decided to adopt the ways of her husband's people and become, as Isabel Burton described her, "more Bedawi than the Bedawi themselves." In some respects the transition was accomplished with ease, for her new life offered all the excitement and adventure she required. In the desert Jane had room to stretch her remarkable stamina and courage to their limits and still find new challenges each day. It did not take her long to discover that a camel race with a Sheik was far more stimulating than a polka with a king. Although a desert hunt bore little resemblance to the *battues* of her Holkham Hall days, there were red-legged partridges, woodcocks, quail, snipes, wild ducks and hares within an hour's ride of Damascus, and Jane astonished the Bedouins with her shooting skill. She impressed them even more by her healing touch with sick or wounded animals.

In deference to an Arab superstition which held that fair hair attracted the Evil Eye, Jane dyed her "crowning glory" jet black and wore it in two plaits that reached almost to her feet. In the wilderness Jane usually dressed in the long, dark blue cotton "Jericho" gown of the tribeswomen, fastened with a cord around the waist; the pointed sleeves, which nearly touched the ground when loose, were tied together behind the waist when the women were working. On her arms Jane, who owned magnificent emeralds and other valuable jewelry, wore the inexpensive Bedouin bangle bracelets, and her head was covered with the traditional dark kerchief.

In time Jane managed to toughen her feet so that she could go barefoot as did the other women in the desert, but she drew the line at the blue facial tattoos which some Bedouins considered a mark of beauty. Dressing and riding like a desert nomad came naturally to Jane, but some of the tasks performed by Bedouin wives involved more of a challenge for a woman who was accustomed to a staff of servants and a personal maid. Nonetheless, she learned to milk the camels, prepare Medjuel's food, stand and wait on him while he ate, wash his hands, hair, face and feet, "glorying in doing so." While the tribe was in the desert, the only distinction made between Jane and the other women was that she was entitled to ride the finest mares while they were mounted on camels or dromedaries. When it was necessary to ride a dromedary, Jane could manage the swiftest with the ease of a man.

A vivid picture of Jane Digby el Mesrab among her Bedouins appears in A. M. W. Stirling's biography of Coke of Norfolk:

> An English lady, who procured an introduction to her, relates how she met her, swathed in a veil and Arab garments, and riding at the head of a cavalcade of wild Arabs—a veritable Queen of Banditti—in surroundings which rendered her gracious, courteous manners, her air of *grande dame* and her sweet low voice more singularly impressive, even though her beauty—all but her glorious eyes— was scrupulously concealed from view. And still her thoughts turned to the life from which she was severed; all her questions were of Holkham Hall, of the relations whom she was fated never again to see. Yet in her strange dual exis- tence she stated that she found a freedom which she loved.

Despite that freedom, there was a side to being a Bedouin wife to which Jane was never able to adjust. Very shortly after she returned from England her husband was called into the desert to investigate rumors of a new war between the Anazeh and the Shammar tribes. Coming so soon after their ecstatic reunion, this separation sent Jane into a complete decline. She worried, wept, fretted and wrote agonizing letters to Medjuel day and night. Her behavior utterly bewil- dered the other Mesrab women, who looked upon desert warfare as a common occurrence and went about business as usual. Jane in turn found their calm, fatalistic acceptance infuriating.

Filled with "triste forebodings," Jane wrote in her journal, "War, oh God, can it be War?" Where was Medjuel and why had he not sent for her as he promised? Was he lying dead in the desert? It was several years before Jane realized that war in the desert was a far less terrible thing than it was in the "civilized" countries, that it was, as E. M. Oddie puts it:

> ...a gentlemanly business, where the property of the enemy, and not his person, was the object of the fight. Killing on a large scale was unknown. The extreme penalty of defeat meant the loss of flocks, herd, tents, tent furniture and mares. Deaths were mainly accidental, though sometimes particularly fiery youths might get in the way of an enemy's lance. The reason why life was so seldom lost in war was partly because firearms were then almost unknown in the desert, and partly because there was a custom of claiming damages for each death at the conclusion of the peace. A tribe which had killed fifty or sixty men would have to pay a heavy ransom at the end of the war. The accounts were settled immedi- ately after the peace, and the *hak el dam* (blood money) was paid in camels, fifty for each death.

Jane found in time that these intertribal skirmishes made life worthwhile for the Bedouin men, who looked upon them as invigorating interludes in an otherwise dull seasonal round. On that first occasion, however, the eighteen days Medjuel was away seemed more like eighteen years, as Jane poured all her tortured feelings into her journal:

> How much is my grief enhanced by the sad thought that I was not very kind to him sometimes! Not attentive enough to his wishes in *little* things, such as not keeping his hours, not washing his hair when he wished it, stingy in little trifles, sometimes irritable and impatient and he is so kind and patient with me! Oh, what would I not now give to see him! And when will this be granted? When? Oh when? Oh, if ever granted that I see him again how differently (with the grace of God) will I behave to him I so really love.

Jane remembered one domestic rift when she had been entirely in the wrong: "My bad temper and bad humor got the better of me and I picked a quarrel with dear Medjuel who was really offended and hurt by my unreasonableness. A sweet reconciliation afterwards took place between us, but I must not trifle with his character!" She bemoaned the fact that she was not as young and beautiful for Medjuel as she had been for the other men in her life. Suppose he were now lying wounded with no one to nurse him. Suppose—even worse—that another woman was nursing him, a lovely young woman of his own race.

On the seventeenth day after Medjuel's departure, a tribesman brought the news to Jane that her husband was safe and on his way back to her. The following morning Medjuel arrived at a gallop and put all her fears to rest by being more loving and tender than ever. ("Oh day of days! My cup of joy spilled over.") The next day Jane noted that her piano arrived from Paris, and she added a prayer that it would please Medjuel and not be a "snare" to her.

Less than a week after Medjuel's return he gave Jane convincing proof that she was at last a bona fide member of the Mesrab tribe. Three English explorers, identified in her journal as Messrs. Pennant, Raley and Radcliffe, arrived in Damascus en route to Palmyra, and Medjuel permitted Jane to make all the negotiations for the escort caravan. When the arrangements were completed, Medjuel rode ahead with half the tribe to prepare the way, and Jane herself conducted the party of Englishmen. This time there were no raids; these clients were treated by the Bedouins as salt-brothers. Jane's pride was boundless when, after an all-night ride through the desert, she brought her travelers within sight of the Grand Colonnade and discovered to her surprise and delight that Medjuel had arranged a fantasia to welcome them. The Englishmen were completely charmed by this rousing reception enacted against the spectacular backdrop of Zenobia's ancient city.

This was the first of many tours Jane and Medjuel led together. If the Bedouin had had any doubts about his English wife's ability to withstand the hardships of life in the wilderness, they were banished now. Like her fictional counterpart, Balzac's Lady Arabella Dudley, Jane had a "constitution of iron." However, she did not attempt the long winter treks (sometimes covering 2000 miles) with her husband's tribe, and Medjuel, little as he cared for city life, usually spent these months in Damascus with her. With the arrival of the first frost in November, the rest of the Mesrabs headed south into the desert with their pots and pans, water skins and other supplies. By December not a camel was seen in the north. These important animals could tolerate cold weather well enough, but they were close grazers; when the aromatic desert shrubs began to lose their leaves, it was time to go where the evergreen shrubs grew. By the middle of April, when the sun was strong enough to scorch the desert grass and the rain pools were drying up, the Mesrabs were back at Homs, where Medjuel and Jane joined them. May was sheep-shearing time, just as July had been at Holkham, and it was also the month when the young camels and colts were sold in the neighboring towns. Jane was an exceptionally good judge of animal flesh—a talent she had begun to acquire during her Norfolk childhood—and the Bedouins of Medjuel's tribe were astounded to discover that their blue-eyed *Umm-el-Laban* was a shrewd trader. It was not long before they came to rely heavily upon the Sitt's opinion in these financial matters.

With only a handful of Europeans in Damascus, and Medjuel's tribe controlling the route to Palmyra, it was natural that nearly every foreign traveler of that period came to meet Jane Digby el Mesrab. In 1859 a party of intrepid tourists who found themselves together at Dimitri's Hotel decided to attempt the difficult journey to Tadmor to see the ruins of Zenobia's capital. Two of the tourists, Emily Beaufort (Lady Strangford) and her sister, had nearly given up the very costly project when they discovered that others among Dimitri's guests had the same ambition. After seeing a portfolio of drawings from Palmyra belonging to a Damascus missionary named Mr. Robson, one of the guests, the well-known painter Carl Haag, told Lady Strangford, "If I am a ruined man all my life, or if I walk there in Bedoueen sandals, I *must* go to Palmyra!" His enthusiasm fired the rest of the group, and the Robsons took them to call on Medjuel to see what might be arranged. Haag's promise to make Palmyra world-famous with his drawings impressed the Mesrabs so much that they offered a bargain rate per head, provided everyone in the hotel joined in. On Friday, October 7, 1859, the caravan set out in high spirits, and, according to Lady Strangford's account, the ancient city lived up to all expectations. There was a large encampment of Anazeh Bedouins at the ruins, which insured the party's safety, so the travelers were fortunate enough to have a leisurely five days at Palmyra instead of the frantic few hours that Jane had had on her first trip there. This episode appears in Emily Beaufort's *Egyptian Sepulchres and Syrian Shrines*, but the author, who became a close and loyal friend of Jane, scrupulously avoided in her book any mention of Medjuel's wife, for fear of causing the old scandals to be dredged up. She did not hesitate, on the other hand, to express in print her admiration for

Sheik Medjuel el Mesrab, and this tribute Jane's brother, Lord Digby, found so touching that he wrote Lady Strangford a letter of thanks.

Carl Haag was not so generous. A native of Bavaria who became a naturalized English citizen, Haag owed his reputation to the patronage of Queen Victoria, who had permitted him to paint her portrait as well as those of Prince Albert and the royal children. In retrospect he appears to have been a better promoter of Carl Haag than a painter, but Jane was sufficiently impressed with his credentials to commission him to paint Medjuel's portrait. The Mesrabs also entertained Haag at their house in Homs and escorted him on a sketching tour in the desert. Some of the pictures Haag painted while in the company of the Mesrabs brought him considerable acclaim in London; a scene of Medjuel's tribe unfolding their black goathair tents, called "Preparing for Encampment," and his "Ruins of the Temple of the Sun at Palmyra" were particular favorites. Haag did not hesitate to advertise his friendship with the notorious Lady Ellenborough. Not satisfied with the facts of his brief acquaintance with Jane, Haag embellished it and in one instance, according to the memoirs of Sir Edwin Pears, claimed that he had been instrumental in bringing about the romance and marriage of Jane and her Bedouin Sheik, although they had been married four years when Haag met them! Eventually such self-serving visitors as Carl Haag caused the normally hospitable Madame Digby el Mesrab to avoid foreign tourists unless they bore letters of introduction from trusted friends or relatives.

One person in Damascus shared with Jane the dubious honor of being a major tourist attraction, but he did not inspire the unkind and highly colored anecdotes that sprang from the English lady's scandal-clouded past. Abel El Kader, hero of the Algerian struggle for independence from France, was the most respected man in the Muslim world. He had arrived in Damascus as an exile while Jane was away in England; upon her return, she and the Algerian refugee became devoted friends. Born the same year as Jane into an aristocratic family of *sherifs* (descendants of Mohammed), El Kader was educated in theology and philosophy. Although he had little military training he suddenly found himself thrust into the forefront of the Algerian resistance. After eluding the French for fifteen years, he was finally captured and imprisoned in the Château d'Amboise overlooking the Loire. The heroic stand of this Algerian had captured the imagination of all Europe, and Jane's old friend Lord Londonderry was finally able to negotiate with Louis Napoleon for the captive's release, provided El Kader would not return to his native land. Surrounded by 500 faithful Algerians, Abd El Kader lived in state in Damascus.

It is not surprising that Jane felt more comfortable in the company of El Kader than that of the Damascene Europeans, most of whom thought their English neighbor was, to say the least, a little eccentric in her enthusiasm for the Bedouins. The foreign colony of Damascus had a tendency to equate the entire native population with its house servants and could not understand why Jane would prefer to be called *Umm-el-Laban* rather than Lady Ellenborough.

(Queen Victoria's posthumous honor to Admiral Digby had also entitled his daughter to be known as the Honourable Jane Digby.)

There were among the Bedouins the normal percentage of unsavory characters. One of the most notorious of these was a brigand named Holo Pasha, whose frequent and successful raids caused much chaos among Anazeh tribes in the Euphrates valley, and it is not difficult to understand why this Bedouin outlaw happened to be on the payroll of the Turkish government. When the news of Holo Pasha's latest forays reached Medjuel in 1858, he was eager to join the fight, and this time he did not leave his wife behind. Unfortunately, the only record Jane left of this desert adventure was a complaint that each time she and Medjuel were certain the bandit was annihilated, he would prove them wrong by staging another raid.

On one occasion in 1859 Medjuel went off into the desert without Jane, and his long, unexplained absence almost cost him his wife. The Turkish pasha had offered him the governorship of Hama, and, wanting to make inquiries before he decided to accept the post, Medjuel left for Hama, expecting to return in a few days. Neither he nor Jane realized at the time that this offer was part of a deceptive government policy to put various towns under the protection of sheiks, who would inadvertently cause divided loyalties among the townspeople. For their favors, the Turkish officials were well paid in silver and horses, and the hapless sheiks would soon find themselves involved in bitter intertribal disputes.

The political machinations of the Turks, however, were the farthest thing from Jane's mind when Medjuel's absence stretched from days into weeks. Whenever her husband was out of her sight for any length of time, she began to brood and worry. Jane's bruising experience with Felix Schwarzenberg had taught her that disenchanted lovers did not always spell out their last farewells, and the experience had left her with a nagging feeling of insecurity. In this feverish state she resembled the lovelorn Arab woman in a Bedouin poem she often heard sung around the campfires:

> The eyes—O Allah!—longing after him,
> Full of sorrow—my heart after him,
> Accursed be the sleep of my eyes after him;
> He fled, and left me no happiness.

Jane tried to make arrangements to join Medjuel but discovered that he was no longer at Hama, and no one could or would tell her where he was. With mounting panic Jane went from one Mesrab tribesman to another seeking information, until she found one whose words horrified her. The Sheik had another wife in the wilderness, this Bedouin told her matter-of-factly, and it was unreasonable of the Sitt to expect him back so soon.

In an agony of despair Jane went to the wife of another Sheik, a woman named Fatima, with whom she had been friendly, and begged her to tell the truth of the matter. Fatima did her utmost to convince the distraught wife that her informant had lied, but her doubts remained. Every day for the next three weeks she rode to the edge of the desert, scanning the horizon, and as each day passed she tortured herself with the thought that if Medjuel had really taken another wife, under the terms of their marriage pact he had agreed to behave in precisely this manner.

During these black days Jane could neither paint nor read to pass the time. Medjuel's relatives came in a body to vow that he had only one wife, their beloved Sitt, but even they could not explain his silence or tell her where he was. The mail from England was not very cheering either. From Fanny Isted came news of the tragic death of Gen. George Anson's widow. The unfortunate lady was a guest of the Isteds and was dressing for a ball at Lord Howe's when she mistook a bottle of laudanum for her tonic and drank a fatal dose. Realizing her error immediately, she rushed down to the drawing room in her negligee and told the Isteds what had happened. A doctor was sent for, but it was too late to counteract the drug. In her letter to Jane Fanny gave a vivid account of walking Isabella Anson up and down trying to keep her awake until her sister-in-law collapsed and died at her feet. All this Jane recorded in her journal, followed by a cryptic note of her own, "Oh, my past life!"

After two months without a word from her husband, Jane reached the break-ing point and announced to Medjuel's people that she would leave Syria alto-gether rather than be subjected to further humiliation and unhappiness. The Mesrab Bedouins were beside themselves; they had come to feel a deep affection for their blue-eyed *Engleysi* Sitt, even if she did make a fool of herself where Medjuel was concerned. Furthermore, Jane's generosity in providing them with the finest animals and the latest weapons had added enormous prestige to the small tribe. When their pleas failed to make any headway with Jane, they sent to Jerud for a close friend of Medjuel, Sheik Mohammed Dukhi of the Wuld Ali Bedouins. With the aid of a little benevolent Arab trickery, the Sheik was able to persuade Jane that she had been tearing her heart out for nothing. He had a message delivered, explaining that Medjuel had been delayed in the desert by the illness of a blood mare. With her passion for horses and her knowledge of their value to the Arabs, this was one excuse Jane could accept. But then a mixup occurred that was highly amusing to everyone but the intended beneficiary of Mohammed's scheme. Another messenger arrived, this one telling Jane that Medjuel was looking for stray sheep. At this explanation the lady became furi-ous, and Eugènie got orders to start packing her mistress' trunks. "Looking for sheep!" she wrote in an angry scrawl, "While I—I who gave him the sheep am here in a furnace of grief and desolation!"

In a last-ditch attempt to delay the flight of his friend's wife, Sheik Mohammed Dukhi urged Jane to remain at Homs for a festival at the little school attended by children of the Mesrab tribe. The school was a project to which Jane had devoted time and money, even teaching classes in the alphabet herself, and she could not refuse this request. She and Mohammed Dukhi were joined at the party by another Sheik, Fares ibn Meziad. Jane's journal describes how the two Sheiks tried with little success to cheer her as they sat under the olive trees watching the schoolchildren playing. Fares was in the midst of telling her fortune with pebbles when a Bedouin galloped up bringing a letter from Medjuel himself.

> A letter from Medjuel! Oh what a moment! And that he was coming in a few hours. I nearly fainted. Then rose, mounted the Saklowyeh [a thoroughbred Arab mare], and rode to the dear Ras el Ain to meet him, the adored, the lost one! Oh God, what shall I render thee for all thy benefits! Oh what a moment of joy was our meeting! What ecstasies of unreserved happiness! We walked together to the Ras el Ain. Oh, what sweet explanations and doing away with all doubts and jealous fears!

Whatever Medjuel told Jane, it was enough to satisfy her completely from the day they met at the fountain on the northern edge of the desert until the next time he exercised his Bedouin independence and rode off without her. Their reunion at Ras el Ain was followed by an idyllic journey together through the valley of the Khabur, a blissful three weeks, before they returned to Damascus. Stories of another wife in the wilderness continued to plague Jane from time to time throughout her life with Medjuel, sending her into new agonies of jealousy and despair, but these black periods were invariably followed by tender reconciliations. She appears to have thrived on these jarring emotional peaks and valleys, and Medjuel, whether by careful design or simply by being his Bedouin self, held the key to Jane as no other man had done.

17

Massacre in Damascus

Damascus is the mole on the cheek of Beauty—
The plumage of the Peacock of Paradise—
The brilliant collar of the Ring-Dove—
The diadem of Allah.

—UNKNOWN ARAB POET

During the sizzling summer of 1860, the country Jane Digby loved so well erupted into a blazing inferno, when 6000 of its Christian inhabitants were cruelly massacred. The grim calendar of events began in the winter of 1859 when bitter cold, snow and sleet brought havoc to Syria, and the misery was compounded by the disastrous spring floods that followed. The wheat was ruined, the olives were blighted, and many Syrians were driven to a starvation diet of grass and shrubs. Famine was still rampant a year later when spring 1860 brought a plague of worms to decimate the desperately needed food crops and bankrupt the silk-growers. Hunger and poverty created a perfect breeding ground for violence, and the laissez-faire policy of the Turks allowed that violence a free rein.

In May of 1860 three men were robbed and murdered at the bridge across the river Owaleh near the ancient town of Sidon. The victims were Druses, members of that strange sect whose esoteric religion was neither Christian nor Muslim. Earlier in the nineteenth century the consummate English eccentric, Lady Hester Stanhope, had lived in bizarre splendor among the Druses of this area and had wielded almost absolute authority over them. But their unusual high priestess had died in 1839, and no one had the power now to prevent the Druses from turning their revenge into a blood bath. To even the score for the deaths at Owaleh a band of Druses killed four Christians from a nearby Maronite settlement. Counter-reprisal led to counter-reprisal in rapid succession until one Sunday in Beirut a barrage of gunfire shattered the early morning stillness and signalled a full-scale Druse uprising. Christians of all denominations and all ages were dragged from their homes and places of worship and slaughtered indiscriminately. Within a week the carnage spread to outlying districts and whole villages were in flames. By the end of June Jane knew she was in serious danger; a week before the flames engulfed her beloved city she wrote: "The Druses and Christians are fighting dreadfully. Should war really break out in Damascus, may strength and faith be given to us who trust in the Lord who is stronger than all evil-doers."

As the tension in Damascus was increasing daily, Medjuel received an urgent summons to Homs, where his first wife was dying, but he was too concerned for Jane's safety to leave her. Two days later his favorite son, Schebibb, arrived to announce his mother's death. Momentarily Jane forgot that her own life was in jeopardy and she began to brood about the dead woman. "Her death does not mitigate my sin in having been the prime cause of Medjuel putting aside the wife of his youth," she wrote. "Plain, accusing words!" Such guilty reflections were violently disrupted when the blood bath came to Damascus.

For several days cryptic symbols had been scrawled on the walls of the Christian quarter and wooden crosses were found trampled in the streets. Numerous complaints were made to the Turkish authorities, but for quite some time they refused to take action. Finally, when they did act, the results were cataclysmic. Early in the morning of July 9 three Muslim youths were seized by the police for some act of vandalism and taken before a magistrate; they were chained together and sentenced to sweep the streets in the Christian quarter, where their offense had been committed. As the young prisoners were herded through the crowded bazaars, excitement and anger mounted among the Muslim population. By the time the prisoners passed before the great Umayyad mosque, all the surrounding shops had been closed. Two merchants suddenly emerged from the mosque and shouted, *"Deen! Deen! Deen Mohammed!"* ("The law! The law! The law of Mohammed!") The battle cry spread like wildfire from street to street, and within minutes an infuriated mob, armed with guns, swords, axes and sticks, was racing toward the Christian quarter. When a fire broke out near the Greek Orthodox church, the Muslim rabble took this as a sign that the quarter was to be burned, and by sunset of that day it was a sea of flames.

When the first news of the rioting reached Abd el Kader that morning, the famous exile and his faithful Algerian bodyguard rushed out into the streets to rescue every Christian they could find. After leading hundreds of them to his well-fortified house, the Muslim hero remained at his gate all night so he would not fail to hear anyone who knocked for refuge. El Kader was unable to stop the carnage, but he saved countless lives, including those of several foreign diplomats. All the consulates of Christian countries were burned to the ground except that of England, which the Turks scrupulously guarded out of deference to their old allies in the Crimean War. The Dutch consul was slain in the streets; the American consul, though severely wounded, was one of those fortunate enough to reach safety with Abd el Kader. One diplomat who showed a certain style in the face of death was the Greek consul, who retreated to the flat roof of his house with a gun, several rounds of ammunition and a bottle of *raki*. Drinking and singing at the top of his voice, he picked off every aba-clad figure who approached his house from either direction until the pile of victims in the street caused would-be attackers to look for easier prey.

In the early stages of the Damascus uprising the main objective of the crowd was plunder, but events took a more ominous turn when the rioters were joined by hordes of wild Druses and Kurds, who swept into the city from the desert. The fame of Jane Digby el Mesrab and the high regard in which she was held in Syria were evident when many of these tribesmen, bent on slaughtering Christians, stopped at the Mesrab house on their way into the city to ask Medjuel if he needed help to protect his *Engleysi* wife. (The Bedouin knew the Druses and Kurds a little too well and, confident that he had enough well-armed and loyal members of his own tribe to defend his home, declined the offers.)

Once the Druses and Kurds were turned loose in the city, the horrors were increased tenfold. Christian females of all ages were ravished in the streets, surrounded by jeering spectators. Their husbands, fathers and brothers were forcibly circumcised and then put to the sword. Some few who agreed to accept the faith of Mohammed were spared, but many instant converts were slain regardless. Churches and convents, filled to suffocation with terrified refugees, were set afire and became human incinerators.

As Jane Digby el Mesrab stood on the roof of her house, watching the smoke rising from the heart of the old city and hearing the sounds of that night of terror, she decided that the time had come for her to make a stand for her Christian faith. She knew that Medjuel loved her and was prepared to defend her with his life if necessary, but she could not ask him to die for some anonymous *giaours*—Christian infidels. This responsibility was hers alone. As soon as daylight came Jane dressed in her Bedouin garments, covering her face with a *yashmak*, or veil, and in defiance of Medjuel's orders rode into the city, accompanied by a single terrified Arab servant who carried several leather water bottles and a basket of food and medicine.

The narrow alleys through which Jane rode were littered with corpses putrefying in the sweltering heat; roving bands of dogs feasted on the dead in bloodspattered scenes straight out of Hieronymus Bosch. There were few people alive in the streets, but for those few Jane did what she could. Aside from her eyewitness descriptions of the Christian quarter, Jane makes no mention of her role in that time of terror. However, Europeans who survived the massacre wrote home that the notorious Lady Ellenborough had risked her life by venturing out in the strife-torn city when she could have remained silent and safe under the protection of her Muslim husband. Word of this latest chapter in the life of Jane Digby eventually reached an old friend—the former king of Bavaria—and Ludwig wrote his son Otto, "What an excellent and brave act of this courageous woman!"

That was not the limit of Jane's role. When, later, she heard of El Kader's rescue operation, she offered to share the expense of feeding the homeless survivors. According to a contemporary account by Col. Charles Henry Churchill, nearly 12,000 refugees of all ages remained for several weeks in the Algerian's stronghold, lying on the bare ground, scantily clothed and exposed to the merciless July sun. These unfortunate people had to be fed, and even El Kader's bounty had its limits. According to the Oddie biography, Jane also gave sanctuary to a number of Christians who appeared at her door.

Jane's commitment had some unhappy consequences. In the five years of her marriage to Medjuel she had never made an issue of her religion; there had been no occasion for it. Now she had made their differences painfully clear, and—much worse—she had defied him. The result was their first real estrangement. Much as Medjuel admired her bravery, he regarded Jane's actions as an insult to him. He had made many concessions to his foreign wife, but there was no place in the world of Islam for independent-minded females. Muslim women were an unfit topic of conversation among most upper-class Arabs, and if a man was forced by circumstances to mention his wife, he apologized by saying *"Ajallak!"*—May God lift you up! (from the degradation of having to hear such a thing spoken"). The Arab men took very seriously the Prophet's declaration that "Men are superior to women on account of the qualities with which God hath gifted the one above the other." Medjuel had lived with Jane too long to believe that, but he had lost face with his people because of his wife's insubordination. As soon as the Damascus uprising subsided, Medjuel left for the desert alone, and he made it very plain that this was punishment for Jane's behavior.

News of the rupture in the Mesrab household reached Sheik Fares ibn Meziad, and the powerful leader of the Hesenneh tribe was delighted to hear of it. Employing the same tactics that had proved successful for El Barak when he acted as Jane's Baghdad guide, Fares waited to make his move until the Sitt Mesrab had passed several lonely and dejected weeks at Homs waiting for Medjuel's return. Then Fares sent his emissary, a tribesman named Schaoury, to present the Sheik's suit. Schaoury turned out to be an unfortunate choice as spokesman, however, because Jane found his manner "most disagreeable." She described her interview with him in her journal: "He spoke of Sheikh Fares' wish to marry me, and of Medjuel's indifference to me, or so it must appear to the world. And perhaps it is so! ... Thy sin shall find thee out." This time Jane did not let her misery overcome her judgment, and she sent the messenger back to Fares with a firm refusal. It was a wise decision—not long afterward Medjuel came back to her, and there was another of those wildly emotional reconciliations. Medjuel had cooled his anger in the desert and realized that the very things that often infuriated him about his English wife were the things that set her apart from every other woman he had known.

Once Medjuel accepted the idea that his wife was not willing under any circumstances to give up her religion, Jane was free to associate herself with the Christian church in Damascus as she had not done before. It was many months before the battered survivors of the great massacre had the courage and the means to return to any formal kind of worship, but when they did, there was a new member of the flock. Early in 1862 Jane attended her first mission service; it was conducted in Arabic by a Dr. Meschaka in a tiny, dimly lit room. Dressed as a Bedouin with most of her face covered by a *yashmak*, Jane took her place at the back and sat on her heels in the Bedouin fashion. She wrote afterward that she hardly understood any of the service because Dr. Meschaka's Arabic was "appalling" and his delivery was "indifferent and poor." The missionaries, who knew the few regular members of their congregation well, realized that the veiled lady at the back was a stranger—and obviously someone of importance. As she was leaving the service, two of the missionaries came to welcome her and were dumbfounded when she answered them in English, introducing herself as Madame Digby el Mesrab. The aristocratic lady asked many questions about the Damascus church and the progress in rebuilding after the tragedy of 1860. When she invited the missionaries to call on her, they accepted eagerly, and from their visits a very different side of life in Damascus began to open up for Jane. Until then her non-Arab acquaintances in the city had been limited to the consular set and a few other resident foreigners. It was ironic that the unconventional Jane should now find some of her closest friends among these hard-working, under-paid messengers of the Gospel, who had come to Syria for reasons so different from her own.

The week following her first contact with the Damascus missionaries Jane received welcome news from another man of the cloth—the Reverend Kenelm Digby. Her brother wrote that his daughter Emily had been married on January 23 to Edward North Buxton, and the young couple was en route to Syria on their wedding trip. During the last week in April the Buxtons arrived in Damascus, and Jane was delighted to have as her houseguests the only relatives who would ever come this great distance to see her. She loved her niece on sight and described Emmie as "charming and unaffected and a perfect lady in manner and mind." The Buxtons were disappointed not to meet their Bedouin uncle, who was at Homs during their brief visit (Jane had delayed her own departure for the desert to entertain the young couple in Damascus). But the newlyweds could not have found a better guide than their "Bedouin aunt" to show them the exotic city that the Arabs called *Shaum Sherif*—the Blessed Place.

For centuries travelers like the Buxtons have been mesmerized by the bazaars of Damascus, a fascinating maze of Eastern treasures, which in Jane's time stretched for a mile from Bab el Jabyah to Bab Sharki along the Suk et-Tawileh ("The Long Bazaar"). This exotic thoroughfare is mentioned in the Bible (Acts 9:11) when the Lord appeared in a vision to Ananias:

> And the Lord said unto him, Arise, and go into the street which is called Straight, and enquire in the house of Judas for one called Saul of Tarsus...

The "street called Straight" is such a labyrinth of peculiar angles and cluttered stalls that Mark Twain said the passage in Acts was "the only irony in the Bible." Nonetheless, the Buxtons found the street enchanting. Striped awnings and old carpets stretched from one building to another, forming a crazy patchwork ceiling overhead; they shaded the narrow street from the glaring sun and gave one the peculiar impression of being outdoors and indoors at the same time. Most of the shops were pigeonholes only six or eight feet square and stacked one atop another, the upper stories being accessible only by ladder. Although the front of each shop was gaily hung with shining brasses or brilliant bolts of Damascus silk, the rear was wrapped in impenetrable gloom. In each tiny emporium a merchant sat cross-legged all day, smoking his *narghile*, drinking coffee, and twirling his beads. A visitor's first impression of the bazaars was of the smell, which hung like smoke in the air—a strange blend of anise, coffee, cardomom, tobacco, pungent spices, and heavy perfume. Combined with all these was a vague odor of age and staleness and sometimes the stench that arose from the filth of the unswept streets.

The variety of merchandise staggered the imagination. There was the water pipe bazaar, displaying *narghile* bowls made of coconuts ornamented with gold and silver; the saddle bazaar with its magnificent brass- and silver-studded leather trappings; the silk bazaar with its bolts of flaming colors; other bazaars filled with exotic jewelry, brasses, marquetry, oriental carpets, clothing, shoes, spices—craftsmen and vendors of like merchandise clustered together in sections spilling over one into the next. Shopping in the Damascus bazaars was not an operation to be hurried through with English efficiency. When a merchant offered coffee to his customers, there was a ritual to be observed. It was not polite to discuss prices over coffee. The "wine of Arabia" was served in handleless cups scarcely larger than a walnut, set in holders of filigreed brass, silver or gold. It was thick and very sweet, and the sediment that filled a good third of the cup was never stirred. It was considered a sign of good breeding here to keep the lips from touching the cup and to suck up the liquid with a loud hissing noise. Only when this ceremony was finished could Jane negotiate for Emmie a pair of pointed-toe, lemon-colored slippers, as soft as kid gloves.

Everywhere the senses were assailed. Added to the sights and smells of the old quarter of Damascus was a ceaseless cacophony of sound. Each of the hawkers making his way through the bazaar employed an eloquent appeal to praise the virtues of his wares. The calls were usually rhyming and sung to a set tune. Often they included one of the ninety-nine sacred titles of Allah. Through the crowded streets went little boys with large trays of sweetmeats on their heads, men with tubs of pickled vegetables, peasants carrying heavy loads of fresh figs, water carriers stooping under the weight of their goatskin bottles, peddlers of cakes and nuts and sherbets and the nosegays that the Syrian gentleman loved to hold literally under his nose (and for good reason!) as he strolled through the streets. All of these were shouting their wares: "O, thirsty ones!" "O, father of a family!" "O, Thou who givest food!" "Allay the heat!" "Rest for the throat!" "Figs as white as jasmine! Fresh as the morning dew!" "Pomegranates for the newly weaned infant!" High above the other sounds could be heard the shrill, nasal song of the pastry vendor—*"Allah er-Razeek!"* ("God is the nourisher!")

—accompanied by the clink of brass bowls rattled against each other, announcing the lemonade sellers. Through the tumult would come periodically the thin, penetrating chant of the muezzin in his lofty minaret, reminding the busy Muslims of their religious obligations. With this the faithful would drop to their knees wherever they happened to be and pray aloud.

Emily and Edward Buxton were able to see Damascus as few travelers of their time saw it, and though they may have found it hard to understand their aunt's marriage to a Bedouin, they at least were convinced that she was entirely satisfied with the arrangement. On May 1, 1862, the Buxtons, loaded with their treasures from the bazaars, left for Beirut. Jane rode with them as far as the top of Mount Salihiyyah, where they had a farewell picnic together. Emmie, who, like her aunt, was a talented and enthusiastic painter, made a last sketch from this lookout point, and then they said their good-byes. The parting left Jane depressed:

> I felt inexpressibly sad as I gazed at her and after her. Ah, thought I, such was I too, once, long years ago, ere mad and sinful passions blighted my existence and cast their poisonous shade on that of others.... My dear and honoured parents, my fond brothers, and now what remains to me in life? My Bedouin husband, my dear and wonderful Medjuel, is fond, faithful and honourable as I could wish, and I am deeply attached to him. But oh, the difference in our religion is a bar to thorough and complete community between us.

The depression did not last. In a few days Jane joined Medjuel at Homs and found him preparing for an attack by Turkish soldiers. When excitement beckoned, regrets over the past were forgotten, everything was concentrated in the thrilling present. For Jane this was the greatest attraction of life in the desert—some matter of extreme urgency, some adventure always offered itself and freed her from the pain of looking backward or the uncertainty of looking forward. When she left Homs that night in May and rode into the desert beside her Bedouin Sheik, the present was all she could ever ask for.

18

A Jealous Wife

Sixty-two years of age, and an impetuous ro-
mantic girl of seventeen cannot exceed me in
ardent, passionate feelings!

—JANE DIGBY EL MESRAB

Desert warfare had become a stimulating sport for the Sitt Mesrab by the year 1862, and it was her money that equipped Medjuel's people to take on Turkish soldiers or rival tribes when the occasion demanded. The Earl of Ellenborough, who had borne "the white man's burden" as Her Majesty's Viceroy of India, would have been outraged to learn that a sizable percentage of the generous allowance he made his former wife was spent on arming a tribe of dark-skinned heathens. Fortunately Jane did not have to make him an accounting. She did, however, make one for herself. In June of 1861 Jane began a very detailed record of where her money went, writing in an outsize notebook (still in existence in Beirut), which she designated on the opening page "Damascus House Book & General Expenses, J. E. Digby el Mesrab." The book covers a ten-year period and reveals a surprisingly practical and efficient side of a person who was so often less than practical in other matters. Every piaster (less than five cents in contemporary American currency) is itemized, and, completely dwarfing the monthly sums paid to servants, the butcher and the baker (which seldom exceeded 500 piasters in all), are a number of strange entries, probably denoting purchases of arms and ammunition for the Mesrabs. They follow a similar pattern and are the only entries in the ledger not spelled out:

720 Bts 593	5000 piasters
02 enfs 2x593 oo	5000 piasters
720 Bts 593	6150 piasters
50 02 nfs 2x2 593 02	5850 piasters
02 enfs 2x2	4920 piasters

It seems likely that "Bts" meant bullets, and "enfs" stood for Enfield rifles. One or two of these entries appear on the ledger about every six months, always prior to Jane and Medjuel's departure for the desert. Smaller amounts were entered from time to time for gunpowder, cartridge belts and gun repair. In a pocket sketchbook where Jane made shopping lists for her trip to England in 1857, the following notation is found: "Adams' registered wadded bullets for revolvers, rifles, carbines, etc. Eley Bros. London. 50 conical, 54 bore." Later she apparently decided to be a little more discreet about such purchases.

Equipping the Mesrabs for desert battles cost considerably more than maintaining Jane's Damascus home, but the desert battles were far more entertaining than those among her household staff. When she and Medjuel returned from the wilderness in the summer of 1862, there was no peace to be found in their small corner of the Prophet's "Earthly Paradise"; their household was at war. The long-suffering Eugènie, who was always left behind to deal with the constant bickering and speedy turnover of the domestic servants, was threatening to leave Jane, because she claimed the job (for which she received her board and the princely sum of $10 a month) was too much for her delicate health. For a few days Jane did everything possible to pamper her maid, but then Eugènie made an impertinent remark and there was a bitter quarrel in which Jane opened up many old wounds: Eugènie had failed to report that she knew of Spiro Theotoky's infidelities; Eugènie had lied about the advances of Hadji-Petros. Eugènie had heard it all before. When the air cleared, she decided to stay on after all, and it could only have been because she could not bear to miss the next installment.

There is little question that Jane needed Eugènie. Sometimes in the face of a domestic crisis, the Englishwoman whose courage was legend would flee to her room and let her maid cope. On one occasion, after a particularly violent battle between the housekeeper and a gardener which ended with the housekeeper departing in a rage, Jane wrote in her diary, "Oh, may God in His great mercy direct Eugènie in the choice of a suitable and proper woman for this house! If He will, He can do all things!" Any housekeeper in this unusual establishment had an awesome task. There were more than 100 cats to be fed (each with its personal dish) besides a large staff, which included at one time or another, according to Jane's records, Bethel, Suzanne, Leilah, Fatima, Bijou, Miriam, Gabrielle, Maria Lou, Ismail, Georgie, Yusef, Afsaad, Nourah, Abdou, Abdullah, and Habib, as well as some temporary day laborers and an indeterminate number of men named Mohammed.

The Damascus account book is a complex mishmash of English, French and Arabic, but it gives a fascinating insight into Jane's life in Syria, covering a range of items from "calico for drawers" (20 piasters) to "one gazelle" (11 piasters). An Italian tailor named Giuseppi, who was paid substantial sums for making Jane's clothes, was finally put on a monthly retainer. The simple Bedouin attire that the Sitt Mesrab wore in the desert gave way in Damascus to European-style gowns of black and purple velvet, scarlet plaid and peacock blue damask, supported by crinoline petticoats and at least "one French corset." The limited menu of the campfire was replaced in the city by such items as artichokes, caviar, veal, lobster, sardines, calf's head, French ham, English mustard, Holland cheese, hot pickles, orange marmalade, sugarplums, special *gâteaux* for New Year's Day, chocolate bonbons, sherry, port, *raki*, beer, and absinthe.

To an unnamed "Américain" who found himself short, Jane once made a loan of 210 piasters. Her charities were entered according to their recipients: "poor leper," "poor Christian widow," "poor German," *"pauvre petit garçon,"* or simply assorted poor (*"pauvres divers"*). Scattered throughout the ledger are small cash gifts (*"cadeaux"*) for errands run or "work well done."

Jane did not count the cost when she bought things to beautify her home—a gold-leaf mirror, two gold-leaf *étagères* (shelves), eggshell china cups, "one large porcelain bowl with butterflies." The house was kept sparkling by frequent applications of whitewash (*"blanchissage"*), but Jane's own cosmetic needs appear to have been few and remarkably simple—cold cream, tooth tincture, kohl, almond soap, Jerusalem soap, hair oil and perfume. Medical expenses in the Mesrab household were almost nonexistent: three boxes of unidentified pills, one bottle of "cod oil," one jar of "ointment," a vaccination for Leilah and a veterinarian's bill.

Many purchases listed in the account book are for the desert—saddles for horses and camels, and luggage, including a large portmanteau—or for the house at Homs, which, though not so large or so luxurious as the Damascus house, was far from humble. (In Jane's sketchbook there is a drawing of the house, a two-story building with *mashrabiyas* at the windows, an outside stairway, and a balcony overlooking a patio with fountain, trellises and shrubs. A sketch of the interior shows a large, elaborately canopied bed.) Jane estimated the expenses for the tent she and Medjuel shared in the desert at 3000 Osman pounds, suggesting that even the primitive life was not so primitive as one might suppose. Changing times in Syria are revealed in a handful of items in the account book: Leilah's vaccination, three telegrams, a red flannel shirt for the gardener, and a bill for "photos." Miscellaneous entries cover a tapir for her "zoo," three parasols and two lottery tickets.

The only thing missing in the ledger is a record of the numerous bribes that someone in Jane's position must have paid on many occasions to various Turkish officials, for this was a necessity of life. She may have concealed this informal income tax under the categories of *cadeaux, pauvres divers,* or *bakshish.* There were times, however, when all the money at her disposal could not buy the government's cooperation. In the late summer of 1862 Medjuel was involved in a skirmish at Tadmor, and Jane learned to her distress that her husband had been arrested by the Turks. All her attempts at bribery through the usual channels failed to get Medjuel released, and she was forced to seek the aid of the British consul, who at that time was Edward Thomas Rogers. The Honourable Mrs. Digby el Mesrab was still considered by most foreigners in Damascus to be a bit eccentric, but she commanded respect, and Mr. Rogers did not dare turn his back on her. Through his negotiations Medjuel was freed. A year later the Bedouin stepped on some Turkish toes again, and the government considered another kind of punishment—denying him entry to either Damascus or Homs under penalty of arrest. Much as her Damascus home meant to Jane, she was fully prepared to go into exile in the desert with the man she loved. Again Mr. Rogers came to the rescue, and Jane joyfully recorded the "precious and unhoped for news" that Medjuel was to be given British protection in the two cities. Occasions such as these raised their *Umm el-Laban* to almost divine status among the Mesrabs.

None of Jane's connections in the West was quite ready to bestow divinity on her, but by this time they had decided that she had settled down, albeit in a somewhat peculiar manner. Through her extensive correspondence with family and friends, Jane was kept well abreast of events in the Western world. Late in 1862 she learned that the Greek army had revolted in October and finally forced King Otto and Queen Amalia to abdicate. Otto died four years later in obscurity, insofar as obscurity could be obtained by a person who insisted on wearing the Greek fustanella in Bavaria. Jane's mother and both brothers now corresponded with her regularly as did Karl and Heribert Venningen.

In 1863 the Baron wrote Jane that their son was engaged to marry the Countess Gabrielle Paumgarten, and the news delighted her. She knew the girl's family well. Gabrielle's mother, one of Lord Erskine's daughters who had befriended Jane in Munich, was married to Count Paumgarten in the same year Jane was married to Karl. The absentee mother wrote a note of congratulation to Heribert, promising him a "little *cadeau*" of a hundred pounds. Less than a week after this happy exchange of letters, however, Jane was plunged into the depths of despair. Lady Andover died on April 29, 1863, and the news came in a telegram from Steely: "Your dear mother has passed away very peacefully at Brighton." Even though Lady Andover was eighty-six and her death could hardly have been unexpected, Jane wept for days. She had lost the one person she could always turn to in time of trouble.

A year earlier Jane had cheerfully delayed her departure for the desert in order to meet the Buxtons. This time she remained in Damascus for a week after Medjuel's departure in order to cry out her tears and compose herself. When she arrived at Homs in the middle of May, she found that Medjuel and the tribe had already left there, and she hurried to catch up with them at Sahin el Asoud. For once the lovers' reunion was not up to standard—Jane was still depressed over her mother's death, and the day after she joined Medjuel, he fell seriously ill.

In the past the Sitt Mesrab with her knowledge of Western medicine had often functioned as the tribe's doctor, ministering to people and livestock alike. Now her skill failed her. She diagnosed Medjuel's illness as typhus after his temperature soared, but despite her treatment her husband continued to grow worse until he was completely delirious. Jane was terrified that he might have cholera, which was always a possibility in Syria. In desperation she finally allowed the Bedouins to practice their ancient remedies. Medjuel's people decided that their Sheik was suffering from *hubta*, a fairly common desert ailment characterized by severe pains in the spine and head and raging fever. The treatment they employed seemed more deadly to Jane than the illness. With a red-hot iron one of Medjuel's kinsmen burned four *misarmi* (brands) on the sick man's head. Jane was appalled at the hissing noise the iron made on her husband's flesh and could hardly bear to watch. Yet miraculously it worked—the Bedouin responded to Bedouin cure. He began to perspire profusely, and the fever was broken.

Aside from Medjuel's second brush with the Turks, which occurred shortly after his illness, Jane had what was for her a fairly uneventful year, and, back in Damascus, her household was running smoothly in the spring of 1864 when she entertained visitors from Bavaria. The Countess de Boury and her husband were touring the Holy Land, and they stayed with Jane for several days. The young Countess was a contemporary of Heribert Venningen and the daughter of another old Munich friend of Jane's, the Countess Lerchenfeld. The visit of the de Bourys was one of the rare occasions when the ageless English romantic was reminded of her years—incredible that her son was past thirty! Heribert, like his father, went in for long engagements, and he wrote his mother that before the wedding took place he planned to visit his fiancée's family in England. In her reply Jane urged him to call on his two Digby uncles, and at the same time she wrote to Edward and Kenelm to expect Heribert. (Jane appears to have remained on excellent terms with her brothers following her 1847 visit in England. Lady Theresa Digby wrote her frequently and in 1865 sent Jane a portrait of Edward.) Whether or not her son saw his English relatives Jane failed to record. At any rate, Heribert and Gabrielle were finally married in 1865, and Jane's first "official grandchild," Karl Venningen, was born January 15, 1866.

The birth of little Karl merited small notice in Jane's diary. She was far more excited over the news from England that one of Kenelm's boys had emigrated to Australia. "My Bedouin nephew Willy interests me most particularly," she wrote, "as his avocation and turn of mind are so closely akin to my own." (Jane was romanticizing here—Willy's trek was more likely prompted by his being one of nine children in a clergyman's family with no inheritance in sight.) Jane's lack of enthusiasm over her grandchild stemmed partly from the fact that time and distance had somewhat isolated Heribert from his mother. At this relatively settled stage of her life Jane might have enjoyed the role of exotic grandmother —if she could have fit it in between desert wars and passionate reunions. She did show affection for Arab children during her life in Syria. The boys and girls of the Mesrab tribe adored their *Umm-el-Laban*, and when a new baby arrived, the Sitt would be among the first to hold it and sing a desert lullaby that would have been singularly inappropriate for her own European grandchildren:

> Come, little Bedawy, sit on my lap,
> Pretty pearls shine on your little white cap.
>> Rings on your ears,
>> Rings in your nose,
>> Rings on your fingers,
>> And henna on your toes.

Jane's Damascus house was a paradise for all children, Bedouin or *Engleysi.* In the 1930s a Professor Crawford, the son of English missionaries to Syria and then a very old man, told biographer E. M. Oddie of a visit he made as a child with his parents to the Honourable Mrs. Digby. The incident was still vivid. Crawford was watching a servant feed the Mesrab animals, and to amuse the little *Engleysi* the Arab began to throw pieces of meat up in the air between two Persian cats, who jumped to catch them. Jane's famous pelican was standing by with his cavernous mouth open, hoping for a windfall, and he got more than he had bargained for. A very startled cat, who had overextended himself in a flying leap, dropped straight into the pelican's pouch. The cat was retrieved with only his pride injured, and the little English boy was left with a marvelous Jane Digby anecdote. He recalled his famous hostess only dimly, but her cat and pelican were indelibly engraved on his memory.

The knowledge that she was a grandmother did not appear to alter Jane's life style or lessen her love of adventure in the slightest; she was soon in the thick of new desert intrigues. Jane's disappointed would-be suitor, Sheik Fares ibn Meziad, raided the Mesrab stables at Homs in the spring of 1866, and he and his tribesmen arrogantly rode the horses through the streets daring the Mesrabs to recapture them. Jane was there, but Medjuel was away when the raid took place, and it was a week before she could get word to him. When she heard he was on his way back, the old magic was again operating: "Medjuel returns! Ah, such are the moments when one forgets all the sorrows and enemies and past months of anxiety in the great bliss of meeting him again!"

Fares had picked his time well, however, since he was in the good graces of the Turks and Medjuel was not. The government was not foolish enough to arrest a Sheik who enjoyed British protection, but the local officials could indulge in all manner of minor harassment without fear of reprisal. When the Mesrab leader appealed to the authorities at Homs for justice, he and Fares were ordered to present their grievances for mediation. Certain of his favored position, Fares flatly refused to return the stolen horses. "And the government cannot do anything to him because of the coming Hadj! How pitiful!" Jane fumed in her diary. (She was referring to a general amnesty preceding the annual pilgrimage to Mecca.) For the time being the Mesrabs were forced to suffer Fares's insolence, and it was a bitter pill to swallow, since most Bedouin men gave their horses a status equal to that of their women. (In a desert ballad a Bedouin sings, "To save my sweetheart I will stab, and I will stab also to save my thoroughbred mare!")

While the matter of the stolen horses simmered, there was a call to action on another front. Holo Pasha, the Bedouin bandit, was raiding again, this time at Afeir, and once more Jane and her husband galloped off to join the fight. According to the ancient custom of Bedouin women who accompanied their men into battle, the Sitt Mesrab, now 59, removed the kerchief from her head and unplaited her long hair, which billowed in the wind like a black silk banner.

When the desert brigand and his ninety men attacked Medjuel's camp, the raiders were thoroughly routed.

The courageous part Jane played in repulsing Holo Pasha was reported to Fares, whose passion for the fascinating foreign woman was, perversely, kindled again. Later that summer, when Jane had to return to Damascus without Medjuel, Fares resumed his campaign to woo her away from the Mesrab Sheik, causing her a great deal of embarrassment and eventually serious trouble.

One evening Jane was having tea in Damascus with Mr. Lucas, a missionary friend to whom she had just lent a hundred pounds for a small business venture in the corn market. The well-meaning Mr. Lucas felt obligated to pass on some electrifying information to the generous lady when in the course of their conversation she spoke of Medjuel's frequent absences. The missionary said he had been told by Gusuf Redouah, Jane's former gardener, that Medjuel had a Bedouin wife named Mehabi. Gusuf had even pointed out the woman to Mr. Lucas, who shortly afterward was aghast to see Mehabi in the Mesrab household. "A clap of thunder would have startled me less," Jane wrote the next day. "I sat *glacée*, and passed the most wretched night, arising with fever in my veins and with throbbing head."

There were three days of torture for Jane while she waited for her husband's return, three days when she could do nothing but review in her mind their strange marriage pact and enumerate all the things that might have caused her to lose Medjuel's love. When the Bedouin finally returned, he faced his wife's accusations with calm and patience—he was accustomed to these scenes by now—and he assured her that in the twelve years of their marriage he had not so much as thought of another woman. Because she so desperately wanted to, Jane believed him:

> Happiness inexpressible and unknown but to those who are condemned to possess my ardent and ungovernable feelings, unchilled, untamed, unsubdued by age, experience of the world and change of every kind! Dear Medjuel returned, and in a long and serious conversation with Mr. Lucas, in the presence of his wife, Mehabi and myself, solemnly denied having any other wife but me since the day I married him up to the present time.

Mr. Lucas was not so easily convinced as Jane, and to satisfy his own doubts he confronted Gusuf Redouah with Medjuel's denial. The gardener finally confessed the Fares ibn Meziad had made up the story and paid Gusuf to see that it reached Medjuel's wife through someone she trusted. Fares, it appears, was willing to use any tactic to win the beautiful Sitt Mesrab for himself.

When her missionary friend reported Gusuf's deception to the Mesrabs and apologized for the unhappiness he had caused them, all was bliss again with Jane and Medjuel. But no matter how many times her husband's fidelity and devotion were proved to her, Jane always sank into a deep depression when he was away from her for any length of time. Medjuel had been called to Homs again later that year when Jane received some sad news from Kenelm. She had already heard from him several months earlier that his wife Caroline had died suddenly. Now Kenelm reported that dear old Steely had died following a long and painful deterioration of mind and body. That her beloved governess ("my firm, sincere and most devoted friend") should have such a tragic and undignified end caused Jane much grief. She forgot Steely's shortcomings and began to dwell guiltily on her own. The death of the prim spinster who had been part of the Digby family for fifty years plunged Jane into another of her *abîmes*, which deepened considerably when she learned that another old friend, Ludwig of Bavaria, had died in Nice on February 28, 1868. Added to her grief was her worry over Medjuel, who failed to appear in Damascus on the appointed date. "Medjuel not returned yet," she wrote, full of misery. "Can I, ought I to go on passing my remains of life thus, in utter uselessness? Not even to Medjuel is my existence of any use."

The day after Jane made this unhappy observation, she discovered that she was needed after all. Medjuel sent word that his favorite son, Schebibb, was seriously ill, and he begged his wife to join him immediately at Homs. In less than an hour she was on her way. For the first time in their life together it was Medjuel who needed comfort. Neither Jane's nor the Bedouins' remedies could help Schebibb, and he died an agonizing death. All of Medjuel's usual calm and resignation abandoned him, and Jane was so affected by her husband's grief that she prayed for his conversion to Christianity "that he might find comfort in the belief of everlasting life." In her diary she described the Muslim funeral and the sealing of Schebibb's tomb: "A sheep was sacrificed and given to the poor; the old sheiks chanted to his memory for the last time—and all is over!"

All was over for Schebibb, but his death was to cause his English stepmother trouble and grief she little anticipated on the day of his funeral. Schebibb left a beautiful young widow named Ouadjid, who became, according to Bedouin custom, part of Medjuel's household. There is no indication that Ouadjid lived with the Mesrabs in Damascus, but she was always with them at Homs and in the desert. She and her father-in-law were drawn together by their mutual mourning, and at first their closeness caused Jane no more than an occasional jealous pang, but the problem of Ouadjid would cast a shadow over the Mesrab marriage for a long time to come.

During the year following Schebibb's death Jane and Medjuel were too much involved with intertribal strife for Ouadjid to cause real friction between them. Jane was in her element:

A day never to be forgotten! Cannon and musketry was heard in the morning, and about twelve dozen Arab horsemen rushed into the town with the too true news that Hassaim Bey had indeed attacked our camp with Ebn Merschid, and after pouring a volley of balls into our tents, had carried off all our camels, but, thank God, had killed none of our men.

A week afterward Jane recorded that Hassaim Bey and his men were taken prisoner at Hama. "This is God's doing," she wrote, "and it is marvelous in our eyes."

In January of 1869 Jane and Medjuel spent an idyllic week encamped among the ruins of Baalbek, the ancient city of the Sun God, where Phoenicians, Greeks, Romans, early Christians and finally Muslims had built their houses of worship. Baalbek, though smaller than Palmyra, was thought by Western travelers who had seen both places to be far more impressive. Lewis Leary called Baalbek "the most beautiful mass of ruins that man has ever seen and the like of which he will never behold again." While Palmyra rose out of the desert oasis, Baalbek was located against a more spectacular backdrop, where the Beka'a plain is highest, widest and most fertile beneath the snowcapped peaks of the Anti-Lebanon. The six giant red granite columns of Baal's temple were at their loveliest when the setting sun bathed them with a golden glow and their long shadows cast a marvelous pattern of light and dark over the ruins. In the outer wall of the Sun God's temple are the three "stones of Baalbek," which were so famous in ancient times that the temple above them became known as the Trilithon.

For Jane Digby el Mesrab, who remembered how unhappy she had been at Baalbek the first time she saw it ("Oh, with what different feelings was I here sixteen years ago!"), the glories of this ancient capital paled before the glories of love. It seemed very fitting to her that of the several temples at Baalbek only the round one believed to have been a shrine to Venus was still intact. Venus was still smiling on Jane when she wrote in her diary on April 3, 1869, "Sixty-two years of age, and an impetuous romantic girl of seventeen cannot exceed me in ardent, passionate feelings!" Happily Medjuel seems to have remained *Nak kaz al-ga'ad*, as the Bedouins called a man who was passionate in sexual intercourse (literally, "a man who dishevels a woman's hair"). And to her husband Jane continued to be as desirable as the woman in the Bedouin love poem:

> *Slender she is and yet fills her dress,*
> *And her breasts lift up her garment.*
> *Oh, how sweet she is while undressing*
> *And while my teeth are pressed against hers!*
> *O woman! Oh! my heart drinks thee*
> *With the same lust as we drink fresh*
>   *water during the great heat.*

From such a pinnacle of ecstasy it was a long way down, and if Jane Digby had never made it all the way to the bottom before, she undoubtedly did so during the five months following this birthday. What happened between April and September of 1869 remains a mystery—the diary and the ledger are blank— but Jane wrote afterward that this period was "one long course of torment and torture not to be experienced or described ... nor shall I ever be able to forget the painful scenes I have passed through." Biographer Oddie in the course of her research in the 1930s came up with two explanations, unfortunately both from people who were hardly in a position to know:

> In the Venningen family there was a story that just once she was unfaithful to Medjuel, and that she suffered at his hands the summary punishment meted out by Bedouin husbands to wives who betrayed Bedouin honor. They say that on her marriage Medjuel made a pact with her, warning her that if ever she reverted to her old tricks she would have no European weakling to reckon with, but a man who on the first occasion would half kill her, and on the second kill her for good. They believed that there was a first occasion, and that Medjuel literally half killed her and carried her off into the wilderness into some sort of penitential captivity from which he threatened she would never return. From the Theotoky family we get a different version, but the theme of the story is the same. They believed that Medjuel discovered her *in flagrante delicto* with another sheik, and that in a mad moment of jealousy he stabbed her.

Oddie was convinced that neither of these stories was correct, and it seems unlikely that Jane would have been tempted to cuckold Medjuel. Although she and her husband were frequently apart, their only long separation occurred when Jane returned to England in 1857, and their wild reunions appear to have more than compensated for lost time. It is possible that the constant intrigues of Sheik Fares caused Medjuel to think that his wife had become *Tamûh* (a married woman who lusts after another man). It is more likely, however, that Jane's violent and unreasonable jealousy of Ouadjid, which she did not admit until sometime later, was the cause of a terrible quarrel and perhaps a severe punishment meted out by Medjuel. April was a month Jane and her husband usually spent at Homs, and life at Homs included Ouadjid. It would have been very easy for the hot-tempered Sitt Mesrab to insult the too young, too pretty and too affectionate daughter-in-law and for Medjuel to come too quickly to Ouadjid's defense.

Among the Bedouins false accusations were punished with whatever penalty would have been given the accused had he or she been proved guilty. Bedouin punishment could be swift and terrible; in the desert vengeance was not left to the Lord. In Alois Musil's weighty study of manners and customs among the Rowalla Bedouins, published in 1928, the author repeats a story he was told of a bloodcurdling act of vengeance that once occurred in Medjuel's camp. Musil's spelling is scholarly phonetic (no two non-Arabs Anglicize an Arab word the same way) and Jane changes nationality, but there is no doubt of the identity:

> In the camp of Meǧwel eben Mesreb, who was married to a French woman, there lived with the Bedouin 'Âfet [Medjuel's son Japhet] a youth named Metḳâl, a native of Irak, working for hire. Suddenly he disappeared. 'Âfet made a search for him but without success. At last he was found by a strange wayfarer with his

head shot through, the corners of his mouth slit, and his ears stuck into his mouth. This showed it to be the deed of an avenger, who was in the camp as a guest at the time and soon made himself known. Having proved that it was his duty to kill Metķâl, he was allowed to go back to Irak in peace.

Jane kept her ears during her long private hell in the desert, and the punishment was finally lifted in late September, when she and Medjuel were reconciled. It was a long time, however, before she could forget the "indecent and intolerable epithet" the Bedouin sheik had flung at her in the heat of anger, and her jealousy of Ouadjid continued to grow and fester.

Despite her suffering, Jane lost neither her passionate love nor her respect for her husband. She was all happiness when she described the journey from her exile back to Damascus: "I rode with Medjuel. I rode behind him on the dromedary, gentle trot all the way, as pleased at the feat as any girl of fifteen."

In December of 1869 peace and contentment reigned in the Mesrab household, and a charming picture of domestic bliss Eastern-style greeted Count Louis de Thurhein when he came to call on the old acquaintance he had known thirty years earlier in Paris as the Lady Ellenborough, the impetuous and lovely mistress of Felix Schwarzenberg. Jane and her visitor reminisced over those faraway days, and from the count she heard for the first time that her daughter Mathilde had been married nearly twenty years to a Baron Bieschin. The only comment Jane made when she recorded this news in her diary was, "So be it." Didi was little more than a dim memory to her mother, who was far more interested in Count de Thurhein's description of the colorful ceremonies that marked the opening of the Suez Canal at Port Said on November 16. The count had just come from Egypt, where he was among the French nobles in the entourage of the Empress Eugènie aboard the *Aigle*, which led the first sixty-eight ships through the canal.

A few days after Thurhein's departure, Jane entertained another visitor, an intrepid Scot named John MacGregor, who was something of a celebrity in the city. Millions of travelers had come to landlocked Damascus down through the centuries, but MacGregor was probably the only one in history to arrive by boat. MacGregor's trip to Damascus was only one of many daring exploits in his canoe, the *Rob Roy*. The Scot, accompanied by seven men, six mules and two horses, brought his little craft by wagon from Beirut to a navigable stretch of the Barada River at the village of Doumah; from that point MacGregor steered his one-man canoe through rapids and irrigation canals to the outskirts of Damascus. Scholar John Brinton gives an account of his spectacular entrance:

> To better savor it, and to prepare for the great moment of arrival in the city, MacGregor stopped on the outskirts by a grassy meadow bank to have his supper. Refreshed and ready for his triumphal entry, he set off again in the *Rob Roy*, paddling slowly toward the center of the city. He sailed under bridges,

around aqueducts, past the Pasha's palace—all under the gaze of the incredulous inhabitants.

He at last reached a stretch of calm water by the garden of Dimitri's Hotel, where he had planned to stay. There a large crowd had already gathered, and a great cheer went up as MacGregor hove into view. When he stepped ashore, he was salaam-ed, shaken, struck on the back, and escorted up the path to the entrance of the hotel. Behind him the *Rob Roy* was picked up by the cheering crowd and deposited in the unnavigable waters of a wide marble basin in the hotel garden, where, her blue sail hoisted and her golden flag flying from the little mast, she was the sight of the town. Even the Pasha with his entire suite came to inspect her, followed by the British Consul.

MacGregor was wined and dined continuously during his stay in Damascus, but the one memorable acquaintance he recorded was "Lady Ellenborough, the English wife of a great Arab chief, who had some thousand spearmen at his beck in Palmyra."

Before the year was out, there was yet another arrival in Damascus, who would prove far more important in Jane's life. Following the retirement of consul Edward Rogers, Her Majesty's government appointed as its representative in the "Prophet's Paradise" a very unusual and highly controversial man. The new consul, Capt. Richard Francis Burton, was a colorful, uninhibited gypsy, who was intolerant of all restraint and who genuinely admired the Arabs. With these qualifications it was natural that he and the Honourable Jane Digby el Mesrab would like each other. As had been the case with Balzac, however, Jane's friendship with Burton (and especially with Burton's wife, Isabel) turned out to be a mixed blessing.

19

◇———◇

Jane and Isabel

*. . . but what was incomprehensible to me was
how she could have given up all she had in
England to live with that dirty little black—
or nearly so—husband.*

—ISABEL BURTON OF JANE DIGBY

The man who was to gain immortality for his monumental translation of the
Arabian Nights came to Damascus under a cloud. By the time Richard Burton
arrived in Syria at the age of forty-eight, he had behind him enough adventure
for a dozen lifetimes, and the number of people he had offended in the process
was equally impressive. Even his most brilliant accomplishments had managed
to make enemies for him. When he was a young officer in India, Burton's
remarkable command of languages and dialects had earned him an intelligence
assignment in the native quarter of Karachi, and to his report on native political
intrigues he added a devastatingly candid treatise on the sexual perversions
practiced in some Indian houses. (This was not the only time he was accused of
writing pornography under the guise of anthropological studies, but in the minds
of many Victorians, who considered the work an unspeakable obscenity, the
Karachi paper marked Burton for life.)

In 1853, the year Jane Digby had first set sail for Syria, Richard Burton sailed
from England disguised as an Afghan Muslim and in Cairo joined a group of
pilgrims on the Hadj to Mecca and Medinah. With his thorough preparation and
the proper spirit of reverence for the religion in which he was a bona fide initiate,
Burton succeeded where Jane's cousin Henry Anson had failed tragically. Even
after his book about his experiences in the Hadj was published, no Arab voice
was raised against him for penetrating their "holy of holies," because the Arabs
felt Burton was one of them. His fellow officers, however, gave him the scornful
title of "Ruffian Dick, the white nigger," and his leanings toward Mohammed did
not endear him to the Church of England.

Returning from a dangerous mission to King Gélélé of Dahomey, where he
was sent to express British disapproval of the monarch's tolerance of human
sacrifice, persecution of Christians, and flourishing slave trade, Burton declared
publicly that he did not consider Dahomey's customs any more barbaric than
those of his native land. (More outrage.) Next, Captain Burton organized and
headed an expedition to find the source of the Nile, but this ended in a bitter

dispute between Burton and his associate on the venture, Capt. John Speke. Speke received the lion's share of the credit and then became a martyr by apparently shooting himself in a hunting accident the day before he and Burton were scheduled to debate their differences before a meeting of the geographic section of the British Association for the Advancement of Science at Bath.

The Burtons came to Damascus from Santos, Brazil, where Isabel Burton had almost singlehandedly run the consulate while her husband was gone for months at a time on expeditions that had nothing to do with his diplomatic post.

For Richard and Isabel Damascus was a dream come true—the first and only time the Foreign Office saw fit to place Burton in a post where his remarkable talents and knowledge of Arabic could be utilized. The problem in paradise was that neither Richard nor Isabel was cut out for the diplomatic gavotte. Pleasing Turks, Arabs, Jews, Kurds, a dozen Christian sects, foreign missionaries and the British consul general at Beirut was too large an order for the professed agnostic and his outspoken, Roman Catholic, Jesuit-oriented wife. It did not help that Burton followed scrupulously his own noble credo:

> *Do what thy manhood bids thee do,*
> *From none but self expect applause;*
> *He noblest lives and noblest dies*
> *Who makes and keeps his self-made laws.*

Isabel had her own very positive ideas of how the consulate should be run. "I saw that English influence in Damascus required lifting a great many pegs higher than our predecessor left it," she declared. "The only member of our own English noblesse the people had hitherto known in Damascus was Lady Ellenborough." With a characteristic lack of modesty Isabel wrote in her account of her life in Syria, "The people loved me, and my chief difficulty was to pass through the crowds that came to kiss my hand or my habit." Maddeningly smug, Isabel Burton was totally unaware that the Arab masses did indeed love her husband (who understood them so well), but the same Arabs were alternately infuriated by the consul's wife (who understood them not at all), or laughing at her.

The contrast between Isabel and Jane, the two most important foreign women in Damascus, was painfully apparent. Jane was admired for wearing the simple dress of a Bedouin wife among Medjuel's people, but it was a joke when the amply endowed Isabel tried to disguise herself as Richard's son in the costume of an Arab boy, fooling no one but herself. Both Jane and Isabel were great animal lovers, but the childless Mrs. Burton (who traveled from London to Damascus with a St. Bernard pup, two brindle bull terriers and "two of the Yarborough breed") was something of a fanatic in her devotion to four-legged creatures. With incredible arrogance she took her horses to the *hammam* (Turkish baths) for their rubdowns, and when she saw anyone treating an animal with less than gentleness (a daily occurrence in Damascus), she flailed the offender with her riding crop.

To Isabel, Jane was always "Lady Ellenborough," the only woman in Damascus of equal social rank with herself, and through some tenuous marital link between the Arundells (Isabel's family) and Lady Andover's first husband, Isabel decreed that she and Jane were cousins. How little Mrs. Burton understood her "cousin," how insufferably Victorian her snobbishness and superiority could be, and what a batch of misinformation she could mix with her facts are all apparent in her lengthy description of Jane:

When I first saw her she was a most beautiful woman though sixty-one years of age [Jane was sixty-three]. . . . She blackened her eyes with kohl, and lived in a curiously untidy manner. But otherwise she was not in the least extraordinary at Damascus. But what was incomprehensible to me was how she could have given up all she had in England to live with that dirty little black—or nearly so— husband. I could understand her leaving a coarse, cruel husband, much older than herself, whom she never loved (every woman has not the strength of mind and the pride to stand by what she has done); I could understand her running away with Schwarzenberg; but the contact with that black skin I could not understand. Her *Shaykh* was very dark—darker than a Persian, and much darker than an Arab usually is. All the same, he was a very intelligent and charming man in any light but as a husband. That made me shudder. It was curious how she had retained the charming manner, the soft voice, and all the graces of her youth. You would have known her at once to be an English lady, well born and well bred, and she was delighted to greet in me one of her own order. . . . I took a great interest in the poor thing. She was devoted to her *Shaykh,* whereat I marvelled greatly. . . . She appeared to be quite foolishly in love with him (and I fully comprehend any amount of sacrifice for the man one loves—the greater the better), though the object of her devotion astonished me. Her eyes often used to fill with tears when talking of England, her people, and old times; and when we became more intimate, she spoke to me of every detail of her erring but romantic career. It was easy to see that Schwarzenberg had been the love of her life, for her eyes would light up with a glory when she mentioned him, and she whispered his name with bated breath. It was his desertion which wrecked her life. Poor thing! She was far more sinned against than sinning.

Even Jane's harshest critics never thought of her as a "poor thing," and Isabel's condescending tone strongly suggests a bit of jealousy. From other of Mrs. Burton's remarks it appears that Jane Digby was everything Isabel wanted to be:

She was *grande dame au bout des doigts,* as much as if she had just left the salons of London and Paris, refined in manner and voice, nor did she ever utter a word you could wish unsaid. My husband said she was out and out the cleverest woman he ever met; there was nothing she could not do. She spoke nine languages perfectly, and could read and write in them. She painted, sculptured, was musical. Her letters were splendid; and if on business, there was never a word too much, nor a word too little. She had a most romantic, adventurous life, and she was now, one might say, Lady Hester Stanhope's successor.

Though Jane was more than twenty years older than Isabel, she gave the appearance of being younger. "She looked splendid in Oriental dress," Mrs. Burton said, "and if you saw her as a Moslem woman in the bazaar you would have said she was not more than thirty-four years of age." Isabel was enormously impressed by Jane's costume at the elaborate wedding ceremony of the Pasha's daughter. The Sitt Mesrab was arrayed in all the spectacular finery described in her will as "my Arab ornaments, belt and jewelry in gold and silver, and my silver gilt headpiece, breast ornament and bridle studded with coral." Isabel was very proud to sit next to her: "By my side, and more thoroughbred looking than anybody, like an Oriental queen, was Lady Ellenborough."

During the two years the Burtons spent in Syria, their closest friends, according to Isabel, were Jane and Abd el Kader. Medjuel always got lower billing in Mrs. Burton's theater because she did not consider him a celebrity in the class of his wife and the Algerian nobleman. (She did, however, manage a few compliments for the Bedouin, who, she admitted, had "a most pleasing face, piercing black eyes, gentlemanly manners and a charming voice." She also allowed that "he speaks the beautiful Bedawi Arabic.") From Medjuel and El Kader, Richard Burton received valuable help in his translation of the *Arabian Nights*, and from Medjuel's English wife Burton learned much about life in the harem. Some of the remarkable information in Burton's introductory essay to the unexpurgated edition of *One Thousand Nights and a Night* may have come from Jane. She could discuss these strange sexual mores candidly with a man like Burton, although she was shocked and disturbed by some of the sexual practices to which many of the aristocratic Arab women were addicted.

If Isabel Burton was offended by these frank discussions, she did not let it show, and her fondest memories of Damascus were of the evenings spent on the roof of her house in the company of Jane and El Kader:

> Often after my reception was over and the sun was setting, we used to ask these two to stay behind the others and have a little supper with us, and we would go up to the roof, where it was prepared, and where mattresses and the cushions of divans were spread about, and have our evening meal; and after that we would smoke our *narghiles*, and talk and talk and talk far into the night.... I shall never forget the scene on the housetop, backed as it was by the sublime mountain, a strip of sand between it and us, and on the other three sides was the view over Damascus and, beyond, the desert. It was all wild, romantic and solemn; and sometimes we would pause in our conversation to listen to the sounds around us: the last call to prayer on the minaret-top, the soughing of the wind

through the mountain gorges, and the noise of the water-wheel in the neighboring orchard.

Isabel, the proper Victorian, admitted freely that she and Jane smoked cigarettes and hookahs ("I must confess to the soft impeachment, despite insular prejudices...").

Abd el Kader and Richard Burton shared many interests and had deep admiration and respect for each other. The Algerian sometimes dined at the Burtons with Jane when Medjuel was away, but there was never any suggestion of a romance between them—the Sitt Mesrab was totally devoted to her husband, and El Kader had five wives in his harem. Both Jane and El Kader were good-natured about being the Burtons' showpieces in Damascus; everyone who visited Isabel and Richard at the consulate sooner or later was taken to meet Lady Ellenborough and the hero of Algeria. This, coupled with the fact that Isabel tried to cash in on her association with Jane in a biography with which Jane flatly denied having anything to do, renders one of Mrs. Burton's statements rather ironic: "As to strangers, she [Jane] received only those who brought a letter of introduction from a friend or relative; but this did not hinder every ill-conditioned passer-by from boasting of his intimacy with the house of Mesrab, and recounting the untruths which he invented, *pour se faire valoir*, or to sell his book or newspaper at a better profit."

Richard Burton was generally very careful not to violate Arab rules of courtesy, but his wife committed some phenomenal blunders in Syria. One of them was reported by Barty Mitford, later Lord Redesdale, who came to Damascus in March of 1871. Isabel was conducting a sightseeing tour of the city for Mitford and several other Englishmen, and she was anxious for the visitors to see a particular tomb inside an old mosque. She was much irritated to discover that the narrow staircase leading to the tomb was temporarily blocked by a Muslim at his prayers. Never one to stand on ceremony for someone she considered an inferior, Mrs. Burton rudely interrupted the man's devotions and threatened to thrash him with her riding crop when he refused to move. Mitford was appalled by her behavior:

What the man muttered I knew not, but I doubt his orisons having taken the shape of blessings. I left the mosque in disgust. If actuated by no higher motive, she should have reflected upon the harm which such conduct needs must work upon her husband, to whom, to do her justice, she was entirely and most touchingly devoted. It is only fair to Burton's memory to show how heavily he was handicapped.

Like all of the Burtons' visitors, Mitford was taken to meet the notorious Lady Ellenborough, and Jane made a far more favorable impression on him than had Isabel:

So many stories had been told about her and her strange life as the wife of an Arab chief, that I expected to see a grand and commanding figure living in a sort of tawdry barbarism, something like the Lady Hester Stanhope of *Eothen* and Lamartine; an imposing personage, mystic, wonderful, half queen, half sybil—Semiramis and Meg Merrilies rolled into one, ruling by the force of the eye a horde of ignoble, ragged dependants, trembling but voracious. No two people could be more unalike. I found Lady Ellenborough—Mrs. Digby, as she now called herself—living in a European house, furnished, so far, at any rate, as the rooms in which we were received were concerned, like those of an English lady; in the desert with the tribe she would be altogether Arab.

The owner was like her belongings; a little old-fashioned, a relic of the palmy days of Almack's; dressed in quite inconspicuous Paris fashion, and very nice to look upon.... she had the remains of great good looks and the most beautiful and gracious old-world manners. She had been a fair beauty, but in deference to the Arabs' superstitious fear of the evil eye, her hair and eyebrows were dyed black.... She asked after the old Lord Clanwilliam—grandfather of the present Earl. How was he? "Wonderful," I said, "cutting us all out skating at Highclere two or three months ago." Lady Ellenborough looked puzzled. "But why should he not?" she asked. "Well!" I answered, "you must remember that he is past seventy years of age." "Dear me! is it possible? That handsome young man!" Her old friends remained in her mind just as she had known them—Lady Palmerston, Lady Jersey, Lady Londonderry—still reigning beauties, queens of Almack's. It was strange to hear a delicately nurtured English lady talking of her life in the desert with "her" tribe. She told us how the summer before a hostile tribe had raided them and stolen some of their mares, and how this next summer they must ride out to avenge the outrage and get back the lost treasures. There would be fierce fighting, she said, and she must be there to nurse the chief should anything happen to him. "In fact," she added, "we have one foot in the stirrup, for we must start for the desert tomorrow morning."... Evidently in this wild, nomad life between the desert and Damascus she had found a happy haven of rest after the adventures of her stormy youth.

Mitford expressed surprise that Jane's husband was "a little man." Like most Westerners he expected "a great lord of the desert" to be tall, and in his few minutes with Medjuel, he did not have the opportunity to observe the Bedouin's intelligence and charm, which gave him a different kind of stature in the eyes of Jane and others who knew the Mesrab Sheik well. Several of the Damascus missionaries were equally shortsighted in their appraisal of Medjuel. Two amusing stories of gaffes made by these Christian messengers have survived. The wife of an English missionary, after being conducted on a tour of the Mesrab house, was thinking out loud when she said, "All this for a barbarian!" Jane overheard the remark, and to ease her visitor's embarrassment, replied, "But he isn't a barbarian really. He has just learned to use a knife and fork!" Medjuel proved that he too had a sense of humor, when two clergymen came to call on Jane. The Reverend J. Mentor Mott (whose bitter conflict with Richard Burton was partially responsible for the consul's recall) rode up to the Mesrab gate with the Reverend W. Parry and hailed an Arab standing nearby to look after their horses while the two were inside. Mr. Parry, knowing the temptation a pair of good horses could be to an Arab, debated at length with Mr. Mott on the wisdom of this move, but the latter did not know how to extricate himself from the arrangement. The two men finally abandoned their horses to the stranger with considerable anxiety. While they were conversing with Mrs. Digby, the suspicious-looking Arab came into the drawing room and was introduced to the flustered ministers as the husband of their hostess. Medjuel greeted them with a smile and said in beautiful English, "Gentlemen, I have handed your horses over to one of my servants. I assure you they will be quite safe."

By the strangest coincidence, Mr. Parry had formerly served as chaplain to the English residents of Pisa and Lucca, and had occupied the tall Italian house where Leonidas Theotoky fell to his death. Mr. Parry's three little girls, who were brought to see Jane a short time after their father's first visit, never forgot her. They had already heard of her son's tragic death, and the story of the Greek boy had made a vivid impression on them. In a scene that might have illustrated a Victorian children's book, the smallest girl sat on the beautiful lady's lap and played with a string of pearls Jane was wearing, while Jane told them about Leonidas and showed them the locket with his curl. With a grave and pious air the sheik's wife warned them they must never slide down bannisters and must always obey their parents. "All my troubles came to me," she said, "because I didn't do what I was told."

In the summer of 1871 Jane was reminded more cruelly of Leonidas when a similar accident took the life of Heribert Venningen's young wife. Karl Venningen wrote that Gabrielle had slipped on the stairs and fallen on some knitting she was carrying. She might have suffered no more than a few bruises, but one of her knitting needles pierced her spine, and she died on May 15 after six weeks of agony. Heribert was left desolate with three tiny, motherless children. The news of Gabrielle's death was a terrible shock to Jane, even though she had never met her daughter-in-law. "Poor Heribert," Jane wrote in her diary, "and the poor little children deprived so early of a mother's care." It did not occur to her that Heribert had also been deprived of a mother's care, almost from the day of his birth, but this newest tragedy in the Venningen family made Jane wonder why someone so young should die when she, who felt "old and useless," lived on. She became so preoccupied with thoughts of death that on June 15 she went to Richard Burton at the consulate and had her will drawn up with two of her closest missionary friends, William Wright and James Orr Scott, as witnesses.

The Burtons had their own troubles that summer. Between the two of them, Richard and Isabel had managed at one time or another to incur the hostility of every faction in Syria, and to make implacable enemies of the two men who carried the most weight—Rashid Pasha, the *Wali*, or Turkish governor-general, and Burton's immediate superior in Beirut, British consul general George Jackson Eldridge. The *Wali* was wary of Burton's tremendous popularity with the Arab masses, who were already restive under Turkish rule; Eldridge was receiving constant complaints against Burton from a variety of sources. Both men felt that "Ruffian Dick" frequently exceeded his authority, meddling in matters that were the domain of the *Wali* or of the Beirut office, and undoubtedly they were right.

If any one group could be called the most instrumental in causing Burton's recall, it was a small group of Jewish money lenders in Damascus, who had the backing of British bankers. According to Isabel's account, Burton was horrified when he was approached by some of these men, seeking his help in collecting bad debts from Arabs, who had been ruined by the 60 percent interest rates. The consul flatly refused to cooperate, and the word was spread that Burton and his wife were rabidly anti-Jewish (there is no doubt that Isabel, in fact, was) and, worse, that the consul was rocking the financial boat. When Jane heard of this attack on the man she admired, she wrote Mrs. Burton a letter, expressing her concern:

My dear Isabel,

I was calling at a native house yesterday, where I found assembled some leading people of Damascus. The conversation turned upon Captain Burton and the present British Consulate. One word led to another; and I heard to my surprise and consternation, that men famed for their *various pecuniary* transactions are boasting about everywhere "That upon *their* representations, *the consul is to be recalled*," and all Damascus is grieved and indignant at them. For my part I cannot, will not believe that her Majesty's Government would set aside a man of Captain Burton's standing and well-known justice and capacity in public affairs, for the sake of these Jews, who are desolating the villages and ruining those who have the misfortune to fall into their clutches. He is also so thoroughly adapted for this Babel of tongues, nations, and religions, and is so rapidly raising our English Consulate from the low estimation in which it had fallen in the eyes of all men, to the position it ought to and would occupy under the rule of an incorruptible, firm, and impartial character like Captain Burton.

. . . Our present Consul is too much a friend to the oppressed, and examines too much everything himself to suit their money transactions. The Consulate for an age has not been so respectable as now, and should you really go, I should think any future Consul would shrink to do his duty, for fear of his conduct being misrepresented at home. You must write me a line to tell me the truth, if you may do so without indiscretion; and people are wanting to write to the Foreign Office and *The Times*, so provoked are they at the lies and duplicity....
With regard to the Arab tribes, they too have an admiration for Captain Burton's dauntless and straightforward dealing, so different from the others....

I had intended to scribble but two lines, and I have been led on till my note has become a long letter. So, goodbye, and I truly hope all these machinations will end in the discomfiture of their inventors.

Your affectionate cousin
Jane Digby el Mesrab

Nothing, however, that Richard Burton's friends in Damascus could do would halt the wheels that had been set in motion, and the blow fell on August 16, 1871. The Burtons were at their summer quarters in Bludan in the Anti-Lebanon when a ragged messenger arrived with the shocking news that the vice-consul from Beirut, William Kirby Green, had already taken over Richard's office in Damascus. Burton rode immediately back to Damascus, unwilling to believe what had happened. When he learned it was true, he left abruptly for Beirut and thence for England, sending his desolate wife at Bludan the famous curt message: "I am recalled. Pay, pack and follow at convenience." In a mad and punishing horseback ride, worthy of Jane Digby, Isabel Burton barely managed to catch the Beirut coach as it was leaving Chtaura so she could join Richard for his last twenty-four hours in Syria before his steamer left for England. The consul's faithful Arab servant Habib, who walked all the way from Damascus to Beirut to tell his master good-bye, arrived at the quay ten minutes too late, and flung himself on the ground at Isabel's feet sobbing hysterically.

It took Mrs. Burton nearly a month to tie up all the loose ends of their life in Syria, and during that time testimonial letters poured in from Richard's staunch admirers, who hoped the consul would be cleared and reinstated. One of the letters the Burtons treasured most highly was a beautiful tribute from Medjuel el Mesrab on behalf of his entire tribe. Isabel finally left Damascus on September 13, and in her own account of her departure, with her usual disregard for facts and her condescending tone, she forfeited any sympathy she may have deserved:

> As half the town wanted to accompany me part of the road, and I was afraid that a demonstration might result, I determined to slip away quietly by night. Abd el Kader and Lady Ellenborough were in on the secret, and they accompanied me as far as the city gates, where I bade them an affectionate farewell. The parting with Lady Ellenborough affected me greatly. I was the poor thing's only friend. As she wrung my hands these were her last words: "Do not forget your promise if I die and we never meet again." I replied, "*Inshallah*, I shall soon return." She rode a black thoroughbred mare, and as far as I could see anything in the moonlight, her large sorrowful blue eyes, glistening with tears, haunted me.

There is no reason to doubt that Jane wept at their farewell, but in the matter of the "only friend," the reverse would have been more accurate, and the "promise" was Isabel's shrewd and dishonest way of backing up her completely false claim that Jane commissioned her to write her biography. The two women parted on the most affectionate of terms and never saw each other again, but two years later the public dispute over Jane's biography shattered their friendship irrevocably.

20

Some Premature Obituaries

Who is this that cometh up from the wilderness,

leaning upon her beloved?

— THE SONG OF SOLOMON

Ever since her mother's death, Jane had dreaded to open letters from the West—it was a rare one that did not bring news of another funeral. Early in 1872 she heard from Kenelm that Lord Ellenborough had died the previous December. It was hard for the woman who had deserted him so long ago (and to whom his name still clung so tenaciously) to think of Edward as a man of eighty-one. "The news of Lord Ellenborough's death moved me to all kinds of sad remembrances," she wrote, "and I felt sad and low as days and years long past rose up before me." Edward's obituaries awakened memories in England too, and for the first time in many years the scandal of the Ellenborough divorce was recalled in the public press. Jane was much irritated to see some letters on the subject of Lord Ellenborough's former wife reprinted from the *Morning Post* in a Levantine newspaper. "Who can think it worth while to keep up such an uninteresting correspondence?" she wrote in her diary.

Fortunately for the Sitt Mesrab, the Syrian present always managed to intrude urgently upon such depressing reminders of her Western past. In that respect Jane was more Arab than she realized—certainly she was in harmony with the philosophy of life Richard Burton discovered in the *Arabian Nights*:

> *Turn thee from grief, nor care a jot,*
> *Commit thy needs to fate and lot,*
> *Enjoy the present passing well,*
> *And let the past be clean forgot!*

During the first months of 1872 the *Wali* loomed large in Jane's present, and if it wasn't a particularly pleasant interlude, at least it diverted her thoughts from her disagreeable publicity. The Turkish governor-general of Syria, no longer having Richard Burton to harass and intrigue against, was amusing himself at the expense of the Mesrabs. A corrupt and greedy man, the *Wali* envied Medjuel the wealth his English wife had brought him; most especially he coveted the beautiful Mesrab horses, many of which Jane herself had broken to the saddle and trained. Several times the Mesrabs sold horses to other Arabs, only to discover later that the buyers were acting in behalf of the *Wali*. Jane was distressed to learn in February that one of her finest mares, named Wrobbski, had ended up in the palace stables. Shortly afterward, when a Turk came to her with an offer for her own personal mare, Midjoumaah, Jane refused it, suspecting that the Turk had been sent by Rashid Pasha. Jane did not want to give up the animal.

Within an hour after the first Turk left, another came with a direct offer from the *Wali* of one hundred twenty Osman pounds. Unfortunately, once the *Wali's* name was brought out into the open, the offer was tantamount to a command, and this time Jane could not afford to refuse, for in doing so she would arouse the Turkish ruler's antagonism toward Medjuel and his tribe. The next day Rashid Pasha's dragoman rode away on Jane's mare. "Midjoumaah, dear Midjoumaah is gone!" she wrote angrily in her diary, "and for twenty pounds less than promised, on account of her little spavin. I am very vexed!" For a while, however, the Mesrabs basked in the *Wali's* favor, and Medjuel was warmly received when he called at the palace to negotiate some tribal business. "Dear Midjoumaah has accomplished her mission," Jane conceded. "The sacrifice has been worth while."

With or without Rashid Pasha's good will, the Mesrabs were almost continually fighting with their neighbors, "wholesomely engaged in internecine war," as one Western cynic put it. The only really variable factor in these conflicts was the enemy. Last year's allies became this year's foes, and, of course, vice versa. During the Burton period in Damascus the Mesrabs had been feuding with the Wuld Ali tribe. Isabel recalled attending a "council of war" at Jane's house, during which Richard tried to settle a dispute between Medjuel and his former friend, Sheik Mohammed Dukhi, the very man who years earlier had come to Medjuel's defense when Jane was so angry over her husband's protracted absence.

Generally, such intertribal quarrels were little more than entertainments for the participants, but in 1873 the Mesrabs became embroiled in a more serious fight. It was so serious, in fact, that when Heribert Venningen wrote his mother that he was contemplating a trip to Syria with his friend Count Arco-Valley ("I am thinking of going with him and being able to see you at long last"), Jane discouraged him because of the danger involved. The Saba Bedouins, to whom Medjuel's people were related, had for many years pastured their flocks in the area around Homs and Hama, while their major rivals, the Rowalla, occupied the adjoining district nearer to Damascus. That particular year, the Rowalla, finding themselves richer than usual in camels, decided they needed more pasturage, and conflict was inevitable. Sheik Sotamm of the Rowalla offered the governor of Hama twice the fee customarily paid by the Saba for their traditional grazing land, and for good measure threw in a gift of some valuable mares. A bargain was struck, and when the Saba Bedouins returned from their winter migration in the south, they found the Rowalla occupying Saba land. This kind of confrontation was sufficiently familiar that it served as a popular theme in Bedouin ballads:

> *I have a land, a paradise for herds,*
> *Met'eb and Sib long for it,*
> *A chief like me must not sleep,*
> *But strive to hold his property.*
> *As long as my comrades can mount their horses,*
> *By Allah, there will be no peace!*

The dispossessed Saba tribe immediately attacked the usurpers, and, in the best Bedouin tradition, the Mesrabs rushed to the support of their kinsmen. But the Rowalla, in turn, were reinforced by Turkish infantry supplied by the governor of Hama. This totally unbalanced the conflict, especially since the Saba and their allies feared savage reprisals if they were to fire on the Turks. In the rout that followed, a number of Saba and Mesrab tribesmen were killed, and the loss of tents, furnishings and animals was a devastating economic blow.

Within a month, however, the defeated Saba were able to rearm, probably at Jane's expense, and to enlist further allies. When they mounted a new attack, the sixty-five-year-old Sitt Mesrab was riding with them. Medjuel was not at all happy with the arrangement, but his wife told him she would rather die with him than live without him, and that was an argument that left no reply. This time the Turks, for reasons of their own, decided to let the Rowalla fight without their help, and the odds shifted strongly to the Saba. In a pitched battle near Jabul, Sotamm's tribe was soundly defeated and forced back to its old territory near Damascus. Both sides suffered heavy losses, however, and in the confusion following the Rowalla retreat, a rumor was spread in the city that the Mesrab's *Umm-el-Laban* was among those killed.

By telegraph the announcement of Jane's "death" was flashed to Beirut and from Beirut on to London, where the notorious Lady Ellenborough had only recently been rediscovered by the press. The few unflattering comments that Jane had inspired a year earlier were high praise compared to the flood of obituaries that now poured forth, making the name of Lady Ellenborough synonymous with Sin. Every piece of old gossip was reexamined and enlarged upon in English, French, German, Greek, Italian, and Turkish, and each journalist felt compelled to add to Jane's romantic career one more husband or lover than had been tallied in print the day before. A fair sample of the notoriety that devastated the proper Victorian Digbys was the article from a Beirut correspondent that appeared in the *Revue Britannique*:

There has just died a noble lady who greatly used, or abused, marriage—Lady Ellenborough—who thirty years ago deserted her first husband and ran away with Prince Schwarzenberg. She retired to Italy where she married six times in succession. She was at her seventh husband when she married in Athens a Greek Colonel, Count Theotoky, who could hold her no longer than the rest, because she was taken up with the *Chef des Pallikaires*, for whom she built a house near Piraeus. Divorce gave her liberty, but this time she profited by it to desert the *Chef des Pallikaires* at the same time as the Greek Colonel, to go voyaging in the Levant. On the way from Beirut to Damascus, her camel driver named Sheikh Abdul appeared worthy of the honor of becoming her ninth spouse. He became it by Arab ceremony, and he was her last. For to him she remained faithful always. During all these matrimonial adventures, Lady Ellenborough conducted a long lawsuit in England against her first husband, a suit which she won in 1855, and which brought her an immense fortune. She died a widow, the camel-man preceding her to the grave, and as she had no children her death enriches numerous nieces and nephews.

In Trieste, where Richard Burton now occupied the British consulate, Isabel read the scathing account in the *Revue Britannique*, and rose with righteous indignation to defend her friend. Her intentions may have been the best when she dashed off a series of letters to the *Times*, the *Pall Mall Gazette*, the Trieste *Zeitung* and the German *Gazette* in Vienna, but in her zeal (and with what appears to be a bit of opportunism), Isabel once more mixed fact with fiction:

> I scarcely know where to begin. But I must do it to keep my promise to her. I lived for two years at Damascus while my husband, Captain Burton, was consul there, and in daily intercourse with the subject of this paragraph. Knowing that after her death all sorts of untruths would appear in the paper very painful to her family—as indeed she was not spared while living—she wished me to write her biography, and gave me an hour a day until it was accomplished. She did not spare herself dictating the bad with the same frankness as the good. I was pledged not to publish this until after her death and that of certain near relatives. But I am in a position to state that there is a grain of truth to a tower of falsehood in the paragraph from Beirut. And inasmuch as Beirut is only seventy-two miles from Damascus, the writer must know that as well as I do.... I cannot meddle with the past without infringing on the biography confided to me; but I can say a few words concerning her life, dating from her arrival in the East, as told to me by herself and by those now living there; and I can add my testimony as to what I saw, which I believe will interest everyone in England, from the highest downward, and be a gratification to those more nearly concerned.

From that point Isabel launched into a reasonably accurate summary of Jane's life in Damascus, and ended with a charming tribute to the lady she so admired:

> ... To the last she was fresh and young; beautiful, brave, refined, and delicate. She hated all that was false. Her heart was noble; she was charitable to the poor. She regularly attended the Protestant church, and often twice on Sundays. She

fulfilled all the duties of a good Christian lady and an Englishwoman. She is dead. All those who knew her in her latter days will weep for her. She had but one fault (and who knows if it was hers?), washed out by fifteen years of goodness and repentance. Let us hide it, and shame those who seek to drag up the adventures of her wild youth to tarnish so good a memory. *Requiescat in pace.*

Mrs. Burton's vigorous defense did not accomplish the desired effect. Not blessed with a sense of humor, she could not foresee the ribald laughter that her flowery statements about Jane ("She was thoroughly a connoisseur in each of her amusements and occupations") were bound to evoke, and few if any of Isabel's readers were willing to lump Jane Digby's scandalous escapades into the category of "but one fault." It was the matter of the biography, however, that really boomeranged on Isabel.

In the spring of 1873, to the utter amazement of everyone in Damascus, Jane Digby el Mesrab, very much alive, came riding out of the desert with her Bedouin husband. Jane had her own share of amazement at the experience of reading her own obituaries, but the shock quickly turned to anger. She wrote Isabel what was evidently a devastating letter (Mrs. Burton never made the contents public), and Isabel tried valiantly in her answer to extricate herself. Jane was not entirely satisfied with the explanation, as she wrote to her sister-in-law, Theresa Digby, on May 21, 1873:

My dearest Theresa,
The last letter from Edward dated 15th March I intended to answer directly, and I shall reserve him a part of this; but a few days after its reception, I was quite overset by the dreadful paragraphs in the papers, and as you may conceive, have been most *intensely* annoyed ever since. The announcement of my death was nothing; I am not superstitious, and no newspaper will kill me a minute before the appointed time, but I deplore the taking up of so much that is painful to all connected with me, so interesting to the *present* generation which from all I hear from others, is far *faster* in style (at least) than what was endured in my day. I am so grieved too for my brother, and cannot conceive *what* enemy can have originated this violence, for I am not conscious of having any, particularly in *this* country, where every class of persons, both here and at Beyrout, Christian and Moslem, high and low, are most friendly, and a general outcry against the author (whoever he was) has been raised. Mr. Green, the Consul, is receiving many letters from people of rank not personally known to him, expressing all sorts of indignation about it and happiness that it has been positively contradicted. I have received myself most kind letters from Lady [illegible], Lady Howard de W. and others. Today I received one from Mrs. Burton from Trieste, explaining the reasons for her "Defense," "the keeping people at bay by telling them that [two words illegible] the real biography and to prevent any more being said upon the subject." I trust hers may be a correct view, but I certainly *always* deprecated every idea of ever publishing anything relating to myself or

my former existence, as you can easily believe, and I never spoke to her at all upon the subject, excepting the answering of some of her queries as to what the world of that day knew, and positively denying some other histories that people had told, and as to "*begging* her to remember *promises*" after my death of *justifying* me, it is pure error, and she knew the *horror* and *aversion* I have to this kind of thing.

The "faster generation" Jane referred to was undoubtedly the high-stepping English society that revolved around the Prince of Wales (later Edward VII), and she seemed to have been unconscious of any irony in her comment. The years had apparently dimmed her memories of Regency rakes and her own circle at Almack's.

In calling a deliberate falsehood an "error," Jane showed more kindness to Isabel than Isabel probably deserved. Those in Damascus who knew both women were not so generous. Feeling ran so high against the unpopular Mrs. Burton that many people in Syria claimed the consul's wife herself was responsible for circulating the false report of Jane's death. Such a story was ridiculous and unfair to Isabel, but the missionaries who had been snubbed by the Catholic Mrs. Burton as too low-class took it to their hearts.

In everything Isabel subsequently wrote about Syria she restated her claim. She was prudent enough, however, to wait until she was certain Jane was no longer alive before reopening the issue. On one occasion in 1884 she wrote that Jane "was my most intimate friend, and she dictated to me the whole of her biography, beginning 15 March, 1871, and ending July 7." In another book, she stated, "We became great friends, and she dictated to me the whole of her biography, and most romantic and interesting it is." Years later, in Isabel's 1893 biography of her husband she was still returning to the subject. Obviously someone was lying, and the facts clearly point to Isabel, who having once told the story was obliged to stick to it. Between mid-March and early June of 1871, the three-month period during which Isabel said the dictation took place, the two women were in Damascus simultaneously for less than three weeks. Isabel left the last week in March to join her husband in a trip through the Holy Land that lasted until the end of May. Jane left for Homs the day after Barty Mitford's visit in March and did not return to Damascus until sometime in June.

The few references to Jane's past that Isabel makes are completely inaccurate. She states, for example, that Lord Ellenborough was an "old man" when Jane was married to him "against her wishes," and that Jane ran away with Prince Schwarzenberg at age nineteen, lived with him "for some years and had two or three children by him." Mrs. Burton knew nothing at all of King Ludwig, Karl Venningen, Spiro Theotoky, or Hadji-Petros. The twenty years that elapsed between Felix and Medjuel are airily dismissed: "I am afraid after that she led a life for a year or two over which it is kinder to draw a veil." Of Jane's Coke relations at Holkham Hall, the title-conscious Mrs. Burton was totally ignorant

—she never even realized during a long acquaintance with the Honourable Henry Coke that he and Jane were related. ("How interested she would have been," Coke wrote after Isabel's death, "had she known that Lady Ellenborough was my niece.") The notes Isabel claimed to have for Jane's biography were never found among her papers, and her "facts" bore no resemblance to the facts as Jane would have given them. Even a casual acquaintance Jane mentioned once in her diary knew more about the Sitt Mesrab's past than did Isabel Burton, and Isabel might have benefited in more ways than one had she read this diary entry:

> I went to Madame Heriguard, and spent the afternoon with her. She is ill, and I was vexed with myself for speaking to her of Felix, the King and bygone days. I neither did the noble-minded Baron justice nor the love I bear the dear sheik. Oh, how necessary it is to put a watch upon the door of one's lips that one may not offend with one's tongue!

There seems no logical reason for Jane, whose candor was so often her undoing, to have lied about the biography. There was, on the other hand, a very good reason for Isabel to have invented the biography. The Burtons depended heavily on income from their writing to supplement Richard's meager diplomatic salary, and the enormous interest shown by the public in the exotic life of Lady Ellenborough must have proved an irresistible temptation to Isabel to earn a little nest egg. What possible harm could a little romantic fiction do the memory of her glamorous friend? Had Jane Digby not been so unexpectedly "resurrected," she might well have emerged in print a redeemed and considerably whitewashed heroine.

However much she deserved her comeuppance, Isabel was deeply embarrassed by Jane's denial and remained sensitive about the subject for the rest of her life. She was not, however, the only one who was embarrassed. Jane's brother Lord Digby was so outraged by the new burst of notoriety that he burned most of Jane's letters in his possession. This rash act does not necessarily indicate that there was another estrangement between Edward and his sister, for a correspondence between Jane and Edward's wife continued. Both Edward and Kenelm Digby received bequests in Jane's will, and Lord Digby was named executor of her estate, but the will had been drawn up in 1871, two years before the storm of publicity broke.

For Jane, the unflattering obituaries had an annoying consequence. Now every casual tourist in the Middle East wanted a glimpse of the infamous Englishwoman, and journalists resorted to every kind of deception to gain admittance to her house. From this time on Jane was extremely wary of strangers from the West, and when she went out in Damascus, she wore Bedouin dress, covering the lower part of her face with a *yashmak*.

Despite her caution, however, the Sitt Mesrab remained hospitable and charm-

ing to visitors who were old friends or who carried satisfactory letters of introduction. One of the latter who met Jane in the spring of 1874 was Heribert
Venningen's friend, Count Louis Arco-Valley—the young nobleman Jane's son
had written about two years previously. Since Louis was on his honeymoon,
however, Heribert did not come along as originally planned. The count ("a fine,
distinguished-looking, and most attractive person," Jane wrote) was the son of
Anna Arco, who had been one of the great beauties of Ludwig's court and a
friend of Jane. He brought to Heribert's mother affectionate greetings from the
Venningens and those few old acquaintances in Munich who wished to be remembered. Jane so enjoyed her conversation with Louis that she immediately
wrote an enthusiastic account of it to Heribert. Within a month she received a
reply from her son, and it brought her "most melancholy intelligence." Karl
Venningen was dead. "My father died as he would have wished to die—in the
saddle," Heribert wrote. The baron, who had loved and forgiven Jane so generously, was a handsome, vigorous man in the prime of life when she last saw him
thirty-four years earlier. ("How quickly life passes, and how often suddenly
terminates.")

Nearly everyone who had played an important part in Jane's life before she
came to Syria was now dead. The faithful Eugènie, who had spanned the gap
from West to East with her vagabond mistress, was no longer with her. There is
no record of why she left, but whatever the reason, she and Jane seem to have
parted on good terms. The last entry in the ledger bearing Eugènie's name
(December, 1868) is for an unusually expensive *cadeau*, possibly a farewell
token of affection and gratitude from the woman she served so well. (Unfortunately, Eugènie had no literary leanings, for her biography of Jane would have
been far more fascinating than any Isabel Burton could have ever written.)
Early in 1869, according to the account book, money for running the Damascus
house—a responsibility that had been Eugènie's—was paid to a new servant
named Gabrielle, and at the same time a cook named Marie was added to the
staff. A manservant named Etienne followed Gabrielle, but he was apparently
another disappointment. The household staff was steadily going downhill, and
Jane longed for the days when Eugènie had been there to shoulder the domestic
woes, especially the hiring and firing. Madame Marie became more and more
insufferable, and in a marvel of redundancy, Jane summed up the cook's character: "She is, I suspect, not very honest, unscrupulous with regard to truth, and
has, added to this, a most unscrupulous and lying tongue." Because she was a
hard worker, however, Marie lasted at the Mesrabs for five years, until Jane
happily caught her stealing some prized dahlias and forthwith gave the woman
"her definite *congé*."

When Admiral Sir James Robert Drummond, commander of the Mediterranean fleet, came to call on his old friend Ianthe in 1874, her household was
still without a cook, and she apologized that she had no one who could prepare a
meal "fit for an Englishman to eat." There was never a shortage of horses at the

Mesrabs', however, and Jane entertained the admiral by lending him her best pony and taking him on one of her delightful tours of Damascus. Drummond had promised Jane eighteen years earlier, when they saw each other in London, that he would come to Syria to meet her Bedouin husband, and he endeared himself to her now by his "spontaneous and unaffected liking for Medjuel." The visit was a very happy occasion, and Jane wrote in her diary after Drummond left, "How refreshing to see again such good kind friends!" The admiral was one of the very few visitors Jane had in Syria with whom she could reminisce over her life in Athens. (One Greek, George Typaldos Cezakis, claimed to have been a guest of the Sitt Mesrab and her sheik in their desert tent, where he was amazed to find the former Ianthe Theotoky dressed as a Bedouin woman, but there is no mention of Cezakis in Jane's papers.)

Two years after Drummond enjoyed the warm hospitality of the Mesrabs, another Englishman, this one a total stranger to Jane, met with a more cautious reception. Sir Edwin Pears, who was at the time foreign correspondent for the London *Daily News* in Constantinople, came to Syria in 1876 and was determined to make the acquaintance of the fascinating woman who had been described to him some years earlier by the painter Carl Haag. Newspapermen were the last people Madame Digby el Mesrab cared to see, and Pears would have had no chance to realize his ambition had he not been fortunate enough to become friendly with Jane's Beirut banker. Twice a year Mr. Heald went to Damascus to deliver in person Jane's income from England, and on this occasion Pears prevailed upon the banker to take him along. Heald warned the correspondent that Jane refused to receive strangers and, to avoid contact with any, had even stopped attending the Anglican church service held at the British consulate, but he said he would try to smooth the way for an introduction. Pears recorded the meeting in his book, *Forty Years in Constantinople*:

> Accordingly, the day after our arrival, we called at her house, which was in the suburbs of the city. He sent in his name. We were shown into a long *sala* or drawing-room. A few minutes afterwards I saw a tall woman enter, who at once gave me the impression of having been strikingly handsome; but a black cloud was over her when she saw that my companion, who had come to pay her the money, had with him a stranger. I subsequently learned that she was then in her seventieth year. My friend explained that it was the first time I had been in Damascus, and that he could not leave me in the street, but that with her permission I might go to the other end of the *sala* while the money due to her was counted, accounts made up, and the proper receipts signed. I offered to leave the house, but she intimated that if I would adopt the course suggested, that would be sufficient.
>
> While business was being transacted between them, I examined several paintings which were upon the wall, and at once recognized two from the hand of Carl Haag. As my form of recreation has long been painting in watercolor, I passed a quarter of an hour very pleasantly in looking at the pictures. Business

being done, I think it probably occurred to the lady that she could hardly be rude to an Englishman in her own house. She came to my end of the *sala*, and after making some banal remarks, the object of which was to remove any idea of discourtesy, I replied by speaking of my enjoyment of the pictures and specially called attention to one where the painter had caught the atmosphere of the desert. She was interested in my criticisms, and recognizing that I knew something of the subject, informed me that the picture in question was painted by her. That broke the ice. We got into an interesting conversation, which ended by her stating that she would have tea on the table every day at five o'clock, and would be very pleased to see me any and every day during the week I proposed to remain in Damascus. She then sent for her husband and introduced us. We became excellent friends, and by his means I was able to get into various mosques and see other sights which I should not have seen but for his assistance.

Pears went several times to have tea with Jane, and found her "a close observer, an excellent talker, with keen flashes of insight and wit." Just as Richard Burton had been, Pears was fascinated with the Englishwoman's knowledge of harem life. Jane told the journalist that while the women of the harem were delightfully childlike in some respects, this quality was most unattractive when it showed itself in "sudden bursts of anger, swift reconciliation, passionate affection, and even hate." (She apparently failed to see any resemblance to herself in this description.)

One story his hostess told him about her unusual life in Syria made a particularly vivid impression on Pears. Once, as a result of a mix-up in orders, the entire Mesrab tribe, numbering in the hundreds, swarmed into Damascus and took over Jane's house, sleeping in every available space indoors and out. Medjuel was away from the city at the time, and could not be reached to straighten things out. Sir Edwin thought such an invasion would have terrified Jane, but she was amused at his reaction. Her only fear, she explained, was that the Turks, being aware of the situation, might take advantage of the opportunity to provoke a one-sided fight by insulting the Sitt Mesrab. Had that happened, she told Pears, her tribe would have rushed to avenge the insult, and the result, a wholesale slaughter, would have been fatal for Medjuel. When Pears repeated this story, which he could not fully understand, to Mr. Heald, the banker told him that the Mesrabs were so fiercely loyal to Medjuel's wife that any one of them would have died for her. Seeing the deep affection and respect that Jane commanded, Sir Edwin left Syria with the impression that "under different circumstances this woman could have exercised a most valuable influence on any society into which she had been thrown."

In the morning of November 17, 1876, a few days after the visit of Pears, a very unusual caller came to the Mesrab house. Emperor Dom Pedro II of Brazil was on a tour of the Middle East, and, like Pears, he wanted to meet the most famous lady in Damascus. The emperor was a tall, handsome, fair-haired man of fifty-one, who cared little for the trappings of royalty. He possessed an insatiable curiosity and was never happier than when conversing with people from whom he felt he could learn. His visit with Jane and her husband was recorded in his diary:

Before lunch I went to the house of Lady Ellenborough who married a Bedouin sheik named Medjuel. The visit was arranged with the excuse that I wanted to see her paintings of Palmyra where she had often been. I met the Sheik first. He had a beautiful, intelligent face, darker than Abd-el-Kader. He is short and he was wearing, as the latter, a ring with a silver mounting and a *sinete* stone.

He showed me his horses of two Arabian strains—I don't think they were particularly handsome—and he talked with me through an interpreter until his wife, who appears to have been very beautiful, arrived.... I asked her to show me the paintings of Palmyra and she quickly went to look for the heavy album in which I admired the beautiful watercolors she had done of Palmyra, Babylon, the Acropolis in Athens and a town on the island of Tinos. She told me her mother had been an outstanding painter in oils. Her own paintings reveal a great artistic talent, and Mrs. Medjuel is a person of great intelligence. I asked her for a picture of her husband and herself as a souvenir, and she told me she had only an old daguerreotype of herself (just what I was hoping for), and she almost ran to bring a picture made in Rome (a spectacularly beautiful face!) and a pencil sketch she had made of her husband, which reveals plainly her love for him and does her credit as an artist. We drank coffee in a room which is attractively decorated in Oriental taste, and they came to the garden door, which is the entrance to their house, to bid me farewell.

Jane was as much taken with the emperor of Brazil as he was with her. In her diary she wrote of Dom Pedro, "Of all the pleasant royalties I have ever come across, he is the pleasantest." This was high praise for a woman who was able to make such comparisons firsthand.

According to all who saw Jane Digby in her last years, her great beauty survived remarkably; her incredible stamina, however, was finally beginning to wane. When she turned seventy in the spring of 1877, the greatest desert war in half a century was raging between the Shammar and the Anazeh, involving every Bedouin in Syria, and for the first time Jane was unable to ride into battle with her tribe. The Mesrabs were in the thick of the fighting, while their *Umm-el-Laban* was left miserable in Damascus, torn between fear for Medjuel's safety and jealousy over his proximity to Ouadjid. Her stamina may have deserted her, but her "beating, burning heart" had not.

21

◆———◆

The Last Three Years

It is now a month and twenty days since Medjuel last slept with me! What can be the reason?

—JANE DIGBY, AGE SEVENTY-THREE

The Syrian desert was relatively peaceful by the beginning of 1878; the tribes had exhausted themselves in battle, and the Turks, who had not fired a single shot, were, as usual, the only real victors. The temporary truce was particularly fortunate for a pair of aristocratic English newlyweds, Lady Anne and Wilfrid Scawen Blunt, who arrived in the Middle East in January, planning to spend two years among the Bedouins. Such an unusual honeymoon was fitting for the granddaughter of Lord Byron, and it was fitting also that near the close of her life Jane should entertain the descendant of the man whose poetry had so long ago fired "pretty little Miss Digby" with dreams of faraway places. Lady Anne shared Jane's admiration for the desert Arabs, and in one of the books she wrote about her adventures—*A Pilgrimage to Nejd*—she described Medjuel's Anazeh Bedouins as "the finest flower of a truly noble race."

When the Blunts came to call on Jane in Damascus, it was through Medjuel's son. In April of 1878, in the tent of Betayen ibn Merschid, Lady Anne and her husband were presented to Japhet el Mesrab, who had fought in the recent wars alongside Sheik Betayen. The "good-looking, extremely polite young man who rode a rather showy colt" (Lady Anne's description) invited the English couple to a meal in his own tent, and the three were quickly on the best of terms. The Bedouin told his guests about his English stepmother and insisted that they look up his family when they got to Damascus. "As regards the stepmother," Lady Anne wrote, "we have constantly heard her spoken of in the desert and always in terms of respect. She is a charitable person, and a providence to her husband's people, supplying them with money and everything they require. Medjuel himself is talked of as an extremely fortunate man, the possessor of boundless wealth, though some think of his marriage as a *mésalliance*, as the lady is not of Arab blood, and consequently not *asil* [noble]."

During the eight months that elapsed between the Blunts' meeting with Japhet and their arrival in Damascus, Japhet's stepmother had herself begun to think of her marriage a *mésalliance*, but for quite different reasons. In April she had moved back to Homs, as was her custom, and was, once more, confronted

237

with Ouadjid, who was then in her early thirties and very lovely. It was hard enough for Jane to listen to Bedouin love songs celebrating youth, ("How sweet the kissing of teeth, if thy sweetheart still be young!"), but her long-smoldering jealousy of Medjuel's daughter-in-law exploded when another tribeswoman casually mentioned to the Sitt Mesrab that Medjuel had once cursed his son Schebibb for being unkind to Ouadjid and had said in the heat of his anger that he wished him dead. Remembering Medjuel's terrible grief when Schebibb died, Jane was now certain that his grief was heightened by guilt and remorse. "It only proves to me how he, Medjuel, must have loved her," she wrote in her diary. Some strange, anguished words (two of which are totally illegible) scrawled across a page in one of Jane's sketchbooks from this period are apparently notes for a letter she was framing to Medjuel, who had the good fortune to be away at Hama when this new domestic crisis erupted:

—Why were you afraid the day her brother came? You must have loved her far more than you ever loved me and she must have known it—is it true that you wished to kill him if he did not divorce her, and that ——————— divorce at last...

Tortured by her bitter thoughts, Jane sent Medjuel a telegram demanding his instant return, and when she received no answer, she left abruptly for Damascus, where a bizarre new problem beset her. With no preliminaries whatsoever, her young and handsome dragoman, Anton, offered his services to console her in her husband's absence, and Jane was more horrified than flattered. She suspected that Anton had been listening to gossip in the bazaars about her scandalous past and had decided the amorous *Engleysi* lady might be ready for a new lover. Disturbed as she was over Medjuel's prolonged absence and the story she had heard at Homs, Jane apparently never considered Anton's proposal seriously, and she dismissed him forthwith. (This incident somehow survived anyway, repeated and embellished until years later *The Complete Peerage* noted that at the time of her death Jane was "contemplating an elopement with her drago-man.")

Several weeks after Jane's return to Damascus, she learned that Medjuel had been near death from another attack of fever in the desert. A missionary friend, the Reverend Mackintosh, had found the Mesrab sheik very ill at Yebrud and with quinine and salt had nursed him until he had recovered sufficiently to travel. Jane was overwhelmed with gratitude when Medjuel told her he owed his life to the Christian missionary's unselfish devotion. "No, none are so really kind and friendly as the people of God," she wrote. "And may God reward them richly, both here and in the world to come." Another passionate reconciliation raised Jane once more to a pinnacle of happiness, and once more there was content-ment in the Mesrab household. Ouadjid was forgotten—temporarily.

By the time Lady Anne and Wilfrid Blunt came to Damascus to pay a call on

Japhet's family, none of the emotional turmoil that had so recently buffeted Jane was evident. Byron's granddaughter was one of the few women who could manage to write about the former Lady Ellenborough without calling attention to Jane's four husbands and indeterminate number of lovers. To Lady Anne the Sitt Mesrab was interesting mainly for having married a Bedouin Sheik and for her knowledge of horses. The young English bride was as passionate a horsewoman as Jane, and she had come to the Middle East primarily to acquire Anazeh stock for the breeding of Arabian horses. The first meeting of the Blunts and the Mesrabs took place on December 7, 1878, and Lady Anne recorded her impressions:

> We have been spending the day with Mrs. Digby and her husband, Medjuel of the Mesrab, a very well bred and agreeable man, who has given us a great deal of valuable advice about our journey. They possess a charming house outside the town, surrounded by trees and gardens, and standing in its own garden with narrow streams of running water and paths with borders full of old-fashioned English flowers—wallflowers especially. There are birds and beasts too; pigeons and turtle doves flutter about among the trees, and a pelican sits by the fountain in the middle of the courtyard guarded by a fierce watch-dog....
>
> The main body of the house is quite simple in its bare Arab furnishing, but a separate building in the garden is fitted up like an English drawing-room with chairs, sofas, books, and pictures. Among many interesting and beautiful sketches kept in a portfolio, I saw some really fine water-color views of Palmyra done by Mrs. Digby many years ago when that town was less known than it is at present.

For the Blunts, Medjuel was the real center of attention, and it was one of the few times that Jane took a back seat to the sheik when English visitors were calling. Lady Anne was far more fascinated by Medjuel's knowledge of the desert and his family history than by his wife's notorious past. He was, she wrote, "a person entitled by birth and position to speak with authority." Like Jane, she had no feelings of racial superiority, and she did not consider her hostess a freak for having an Arab husband. Both Blunts were much impressed with Medjuel's manner and appearance, and neither thought of him as a "little man." "The Bedouin Arab of pure blood," Lady Anne wrote, "is seldom more than five feet six inches high; but he is long-limbed for his size; and the drapery in which he clothes himself gives him full advantage of his height. In figure he is generally light and graceful."

There was no one in Damascus, according to Lady Anne, who could give better advice on travel in the Syrian desert than Medjuel. It was Jane's husband, not Jane, of whom Anne Blunt had the most to record:

> The strange accident of his marriage with an English lady has withdrawn him for months at a time, but not estranged him from the desert, and he has adopted

little of the townsman in his dress, and nothing of the European.... It is also easy to see that his heart remains in the desert, his love for which is fully shared by the lady he has married; so that when he succeeds to the Sheykhat, as he probably will, for his brother appears to be considerably his senior, I think they will hardly care to spend much of their time in Damascus.

It did not occur to Lady Anne that Medjuel's wife was then seventy-one and that her days of riding off into the desert with her Bedouin tribe were over. Lady Anne's courage, horsemanship and youth were probably reminders to the Sitt Mesrab of what she had been, and when the Blunts left Damascus, according to the Oddie account, Jane wept that she could no longer keep the pace of desert life. The worst part of her enforced retirement was that Medjuel, who was only a few years younger, was still able to make the long, hard rides, and as always she was desolate each time he was away. There were no more protracted separations, however, and each short one was followed by a joyful reunion. Medjuel seldom returned from the desert without some gift to show his wife that she was constantly in his thoughts. For her seventy-third birthday, in April of 1880, he brought her the most beautiful horse that she had ever seen—a thoroughbred Saklowyek mare in foal. "If she does not suit me, I shall never get a horse that does," Jane wrote.

Despite these frequent demonstrations of Medjuel's affection, his possessive wife continued to be tormented by jealousy of Ouadjid. Early in the summer of 1880 Schebibb's widow died of a fever in the desert, but not even this seemed to give Jane peace of mind. It was only in August, nearly two months later, that Medjuel decided to tell Jane of Ouadjid's death, and the fact that he had withheld the news from her all that time suggested that he had felt the loss too deeply to discuss it. Jane was miserable to think he might have cared so much. "I am jealous of her memory," she confessed in her diary. "I strive for a feeling of pity and thankfulness rather than of hatred gratified." For thirteen years Jane had been tormented by suspicions of a romance between her husband and Ouadjid, and she was never completely convinced by Medjuel's frequent denials. Whether or not her suspicions were justified remains a mystery, but Jane's hatred for Ouadjid was reason enough for her husband to avoid the subject of his daughter-in-law under any circumstances.

In the fall of 1880, an English diplomat, Sir Valentine Chirol, called on Jane. Sir Valentine thought Jane older than she actually was (he was the only person who erred in this direction), but his description of her suggests that he was basing her age more on his memory of dates than on her appearance:

When I made her acquaintance she must have been getting on for eighty, but so long as her Turkish yashmak concealed the lower part of her face, her ivory white and almost unwrinkled brow, her luminous eyes and the fine line of her aquiline nose still preserved traces of the beauty which had captured so many hearts in many lands and the highest places. Not only was she well read, but the world had been to her a strangely interesting book, of which she still seemed to enjoy turning over many of the old pages with a disarming simplicity, as if they belonged not to her own but to some one else's life. She had also a keen sense of humor, and when I once suggested that she ought to write her memoirs, she replied with a chuckle that she was afraid they would be "a very naughty edition of the *Almanach de Gotha*," and then added rather primly that a prayer-book would be more suitable for her declining years.

Chirol disagreed with Jane's comparison of herself to Lady Hester Stanhope, for he felt that the Sitt Mesrab had a far happier life ("though it could hardly be called commonplace") than the freakish spinster who had been high priestess to the Druses. Unlike Lady Hester, who had lived and died in a bizarre fashion, Sir Valentine wrote that Madame Digby in her later life "resumed the pursuits of a refined Englishwoman." Chirol was referring to Jane's gardening, needlework and watercolors, but he would have been considerably surprised to know that shortly after his meeting with her, the woman who was approaching her seventy-fourth birthday complained bitterly in her diary, "It is now a month and twenty days since Medjuel last slept with me! What can be the reason?" (In some respects the Bedouin was showing his age more than Jane.)

Either because of his own advancing years or because he had a presentiment that Jane's days were numbered, Medjuel stayed at his wife's side during the spring of 1881, making only one short trip to Homs on tribal matters. Mary Mackintosh, the missionary who was now Jane's closest friend in Damascus, had gone to England to convalesce from an illness, leaving a void in Jane's life, unexpectedly filled when a slight acquaintance, a Turkish widow, died and left the custody of her little daughter Fatima to the wealthy and generous Sitt Mesrab. Had the woman known Jane's record as a mother, she might have had second thoughts, but Jane was delighted with the legacy and proved to be a responsible guardian. Her first concern was Fatima's education, and she battled with the Turkish government, which did not want the child converted to Christianity, for permission to enroll her in the Mackintosh school. Since it was Jane's money that was to pay for Fatima's education, the government finally relented.

Years of such openhandedness had finally begun to tell on Jane's seemingly unlimited wealth, and in May of 1881 she noted that she was distressed to refuse a loan of a hundred pounds to an unnamed friend. The friend already owed a hundred pounds to Jane and two hundred to Medjuel, but she was not worried about repayment. She simply did not have the cash to spare. Jane had recently paid a sizable sum to the Protestant cemetery authorities for the purchase and maintenance of a plot for herself, knowing that Medjuel with his Muslim beliefs could not be expected to tend her grave or to lie beside her in Christian ground.

Late in July of that year the woman who had lived in very good health under the most primitive of conditions fell ill with a virulent dysentery. Medjuel was with her, but all her close friends had fled the devastating heat of Damascus for the cooler, healthier climate of the Lebanon mountains. The only nurse Medjuel could find was an Armenian woman whose husband was with the Mission to the Jews. Jane did not know her well and did not particularly like her; the woman had shown herself in a bad light a few months earlier when Jane was donating some clothes to the mission. "I was surprised, distressed and disappointed at her indiscretion about the dresses—almost asking for things," she wrote at the time.

There were no miracle drugs in Damascus in 1881, and Medjuel was forced to watch helplessly as his wife grew weaker each day. Sometimes Jane would ask to be carried outside to the *liwan*, where she could see from her couch the gardens she had so lovingly planned and tended, and what was left of the curious menagerie she had collected. Her fierce Kurdish hound left off his continual harassment of the pelican to lie down soberly, close to his mistress who could subdue him with her soft, sweet voice, now barely audible. Not only had Jane's stamina deserted her, but apparently her will to live had gone too. Once she could no longer ride into the desert beside her Bedouin husband, once the *yashmak* had to be used for concealment rather than disguise, once the great adventures were behind rather than ahead, she could find little reason to go on. On August 11, 1881, the tempestuous life of Jane Digby came to a remarkably serene close.

Epilogue

Thus lived—thus died she;
Never more on her
Shall sorrow light, or shame.
—LORD BYRON

Following the hastily arranged Anglican funeral and his dramatic graveside farewell, Medjuel rode off into the desert to mourn his wife in his own fashion, among the Bedouins who had respected and loved her. For the ritual feast a lamb was killed, and afterwards one of the finest Mesrab camels was sacrificed in her memory.

The beautiful house just outside the Damascus walls meant nothing to Medjuel with Jane gone; the time spent there had been little more than a concession to his English wife. A cynical story was told in Syria that the Bedouin deliberately grazed his camels on the rare plants in Jane's garden before he rented the house to the Reverend J. Segall of the London Jews Society, but this seems unlikely. If Jane's beloved dahlias became camel fodder, it could have happened while Medjuel mourned in the desert, leaving no one to supervise the house and the animals.

In April of 1882 Jane's will was probated in London, and her estate was valued at six thousand and twenty-two pounds, two shillings and sixpence. This was the document witnessed by Dr. William Wright and James Orr Scott in the presence of Richard Burton eleven years earlier:

I, Jane Elizabeth Digby el Mesrab, of Damascus, in Syria, Wife of the Sheik Medjuel el Mesrab, declare this to be my last Will and Testament. I give to my husband, as a token of my respect and regard, my house, stables, gardens and premises situated near the Bab Menzel Khassabb in the City of Damascus, together with all furniture, plate, linen, coppers, carpets, saddlery and household goods, my horses, dromedaries and other livestock, my gold watch and chain, large ruby ring, and Arab ornaments, belt and jewelry in gold and silver and my silver gilt headpiece, breast ornament and bridle studded with coral, and my silver gilt ewer and basin, together with the sum of one thousand pounds (being a moiety of the legacy of two thousand pounds bequeathed to me by my dear mother). I bequeath the sum of one thousand pounds (being the other moiety of the said legacy), my diamond necklace and earrings, my emerald and diamond bracelet and my silver gilt dressing box to my son Heribert, Baron de Venningen, Ulner, and I bequeath my colored diamond sprig for the head, and earrings, and my chrysolite necklace, together with the portraits of my dear father and mother, and the miniature of my brother Lord Digby to my said brother, Lord Digby. And I give to my brother Kenelm Henry in token of my affection my large turquoise ring, my silver and gilt inkstand and my colored sketches in Switzerland and Palmyra. I give all the residue of my estate and effects whatsoever after payment thereout of my just debts and testamentary expenses, unto my said husband absolutely. And I appoint my said brother Lord Digby Executor of this my Will. In witness thereof, I, the said Jane Elizabeth Digby el Mesrab, the Testatrix, have, to this my last Will and Testament, set my hand, this fifteenth day of June, in the year of Our Lord, one thousand eight hundred and seventy-one.

After Heribert's legacy was paid, the balance remaining in Jane's estate was sent to Medjuel, delivered in packets of five hundred gold sovereigns each, stamped with the consular seal. The Bedouin's indifference to the money was further proof that he never had designs on his wife's fortune. Only when he wished to buy camels for his tribe did he remember the packets, and then he would spill one open to pay. When he died a few years later, some of the packets, still unopened, were found under his pillow. There was nothing avaricious about Medjuel, and, by Western standards, he appears to have had little money sense. To the friends in Damascus whom he knew Jane cared for he gave generously of her jewelry and other personal belongings not mentioned in the will. Before renting the house he sold what was left in it for a fraction of its value. It was said that rings worth hundreds of pounds went for a few piasters.

In her biography of Jane, E. M. Oddie wrote that a Damascus hotel keeper claimed to have been bribed by a relative of Jane's named Ellenborough to break into the house shortly after Jane's death to get an album or diary. This seems suspect. The unidentified originator of the story was apparently unaware that Jane's family name was Digby, not Ellenborough, and the relative who would have been most interested in suppressing any intimate memoirs was Jane's brother Edward, who as her executor would, in any case, receive all her papers to dispose of as he saw fit.

Medjuel was more than scrupulous in carrying out the terms of his wife's will. To Heribert in Bavaria the Bedouin sent valuable emeralds other than those specified in the will, and the stunning miniature portrait of Jane by James Holmes as well. Kenelm Digby received all of his sister's sketches, not just those of Palmyra and Switzerland as she had designated.

Correspondence now in the possession of the Digby family reveals that following Jane's death, Lord Digby went to a great deal of trouble to locate Mathilde Selden (Didi), Jane's illegitimate Schwarzenberg daughter. His motive is not clear, but he may have felt that the niece he had never seen would have a claim against her mother's estate, even though she was not mentioned in Jane's will. Through the law firm of Bennett, Dawson and Bennett, Lord Digby was able to contact in Bohemia a Madame A. de Ranchy, who was a personal friend of Mathilde. According to Madame de Ranchy's reply, Didi had "inherited the beauty of her mother to whom she is said to bear a great likeness, and the mental gifts of her father." Mathilde was well aware, Madame de Ranchy wrote, of the identity of her mother, "for whom she always had a longing," and she had once asked her friend to bring her from Munich a photograph of the Stieler portrait of Lady Ellenborough. The photograph, she added, was a very poor one and not very satisfactory. Lord Digby was evidently so touched by this story that he sent Didi a miniature of her mother. At the time of this correspondence in 1883, the domineering Princess Mathilde Schwarzenberg was a very old woman, but she was still clearly in charge of her namesake, for the fifty-three-year-old Didi explained that she had delayed responding to Lord Digby's first letter until she had received the approval of the princess.

Many years ago Jane's Damascus house near the Bab Menzel Khassabb was destroyed to make way for tram lines, but her grave can still be seen in the Protestant cemetery, between that of the historian Henry Thomas Buckle and a Countess Teleki. (Both Buckle and the countess were tourists in Damascus when they were suddenly taken ill and died.) The tombstone bears the inscription, "Jane Elizabeth, daughter of Admiral Sir Henry Digby G.C.B., Born April 3, 1807, died August 11, 1881. My trust is in the tender mercy of God for ever and ever." Another stone, placed by Medjuel at the base of the cross, is inscribed with Jane's name in Arabic. There are still walnut trees in the cemetery, but nothing is left of the Pride of India and damask roses that Dr. William Wright described when he visited the graveyard a few years after Jane's death. According to Dr. Wright's account, Jane's lasting resting place did not enjoy the tranquillity usually accorded the dead:

> In the midst of the chaos of neglected, open graveyards, a closed substantial door [to the Protestant section of the Jewish cemetery] is a mark for fanatics, and so the cemetery is thickly peppered with shots and slugs, and blue bullet marks appear on the stones at each side, showing fanaticism in excess of skill; and sometimes the gate used to be smashed in several times a year.

Neither Jane's death nor the twenty-five years of fidelity to her Bedouin husband that preceded it could still the shrill voice of scandal her name continued to evoke. When her death became known outside Damascus, the journalists who had found Jane such fascinating copy eight years earlier were not disposed to let the lady exit without fanfare. A Middle East correspondent of the German *Gazette* rose to the occasion, writing from Beirut: "I met today an old acquaintance, the camel-driver, Sheik Abdul, and he told me that his wife was dead. Her name was once known through all the East. Sheik Abdul is the ninth husband of Lady Ellenborough, whom I met for the first time about thirty years ago at Munich, just after she had eloped with Prince Schwarzenberg from the residence of her first husband. She then went to Italy, where as she told me herself, she was married six times in succession."

Such stories gave new zest to a nearly forgotten scandal. No one really cared if the six husbands in Italy were fictitious, nor did it matter that the "camel-driver" was every bit as blue-blooded in his part of the world as his English wife was in hers. Even *The Complete Peerage* had the facts hopelessly garbled:

> The cause of her divorce was her adultery with Prince von Schwarzenberg, with whom her husband fought a duel, and from whom he recovered damages for 25,000 pounds in an action for crim. con. On his abandonment of her, she next became mistress of Ludwig I, King of Bavaria. She m., 2ndly, 10 Nov., 1832, Karl Theodor Herbert, Baron de Venningen, Prime Minister of Bavaria, who committed suicide when she left him. She m., 3rdly, Sheikh Medjwal el Mizrab, an Arab general in the Greek army. She d. in Damascus of dysentery, 11 Aug. 1881, aged 74, being then contemplating an elopement with her Dragoman!

Burke's Peerage identified Jane's first two husbands correctly and then fell apart at the seams: "She was married thirdly, to General Sheik Medjuel of the Greek Army, and fourthly, to Medjouell, an Eastern gentleman."

These erroneous "statistics" were faithfully copied by many authors and served for years as the main source of information about Jane Digby. Matters were not helped by her harassed and misguided brother, who had burned most of her papers in his possession. He did not realize in his haste that he was leaving only the sordid public records in the newspapers and the Parliamentary minutes of Lord Ellenborough's divorce suit, which added up to a very one-sided portrait. So much myth began to cloud Jane's life story that even her own cousin, Anna Maria Stirling, writing a biography of their famous Coke grandfather, was unable to separate fact from fiction in the vignette she gave of Jane. In many respects Jane's family knew less about her than comparative strangers, because of their conspiracy of silence on the subject of their notorious kinswoman. This family policy reached as far back as the 1850s, when Edmond About's book, *La Grèce Contemporaine*, was translated into English, and someone among the Cokes or Digbys managed to see that every anecdote involving Jane was deleted.

Nearly a hundred years after Jane's death, the Digbys, the Cokes, the Venningens and the Theotokys—even the Schwarzenbergs and the Ellenboroughs— are no longer reluctant to talk about the intriguing lady who ties them all together. (It was not this way just a generation ago, when in many of these noble houses Jane's name was not allowed to be mentioned.) With these doors finally unlocked, a far more complete picture of Jane has emerged than could ever before be presented.

The present Lord Digby, a great-grandnephew of Jane, lives with Lady Digby and their children at Minterne House in Dorset, the family seat where Jane was once banished with Steely following her separation from Lord Ellenborough. In the Muniments Room at Minterne are some of Jane's papers that escaped the Victorian bonfire: a notebook of poetry, some sketchbooks, a few letters and legal documents. Someone in the family, possibly Lady Theresa Digby, wrote a brief chronological history of Jane's years in Europe, apparently based on letters that were afterward destroyed. The delightful Thomas Barber portrait of Jane and her brothers, painted in 1816, hangs in Minterne's magnificent drawing room, and two of Jane's watercolors of Palmyra are on the wall in an upstairs bedroom. Lord Digby's sister Pamela (Jane's great-grandniece) was formerly married to Sir Winston Churchill's son Randolph and is now the wife of Averell Harriman. The present Earl of Leicester, a distant cousin to Jane, occupies palatial Holkham Hall in Norfolk, which is open to the public one day a week during the summer. The dowager Lady Ellenborough, whose late husband was descended from a nephew of Jane's husband, Edward Law, now lives in London, and although she is no relation to Jane, she has become deeply interested in the life of "that other Lady Ellenborough."

The largest known collection of Jane's personal papers is in Munich. King Ludwig I, the great romantic, kept most of the letters and notes from his lovely Ianthe; there are more than seventy of them in the *Geheimes Hausarchiv*, the secret archives, of the Wittelsbach family, in the keeping of Ludwig's direct descendant, His Royal Highness, Duke Albrecht of Bavaria. Tambosi's, where Jane and Ludwig first met, is operating today as the Cafe Anast, and is still a favorite meeting place. Although the Nymphenburg Palace is now a state museum, Duke Albrecht is entitled to the use of the south wing. Occasionally he gives a private reception there in the evenings, when the fountains are floodlit and the sound of music and laughter carries through the south gallery to the pavilion where Jane's portrait by Joseph Stieler hangs—the famous Schönheiten, the Gallery of Beauties. In the daytime the corridors of the magnificent Wittelsbach summer residence resound to the heavy footsteps of hordes of tourists, who gaze with awe at the English beauty with the golden ringlets, the classic features and the dreamy look in her azure eyes. Tour guides recount Jane's romantic odyssey in several languages with small regard for fact. So the elegant lady in the deep blue *gros de Naples* gown with a jeweled *ferronnière* resting like a crown on her brow continues to inspire fiction.

On a quiet residential street within walking distance of the Nymphenburg lives Frau Ilse Horner, a great-great-granddaughter of Mathilde Selden, the illegitimate child of Jane and Felix Schwarzenberg. Frau Horner, who fled from the Russian advance into Czechoslovakia at the end of World War II, managed to save her copy of Mathilde's portrait. There are today more than seventy living direct descendants of Jane and Felix through their love child—quite a lineage from a man who never married.

Jane's closest living relative is her great-granddaughter, the Baronin Gabriella Venningen, whose home is just outside Munich in Pöcking. The Baronin and Frau Horner have been friends since the day the Czechoslovak refugee looked in the Munich phone book to find some of her English ancestor's Venningen descendants, and the two women refer to each other as "cousin." (The females of Mathilde's branch married and had children quite young, while the Venningen males married late, which accounts for the difference in the number of generations separating the Baronin and Frau Horner from Jane.) The former Schloss Venningen in Weinheim now serves as the city hall, and for some years the seat of the Barons von Venningen has been located in Upper Austria in the hamlet of Riegerding, six miles from Ried-im-Inkreiss. There the young Baron Karl Venningen, Jane's great-great-grandson, raises black angus cattle and oversees the brewing of Venningen beer. One of the family treasures at Riegerding is the Holmes miniature of Jane Digby at age twenty-one, which Medjuel sent to Heribert so long ago.

The tall Italian house in Bagni di Lucca where Leonidas Theotoky fell to his death is now boarded up; a sign identifies it as the English church. The English colony that flourished there in the nineteenth century has long since disappeared and with it the need for an Anglican place of worship. No trace can be found of Leonidas's grave. Members of the Theotoky family say that since the tragedy of little Leonidas, one Theotoky male in each succeeding generation has met a violent death.

The present house at Dukades on the island of Corfu is a later structure than the one in which Jane and Spiro lived, and it has been uninhabited since a series of military occupations during World War II. The rambling mansion is fast deteriorating, and the gardens Jane laid out have long been overgrown, but a proud Corfiote caretaker is happy to spin a few highly imaginative stories of the beautiful Ianthe Theotoky. He shows his visitors a handle-less sauce dish from the white porcelain dinner set with the Theotoky crest in gold, which Jane had made to order. In what was once the library a heap of magnificent leather-bound books, some undoubtedly the handiwork of Spiro, lie moldering on the floor. The bearded Greek Orthodox priest of the small village will point out the vault in the chapel wall where the handsome Count Spiridion Theotoky lies buried with none of his wives (some say he had three) beside him.

Countess Eleni Theotoky, whose late husband was a great-grandnephew of Spiro, makes her home in the town of Corfu, and has kept a few pieces of the gold-banded dinner set intact. She is a great admirer of Jane Digby and during a visit to the Middle East before World War II made a pilgrimage to Jane's grave. The portraits of Spiro, Jane, and Leonidas, made at the beginning of their tragic summer in Italy, are now in the possession of the present Count Spiridion Theotoky in Athens.

One afternoon in the spring of 1974 Countess Eleni Theotoky, Frau Ilse Horner, the Baronin Gabriella Venningen, and I met in Munich for tea to discuss the fascinating Englishwoman in whom we four share an interest. This interest was given new impetus in 1972 by a Bavarian television series on the life of King Ludwig I. In the installment dealing with Jane Digby, the Baronin was interviewed along with Lord Digby, and thousands of Bavarians heard for the first time some tantalizing fragments of the life of Lady Ellenborough.

No tangible trace of Jane can be found among the Syrian Bedouins today, but the *Umm-el-Laban* remains a legend in the Mesrab tribe. When the present Lord Digby was in the Middle East during World War II, he found a member of the tribe who was able to draw from memory a sketch of the house Jane and Medjuel had lived in at Homs.

The ancient desert city of Palmyra is not so difficult to visit today as it was when Jane made her first trip there with the Mesrab Bedouins. A strong-willed French noblewoman, the late Baroness d'Andurin, built a tourist hotel, the Zenobia, in the heart of the ruins, and the only hardships now are said to be indifferent service, brackish plumbing, and the sulfurous stench of the oasis water. Jane's Damascus account book was preserved by the alertness of M. John Joly of Beirut, who discovered it gathering dust in a desk drawer when the firm that had handled Jane's business affairs was moving to a new office.

Bits and pieces of Jane Digby's story have come from sources so diverse and through coincidences so incredible that one might be tempted to believe that the lady who "loved not wisely, but too well" was pulling a few of the strings herself. It is undeniable that during her seventy-four years Jane touched in some way the lives of many people in many places, but the greatest proof of her peculiar brand of magic is the fact that nearly a hundred years after her death her adventures capture the imagination of everyone who hears them.

To those who really knew Jane Digby she was a far different person from the naughty lady depicted in the tabloids. One devoted friend—Lady Emily Strang-ford—described the other Jane in a black-bordered letter of condolence to Lord Digby when his sister was erroneously reported dead in 1873:

It is a pleasure for me to record on paper more freely than could be done in print how truly I was attached to her, how worthy, how fully worthy I found her of all love and affection and respect.... When I first met her I knew nothing whatever of her previous history—she herself told it to me before we parted; by that time I had learned to love and admire her for what I saw her to be. She was in a difficult position for one less unselfish, less devoted than she was to fill worthily —how she did fill it only a few people know. She had a wonderful power of contentedness and an unselfishness that I believe could never be outdone. She carried out a simple, unaffected, quiet, beautiful, useful life, finding her happiness in doing good to all of those who came near her, amply repaid by her husband's love and the affectionate respect of all who knew her. I have heard most of the lies told of her by people resident at and passing through Damascus, and I know the value of each. I know how some of them hurt her—and how gently and well she bore them. Her grateful loving friendship for those who loved and respected her was touching with its simplicity and tenderness.... But for herself I believe her death will be her infinite gain. The wrongs that she did and the wrongs that were done to her will be more equally judged in the balance than have been before to say nothing of the gentle, faithful life during the past sixteen or seventeen years that may well have wiped out some of the past.... Few will mourn for her in England—very many will weep for her and miss her sorely in Syria. It may be that silence is her best epitaph, but I could not ever hesitate to bear my testimony to her goodness if it was in any way needed or wise to express it.

If Jane was not entirely the saint that Lady Strangford believed her to be, neither was she the black sinner nor the nymphomaniac that she has sometimes been portrayed. "The misfortune of my nature is to consider love as all in all," she wrote to Ludwig. She wanted above all else to give herself completely to the man of her choosing, but in the act of giving there was a fierce possessiveness that could stifle the love she prized so highly. Love was always the dominant theme of her life: love pursued, love won, love rejected, love turning to ashes then rising to beckon her again. Despite her many defeats, she remained her own woman—she followed neither "the highway of virtue nor the miry path of the courtesan." She followed the dictates of her heart. No one has ever done that with more style than Jane Digby. Lord Byron said:

> *Is it not better thus our lives to wear*
> *Than join the crushing crowd?*

Notes

These notes are intended to serve as an informal guide to the reference material used in the writing of Jane Digby's biography. Most of Jane's personal papers are found today in the Muniments Room of Minterne House, Dorset (seat of Lord Digby), and in Munich's *Geheimes Hausarchiv*, where more than seventy of her letters to King Ludwig I of Bavaria are preserved. The diaries Jane kept during her life in Syria have been lost, but quotations and a narrative of events taken from them were recorded in a 1936 biography, *The Odyssey of a Loving Woman*, written by the late E. M. Oddie. An unknown member of the Digby family in the nineteenth century made a synopsis of Jane's European years from letters now destroyed, and this synopsis will be referred to as the *Digby Chronology*. Another source frequently mentioned is *Vingt-Cinq Ans à Paris* by Count Rodolphe Apponyi, which will be designated as the *Apponyi Journal*. When a source is cited in the text, it will not always be repeated in the notes, and general historical sources will not be cited.

Prologue

The story of Jane's Damascus funeral is from the description found in Oddie, and Sir Richard Burton's phrase is quoted in *The Wilder Shores of Love* by Lesley Blanch. Other direct quotations are from *An Account of Palmyra and Zenobia* by Dr. William Wright and *La Grèce Contemporaine* by Edmond About.

Chapter 1

Most of the material concerning the Coke family is from C. W. James's *Chief Justice Coke* and A. M. W. Stirling's *Coke of Norfolk and His Friends*. "Cavalier Intellectual," an article in the November 1972 issue of *MD*, provides an excellent profile of Sir Kenelm Digby, and another source is E. W. Bligh's *Sir Kenelm Digby and His Venetia*. The Graham Greene quotation is from *Lord Rochester's Monkey*, and the description of Sir Everard Digby at Oxford is found in Catherine Drinker Bowen's *Francis Bacon*. For John Aubrey's comments, Oliver Lawson Dick's edition of *Aubrey's Brief Lives* was used. Other sources for this chapter include *In English Homes*, Vol. III, by Charles Latham and *Burke's Peerage*. Anecdotes concerning Lady Andover are found in Mrs. Stirling's book; the naval exploits of Capt. Henry Digby are discussed by both Stirling and Oddie. Sir Kenelm Digby's quotations came from his *Private Memoirs*.

Chapter 2

Background material for the Regency came from several sources, including J. B. Priestley's *The Prince of Pleasure*, Arthur Bryant's *The Age of Elegance*, and Christopher Hibbert's two-volume *George IV*. Stories of life at Holkham Hall are found in Stirling's *Coke of Norfolk* and Anna Maria Wilhelmina Pickering's *Memoirs*. Jane's childhood letters are preserved at Minterne, and the description of her at age thirteen comes from Thornton Hall's *Romances of the Peerage*. Also in Hall's book are the stories of Jane's adventure with the gypsies and her alleged attempted elopement with a Holkham stable groom.

Chapter 3

Background sources include Elizabeth Longford's *Wellington, Pillar of State*, and the previously mentioned works of Priestley, Bryant and Hibbert. The Albert H. Imlah biography, *Lord Ellenborough*, was the major source for the portrait of Jane's first husband, and the poetry written by Jane and Edward was found in Jane's notebook at Minterne. Wording of the special marriage license came from Oddie, and About's quote is found in *La Grèce Contemporaine*. Other quotations are taken from *The Creevey Papers*, *The Journal of Mrs. Arbuthnot*, *The Reminiscences of Lady Dorothy Nevill*, *Correspondence of Mr. Joseph Jekyll*, *Almack's*, and *Letters of Harriet, Countess Granville*.

Chapter 4

The romance between Jane and Frederick Madden was revealed in Madden's diaries, now at the Bodleian Library, Oxford. Reminiscences of life at Holkham Hall during the reign of the "White Lily" came from *Coke of Norfolk*, *The Letter-Bag of Lady Elizabeth Spencer Stanhope*, the Pickering *Memoirs*, and Sir Algernon West's *Memoir of Sir Henry Keppel, G.C.B.* Jane's poem is another from the Minterne notebook. Henry Anson's ill-fated Syrian adventure and details of the 1827 publication of Sir Kenelm Digby's memoirs are related in Oddie. Other sources for this chapter were Imlah's *Lord Ellenborough* and *The Creevey Papers*.

Chapter 5

Prince Felix zu Schwarzenberg by Adolf Schwarzenberg, and Edward Crankshaw's *Fall of the House of Habsburg* provided material for the description of Prince Felix. The characterization of the political scene in London of 1828–1829 was drawn from Lord Ellenborough's *Political Diary*, Longford's *Wellington, Pillar of State*, and Hibbert's *George IV*. Details of the meetings between Lady Ellenborough and Prince Schwarzenberg are fully documented in the Parliamentary records of the Ellenborough divorce bill. Those records also contain Jane's two letters to Ellenborough, as well as an outline of Jane's actions in the months immediately following the Ellenboroughs' separation. Contemporary comments are from *The Creevey Papers*, the *Apponyi Journal*, and *The Reminiscences and Recollections of Captain Gronow*. The anecdote concerning Felix Schwarzenberg's nickname "Cadland" came from the *Correspondence of Mr. Joseph Jekyll*. The poem Jane wrote to Felix is in the Minterne notebook.

Chapter 6

Testimony in the Parliamentary hearing on the Ellenborough divorce bill is found in the *Report of the Minutes of Evidence*, printed by order of the House of Commons. A lively description of the debate on the divorce in both houses is given by Horace Wyndham in *Judicial Dramas*. Other sources include Oddie, files of the *Times*, Longford's *Wellington*, and Hibbert's *George IV*. Contemporary comments are from *The Journal of Mrs. Arbuthnot* and *Correspondence of Princess Lieven and Earl Grey*. Lord Ellenborough's poem and other sidelights of his personal life came from the Imlah biography.

Chapter 7

Packet boat travel from England to the Continent around 1830 is described in detail by W. M. Thackeray in *Vanity Fair*. Jane's trip to Basel is documented in the *Digby Chronology*, and the story of Mathilde Selden's birth was verified by Frau Ilse Horner of Munich, a direct descendant of Jane's illegitimate daughter. Schwarzenberg material is found in Crankshaw's *Fall of the House of Habsburg* and the biography by Adolf Schwarzenberg. Background material for Paris in the 1830s is found both in Oddie and in *The Wilder Shores of Love* by Lesley Blanch. Other sources include *Prometheus, The Life of Balzac* by André Maurois, Lady Blessington's *An Idler in France*, and the *Digby Chronology*. Jane's poem to the infant Felix is among those in the Minterne notebook, and her comment on Felix Schwarzenberg's treatment of her is from a letter, now lost, quoted in Oddie.

Chapter 8

Descriptions of Munich and of Ludwig I, King of Bavaria, are based mainly on Luise von Kobell's *Unter den vier ersten Königen Bayerns*, Carl Fernau's *München Hundert und Eins*, and Georg Jakob Wolf's *Ein Jahrhundert München*. Some material came from two biographies of Lola Montez—*The Uncrowned Queen* by Ishbel Ross and *Lola Montez* by Amanda Darling—and from Count Egon Caesar Corti's biography, *König Ludwig von Bayern*. All of Jane's letters excerpted in this chapter are found in the *Geheimes Hausarchiv* in Munich. The quotations from the Marchesa Florenzi and her maid Gita are from *König Ludwig I und die Schönheiten Seiner Galerie* by Hans Thies. Other sources include Oddie, the civil registry of Palermo, Sicily, the *Almanach de Gotha* and a registry of Bavarian noble families, *Genealogisches Handbuch des in Bayern emmatrikulierten Adels*.

Chapter 9

The most complete documentation of the relationship between Jane and the famous French novelist is found in Herbert J. Hunt's "Balzac and Lady Ellenborough," in the July 1958 issue of the Oxford University *French Studies*. Hunt included in his article all the known references to Jane in Balzac's correspondence, as well as the full text of Jane's letter to Balzac. Jane's other letters that are quoted in this chapter are in the *Geheimes Hausarchiv*. Passages from Balzac's *Lily of the Valley* are from the English translation by Clara Bell and James Waring. Munich background material was compiled from the German works of Luise von Kobell and Carl Fernau, previously cited. Other sources include the biography of Balzac by André Maurois and *Vie de Balzac* by André Billy. The story of Marguerite Gardiner, Countess of Blessington, is chronicled in Michael Sadleir's *Blessington-D'Orsay*.

Chapter 10

All Jane's letters to Ludwig that are quoted in this chapter are in the *Geheimes Hausarchiv*, with the exception of the one complaining about how her portrait was hung. This letter, for some curious reason, found its way to another section of the Bavarian State Archives. Jane's quarrel with Karl Venningen and the baron's comment on his wife toward the end of the chapter are both found in Oddie, as is the anecdote of King Otto and the Acropolis. Background for Otto's accession to the Greek throne was compiled from *Modern Greece* by John Campbell and Phillip Sherrard, and George Finlay's *History of Greece*. The history of the Corfiote Theotokys was provided by the Countess Eleni Theotoky and members of her family, with some additional information from Nondas Stamatopoulos in his book, *Old Corfu*. Jane's stay at Schwetzingen was recorded by Count Corti in his Ludwig biography, and the legend of her equestrian feat is found in *König Ludwig und die Schönheiten Seiner Galerie* by Hans Thies. Other sources are the *Apponyi Journal* for the duel story and Stirling's *Coke of Norfolk* for information on Jane's English family in the year 1837.

Chapter 11

The Baden paternity document, Karl Venningen's letter to Jane and the *Digby Chronology* are all preserved at Minterne. The Balzac quotation is from *The Lily of the Valley*, and Charles Dickens's words are taken from *A Tale of Two Cities*. Edmond About's story about Jane's Greek Orthodox baptism is found in *La Grèce Contemporaine*, and his description of Santorini wine comes from *The King of the Mountains*. A picture of Tinos as it was in 1841 was provided by Alexandre Buchon in *Voyage dans L'Eubée, Les Iles Ioniennes et Les Cyclades en 1841*. Background material on Corfu came from *The Enchanted Island of Corfu* by Marie Aspiati and from *Old Corfu* by Nondas Stamatopoulos. The quotation from Lawrence Durrell is found in *Prospero's Cell*. Details of the 1843 coup d'état in Athens are given in Campbell and Sherrard's *Modern Greece*.

Chapter 12

Most of the descriptions of Othonian Athens and of King Otto and Queen Amalia are taken from the English translation of Edmond About's *La Grèce Contemporaine*, which was published in Edinburgh in 1855 under the title of *The Greeks of the Present Day*. The original French edition, however, had to be consulted for About's references to Ianthe Theotoky, as every one of them was mysteriously deleted from the English version. About's *King of the Mountains* contains a colorful, if partially fictitious, picture of life among the Pallikari. Works providing a general background are Finlay's *History of Greece*, Campbell and Sherrard's *Modern Greece*, *La Grèce du Roi Otho* by Edouard Thouvenal and *The Greeks of Today* by Charles Tuckerman. Other sources include Oddie, the *Digby Chronology* and Crankshaw's *Fall of the House of Habsburg*.

Chapter 13

In this and the following chapters, direct quotations and personal feelings attributed to Jane, unless otherwise cited, are from Jane's diaries, as quoted and interpreted by Oddie. Bedouin poems and songs are recorded in Alois Musil's study of *The Manners and Customs of the Rwala Bedouins*. Any letters Jane may have written her family about her travels in Syria were evidently among those destroyed; fortunately, however, accounts of caravan life and detailed descriptions of many of the places Jane visited have been provided by some of her contemporaries—Isabel Burton in *The Inner Life of Syria*, and Emily Beaufort, Viscountess Strangford, in *Egyptian Sepulchres and Syrian Shrines*. Both these Englishwomen saw Palmyra not long after Jane's first trip there; other descriptions are found in Lewis Gaston Leary's *Syria, the Land of Lebanon* and Dr. William Wright's *Account of Palmyra and Zenobia*. A reference to Lady Hester Stanhope's claim to having been crowned "Queen of the Desert" appeared in the September/October 1970 issue of *Aramco World*.

Chapter 14

Jane's brief affair with El Barrak is related in Oddie, and a profile of the colorful Col. Henry Creswick Rawlinson is found in James Norman's *Ancestral Voices*. The letter from Jane to Lady Theresa Digby is among the Minterne documents. Other sources for this chapter include Beaufort's *Syrian Shrines*, Isabel Burton's *Inner Life of Syria*, and Mary Mackintosh's *Damascus and Its People*.

Chapter 15

The Oddie biography contains the only personal record known today of Jane's return to England in 1857. Background information on London during this period is found in the delightful *Victoria's Heyday* by J. B. Priestley. The quotation from Jane's farewell letter to her mother was taken from *Unwise Wanderer*, a fictionalized version of Jane's life written by Leila Mackinlay, who included some factual material in her novel.

Chapter 16

Jane's diary, as quoted by Oddie, is the source of personal material in this chapter. The description of Nicolas Bassoul's hotel in Beirut is from an article in the November/December 1973 issue of *Aramco World*, "From Khans to Khiltons." A house plan of Jane's Damascus residence, sketched by Jane herself, is among her sketchbooks at Minterne, and a microfilm of her household ledger, covering ten years of her life in Syria, is in the possession of John Brinton of Beirut. Other information and quotations are taken from Beaufort's *Syrian Shrines*, Isabel Burton's *Inner Life of Syria*, Sir Edwin Pears's *Forty Years in Constantinople*, and Lord Redesdale's *Memories*.

Chapter 17

The most vivid eyewitness account of the massacre in Damascus is found in Col. Charles Henry Churchill's *The Druzes and the Maronites*, but the anecdote about the Greek consul was related by Lesley Blanch in *The Wilder Shores of Love*. Hans Arthur Thies in his book about the Schönheiten Gallery recorded the deposed King Ludwig's comment on Jane's bravery; and the Bedouin poems are quoted in Musil's study of the

Rowalla tribe. Colorful descriptions of the Damascus bazaars are given by Lewis Leary in *Syria, the Land of Lebanon* and by Isabel Burton in *The Inner Life of Syria.*

Chapter 18

Jane's household expenses are taken from the Brinton microfilm of her ledger and the brief notation in her sketchbook, now at Minterne. Mary Mackintosh recorded the Bedouin mother's song to her infant child, and the other Bedouin poems and songs are from Musil's work. A fascinating description of Baalbek is found in Leary's *Syria, the Land of Lebanon,* and a delightful account of the intrepid John MacGregor and his canoe, the "Rob Roy," appears in John Brinton's article, "Sailing to Damascus," in *Aramco World,* July/August 1972 issue.

Chapter 19

The two years Richard and Isabel Burton spent in Damascus are documented in many books. The ones that provided most of the material in this chapter are *The Life of Captain Sir Richard F. Burton* and *The Inner Life of Syria* by Isabel Burton; *The Romance of Isabel Lady Burton* by W. H. Wilkins; *The Wilder Shores of Love* by Lesley Blanch, and *The True Life of Captain Sir Richard Burton* by Georgina Stisted. (Stisted was Burton's niece, and the title she chose for her biography, published three years after Isabel's biography of Richard, reveals clearly what Richard's family thought about his wife.) The comments of Barty Mitford (later Lord Redesdale) on Isabel and Jane are found in Lord Redesdale's *Memories.* Anecdotes about Jane, Medjuel and the Damascus missionaries are recorded in Oddie. The letter Jane wrote to Isabel is included in Isabel's biography of Richard.

Chapter 20

The controversy between Jane and Isabel is discussed in Oddie, Blanch, Wilkins, Stisted and both of Isabel Burton's previously cited books. Newspaper accounts of Jane's "premature" death are included in Oddie and Blanch, but Jane's letter to Lady Theresa Digby on the subject, found at Minterne, has not been previously published. The quotation from Dom Pedro is an excerpt from his diary, now at the Museu Imperial in Petropolis, Brazil, and Sir Edwin Pears's meeting with Jane is described in *Forty Years in Constantinople.*

Chapter 21

The story of Jane's passionate jealousy of Ouadjid was taken by Oddie from Jane's diary. Lady Anne Blunt's quotations are from two of her books about her Syrian travels: *A Pilgrimage to Nejd* and *Bedouin Tribes of the Euphrates.* Jane's sketchbook referred to in this chapter is now at Minterne, and her fascinating complaint about Medjuel's lack of ardor is preserved from her diary in the Oddie biography. Sir Valentine Chirol reported his visit with Jane in a book of his reminiscences, *Fifty Years in a Changing World.*

Epilogue

Jane's will is included in the Oddie biography, and the description of her grave is found in *An Account of Palmyra and Zenobia* by her missionary friend, Dr. William

Wright. The correspondence concerning Lord Digby's search for Mathilde Selden is among the Minterne documents, as is the black-bordered letter of condolence from Lady Strangford. Most of the Byron quotations scattered throughout this book are from *Don Juan*.

Sources

About, Edmond. *La Grèce Contemporaine*. Paris, 1863.

——. *The Greeks of the Present Day*. Edinburgh, 1855.

——. *The King of the Mountains*. New York, 1902.

Apponyi, Count Rodolphe. *Vingt-Cinq Ans à Paris*. 3 vols. Paris, 1913–1914.

Arbuthnot, Harriet. *The Journal of Mrs. Arbuthnot*. Edited by Francis Bamford and the Duke of Wellington. 2 vols. London, 1950.

Aspiati, Marie. *The Enchanted Island of Corfu*. Corfu, 1968.

Aubrey, John. *Aubrey's Brief Lives*. Edited by Oliver Lawson Dick. Ann Arbor, 1957.

Balzac, Honoré de. *The Correspondence of Honoré de Balzac*. Translated by C. Lamb Kenney. 2 vols. London, 1878.

——. *The Lily of the Valley*. Translated by Clara Bell and James Waring. Philadelphia, 1878.

Beaufort, Emily A. (Viscountess Strangford). *Egyptian Sepulchres and Syrian Shrines*. London, 1874.

Billy, André. *Vie de Balzac*. Vol. I. Paris, 1959.

Blanch, Lesley. *The Wilder Shores of Love*. London, 1954.

Bligh, E. W. *Sir Kenelm Digby and His Venetia*. London, 1932.

Blunt, Lady Anne. *A Pilgrimage to Nejd*. 2 vols. London, 1881.

——. *Bedouin Tribes of the Euphrates*. 2 vols. London, 1889.

Bowen, Catherine Drinker. *Francis Bacon*. Boston, 1963.

Brinton, John. "Sailing to Damascus." *Aramco World*. July/August, 1972.

Brodie, Fawn M. *The Devil Drives: A Life of Sir Richard Burton*. New York, 1968.

Bryant, Arthur. *The Age of Elegance*. New York, 1950.

Buchon, Alexandre. *Voyage dans L'Eubée, Les Iles Ioniennes et Les Cyclades en 1841*. Paris, 1911.

Burton, Isabel. *The Inner Life of Syria, Palestine and the Holy Land*. London, 1884.

———. *The Life of Captain Sir Richard F. Burton.* 2 vols. London, 1893.

Bury, Lady Charlotte. *The Exclusives.* London, 1830.

Campbell, John and Sherrard, Phillip. *Modern Greece.* New York, 1968.

Channon, Henry. *The Ludwigs of Bavaria.* London, 1952.

Chirol, Sir Valentine. *Fifty Years in a Changing World.* London, 1927.

Churchill, Col. Charles Henry. *The Druzes and the Maronites.* London, 1862.

Corti, Conte Egon Caesar. *König Ludwig von Bayern.* Munich, 1960.

Crankshaw, Edward. *The Fall of the House of Habsburg.* New York, 1963.

Creevey, Thomas. *The Creevey Papers.* Edited by John Gore. London, 1934.

Darling, Amanda. *Lola Montez.* New York, 1972.

Digby, Sir Kenelm. *Private Memoirs.* London, 1827.

Durrell, Lawrence. *Prospero's Cell.* London, 1962.

Ellenborough, Lord. *A Political Diary 1828–1830.* Edited by Lord Colchester. 2 vols. London, 1881.

Fernau, Carl. *München Hundert Und Eins.* Munich, 1840.

Finlay, George. *A History of Greece.* 7 vols. New York, 1970.

Gardiner, Marguerite, the Countess of Blessington. *An Idler in France.* London, 1841.

———. *The Two Friends.* London, 1835.

Granville, Lady. *Letters of Harriet Countess Granville 1810–1845.* Edited by the Honourable F. Leveson Gower. 2 vols. London, 1894.

Greene, Graham. *Lord Rochester's Monkey.* New York, 1974.

Gribble, Francis Henry. *Balzac, the Man and the Lover.* New York, 1930.

Gronow, Rees Howell. *The Reminiscences and Recollections of Captain Gronow.* Edited by Joseph Raymond. London, 1964.

Hall, Thornton. *Romances of the Peerage.* London, 1914.

Hibbert, Christopher. *George IV.* 2 vols. New York, 1974.

Hudson, Marianne. *Almack's.* 3 vols. London, 1887.

Hunt, Herbert J. "Balzac and Lady Ellenborough." *French Studies.* Oxford University. July 1958.

Imlah, Albert H. *Lord Ellenborough.* Cambridge, Mass., 1939.

James, Charles W. *Chief Justice Coke, His Family and Descendants at Holkham.* London, 1929.

Jekyll, Joseph. *Correspondence of Mr. Joseph Jekyll.* London, 1894.

Keppel, Sir Henry. *Memoirs of Sir Henry Keppel, G.C.B.* Edited by Sir Algernon West. London, 1905.

Kinglake, William. *Eothen.* London, 1847.

Kobell, Luise von. *Unter den vier ersten Königen Bayerns.* Munich, 1894.

Latham, Charles. *In English Homes.* Vol. III. London, 1909.

Leary, Lewis Gaston. *Syria, the Land of Lebanon.* New York, 1913.

Lieven. *Correspondence of Princess Lieven and Earl Grey.* Edited by Guy Le-Strange. 3 vols. London, 1890.

————. *The Lieven-Palmerston Correspondence.* Edited and translated by Lord Sudley. London, 1943.

Longford, Countess Elizabeth. *Wellington, Pillar of State.* New York, 1972.

Ludwig. *Gedichte Ludwigs des Ersten, Königs von Bayern.* Munich, 1939.

MacGregor, John. *The Rob Roy on the Jordan.* London, 1876.

Mackinlay, Leila. *Unwise Wanderer.* London, 1951.

Mackintosh, Mary. *Damascus and Its People.* London, 1883.

Maurois, André. *Prometheus, The Life of Balzac.* New York, 1965.

Mavrogordato, John. *Modern Greece.* London, 1931.

Musil, Alois. *The Manners and Customs of the Rwala Bedouins.* New York, 1928.

Nevill, Lady. *The Reminiscences of Lady Dorothy Nevill.* Edited by Ralph Nevill. London, 1906.

Norman, James. *Ancestral Voices.* New York, 1975.

Oddie, E. M. *The Odyssey of a Loving Woman.* New York, 1936.

Pears, Sir Edwin. *Forty Years In Constantinople.* London, 1916.

Pickering, Anna Maria Wilhelmina. *Memoirs.* Edited by Spencer Pickering, F. R. S. New York, 1904.

Priestley, J. B. *The Prince of Pleasure and His Regency.* New York, 1969.

————. *Victoria's Heyday.* New York, 1972.

Redesdale, Lord (Algernon Bertram Freeman-Mitford). *Memories.* 2 vols. London, 1915.

René, Benjamin. *Balzac.* Translated by James F. Scanlan. New York, 1927.

Ross, Ishbel. *The Uncrowned Queen: Life of Lola Montez.* New York, 1972.

Rumbold, Sir Horace. *Final Recollections of a Diplomatist.* London, 1905.

Sadleir, Michael. *Blessington-D'Orsay.* London, 1947.

Schwarzenberg, Adolf. *Prince Felix zu Schwarzenberg.* New York, 1946.

Sitwell, Sacheverell, ed. *Great Houses of Europe.* London-New York, 1970.

Spencer-Stanhope, Lady. *The Letter-Bag of Lady Spencer-Stanhope.* Edited by A. M. W. Stirling. 2 vols. London, 1912.

Stamatopoulos, Nondas. *Old Corfu.* Athens, n.d.

Stirling, A. M. W. *Coke of Norfolk and His Friends.* 2 vols. London, 1912.

Stisted, Georgina M. *The True Life of Captain Sir Richard Burton.* London, 1896.

Thackeray, William M. *Vanity Fair.* Boston, 1963.

Thies, Hans Arthur. *König Ludwig I und die Schönheiten Seiner Galerie.* Munich, 1954.

Thonger, Richard. *A Calendar of German Customs.* London, 1966.

Thouvenal, Edouard. *La Grèce du Roi Otho.* Paris, 1890.

Tuckerman, Charles. *The Greeks of Today.* New York, 1872.

Wilberforce, Edward. *Social Life in Munich.* London, 1864.

Wilkins, W. H. *The Romance of Isabel Lady Burton.* 2 vols. London, 1897.

Wolf, Georg Jakob, ed. *Ein Jahrhundert München 1800–1900.* Munich, 1921.

Wright, William. *An Account of Palmyra and Zenobia.* London, 1895.
Wyndham, Horace. *Judicial Dramas.* London, 1927.

Other Sources

Personal papers of Jane Digby, Muniments Room, Minterne House, Dorset; letters and notes from Jane Digby to King Ludwig I of Bavaria, *Geheimes Hausarchiv,* Munich; diaries of Sir Frederick Madden, Bodleian Library, Oxford University; the diary of Emperor Dom Pedro of Brazil, Museu Imperial, Petropolis, Brazil; British Foreign Office files; files of the *Times* of London; Jane Digby's Damascus account book, on microfilm in the possession of John Brinton, Beirut; *Burke's Peerage*; selected articles from *British History Illustrated*, MD, and *Aramco World*; official guide books to the Nymphenburg Palace, Schwetzingen Palace, and the Residenz, Munich.

Index